Advertising in Asia

Advertising in Asia

Communication, Culture and Consumption

Edited by **KATHERINE TOLAND FRITH**

IOWA STATE UNIVERSITY PRESS / AMES

This book is dedicated to my father,

John M. Toland (1911–1986),

who introduced me to advertising.

Katherine T. Frith received both Master of Education and Doctor of Education degrees from the University of Massachusetts. Before joining academia, she worked in the professional world of advertising as a copywriter. She has taught advertising at two major American universities and has been Chair of the Advertising Department at Pennsylvania State University, University Park. Frith was a Fulbright Professor in both Malaysia and Indonesia.

© 1996 Iowa State University Press, Ames, Iowa 50014

♾ Printed on acid-free paper in the United States of America

First edition, 1996

Library of Congress Cataloging-in-Publication Data

Advertising in Asia: communication, culture and consumption / edited by Katherine Toland Frith.—1st ed.
        p.   cm.
    Includes bibliographical references and index.
    ISBN 0-8138-2888-0
    1. Advertising—Asia.
  HF5813.A74A38   1996
  659.1′095—dc20

96-20836

Last digit is the print number: 9 8 7 6 5 4 3 2 1

CONTENTS

Contributors, **vii**

Foreword, **ix**

Preface, **xi**

1 Introduction: Dependence or Convergence?, **3**
    KATHERINE TOLAND FRITH

2 Advertising in Japan: Changing Times for an Economic Giant, **11**
    OSAMU INOUE

3 Advertising in Hong Kong, **39**
    ERNEST F. MARTIN, JR.

4 Advertising in China: A Socialist Experiment, **73**
    HONG CHENG

5 Advertising in Taiwan: Sociopolitical Changes and Multinational
    Impact, **103**
    JAMES TSAO

6 Advertising in Korea: International Challenges and Politics, **125**
    KWANGMI KO KIM

7 Advertising in India: The Winds of Change, **155**
    SUBIR SENGUPTA AND KARTIK PASHUPATI

8 Advertising in the Philippines: Communication, Culture and
    Consumption, **189**
    ELENA PERNIA

9 The Blossoming of Advertising in Thailand, **223**
    M.L. VITTRATORN CHIRAPRAVATI

10 Malaysia: Advertising in a Multiracial Society, **241**
    TECK HUA NGU

11 Advertising in Indonesia: Unity in Diversity, **259**
    KATHERINE TOLAND FRITH

12 Advertising in Singapore, **273**
    FELIX STRAVENS

Index, **293**

CONTRIBUTORS

Hong Cheng

Assistant Professor, Department of Communication
Bradley University
Peoria, Illinois

M.L. Vittratorn Chirapravati

Department of Public Relations and Advertising
Faculty of Communication Arts, Chulalongkorn University
Bangkok, Thailand

Katherine Toland Frith

Chair of Advertising, College of Communications
The Pennsylvania State University
University Park, Pennsylvania

Osamu Inoue

Director, Asia Project Office, Overseas Strategy and Planning Division,
    Dentsu Inc.
Tokyo, Japan

Kwangmi Ko Kim

Assistant Professor, Department of Communication
Appalachian State University
Boone, North Carolina

Ernest F. Martin, Jr.

Head, Department of Communication Studies
Associate Professor of Public Relations and Advertising
Hong Kong Baptist University
Hong Kong

Teck Hua Ngu

School of Mass Communications, Institute Technology MARA
Shah Alam, Malaysia

Kartik Pashupati

Assistant Professor, Department of Communication Arts
University of West Florida
Pensacola, Florida

Elena Pernia

Associate Professor and Past Department Chair
College of Mass Communications
University of the Philippines
Diliman, Quezon City, Philippines

Subir Sengupta

Assistant Professor, College of Communications
The Pennsylvania State University
University Park, Pennsylvania

Felix Stravens

Executive Director of the Institute of Advertising
Republic of Singapore

James Tsao

Assistant Professor, Department of Journalism
University of Wisconsin-Oshkosh
Oshkosh, Wisconsin

Norman Vale

Director General, International Advertising Association
New York, New York

FOREWORD

TODAY that large geographic area commonly called Asia-Pacific is rapidly developing and with it all, a rapidly evolving consumer market is emerging. This did not occur overnight. It required almost five decades, encompassing the conclusions of World War II, the Korean War and the Vietnam involvement, for individual countries to dedicate the time to rebuild infrastructures to peaceful, industrial and consumer goods markets.

We have been witness to some dramatic changes as free-market economies have been defined and taken their place in this vast arena. The "Tigers," People's Republic of China and other pockets of strength, present Asia as an open opportunity to those companies and individuals with foresight and patience. The scale of opportunity is tremendous when considering the enormously large blocks of population. In February 1994, China and India alone accounted for 2.1 billion people or 37 percent of the world's population. Include the area's other countries in different stages of industrial/consumer development and the prospects for the future are buoyant.

As well, each market dynamic has contributed to the development and growth of the marketing communications industry. Today individual markets lead to Pan-Asian opportunities beyond the launch and sustaining phases. Where marketers venture, advertising agencies follow and the media grow. Together they represent a significant economic force in manufacturing, jobs, revenues and taxes.

This evolution has led to a new vocabulary. Consider satellite telecasting, wide-band blockage, enlarged footprints, interactivity, information superhighway, webs, high definition, digitalization and the rapid transfer of knowledge and techniques. All of these new technologies are emerging ways to reach the empowered consumer. *Advertising in Asia* is the first book to present in-depth studies of how advertising operates on a country-by-country basis.

Each of the eminent contributors has done an impressive job of describing the context for advertising in one country. Taken as a whole, we begin to see both similarities and differences in the philosophies, cultures, ideologies and approaches to economic growth throughout the region.

This book then is a must for anyone with an interest in acquiring an in-depth knowledge of each market. As the first-ever presentation by such an eminent group of authors, it is recommended reading for marketers, educators, journalists, students and government officials interested in the dynamics of economic growth and marketing communications in this region.

Also, the International Advertising Association is pleased to have had early exposure to this book and the opportunity to share some of our perspective. You can be certain that this publication has a prominent place in our resource center.

NORMAN VALE, *Director General*
International Advertising Association

PREFACE

OVER the past few decades many Asian countries have experienced unprecedented economic growth owing in large part to the opening up of these markets to foreign investment. The gradual buildup of multinational business activity and the resultant transformation of consumer behavior in this region have made it one of the major growth centers for international advertising and marketing. Because this region contains over half the population of the world, Asian markets have become particularly attractive to multinational businesses and advertising agencies. Although many authors have pointed to the opportunities for advertisers in Asia, the actual details of how the industry interfaces with the local culture and political structures in these diverse countries have received little attention.

Advertising in Asia addresses a blind spot in the communications and advertising literature by offering an in-depth analysis of one area of the world that is now of particular interest to practitioners and scholars—Asia. The purpose of this book is not merely to outline the challenges and opportunities for advertising in this region, but to stimulate discussion about the practice of advertising in non-Western cultures. The chapters in this book have been written by practitioners and scholars from throughout Asia who are eminent authorities in their fields. These authors examine the unique political, cultural and religious systems that create the context for advertising in Asia and describe the unique historical and political context within which the practice of advertising takes place.

Because of Asia's vast size and uneven development, we cannot attempt to cover every country; however, the book contains chapters on the more developed countries: Japan, Hong Kong, China, Taiwan, Korea, India, Malaysia, Indonesia, Thailand, Singapore and the Philippines. In sampling these countries the reader will be exposed to most of the underlying issues that affect advertising in Asia. By examining the issues related to political systems, national development policies and the social, cultural and philosophic underpinnings that impact on advertising in the region, this book attempts to extend our understanding of how the intersecting variables of culture, communication and consumption are played out within the Asian region.

In shaping this selection of chapters I must, first of all, thank the wonderful group of authors who have spent countless hours of their precious time developing, writing and rewriting their drafts. I was most fortunate to be able to work with such a talented and dedicated group of scholars and practitioners. In addition I gratefully acknowledge the support of the administration at the College of Communications of The Pennsylvania State University and that of my graduate students who are forever teaching me about the practice of communications in Asia. I must also thank David Adams and the staff at CIES (Council for International Exchange of Scholars) in Washington, D.C., who helped me so much with my Fulbrights to Malaysia and Indonesia, and the faculties at the Institute of Technology MARA in Malaysia and the Institute of Technology Bandung in Indonesia for sharing their resources and expertise with me. I want to thank Pak Islan in Indonesia for inviting me to spend a summer as a visitor at InterAdmark, Mr. Osamu Inoue for treating me as an honored guest and allowing me to participate in the workings of the agency and John Crossby for kindly putting me up in his home. I must also recognize the contribution of my father to my career. I should thank him for sharing with me his delight in the world of advertising, for assisting in getting me my first internship at Doyle Dane Bernbach in New York and for encouraging me to get a doctorate and teach advertising. He was my inspiration and remains so to this day. Last, and not least of all, I acknowledge the love and support of my family, this group of world travelers and great adventurers who have traveled with me to Asia and share my love of this region. Thank you Michael, Giles and Sebastian; I could never have done this without you.

Advertising in Asia

1

Introduction:
Dependence or Convergence?

KATHERINE TOLAND FRITH

Over the past few decades Asia has experienced the most dynamic economic growth of any region in the world. Although the East Asian economies accounted for only 4 percent of the world's gross national product (GNP) in 1960, by 1991 they had reached some 25 percent. By the turn of the century, they are expected to account for one-third of the total world GNP. Some experts predict that East Asia could grow twice as fast economically as the United States and three times the rate of Europe (Business America 1994). Add to this the nations in the Association of Southeast Asian Nations (ASEAN), and the figures are even more impressive. The World Bank estimates that over the next 5 years, Asia will account for more than half of the global GNP growth and half of the global trade growth (Business America 1994).

This rapid economic growth has been accompanied by a dramatic increase in advertising. Today billions of U.S. dollars are spent on mass media advertising in the region, all aimed at enticing the burgeoning middle class to consume everything from perfumes to Pentiums. The gradual buildup of multinational business activity has resulted in a transformation of consumer behavior as the region shifts from traditional to mass-market. and advertising is positioned at the center of this change. The purpose of this book is to examine the practice of advertising in the Asian region, including issues related to political systems, national development policies and the social, cultural and philosophical underpinnings that impact on advertising and advertising regulations in the region.

Dependency Theory

There has been a wealth of articles and books on the economic miracle of Asia; however, there has been little comprehensive work done on the practice of advertising in the region. Michael Anderson's book, *Madison Avenue in Asia: Politics and Transnational Advertising,* provides an excellent starting point for

3

our discussion. Published in the mid-1980s, Anderson's book provides an analysis of the situation that existed in this region in the 1970s and very early 1980s and describes, quite accurately, the most pressing concerns of those decades relating to the impact of advertising on Third World development:

> The impact of the transnational corporations (TNCs) on the needs and aspirations of Third World masses living amidst scarcity and poverty is not always encouraging. The consumption gap between the few rich and the many poor continues. Progress toward reducing the cultural shock, eliminating poverty and other forms of inequality, ensuring citizens full participation in their nations' decision-making process or fostering national self-reliant action has been slow at best. The debate generated by this book should help contribute to a better understanding of some of these consequences of today's world order. . . .
> (Anderson 1984, 25)

In his book Anderson views the situation in Asia through the lens of dependency theory, which takes into account the structures of social relations and social power and the impact of these structures in contributing to underdevelopment. He uses Galtung's structural theory of imperialism to describe the impact of transnational advertising on the periphery nations of Asia. This theory supports the notion that under economic colonialism, "center" nations, particularly the United States, Britain and Japan, to a large extent controlled the economies of the developing or "peripheral" nations. From our perspective in the mid-1990s, however, the rise of the Four Dragons (South Korea, Taiwan, Hong Kong and Singapore) as areas with the greatest sustained economic development in the world might raise some challenging questions about the final outcome of the modernization process in Asia. In fact, today,

> the Four Dragons are providing thirty-one percent of all foreign investment in the countries of ASEAN . . . they are now responsible for the largest capital transfer in the region, exceeding that of both Japan and the United States.
> (Tu Wei-ming 1991, 8)

In addition Tu points out that by 1990, all indications suggested that the average per capita income in Hong Kong had already surpassed that of its colonial ruler, the United Kingdom. In effect we may be witnessing the periphery as the center.

One of the most interesting aspects of economic growth in East Asia has been the connection between culture and economic growth. Although the "Greater China" discussed in chapters 3 and 5 of this book has been described geographically as including Taiwan, Hong Kong, mainland China and Singapore, Tu extends this concept to include all the universes that make up a "Cultural China." In this symbolic rather than geographic region, he includes not only the People's Republic of China (PRC), Taiwan, Hong Kong and Singapore, but also the Chinese diaspora scattered as an ethnic minority throughout Asia. This geographically diverse group is held together by a set of cultural values that are described quite well by Ernest F. Martin, Jr., in his chapter on Hong Kong advertising (Chapter 3).

In addition to sharing cultural values, this group is also responsible for much of the economic growth in the region. As Tu notes, "The Chinese constitute not only the largest peasantry in the world today but also the most mobile merchant class" (Tu Wei-ming 1991, 8). And it is through these lines of cultural connections that much of the current economic growth is occurring. The recent economic phenomena in the Asia-Pacific region may not be explained primarily along geographic and political lines from center to periphery—as the dependency theorist of previous decades argued; it may, in fact, be strongly influenced by cultural connections.

Another concern expressed by authors in the 1980s (Anderson 1984; Janus 1986) is that advertising promotes the consumption of nonessential products and concentrates economic power into the hands of a few large transnational corporations TNCs. The argument is, in effect, that advertising gives transnational products the advantage in foreign markets, and these products compete with local products—often replacing cheaper, more durable and sometimes more nutritious or ecologically sound products with costlier ones in fancier packaging (Frith and Frith 1990). The argument continues that transnational advertising drives out local competition and perpetuates monopolies by preventing smaller firms—often local ones—from entering the market because these smaller firms do not have access to sufficient capital to provide for the high cost of advertising. The ultimate result, the critics argue, is the greater transnational penetration of the economy as a whole.

Although there are countless examples of apparently successful multinational brands in Asia, there is also, in fact, a great deal of myth to the belief that multinational corporations are always successful in cracking through the resistance of Asian culture and politics. As one Canadian newspaper suggests:

> But the great myth that Asia is a vast untapped mine of potential customers waiting for Western manufactured multinational products may turn out to be just that—a myth.
>
> (Manthorpe and Southam 1995, B5)

Asian countries maintain a plethora of regulations, local customs and long-standing relationships or connections that often frustrate and confound the foreign company eager to break into these markets. In confronting Asia, most foreign enterprises face numerous subtle and not so subtle challenges such as the Korean *chaebol* described by Kwangmi Ko Kim in Chapter 6; the importance of local business connections described by Ernest Martin, Jr., in Chapter 3 and James Tsao in Chapter 5; and the embedded bureaucracies described by Osamu

Inoue in Chapter 2 and Hong Cheng in Chapter 4. While dependency theorists were able to argue that in principle advertising gave transnational products the advantage in foreign markets, experience in Asia, at least, has proven that this is no longer always the case.

Furthermore the trade connections between Asian nations have improved in recent years to the point that more Asian products now go to other Asian countries than at any time in the past. With the introduction of economic alliances such as the ASEAN Free Trade Area (AFTA) agreement signed in January 1992, trade tariffs between member countries are being phased out. Thus, rather than holding all the power, as the dependency theorists suggested, the power of transnational corporations to monopolize these markets is often held at bay by national development policies. This is not to argue that those corporations that have already established longstanding relationships with host countries in Asia have not been successful (Marlboro is, after all, the world's largest-selling cigarette), but rather to note that success is no longer assured merely by the fact that a corporation is Western or transnational. In fact, as Manthorpe and Southam (1995) point out, in dealing with Asian governments Western officials used to "go in with lists of political prisoners we wanted released, today we go in with lists of [our] companies that want contracts" (Manthorpe and Southam 1995, B5). In other words the balance of power is shifting, and the ability of Western governments and transnational corporations to "perpetuate dominance over weak nations" (Anderson 1984, 87) is diminishing.

Another area of concern to critics over the past few decades has been the employment practices of transnational advertising agencies (TNAAs). It has been suggested that the concept of media "professionalism" was merely a cover for expatriate management. Dependency theorists charge that media professionalism, along with the transfer of technology from the First World, is a part of the dominant ideology in the general stream of cultural dependence. Without a doubt, historically there has been a division of labor in the structure of TNAAs. Generally, expatriate experts have been brought in and have taken the executive positions, whereas local media practitioners have held low-status positions and have been offered little in the way of executive experience. In Anderson's analysis this structure contributes to dependency. In recent years, however, there has been some evidence to suggest that this employment trend is changing. Although in the past, transnational agencies handled primarily transnational clients, today agencies need local business to compete, and in order to attract local business in Asia, agencies need to develop contacts with local people. This is best done through local managers. In China the term for new capitalism is *guanxi*, which means "network" or "connections." Here, in *Advertising in Asia: Communication, Culture and Consumption*, the authors from Korea, Taiwan, Thailand and Japan all allude to the fact that business contacts are crucial to business success in their countries. In Thailand more that half of Ogilvy and Mather's clients are now Thai nationals. As M.L. Vittratorn Chirapravati points out in Chapter 9 on Thailand, the 1990s have been called the "Thai Era" in advertising. The largest

TNAAs in Thailand all now have Thai chief executives. Leo Burnett, one of Thailand's largest agencies had only four expatriates among its staff of 210 employees (*The Economist* 1992). Again, although it would be dishonest to suggest that the transnational agencies do not hold great power throughout the region, there is evidence from Taiwan, Thailand, Singapore, India and Malaysia that management in TNAAs is becoming a shared endeavor: The days of merely translating foreign campaigns developed by copywriters at corporate headquarters in center countries, or as Anderson (1984) suggests, "standardized commercial products that can be packaged and widely syndicated by TNAAs" (51) are long gone.

Another criticism that emerged in the 1970s and 1980s was that transnational advertising was responsible for the spread of consumer culture. Advertising has been charged with creating an increasing gap and disharmony of interest between the "haves" and the "have nots." The argument here might be that with or without advertising (and, as noted in Chapter 11, Indonesia was without TV advertising for almost 10 years because of the government's belief that this criticism held true) the gap between the rich and poor has been shrinking in most parts of Asia. The number of families living below the poverty line in most countries in Asia is decreasing. Although economic growth in East Asia has been phenomenal, ASEAN nations have also experienced fast economic development. The annual real GDP growth for the period from 1985 to 1990 averaged 8.6 percent for Singapore and 6.8 percent for the ASEAN Four—Indonesia, Malaysia, Thailand and the Philippines (Pierson 1994). Even the so-called "underdeveloped" countries such as Vietnam are experiencing impressive economic growth (8 percent per year). As Hill (1994) points out regarding the ASEAN countries:

> The benefits of rapid development in the four growth economies have been distributed reasonably widely, in turn ensuring a cohesive social order and widespread community acceptance of the desirability of growth. Moreover, the relationship between growth and the decline in poverty incidence is very clearly a strong one.
>
> (Hill 1994, 853)

In fact, if advertising has contributed to economic growth, then it can also be credited with helping to decrease the gap between the haves and the have nots. Which brings us to the final criticism of transnational advertising, which emerged in the 1970s and '80s:

> The sheer volume and effectiveness of TNAAs advertisements have been said to introduce or condone aggressiveness, materialism, romanticism, elitism, racism, conformism, and so forth, and such beliefs have been said to gradually contribute to the creation of a new, elite-oriented culture that has nothing to do with the indigenous one it is rapidly replacing.
>
> (Anderson 1984, 64)

Of all the criticisms of advertising this one is most worrisome because although it is hard to argue against the positive benefits of economic growth, it is equally hard to argue for the destruction of indigenous culture. And there is no doubt that advertising has contributed to the creation of a lifestyle segment, particularly among the young in Asian countries, heavily oriented toward Western culture. As *The Economist* (1992) notes:

> If there is one thing that unites this diverse region it is the emergence of an affluent middle class. These new consumers are young, status-conscious and interested in image as well as product.
>
> (*Id.* 1992, 85)

In advertising's defense, this emerging segment is not just the creation of advertising agencies, but that of all the culture industries including television, movies, rock videos and music. The question that seems most relevant, however, is what is being lost and what is being gained? On the one hand, without a doubt foreign cultural influences through the mass media have affected the style of dress and address in Asia. Modes of communication have changed, but whether or not deep moral values have eroded in Asia as the result of advertising and the mass media is difficult to assess. Many of the authors in this book discuss the deeply held cultural values that run throughout Asian cultures and these authors affirm the strong hold of these values. Although styles of clothing and modes of address may have changed in the last few decades, the importance of family, religion and cooperation seem to have held firmly throughout the region. As Felix Stravens notes in Chapter 12 there are good and bad Asian values and there are good and bad Western values. Arriving at a balance seems to be a theme that occupies nearly all of the authors in the book and which underscores the relevance of this discussion throughout the region.

Convergence

As we move toward the 21st century, we are beginning to see the emergence of a new vision that challenges the assumptions of dependency theory. Within this new structure, higher levels of cooperation between nations as well as new forms of communications technology are creating a form of global integration that is unprecedented in the history of the world. James Carey (1989) described two views of communications—the transmission model and the ritual model. The so-called "old media" such as radio, television and newspapers fall within the transmission model in that they have, by their very nature, promoted a one-way, top-down transmission system that theoretically gave rise to a passive audience and a powerful media. Much of the criticism of advertising voiced in the past was rooted in the notion of a passive audience and a powerful medium.

Carey's other model describes the ritualistic aspects of communication and the relationship of communication to the development of communities.

> A ritual view of communication is directed not toward the extension of messages in space but toward the maintenance of society in time; not the act of imparting information but the representation of shared beliefs.
>
> (Carey 1989, 18)

The "new" media, available through telephone, satellite and computer provide for interaction and allow greater dialogue between sender and receiver than has ever before been possible (Elmer-DeWitt 1995). Marshall McLuhan's vision of a "Global Village," first articulated in 1962, may be coming to fruition through these new technologies, which create the possibility of convergence and a global integration that transcends national boundary and individual culture. Meyrowitz in *No Sense of Place* (1985) argues that the new media redefine the notion of social position and place, divorcing experience from physical location and bringing together otherwise disparate groups through communications. Whereas earlier forms of mass communication formed a genuinely fragmented set of human social conditions, we now appear to be moving into a world, "in which humankind in some respects becomes a 'we,' facing problems and opportunities where there are no 'others'" (Giddens 1991, 27).

What role does advertising play in this vision? If capitalism has been the fuel for economic growth, then advertising has been the match that sparked the fire. As a form of public communication, advertising transcends nationality and ethnic origin. Although some might wish that the language that finally transcended all national boundaries was of a more spiritual nature, the reality is that advertisements for products such as Coca-Cola and blue jeans have been creating "communities of interest" across geographic regions, and have penetrated villages and towns where religious messages would never have been allowed. And it is these discourses—not just about products and services, but about lifestyles—that have had the greatest impact in creating a worldwide "culture" of convergence that is emerging today.

As new media technologies move us from the top-down, one-way message model to a more democratic and interactive mode of communicating, we shall see advertising change. Some of the power previously attributed to advertising may give way to new channels of discourse that are less dependent on the external factors of what one wears and what one consumes, and more dependent on what one thinks. If this book helps pave the way for this vision of the future, then the effort of all the authors is, indeed, an eminent contribution.

Bibliography

Anderson, M. 1984. *Madison Avenue in Asia: Politics and Transnational Advertising.* Teaneck, NJ: Fairleigh Dickinson University Press.

Business America. 1994. Asia, APEC, and the Pacific Community: A New World Dawns. Washington, DC: U.S. Dept. of Commerce, November, p. 4.

Carey, J.W. 1989. *Communication as Culture: Essays on Media and Society.* Boston: Unwin Hyman.

The Economist. 1992. Advertising in Asia: Full of Western Promise, 325 (7785): 84–85.

Elmer-DeWitt, P. 1995. Welcome to Cyberspace. *Time,* Spring, Special Issue, pp. 4–11.

Frith, K.T. and M. Frith. 1990. Western Advertising and Eastern Culture: A Confrontation in Southeast Asia. *Current Issues and Research in Advertising,* 12 (1&2): 91–93.

Giddens, A. 1991. *Modernity and Self-Identity: Self and Society in the Late Modern Age.* Cambridge, U.K.: Polity Press.

Hill, H. 1994. ASEAN Economic Development: An Analytic Survey: The State of the Field. *The Journal of Asian Studies,* 53: 832–866.

Janus, N. 1986. Transnational Advertising: Some Considerations on Its Impact on Peripheral Societies. In: Atwood, R. and E. McAnany, eds. *Communications and Latin American Society: Trends in Critical Research 1960–1985.* Madison, WI: University of Wisconsin Press.

McLuhan, M. 1962. *The Gutenberg Galaxy.* Toronto: Toronto University Press.

Manthorpe, J. and N. Southam. 1995. "Balancing Act." *The Montreal Gazette,* July 16, p. B5.

Meyrowitz, J. 1985. *No Sense of Place.* Oxford: Oxford University Press.

Pierson, M.Y. 1994. East Asia: Regional Economic Integration and Implications for the United States. *Law and Policy in International Business,* 25 (3): 1161–1185.

Tu Wei-ming. 1991. Cultural China: The Periphery as the Center. *Daedalus,* 120 (2): 1–32.

2

Advertising in Japan: Changing Times for an Economic Giant

OSAMU INOUE

Introduction

The year 1995 was an epoch-making year in Japan, marking the 50th anniversary of the end of World War II. Having experienced 50 years of peace, Japan has been able to transform itself into one of the most economically advanced countries in the world. Recent globalization of the economy, deregulation and the constant escalation of the yen have been accelerating drastic changes among consumers, advertisers and the communications systems in Japan. How have things changed? What kinds of impacts are those changes having on advertising, and which directions will the Japanese advertising industry follow? These are questions this chapter tries to clarify.

Geographic and Strategic Setting

Japan is an island nation made up of four main islands (Honshu, Shikoku, Kyushu and Hokkaido), which are linked together by bridges and tunnels. Together with more than 4,000 smaller islands they are collectively referred to as the Japanese Archipelago. In terms of land mass, Japan is about 378,000 square kilometers (146,000 square miles), making it slightly larger than Malaysia and one twenty-fifth the size of the United States. A mountainous country, only 30 percent of Japan's land is habitable, making the population density of cities extremely high.

Japan is divided into 47 administrative units or prefectures, among them Tokyo, Osaka, Kyoto, and Aomori. The country's population of 124.3 million makes it the seventh largest in the world. Approximately one-quarter of the population is concentrated in the greater metropolitan area of Tokyo, which is the capital city and the center of all political, economic and cultural communications. Most of the inhabitants of Japan are racially homogeneous, speaking one common language. Nearly all Japanese complete 9 years of compulsory education. Japan's high literacy rate facilitates the immense power of the printed word and has contributed greatly to the penetration of mass media.

Economic Growth and Contributing Factors

Over the past 50 years the Japanese have been successful in their efforts to transform Japan into one of the world's most affluent countries in the world. Although currently facing various problems such as high prices (by international standards), a scarcity of housing space, long working hours and urban congestion and pollution, foreign economists have unanimously observed that Japan has attained an "economic miracle." This economic miracle has occurred in four developmental stages:

1. THE RECOVERY PERIOD (1945 THROUGH THE MID-1950s)

During this time the occupying Allied Forces introduced three democratization policies into Japan: *Zaibatsu* dissolution; reformation of agricultural land; and labor reform. All of these laid the foundation for the post-war economy. The *Zaibatsu* were large capital-holding groups that controlled the wartime Japanese economy, and their dissolution brought about open and free competition among business enterprises.

In 1947 during the immediate post-war period, under the guidance of the United States, Japan enacted an Anti-Monopoly Act based on the principle of absolute prohibition of monopolies. In 1953 following the signing of the United States–Japan peace treaty, the law was extensively revised to change it from one based on the outright prohibition of monopolies to one aimed at preventing monopolistic abuses. In the 1970s the Anti-Monopoly Act was again revised for the third time to establish a penalty system for cartels, oligopolies and other monopolistic practices. The Anti-Monopoly Act has played an important role in promoting fair and free competition by excluding monopolies and unfair business practices in the post-war economy. More importantly, Japan's policies were influenced by the U.S. occupation forces, which gave basic guidance to the post-war Japanese economy, as well as by external conditions under the free-trade system maintained by the leadership of the United States.

Agrarian land reform during the 1940s made agricultural modernization possible by abolishing old landlord–tenant farming systems. The Trade Union Law, Labor Relations Adjustment Law, and Labor Standards Law were enacted by labor reform policy, and improved the worker's status and helped maintain stable management–labor relations. Coal and steel were the two most fundamental industries on which a major part of the material, financial and labor resources was focused under the priority production system.

With the outbreak of the Korean War in 1950, recovery was assisted by the special procurements needed for U.S. forces stationed in Japan, and the GNP reached the pre-war level by the mid-1950s.

2. RAPID GROWTH PERIOD (MID-1950s THROUGH THE 1960s)

From 1955 to the late 1960s the average annual growth rate of Japan's GNP was nearly 10 percent. During this period heavy industries developed rapidly, and GNP growth averaged 8 percent for the next 10 years. By the mid-1960s, Japan had attained one of the highest economic growth rates in the world and had the second-largest GNP in the free world by 1968. Domestic markets for durable household goods such as TV sets, washing machines and refrigerators reached a near-saturation level during this period, and automobile ownership climbed to nearly 10 million by 1965.

By 1962, liberalization of imports had reached 88 percent. Japan had reshaped its economic relations with the rest of the world through a lifting of foreign-exchange restrictions and a freeing of capital investment. With the latter half of the 1960s, the country began consistently maintaining a favorable international balance of payments.

3. STABLE GROWTH PERIOD (MID-1970s THROUGH 1980s)

After the oil shocks of 1973, Japan's growth slowed by about 4 to 5 percent between 1975 and 1987, but there were still advances made in high-tech industries, as well as expansion of service industries. The higher appreciation of the yen that began in 1973 forced Japan to readjust its economic structure, which had been highly dependent on exports. A second oil crisis in 1979 further disrupted the world economy. To overcome these crises, Japanese industries focused on the development and application of energy conservation and automation technologies. While economic growth slowed to a more moderate pace, in 1980 the Foreign Exchange and Foreign Trade Control Law was revised in response to the rapid liberalization and internationalization of the financial and capital markets, and companies were able to diversify their fund sources.

4. DOMESTIC DEMAND-LED ECONOMY (MID-1980s ONWARD)

As vigorous exporting has continued to increase the country's trade surplus since the mid-1980s, Japan has been under constant pressure to curb its exports and expand imports. Taking advantage of the higher yen, the fall in oil prices contributed to the stabilization of domestic prices. This stability promoted greater consumption and investment, in turn sparking higher land and stock prices and bloating the book values of Japanese assets. In 1986, the economy entered a period of sustained growth called the Heisei Boom, which lasted a nearly record-long period of 57 months. With higher asset evaluation, people became more interested in luxury items such as extravagant automobiles, big-screen TV sets and other examples of conspicuous consumption. The overblown economy eventually burst, however, and stock and real estate markets plunged, leading to a recession. Still, due to the higher appreciation of the yen, Japan's per capita GNP (when translated into dollars) overtook that of the United States in 1987.

Today Japanese consumer prices are said to be the highest of any other country in the world. According to the consumer price index of the Japanese Management and Coordination Agency, except for the cost of education and housing, the cost of fuel, water, household furniture and furnishings, and health care have all risen relatively steadily over the last 30 years. In June 1994 the yen-to-dollar rate broke through the $1 = ¥100 point and plunged to the record level of 90 some yen to the dollar. The rising yen has forced the export business to squeeze profits, and has served as an impetus for Japanese firms to move overseas. In other words it has contributed to the "hollowing out" of Japanese industry. On the other hand, the strong yen can play an important role in structural adjustments to the economy and improved living standards.

A number of factors have contributed to Japan's economic success, but one in particular that has been especially conducive to rapid development has been the Japanese-Style Industrial Policy. Western scholars and journalists who have researched Japan's economic success almost without exception give much of the credit to the country's skilled bureaucracy. The Ministry of International Trade and Industry (MITI) is regarded as the authority leading Japan's industries and promoting exports in tandem with *sogo-shosha* (major trading firms). The Japanese bureaucracy is perceived as highly capable, and in large part has been responsible for giving appropriate guidance to the private sectors in place of the capable politicians. Among the reasons that Japan's bureaucracy has worked so well are that it has attracted outstanding people, it has considerable authority in drafting policy, and it enjoys the trust of the private sector.

A capable bureaucracy is not a recent development in Japan. The foundation for Japan's development into a modern nation was to a large extent laid during the peaceful years of isolation during the feudal period. The experience gained by the ruling warrior class of this period accounted for the presence of men capable of running the new bureaucratic government and its institutions. In postwar Japan, most conspicuous were the conservative politicians who formed the Liberal Democratic Party and who stayed in power for as long as 4 decades. This longstanding continuity has helped the bureaucracy plan and maintain long-term policies for the government.

Japanese bureaucrats work for the same office on almost a lifetime basis, whereas politicians change frequently, depending on election results. During Japan's post-war history, from the Higashikuni cabinet in 1945 through the Murayama cabinet in 1994, there have been 24 cabinets formed, which means that approximately every 2 years a new cabinet has been born over the past 50 years. Judging from the fact that ministers have changed more frequently than premiers, it would have been almost impossible to carry out consistent policies without the existence of capable and experienced bureaucrats in place of constantly changing policymakers.

Historical Growth of the Advertising Industry

PRE-WAR PERIOD

The establishment and popularization of the mass media have been a driving force in the development of advertising as a modern industry. The first newspaper advertisement placed by a Japanese company in a Japanese-language newspaper appeared in 1867. The first advertising agency is said to have been founded in 1873, although this firm's main lines of business were news wire service, shipping and insurance—advertising was just a sideline.

The first truly professional advertising agencies were founded in the 1880s and 1890s, including Kohodo in 1886, Kokoku-sha in 1888, Man-nen-sha in 1890, Hakuhodo in 1895 and the forerunner of Dentsu in 1901. Japanese major newspapers were born one after another, starting with the forerunner of the *Mainichi Shimbun* in 1872, the *Yomiuri Shimbun* in 1874 and the *Asahi Shimbun* in 1879. These soon began to strengthen their efforts to increase their circulation, as well as their advertising revenues.

In 1892, the first weekly magazines started: the *Weekly Asahi*, the *Sunday Mainichi* and the *Weekly Yomiuri* all appeared. The primary advertisers in those days were cosmetics, pharmaceuticals and publications. The skills of advertising expression were gradually being refined through these publications.

In 1925, radio broadcasting began. Although commercial broadcasting was legally banned in Japan, it was experimented with both in Taiwan from 1932 to 1937, and in Manchuria from 1936 until 1940 during the Japanese occupation period. These experiments with commercial broadcasting contributed to the later development of post-war commercial broadcasting.

THE POST-WAR PERIOD

The advertising industry, together with newspapers and magazines, went through a severe austerity period immediately after World War II, largely because of the shortage of paper. When the paper industry was decontrolled in 1951, the advertising industry, as well as the general industries, was rejuvenated by the recovery of the mass media. Above all, the launching of commercial broadcasting acted as a springboard for the massive development of the advertising industry. As a part of the democratization policies, commercial broadcasting was initiated under the auspices of the Allied Forces, and licenses were given to 16 firms including Radio Tokyo, Bunka-Hoso, Shinnihon Hoso and Chubu Nihon Hoso—all in 1951. By the end of 1952, total advertising expenditures for radio had already exceeded those for magazines, and radio became the number two advertising media, right behind newspapers.

In August 1953 Nippon Television Network (NTV) was established as the first commercial TV network, but total household TV units in the Tokyo area numbered only about 3,000. In April 1955 Tokyo Broadcasting System (TBS) started its TV operation and, by that time, total household TV units had reached more than 50,000. By then television sets were increasingly being produced as a typical home electric appliance, and the total number of TV reception contracts for Nihon Hoso Kyokai (NHK) exceeded one million by May 1958. This rapidly growing trend was further accelerated by the televised wedding of Prince Akihito. Television sets reached the 3 million mark by October 1959. Advertising expenditures on TV also grew rapidly during this period and exceeded those for newspapers, taking a 34 percent share of total advertising expenditures by 1975.

INTRODUCTION OF MARKETING

During an early stage of the period of rapid economic growth, the theory of marketing was introduced as a way of eliminating the old business practice of space brokers. The modernization of the Japanese advertising industry then ensued in three stages. The first was an introduction of basic research techniques and the establishment of a research department in most advertising agencies. The second step was an improvement of creative techniques from the standpoint of marketing, and the introduction of an independent creative department to the agency environment. The third step was the AE (Account Executive) system introduced from the United States, which did not necessarily match Japanese indigenous practices; the account service system was strengthened by the deeper involvement in marketing planning by the advertisers themselves.

Thus, since the late 1950s Japanese advertising agencies have modernized themselves into full-service agencies, in line with the introduction of widely accepted marketing theories and techniques.

INTERNATIONALIZATION

Foreign-based advertising agencies started their operations in Japan in the late 1950s. J. Walter Thompson opened its Japanese branch in 1956, followed by the joint venture between McCann-Erickson and Hakuhodo in 1960, and another joint venture, Grey-Daiko, in 1963. In 1971, 100 percent capital liberalization was implemented, and both BBDO and Young & Rubicam started their Japan operations in 1972.

In the meantime some of the major Japanese agencies, such as Dentsu, Hakuhodo and Asatsu, had begun to expand their services outside Japan in accordance with the increasing number of Japanese products being exported abroad. Since the 1960s these agencies have established footholds mainly in Southeast Asia. However, except for just a few of the top Japanese agencies, there has been very little expansion on a worldwide basis.

Compared with the rapid internationalization of Japanese manufacturers in general, Japanese advertising agencies on the whole have encountered some constraints to expanding their international networks. In addition to the linguistic and cultural barriers, the limited categories of primary Japanese export products, such as automobiles, electric appliances, and computers and cameras, have constrained Japanese agencies. The mature advertising industry in the United States and Europe made business opportunities for the newcomer foreign agencies fewer and harder to come by. Recently, therefore, Japanese advertising agencies have tended to focus mainly on their neighbors in the Asia-Pacific region, where wider categories of Japanese products are marketable and potential business opportunities are growing. In addition there is less of a cultural barrier to Japanese agencies in this region of the world. One other way in which Japanese agencies have been able to expand is through joint-venture arrangements between Japanese and Western agencies such as Dentsu, Young & Rubicam (DY&R), which is able to handle both local and international clients and thereby overcome cultural barriers.

Main Features of the Japanese Advertising Industry

Japan is the second largest market next to the United States in terms of total advertising expenditures. During the early stages of the post-war economic recovery period, the Japanese advertising industry learned a great deal from U.S. marketing and public relations theories in order to modernize their own industry. The Japanese advertising industry has also developed its own business systems, however, some of which are very unique in comparison to other countries. The following are several of the main characteristics of the contemporary Japanese advertising industry.

MAJOR AGENCIES TAKE THE LION'S SHARE OF THE MARKET

According to an MITI survey there were 4,898 advertising agencies operating in Japan as of 1992, and advertising expenditures for that year were approximately 5,461 billion yen. The combined billings for the top five agencies—Dentsu, Hakuhodo, Tokyu Agency, Daiko and Asatsu—are 2,259 billion yen, which is more than 41 percent of the total Japanese expenditures. The top 10 agencies' combined billings are 2,746 billion yen, or more than 50 percent of the total advertising expenditures. There is no such oligopolic situation in other countries, whether in the West or other parts of Asia except for Korea, and the most conspicuous example is Dentsu, the largest advertising agency in Japan.

According to *Advertising Age* (1993), 10 Japanese agencies or their joint ventures are listed in the world's top 30 advertising organizations for 1993 (Table 2.1). Dentsu has maintained the number one ranking in terms of billings among single agencies worldwide for the past 20 years. Dentsu's billing share among the total advertising expenditures in Japan was about 22 percent in 1993, and Dentsu's unique position is explored further at the end of this section (see Dentsu's Role in the Advertising Industry).

Table 2.1. World's Top 30 Advertising Organizations, 1993

Rank	Name	Headquarters	Worldwide Gross Income (billion US$)	Change vs 1992 (%)
1	WPP Group	London	$2,633.6	1.6
2	Interpublic Group	New York	2,078.5	1.2
3	Omnicom Group	New York	1,876.0	3.1
4	Dentsu Inc.	Tokyo	1,403.2	1.1
5	Saatchi & Saatchi	London/New York	1,355.1	−3.0
6	Young & Rubicam	New York	1,008.9	−4.7
7	Euro RSCG Worldwide	Neuilly, France	864.8	−7.2
8	Grey Advertising	New York	765.7	5.2
9	Hakuhodo Inc.	Tokyo	667.8	9.7
10	F,C & B Communications	Chicago	633.7	−4.2
11	Leo Burnett	Chicago	622.4	−3.3
12	Publicis/Publicis–FCB	Paris	572.0	−8.2
13	D'Arcy Masius Benton & Bowles	New York	553.6	−0.9
14	BDDP Group	Boulogne, France	278.8	−4.8
15	Bozell Worldwide	New York	269.9	9.1
16	Tokyu Agency	Tokyo	181.8	−2.0
17	Daiko Advertising	Osaka	181.5	3.2
18	Asatsu Inc.	Tokyo	171.3	3.3
19	Ketchum Communications	Pittsburgh	140.4	5.7
20	Dai-Ichi Kikaku	Tokyo	135.3	−10.7
21	Dentsu, Young & Rubicam Partnerships	New York, Tokyo	124.5	−5.9
22	Chiat/Day	Los Angeles	122.1	2.8
23	N W Ayer	New York	108.5	−7.7
24	Yomiko Advertising	Tokyo	108.1	6.7
25	Cheil Communications	Seoul	106.6	3.0
26	I & S Corp.	Tokyo	105.0	−8.7
27	Gold Greenlees Trott	London	100.3	−0.4
28	Ayer Europe	London	96.0	−15.3
29	TMP Worldwide	New York	92.0	4.6
30	Asahi Advertising	Tokyo	91.6	−2.5

Source: *Advertising Age,* 1994.

NO "ONE PRODUCT PER CATEGORY" SYSTEM

Unlike other countries, Japanese agencies handle more than one product or client within the same product category. This is partly because advertising agencies first developed as space brokers for the Japanese newspapers, but there are also cultural aspects that explain this difference. Lifetime employment is a business practice unique to Japan. Whereas in other countries any employee, including management, can move from one agency to another at any time, in Japan it is not unusual for the same account team in the same agency to handle the same account for more than a few decades (as long as the client requests so and team members do not reach the mandatory retirement age).

The lifetime employment system and the Japanese-style agency–client relationship, which maintains strict client confidentiality, have been the main reasons why clients stay with the same agency for many years. However, recent changes in the business environment have affected the traditional employment system, which may also affect this relationship in the future.

WIDER RANGE OF AGENCY SERVICES

Today the so-called "below-the-line" services are a growing business area both in Japan and in the West, and it is not unusual to include sales promotions and public relations in the Japanese agency's services. Since the mid-1960s the major Japanese agencies have been handling these newer areas of business, such as sports events, street festivals, conventions, expositions and film productions. Often agencies have in-house specialists to handle such tasks. Whereas advertising agencies in other countries tend to focus on the mass media and assign below-the-line work to outside companies, Japanese agencies traditionally handle a wider range of services in-house, in order to meet the demands of their clients. As competition among agencies gets tougher and tougher, these services are getting more sophisticated and diversified each year. As an indication of the expansion of services beyond traditional advertising, Dentsu, for example, adopted "total communication services" as its corporate slogan and changed its English name from "Dentsu Advertising" to "Dentsu Inc." in 1978.

NO WESTERN AGENCIES ARE IN DOMINANT POSITIONS

Unlike most other Asian countries, where Western-based foreign agencies have achieved a dominant position, foreign agencies have never taken a significant share of the Japanese advertising market. Although the market has been open to foreign investors since the 1960s, none of the mega-agencies have been ranked among top positions in agency billing (Table 2.2). One exceptional case was McCann-Erickson Hakuhodo, the U.S.–Japanese joint venture. This agency ranked number nine among the top 10 largest billing agencies in 1993, but the joint venture was dissolved in 1994.

Besides the language problem, the indigenous business culture might also be a major reason why Western agencies do not play key roles in Japan. In other Asian markets such as Singapore, Hong Kong, Malaysia and the Philippines, there has been no crucial language barrier, and it was thus much easier for the Western agencies to establish business footholds there.

Although there are no unfair business practices as such in the advertising marketplace, the recent movement toward relaxation of the restrictions in the overall Japanese market, as well as the changing business environment, should bring more openness for the foreign-based agencies.

MEDIA-BUYING PRACTICES

In Japan there are no media-buying companies or media representatives (except for some foreign-based media) as there are in Western countries, especially the United States. In Japan a large number of media staff work in agencies' media divisions where they function both as media buyers and media representa-

Table 2.2.   Japan's Largest 30 Advertising Agencies in Billing

1993 Rank	Name	Billing 1993 (billion yen)	1992 (billion yen)	Approximate % Change
1	Dentsu	1,123.4	1,198.3	-6.2
2	Hakuhodo	525.8	553.6	-5.0
3	Tokyu Agency	167.0	192.8	-13.4
4	Daiko	159.6	169.3	-5.7
5	Asatsu	141.0	147.9	-4.7
6	Yomiko	103.1	110.3	-6.5
7	Dai-Ichi Kikaku	95.5	102.0	-6.4
8	I & S	92.0	108.5	-15.2
9	McCann-Erickson, Hakuhodo	86.7	90.6	-4.3
10	JR Higashi Nihon Kikaku	76.2	77.2	-1.4
11	Asahi Advertising	66.6	73.9	-9.9
12	Oricom Advertising	48.2	51.9	-7.2
13	Sogei	43.1	43.6	-1.0
14	Chuo Senko	40.3	45.7	-11.7
15	Nihon-Keizai-Sha	39.9	45.9	-13.0
16	Man Nen Sha	37.5	37.9	-0.9
17	Kyodo Advertising	37.2	40.5	-8.2
18	Nippo	36.1	34.9	+3.6
19	Dentsu, Young & Rubicam	34.7	39.3	-11.7
20	Tokyu Agency International	34.4	36.6	-6.2
21	J.W. Thompson	34.3	34.0	+1.0
22	JIC	30.6	33.8	-9.5
23	Nihon Keizai Kokoku Sha	30.6	32.4	-5.8
24	Meitsu	27.5	30.3	-9.5
25	Ad. Melco	26.2	29.9	-12.3
26	Sankosha Co., Ltd	23.0	24.3	-5.2
27	Kyoei Ad International	22.4	24.0	-6.6
28	Sankosha Advertising Agency	22.0	23.6	-6.5
29	Shintsu	21.6	22.5	-3.6
30	Nanbokusha	20.2	21.2	-4.5

Source: *Advertising Age,* 1994.

tives. Advertisers buy media through advertising agencies, which generally receive a 15 percent commission. In addition to the media-buying operation, some agencies—such as Dentsu—are often deeply involved in the planning and production of new publications, as well as television and radio programs. As a result, a certain issue of a certain magazine or a certain program of some national television network may be solely booked by a particular agency's clients, and thus is unavailable to clients of other agencies.

DENTSU'S ROLE IN THE ADVERTISING INDUSTRY

Dentsu was founded in 1901 and started its business as a telegraphic news service agency, as well as an advertising agency. The uniqueness of Dentsu is not attributable to its large share of the industry, but to the leading role it has played in advertising and related industry development in Japan. The following are some examples:

• In 1946, Dentsu began publication of *Dentsu-Ho,* which is the oldest and largest trade paper (with 30,000 circulation) in the Japanese advertising industry. Today it functions like the *Advertising Age* of Japan.

• In 1948, The Dentsu Advertising Award was established. This is the most prestigious advertising award in Japan, given annually to advertisers with the most-outstanding creative techniques, regardless whether or not they are clients of Dentsu.

• In 1949, The Dentsu Advertising Essay Contest for Students was established with the support of the Ministry of Education in an effort to stimulate high school and university students' interest in advertising.

• In 1951, Radio Tokyo was started as one of the first commercial broadcasting stations in Japan, as a result of the initiative of Mr. Yoshida, then President of Dentsu.

These are just a few examples of Dentsu's activities. The agency has also taken initiatives in establishing various industry organizations such as the Audit Bureau of Circulation, an organization that provides auditing and endorsement of the circulations of member newspapers and magazine publishers; the Japan Advertising Agency Association, an organization made up of members from the main advertising agencies in Japan; and Japan Advertising Review Organization, which provides screening and guidance to advertisers on inquiries related to the content of advertisements and product labeling. In addition Dentsu has created various industry publications, such as Japan's total annual advertising expenditure tally—the Dentsu Advertising Annual; the Japanese Newspaper Annual; the Japan Marketing and Advertising Year Book (in English); and other assorted publications concerning the Japanese advertising industry. These publications are circulated not only to the advertising industry, but also to schools and public libraries all over Japan, and in foreign countries as well. Dentsu is thus unique in the sense that it has dedicated itself to upgrading the overall advertising industry, as well as functioning as a spokesperson for the industry as a whole in Japan.

The Japanese Cultural Context

In order to understand the context for advertising, it is first important to describe the cultural situation in Japan. Japan is a homogeneous society in terms of race, language and culture. There is no single religion or ideology that dominates Japan the way Islam does in Indonesia, or Communism does in China. Since the Meiji Restoration of the 19th century, Shinto came to be regarded as the national religion of Japan and the Emperor became deified. However, after World War II the practice of religion was separated from the functions of state, and the present constitution declares that the Emperor is merely the symbol of the state. The Japanese constitution guarantees religious freedom and this guarantee is strictly maintained. Therefore, there is no state religion and no connection between national and religious functions.

Unlike the followers of many other religions, most Japanese are adaptive regarding religious beliefs and do not consider it contradictory to follow more than a single religion at one time. The birth and marriage ceremonies of most Japanese, for example, are Shinto, whereas funerals are Buddhist. The same person may pay his respects to a Shinto shrine on New Year's Day, visit a Buddhist temple during the Bon Festival of the Dead in summer, and celebrate Christmas at the end of the year. Japanese feel no pangs of conscience for such behavior. This attitude toward religion has prompted some large temples and shrines in the Tokyo area to become advertisers. Toward the end of each year, they will use mass media such as TV to solicit larger numbers of worshippers on New Year's Day.

Currently Japan has a total of 118 million Shintoists, 89 million Buddhists, and 1.51 million Christians. But because the country has a total population of just 124 million, the statistics seem to indicate that a significant number of people worship multiple religions at once. As Mr. Taichi Sakaiya (1993) points out in his book, *What is Japan*, this kind of adaptive and situational religious behavior seems to characterize the Japanese people.

JAPANESE GROUP CONSCIOUSNESS

Former U.S. Ambassador to Japan Dr. Edwin O. Reischauer has pointed out that the Japanese tend to put group interests before personal ones. It is also widely acknowledged that Japanese group-consciousness is related to Japan's longstanding culture of rice cultivation. Rice cultivation required collective labor: Water maintenance and management required the people to work in groups and communal allocation. In a traditional rice-cultivating agricultural society, individuals and families could not survive independently of the group. All this instilled in the agricultural workers a consciousness of belonging to their localized farming communities, and among the warrior class of belonging to a clan. Also, with the spread of the Confucian ethic from China there was a strengthening of the concept of belonging to a family group or a clan.

Against this historical background, the modern employee's sense of belonging to the company is further fostered by the system of lifetime employment, his ranking according to the number of years of service and the internal welfare schemes, which are features of company management in Japan. This group-consciousness has underpinned the homogeneity of the Japanese and can be seen in various fields of the Japanese society such as schools, business firms and even professional sports teams. Instead of promoting individual originality, the sense of unity or team work as a group has been encouraged, especially in school education.

Although this tendency has been criticized by Westerners as "standardization of education sacrificing individualism," it has been regarded by the Japanese as highly instrumental in maintaining a competitive edge in the mass production system. The standardization of labor quality is the most efficient way to upgrade productivity of mass manufacturing as well as mass marketing.

JAPANESE HOMOGENEITY

It is often pointed out that the Japanese have a habit of not giving a clear yes or no answer. In comparison, Westerners are more likely to express their opinions openly in a self-asserting way. The Japanese tend to speak and act only after due consideration has been given to the other person's feelings and point of view. The fact that the Japanese behave in this way and take these attitudes for granted in their dealings with one another can be partly explained by their homogeneity and a tradition of avoiding unnecessary friction. Japanese do not want to be different, and pay special attention to their appearance in front of others. It takes courage to behave conspicuously. These attitudes are also applicable to the modern Japanese lifestyle. People are so susceptible to fashion that once something new starts successfully in Tokyo, it spreads all over Japan within a very short period of time. Most Japanese feel a need to pursue a similar standard of living, behavioral norms and values. Thus, homogeneity and group-consciousness have been used to explain the underpinnings of Japanese consumer behavior to a great extent and have made the highly mass-consumption society possible.

GIFT-GIVING AND ENTERTAINMENT CUSTOMS

Gift-giving and entertainment customs are unique aspects of the Japanese culture and, to a large extent, are important to an understanding of Japanese consumer behavior. Gift-giving in Japan involves elaborate rules and is part of a larger system of social exchange, and entertainment takes up a significant portion of companies' and individuals' expenses in business. These social expenses might appear exorbitant, but both customs are constantly affecting the consumption patterns of the Japanese, and are one of the major sources of the nation's tax revenue.

Traditionally, there are several gift-giving seasons during the year: New Year's Day (*Otoshi-Dama*), year-end gifts (*seibo*), and mid-year gifts (*chugen*). Year-end and mid-year are the two biggest sales seasons in the year for most retail outlets. During these two seasons gifts are customarily presented to one's social superiors such as a teacher at school, a marriage go-between, or a business client. Gift-giving expenses are indispensable items for both household and company budgets.

Recently, Christmas and St. Valentine's Day have become popular, transforming Western customs into Japanese ways. Both of them are now trendy gift-giving and entertainment occasions, in addition to the more traditional ones. They have also become major sales occasions for the confectionery industry. Chocolate is a typical gift item for St. Valentine's Day, and the average household spends more for chocolates during the month of February than any other time of the year.

It is also a customary practice for the Japanese to bring gifts when they travel or visit someone, regardless of whether it's a business or social occasion. Proper social manners also dictate that you offer some gifts when you visit someone to ask a favor.

At significant stages of human life such as birth, school entrance, coming of age, and marriage, as well as at funerals, return gifts (*kaeshi*) are required. This return-gift custom creates additional gift-giving occasions. Weddings, for example, involve both gift-giving and entertainment, and are good business opportunities for the hotels and halls with banquet facilities. The average spending for a wedding ceremony at Tokyo hotels ranges from 7 million to 8 million yen (approximately U.S.$70,000–80,000). The invited attendants are usually expected to give gift money of approximately 20,000 to 30,000 yen (approximately U.S.$200–300) per person. The attendants, in turn, receive return gifts worth about half of the value they gave.

Corporate entertainment is another business custom that requires a significant outlay of money. Together with gift-giving, entertainment is a common way of showing gratitude to a company's customers. Typically, the entertainment consists of an invitation to a substantial meal at a high-quality restaurant, followed by one or more visits to Japanese-style bars or night clubs. All major Japanese cities have their entertainment districts containing expensive Japanese-style restaurants (*ryotei*) and Kara-oke bars where business entertainment is conducted. Entertainment expenses are also incurred for occasions such as welcome and farewell parties, promotions, and changes of assignment.

Another favorite method of corporate entertainment is the golf outing. The Japanese often consider golf a business skill, inviting clients to expensive golf courses. Because of the relatively long recession following the collapse of the "bubble economy," the Japanese have been cutting back on their entertainment expenses lately, but that does not mean they have stopped spending altogether for such social expenses. According to a survey by the National Tax Administration, total entertainment expenses for companies in Japan from February 1993 to January 1994 were approximately 5.9 trillion yen, which is 4.2 percent less than the previous year, and a little higher than the total advertising expenditures for Japan during the same period.

CHANGING LIFESTYLES

For years the Japanese have admired the American way of life and have worked hard to catch up with American middle-class lifestyles. As Japan's per capita GNP has grown, many of the riches of the American way, with the exception of housing, now have been acquired. Nevertheless, according to various public opinion surveys many Japanese do not actually feel affluent.

The Heisei-era economy and the subsequent collapse of the bubble economy have had an unprecedented impact on lifestyles and consumption patterns of the Japanese. The bubble collapse left a strong psychological imprint. Consumers have become more price-conscious and generally more conservative in their purchasing habits. The consumption boom period was an era of conspicuous consumption, and people tended to purchase brand-name products and services that demonstrated their more affluent lifestyle. By increasing consumption, consumers acquired luxury goods that had been hitherto out of their reach. As a result of the bubble collapse, though, people seem to have become more introspective, and this new attitude has led to a number of changes in Japanese consumer behavior. Old standards for product selection have collapsed and new yardsticks have emerged. People have become more selective, and the biased view that expensive things are better has largely disappeared. Consumers have started to grope for what may be called their own way of life; they have started to recognize what is truly necessary to fulfill their basic life needs and that purchasing things is only a part of what brings pleasure in life.

Through such changes in consciousness, new lifestyles among the Japanese are being formed. Consumers in Japan are looking for new values, focusing on mental affluence, after having reached a saturation point in material affluence. Long-term social trends are also underpinning the changes in consumer consciousness. These include a rapidly aging society, increased leisure time, the social advances of women, increased health consciousness, rising interest in the global environment, and internationalization. Among these changes, the increase in leisure time, in combination with recent moves toward work-hour reductions, will be an important factor in changing lifestyles.

Following the lessons learned during the bubble economy period, Japanese consumer attitudes now more widely reflect purchasing intentions that could be described as "lower prices for quality products," and an emphasis on value that could be described as "paying what products are worth."

Another changing aspect of the post-bubble economy can be seen in the recent development of "private brands" by some major supermarkets such as Daiei, Ito-Yokado and Seiyu. Also, the introduction of an "open-pricing system" has been initiated by retail stores, which have replaced the manufacturers in determining retail prices. Both of these trends were created under the influence of changing consumer attitudes, as well as price differentials between domestic and foreign markets.

Social and Cultural Constraints on Advertising

Although freedom of speech and expression are guaranteed by the Japanese constitution, there is no established precedent that says this freedom of expression is applicable to advertising. Aside from legal restrictions, advertising is constrained by various habits and unwritten rules based on cultural values that are observed by the majority of the Japanese. These include indirect speech; use of words or expressions that have positive connotations, and avoidance of words with negative connotations; and concern over words and expressions that are considered discriminatory.

In terms of indirect speech, the Japanese tend to avoid straightforward statements, even though they might have distinct opinions about something. Instead they will use indirect phrases or euphemisms, and these roundabout ways of expression are generally considered more appropriate for polite conversation. Although occasionally criticized as being ambiguous, these efforts to soften a statement of opinion reflect basic Japanese attitudes derived from the group consciousness and homogeneity.

Unlike Americans, it is very rare for the Japanese to have a face-to-face debate between two rival candidates during an election. Instead roundtable discussions among several speakers are common as a means of exchanging opinions. Candidates usually try to avoid direct conflict between the competitors, and prefer to talk in harmonious tones. The same frame of mind is true in advertising. The so-called "soft-sell" approach is more common than a direct appeal to reason.

It is only recently that comparative advertising has been legally allowed in Japan. While American-type comparative advertising has begun to appear in the Japanese media, the tendency toward indirectness is a deep-seated cultural preference. Certainly, the preponderance of soft-sell, image advertising will remain the norm. As a Japanese saying points out, "The nail that sticks out gets pounded down." In a group-oriented society, one who rises even a little above his fellows becomes the object of punishment or ostracism.

In addition to indirectness there are certain words and expressions that have certain connotations and therefore should preferably be avoided in advertising. For example, certain numerals are to be avoided on certain occasions; these include the number four (4), pronounced *shi,* which means death, and the number nine (9), pronounced *ku,* which means pain. Hospitals or hotels often do not have rooms numbered four or nine, or, as well, 13, which is an unlucky number from the Western tradition. Marketers and advertisers often avoid use of any of these numbers or dates for scheduling of new product or campaign launches.

When setting up certain events, particular days of the lunar calendar are also to be avoided, such as a wedding on *Butsu-Metsu* (Buddha's death) or a funeral on *Tomo-Biki* (to hold a funeral on this day is said to be inviting another death).

Traditionally, people also pay attention to associations with nature. Certain kinds of plants, trees and flowers are regarded as symbols of good or bad luck, and certain kinds of animals are believed to possess particular personalities or powers. Pine trees, bamboo and plum trees in combination signify good fortune, and are used in flower arrangements or bonsai on festive occasions such as New Year's Day. Use of these plants or trees in advertisements would have a pleasing effect on the audience. Very often, this same threesome, *Sho-Chiku-Bai,* is used in restaurants as names for the three ranks of quality and prices of its dishes.

Animals also have certain connotations that must be understood by advertisers. Both dogs and cats are popular as pets, but sometimes the use of the word can have a double meaning. The Japanese word for *dog* can be a synonym for "spy" or "dupe," and the word for *cat* is a synonym for "someone seeking revenge." Although in the West animosity between cats and dogs is assumed, in Japan this animosity is thought to exist between dogs and monkeys.

Another animal, the horse, has traditionally been treated as a sacred creature at Shinto shrines. On the other hand, the horse is often considered to be a stupid creature, as epitomized in the word *baka*, written with the characters for "horse" and "deer." The cow symbolizes dullness and slowness; to walk like a cow means to walk extremely slowly, whereas the rabbit is compared with a person who runs away very quickly. Both *tanuki*, or the Japanese raccoon, and *kitsune*, or fox, are believed to be able to change their appearances into human form and trick people. Both cranes and turtles are said to live long lives, and they symbolize longevity. To misuse one of these animals symbolically in an advertisement could create negative impressions for the advertiser. Although the Japanese tend to avoid identifying with any single religious doctrine, they have a cultural reverence for all things that originate from their deeply rooted, mystical affinity with nature and their belief that prayer can bring tangible, worldly benefits.

Finally, discriminatory words and expressions can be problematic in Japan and must, therefore, be avoided in advertisements. From the 1970s through the 1980s a movement protesting discriminatory attitudes and expressions intensified, and as time has gone by, the content and the targets have greatly expanded. This movement covers many issues, including the disabled, sexual harassment, the elderly, child abuse, minorities and various other human rights issues. A number of associations and activist groups have protested against business firms or local municipal government offices for their discriminatory policies on employment or advancement. In response, some of these companies and public offices have set up internal organizations called Anti-Defamation Departments and have begun employee education sessions to cope with these issues. Because of the barrage of protests and complaints, one of the major newspapers, the *Yomiuri Shimbun*, published a guidebook, *A Brief List of Discriminatory Expressions, Uncomfortable Words, and Words to Be Used with Caution*, in 1993.

These issues can affect advertisers. For example, poster advertisements and TV commercials for some whiskey products were condemned by a women's liberation group because the model was allegedly associated with a rape scene. All such advertisements were pulled from the media in 1989.

Most of the mass media have their own self-restrictive codes on similar issues. However, Mr. Kenji Kobayashi, one of the pioneers of *Buraku* (the minority) issues, points out that the issues are not a matter of words, but of the intentions of discrimination. Overly sensitive reactions on these matters by mass media might lead to self-censorship. Thus, too much concern with social constraints might also lead to restricting the creativity and originality of advertising expressions, and might eventually block the free interchange of ideas.

Advertising Regulations and Regulatory Process

Advertising regulations in a true sense were born in Japan after the establishment of the Anti-Monopoly Act in 1947. The Japan Fair Trade Commission (JFTC) enacted the Act Against Unjust Premiums and Misleading Representations (*Keihyoho*) in 1962 as a complement law to the Anti-Monopoly Act in order to prohibit misleading or false indications and advertising. Regulations against false and misleading advertising are mainly based on this law.

The MITI and JFTC are the major authorities concerned with the advertising industry, and these bodies are responsible for enforcing the Act Against Unjust Premiums and Misleading Representations and the Anti-Monopoly Act.

Part of the authority for enforcing the law has been shared with the prefectural office since 1972. The regulations that enable consumers to select merchandise using their own judgment, based on reasonable and open information, are called "fair competition rules." These rules are subject to self-regulation in each industry, and have been implemented by the approval of JFTC (*Keihyoho*, Article 10). However, regulations under the Anti-Monopoly Act and the *Keihyoho* only control misleading indications or extravagant advertising.

Advertising Self-Regulation

The fair competition rule in Japan was modeled after the Federal Trade Commission's system in the United States. This system operates under the assumption that violations occur mainly as a result of competition within a particular industry. The fair competition rule was regarded as an effective way to set up a self-regulatory standard of proper business practices by the industries themselves. The rules encourage an industry to establish mutual checks and balances and to prevent improper competition by enforcing the self-regulatory rules. The Fair Competition Council has been organized by the members of the participating industries to implement the rules.

In 1974, the Japan Advertising Review Organization (JARO) was founded as a self-regulatory organization consisting of advertisers, media, advertising agencies and producers of advertisements. Their activities include (a) receiving and processing inquiries and complaints concerning advertisements and representations; (b) monitoring and giving guidance on advertisements and representations; (c) compiling standards for advertisements and representations; (d) promoting cooperation and linkages between advertisers, media and advertising agencies; (e) doing liaison work with consumer groups and administrative offices; (f) engaging in education and public relations activities for companies and consumers; (g) establishing a role as an information center; and (h) effecting other tasks that may be deemed necessary. Review and processing functions for complaints and inquiries from consumers and companies are shown in Figure 2.1.

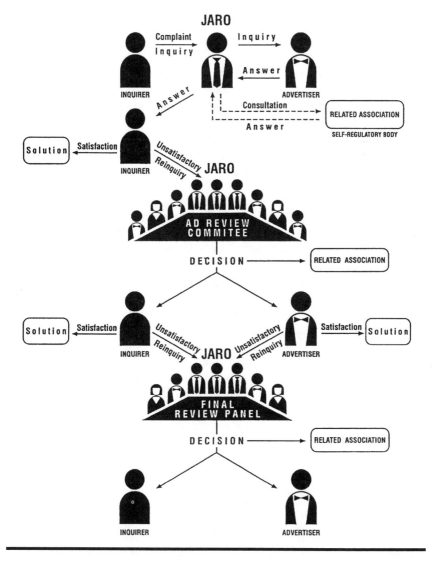

Fig. 2.1. Process of handling complaints by JARO. (Source: Japan Advertising Review Organization (JARO), 1994.)

This structure was modeled on the Council of Better Business Bureaus (CBBB) as it exists in the United States, but what makes the CBBB different from JARO is the following. In the United States, if the matter is not settled after the examination, and the advertiser will not agree to change or pull out the offending advertisement(s), the CBBB is eventually supposed to put the matter into the hands of a higher administrative body made up of industry representatives. In the case of JARO's review system, however, the final decision-making body, called the Final Review Panel, is composed of seven academics who are not members of JARO. Their decision is final and will simply be reported to the concerned organizations and administrative bodies, because the administrative bodies are not supposed to be involved in the final settlement.

During 1993 the total inquiries received by JARO numbered 3,725, and 25 percent of those were complaints. According to JARO, the most frequently mentioned issues in 1993 were (a) membership club recruitment; (b) advertising and related matters; (c) food; (d) human resources recruitment; (e) mail order sales; (f) requests for inquiry and introduction; (g) questions regarding JARO; (h) part-time job recruitment; (i) prizes and premiums; and (j) financial and insurance matters.

There are many other self-regulatory organizations that function in various industries, including advertising and media, and each industry's organization has its own code of ethics or an agreement on advertising activities. Some examples of advertiser organizations include (a) The Federation of Bankers Associations of Japan (*Zenginkyo*), set up by the self-regulatory agreement on advertisements in 1968; and (b) The Federation of Pharmaceutical Manufacturers Associations of Japan (*Zenyakuren*), which created a self-regulatory agreement on advertising for over-the-counter medical and pharmaceutical products in 1964.

In the case of media self-regulation, the Japan Newspaper Publishers and Editors Association instituted the Newspaper Advertising Ethics Principles in 1958, and set up the Newspaper Advertising Review Council in 1971. The National Association of Commercial Broadcasters in Japan established the Radio Broadcasting Criteria in 1951, and formulated an expanded set of self-regulatory criteria extending control to television commercials and others in 1990. Each major medium has established its own self-restrictive criteria on an in-house basis, but usually does not open those criteria to outside scrutiny.

Deregulation and Advertising

Prior to the 1980s, Japan had extensive government regulation of private sector activities in industries and areas that were regarded as having an important impact on consumer welfare. Compared with the United States and Europe, deregulation was slow in coming to Japan because the priority had been on maintaining standards of safety and health. However, after experiencing the sluggish economy brought about by the rising yen, consumers and consumer groups that had formerly approached deregulatory measures with caution began reconsidering their views toward innovations such as coupon advertising and comparative advertising, which previously had not been practiced in Japan.

Coupon advertising, or the coupon redemption system, had been prohibited in Japan because it was regarded as a kind of "premium item" that was not consistent with fair competition. However, at meetings held by Structural Impediments Initiative, the United States criticized the Japanese policy toward couponing as a nontariff barrier hindering foreign products coming into the Japanese market. Mainly because the U.S. government insisted on a review of this policy, the JFTC lifted the ban on newspaper coupons in October 1994, 3 years after the ban on magazine coupons had been lifted.

Under the terms dictated by the JFTC, the maximum discounted price with a coupon is 50 percent and the maximum sampling price is 300 yen per item. However, marketers must still overcome some image problems with couponing because in the past, the Japanese consumer has tended to believe that a couponed product was defective or overpriced to begin with. Once consumers realize, however, that the actual prices are being discounted with coupons, they should provide more support for the continued growth of this marketing tool.

Deregulation in the advertising field has also recently led to the introduction of comparative advertising. Comparative advertising is advertising that describes the superiority of a product or service by referring to competitors. Previously it had been virtually prohibited both from a legal and business standpoint in Japan. In connection with the trade conflict in April 1986, and under growing criticism by foreign firms that had been claiming that their effective advertising was being hampered, the JFTC announced "the guidelines of comparative advertising." The JFTC has actually lifted the ban, with the condition that the content must be proved from an objective point of view. Recent examples of comparative advertisements appearing in Japan include:

1) The newly established DDI corporation ran newspaper advertising in April 1992, describing their new long-distance telephone charges and comparing their rates to those of their competitors.

2) Pepsi television commercials that ran in the spring of 1992 showed U.S. rap singer M.C. Hammer turning into an old-fashioned crooner upon sipping a Coca-Cola. This commercial was pulled by the stations after a complaint by Coca-Cola.

3) In 1992, GM Japan ran a print advertisement in several major newspapers making a direct comparison between Cadillac Seville and Nissan Infiniti in terms of quality, price and fuel efficiency. This was the first of its kind in terms of comparative advertising.

At this moment the possibility of these types of advertising prevailing in

Japan appears rather limited. Some critics have mentioned that because Japanese advertising agencies handle more than one client in the same product category, it would be difficult to run comparative advertising. But a more important reason why Western-style comparative advertising probably will not prevail is because of the Japanese personality. The Japanese tend to show reluctance to firms flattering themselves by demonstrating their superiority, even though their assertions are correct, as Mr. Kiyoshi Kogure of McCann-Erickson, Hakuhodo, pointed out in the *Nikkei Sangyo Shimbun,* March 12, 1993: "Although product superiority is convincing, the Japanese believe it is better for advertisers to be modest and cautious, so that their advertisements are not regarded as slanderous to their competitors."

The Japanese tend to prefer emotional and ambiguous expressions, and advertisers would rather demonstrate their comparative advantages in humorous or roundabout ways instead of identifying their competitors directly. This attitude is deeply related to the subject of indigenous Japanese cultural values that was described in the earlier section. In this sense Japanese comparative advertising will almost certainly take its own distinctive course different from the American way, even though more direct comparative advertising might be welcomed by consumers in the future.

General Characteristics of the Mass Media

According to Article 21 of the Japanese constitution, freedom of speech is guaranteed in the press and all other forms of expression. The constitution states that no censorship shall be maintained. During World War II, having experienced such hardships as censorship, interventions and various restrictions, mainly by the military government, the Japanese press was concerned about government controls and restrictive policies toward media. Under the current democratic system, no such strict control of media industries is allowed as a whole, but there are some rules and regulations on mass media, especially broadcasting operations.

NEWSPAPERS

The Japan Newspapers Publisher and Editors Association has 122 members who publish in total 52,433,000 copies of daily papers. This number substantially exceeds that of the total Japanese households namely 1.22 copies per household. Most of these newspapers are delivered door to door.

The Japanese newspaper industry is in many ways unique when compared with other countries. Japan has a number of major national newspapers including *Asahi, Mainichi, Yomiuri, Nikkei* and *Sankei,* as well as influential local newspapers. The circulation of the Japanese national newspapers reaches a magnitude unequaled in any other country in the world (Table 2.3).

Table 2.3. Circulation of the Five National Newspapers in Japan, 1993

	Morning Edition	Evening Edition
Asahi	8,228,960	4,532,091
Mainichi	4,008,565	1,962,501
Yomiuri	9,874,315	4,513,380
Nikkei	2,921,855	1,714,125
Sankei	1,904,987	960,051

Japanese newspapers can be classified into three categories: national, block and regional according to the size of circulation areas. These national, block and regional papers have been labeled **general interest** papers due to the fact they provide wide coverage of current events, business, politics, overseas news, culture and sports. In addition there are also a variety of **special interest** papers that offer information on a wide range of specific subjects. For example, sports papers primarily focusing on sports, entertainment and leisure, and trade papers cover specific industries.

MAGAZINES

In 1993, 2,379 monthly magazines published 2,985,330,000 copies, and 81 weeklies published 1,930,510,000 copies; 169 new magazines were launched. As many as 21 magazines (13 of which are comics) have a circulation of over one million copies in the domestic market alone. Members of the advertising departments of the main magazines and advertising agencies belong to the Magazine Advertising Association of Japan, a group whose purpose is to codify magazine advertising ethics, award prizes for outstanding ads, and host seminars and essay contests.

Japanese magazines can be broadly classified as follows:

1) **General interest magazines**: monthly or weekly publications that provide wide coverage of issues relating to politics, economics, arts, sports as well as news and events. Some of these are characterized by their orientation toward literature, business, and so forth.

2) **Segment magazines based on demographic criteria**: Publications for young men or women, housewives, families, elderly people, and so forth.

3) **Segment magazines based on tastes or types of information**: Fashion, interior decoration, local information, recent trends, and so forth.

4) **Special interest magazines**: Cover specific subjects including finance, music, housing, architecture, automobiles, cooking, science, tourism and sports.

5) **Magazines in specific editorial styles**: Photogravure, weeklies, comic magazines, book-like magazines called "mooks" (neologism derived from magazine and book).

Recently, an increasing number of joint ventures with foreign magazines have given birth to new publications including *Forbes Japan, GQ Japan,* and *Global Business* (Japanese version of *The Economist*) and *National Geographic.* Another recent trend is a growing number of the so-called "controlled magazines" such as credit card membership magazines, luxury target magazines and in-flight or on-board magazines. There are approximately 30 magazines in this category.

Japanese magazines are sold mainly in book stores and station kiosks. Few magazines are sold through subscription. Recently, convenience stores—which are gradually spreading throughout the country—have become popular magazines outlets.

BROADCAST MEDIA

The Broadcast Act, The Wireless Telegraphy Act and the related regulations enacted in the 1950s are supervisory laws and the Ministry of Posts and Telecommunications is the authority concerned with the broadcasting industry. Broadcasting operations are fundamentally controlled by the licensing system and all broadcasting stations are required to get their licenses from the Ministry when they start operations and to renew these licenses every 3 years.

Nihon Hoso Kyokai (NHK) is the nonprofit public corporation and operates broadcasting stations based on the income from a viewing fee collected from all television set owners. The corporation is obliged to get approvals from Diet on the budget and program planning. Although NHK is required to provide nationwide services, either by AM and TV, or by FM and TV, other broadcasting companies have been granted permission to operate commercial broadcasting operations and support themselves by advertising revenue. Each commercial station is, in principle, given a license on the basis of serving one local prefecture. Commercial broadcasting operations are divided into three categories: (1) a single radio operation based on either AM or short wave or FM, (2) a single TV operation, (3) a double operation of AM radio and TV. Regarding the programming of both NHK and commercial broadcasting stations, there are detailed regulations about the program content and the journalistic attitude toward social, political matters by the stations in accordance with Article 44 of the Broadcast Act.

RADIO

Today there are 92 radio stations broadcasting across the country and 47 of these are AM, 44 are FM and one is short wave (April, 1994). AM broadcasting is nationwide, with some wide-coverage stations reaching several prefectures and many local stations each serving one prefecture. Two dominant national AM networks, JRN (Japan Radio Network, the key station of which is the Tokyo Broadcasting System) and NRN (National Radio Network, lead by Nippon Broadcasting and Culture Broadcasting) share the overall market while several independent local stations serve their specific audiences.

FM broadcasting primarily serves the main metropolitan areas, thus it may be characterized as an urban medium. There are in total 44 FM stations across Japan, of which 33 belong to JFN (Japan FM Network, lead by TOKYO-FM). These affiliated stations purchase optional sponsored network programs as well as JFN's coproduced programs to organize programming schedules in combination with their own live shows or local information programs. Independent FM stations, including J-WAVE, inaugurated in 1989, stress their policies concerning program individualization; some of them have also joined together to form networks.

The number of radio sets in Japan is estimated at 182,000,000, of which 124,000,000 are ordinary radios and 58,000,000 are car radios. The typical Japanese household owns as many as 4.4 radio sets. New technology has actively influenced radio broadcasting techniques, evidenced by the introduction of multiplex FM broadcasting and encoded transmission. Within the last 2 years, 11 major AM stations started broadcasting in stereo.

The rating survey in 1994, using the same standards for AM and FM broadcasts, showed an overall rating of 8.2 percent; 8.5 percent on weekdays; 7.9 percent on Saturdays; and 6.9 percent on Sundays. A 1 percent radio rating corresponds to an audience reach of 830,000 people (males and females aged 12 through 59) across the country, including 270,000 in Tokyo metropolitan areas and 150,000 in Osaka areas. In Japan the average household owns one or more cars, over 90 percent of which are equipped with radios. Although the ratings of car radios are not tracked, they can be expected to be considerably high. The overall radio listening rates show three peak periods during the day: 7:00–8:00 a.m., 10:00 a.m.–12:00 noon, and 1:00–4:00 p.m.

In general the highest ratings for AM radio are held by traffic information programs for commuters (6:00–9:00 a.m.), evening baseball broadcasts and midnight programs targeted toward teenagers and college students (after 11:00 p.m.).

TELEVISION

There are presently 120 commercial TV stations, of which 48 are VHF and 72 are UHF. Five key stations (NTV, TBS, CXT, ANB and TX) each operate a national network. Households owning television sets number 42 million (99.7 percent of total households in Japan) and 99.2 percent of these own color sets. Of all the advertising media, television is the most popular not only in terms of exposure rates, but also in terms of exposure time. The typical household watches television for over 8 hours per day, while individuals average nearly 4 hours per day. Viewing rates show three peaks during the day; morning, noon and evening. Nearly 80 percent of all households watch television, particularly between the hours of 8:00 and 9:00 p.m.

The development of a rating survey by Video Research and Nielsen using audience meters has allowed stations and advertisers to pursue more-accurate advertising effectiveness. At the same time, however, the excessive pursuit of quantitative effectiveness has given rise to public criticism of television programs.

This has in turn led to the recent issue of the "quality of audience." In response to such demands on the part of both audiences and advertisers, stations are striving to develop quality programs. Recently each station has begun putting greater emphasis on news and information-oriented programs, and these increasingly account for a significant percentage of all broadcasts.

NEW ELECTRONIC MEDIA

There are three satellite channels [two of these belonging to NHK, and another to Japan Satellite Broadcasting Co. (JSB)] that began operations in April 1991. In August 1992, 4.3 million households were subscribing to NHK's satellite broadcasting and one million households to JSB.

Initially satellite broadcasting could be received by households only via cable television (CATV). But in April 1992 a new system was developed enabling individual reception. As a result there are 20 cable television network companies linked to communications satellites, of which six have had their licenses approved.

Total CATV household penetration is 9.2 million. CATV was originally introduced to serve areas with poor reception. There have been 147 urban-type CATV licenses approved, of which 130 started operations during 1993 (household penetration 1.6 million). NHK contract viewership is 4.7 percent. Terrestrial broadcasting, however, still predominates over satellite and CATV broadcasting. New electronic media (CATV, Videotext and Teletext) advertising expenditures totaled 11.9 billion yen in 1993, up 4.4 percent from the previous year, for the second consecutive year of growth. Despite four new CS (communications satellite) TV stations and CATV program suppliers, bringing the industry total up to 10, national advertisers have not shown aggressive support for this medium, resulting in its maintaining only a 0.2 percent component ratio among total advertising expenditures unchanged since 1987.

ADVERTISING ASSOCIATIONS

In addition to the advertising organizations mentioned earlier in this chapter, there are a number of others that should be noted. The Advertising Federation of Japan is an organization that includes advertisers, media and advertising agencies. Its aims are to uphold advertising ethics, to conduct research on the industry and to act as a liaison between the industry and government and consumers; The Japan Advertising Council, which appeals to society through advertising for understanding of and cooperation in addressing social welfare problems; The Nippon Arts Council, whose members are made up of art directors, designers, copywriters and other creatives who cooperate to achieve common goals and study new advertising techniques; the All Japan Radio & Television Commercial Council, which holds annual award ceremonies and seminars; and the Japan International Advertising Association, which contributes to the promotion of international trade through the improvement of international advertising standards in Japan. This group cooperates with other international advertising organizations through the introduction of the latest technology and information. In addition to the organizations directly involved with advertising, there are also a number of groups that indirectly are related to the advertising industry such as The Japan Marketing Association, which is made up of representatives from the advertising industry and related industries as well as university scholars, and The Public Relations Society of Japan, whose goals are to improve the moral and ethical standards of the profession and to educate people through seminars and exchanges of personnel with overseas organizations.

Conclusions

For the past 50 years, Japanese consumers have admired the lifestyles of the advanced Western countries and have sought materialistic affluence. Having achieved one of the highest living standards in the world, and having now experienced the bubble economy and subsequent collapse, the Japanese are in search of new life values, focusing on "mental" affluence.

In the advertising field Japan has learned a great deal from the United States in terms of modern theories and techniques, and it has become today the second-largest advertising market, following the United States. However, the increasing trends toward globalization and international dependence have prompted Japan to deregulate and open its markets. Under these circumstances, the Japanese advertising industry is also trying to develop its own technologies and culture.

The role of advertising has developed from a mere means of sales promotional activities into more-diversified communications. Preparing for the 21st century, advertising is also being applied to help solve global issues such as conservation of energy and the environment, as well as social welfare problems concerning the aged, the physically challenged, fatherless families, traffic victims, and education. Public affairs communications will become increasingly important, and Japan should play a key role in promoting these activities as a member nation of the Asian Region from now on.

Bibliography

Advertising Age. 1993. Annual Report, April 14, p. 28.
Advertising Age. 1994. Annual Report, April 11, p. 26.
Dentsu Advertising Annual '94/'95. 1994. Tokyo: Dentsu Inc.
Guide to the 4 (Four) Mass Media in Japan. 1993. Tokyo: Dentsu Inc.
Handbook for New Employees. 1992. Tokyo: Dentsu Inc.
Handbook for New Employees. 1994. Tokyo: Dentsu Inc.
Japan 1992 Marketing and Advertising Yearbook. 1991. Tokyo: Dentsu Inc.
Japan 1993 Marketing and Advertising Yearbook. 1992. Tokyo: Dentsu Inc.

Japan Almanac 1995. 1994. Tokyo: Asahi Shimbun, October.

Japanese Newspaper Annual '94/'95. 1994. The Japan Newspaper Publishers and Editors Association. Tokyo: Dentsu Inc.

Journal of Japanese Trade & Industry. Japan Economic Foundation. Tokyo.

Kokoku no Hyogen to Houki [Rules and Regulations on Advertising Expressions]. 1980. Tokyo: Dentsu Inc.   ˎ

Media-Data Handbook. 1992. Tokyo: Dentsu Inc.

Media-Data Handbook. 1995. Tokyo: Dentsu Inc.

NichiBei Sangyo Hikaku ni Kansuru Chosa Kenkyu Hokokusho [A Research Report on Comparison Between Japanese and U.S. Industries]. 1985. Tokyo: Japan Economic Research Center, March.

Nikkei Sangyo Shimbun. 1993. "Four Principles of the Japanese Style Comparative Advertising, i.e., 'Modesty,' 'Objectivity,' 'Consumer's View Point' and 'To Avoid Provocation'," March 12, p. 24.

Sakaiya, Taichi. 1993. *What is Japan?* Translated by Steven Karpa. New York: Kodansha America.

Seeking New Values: Tasks for the '90s. 1990. Tokyo: Dentsu Institute for Human Studies, January.

Shohisha Dantai no Gaiyo [An Outline of Consumer Organizations]. 1993. Japanese Economic Planning Agency. Tokyo.

Woronoff, J. 1990. *Asia's "Miracle" Economies.* Tokyo: Yohan Publications, Inc.

3

Advertising in Hong Kong

ERNEST F. MARTIN, Jr.

Introduction

As a key center of commerce, Hong Kong is a focal point of Southeast Asian business development and is one of the world's most dynamic economies. This small outpost in southern China is one of the least regulated free-enterprise systems in the world. Along with its rank as one of the largest container ports in the world, and its longstanding position as a major international financial center, Hong Kong is also the prime business, communications and marketing center for the region. The only natural resources are its deep-water harbor and favorable geographic location on China's southeast coast. With these limited resources Hong Kong is not only a thriving industrial and commercial center in its own right, but is also the gateway to the rapidly expanding economy of the People's Republic of China (PRC) and mainland East Asia.

Hong Kong is a major financial capital of Asia for a number of reasons in addition to its natural harbor. The communication and transportation infrastructures are well developed. The legal system, founded on British common law, was designed for business and trade. As the largest port of entry to the PRC, it is the trade conduit between Taiwan and China, two long-time antagonists whose economic interdependence is increasing. Additionally, the people of Hong Kong are culturally disposed toward business. It continues to be the center of Western business interests in East Asia, and English is the official second language, making it highly accessible to Westerners.

HISTORICAL CONTEXT

The modern era of Hong Kong began for the sole purpose of trade. In the 1840s British East India Company traders established Hong Kong as a trading outpost and the British port of entry to China. Britain declared it a free port in 1841, using it to bring in large amounts of opium produced in India, thus depleting Chinese silver reserves and creating an epidemic drug problem.

Britain won Hong Kong Island, in perpetuity, from China in 1842 after the First Opium War (Treaty of Nanking). The British gained control of the Kowloon

Peninsula by the Convention of Beijing in 1860. The New Territories adjoining Kowloon and 235 adjacent islands were obtained by the British in 1898 (the Second Convention of Beijing) with a 99-year lease for the land. This was one of the many unequal treaties forced on the corrupt and crumbling Qing Dynasty, enlarging the entire British possession to the 415-square-mile area that is today called Hong Kong.

During the first half of the 20th century, Hong Kong's position as a trade center declined relative to Shanghai. After the Communist victory in 1949, the colony once again regained its prominence. Beginning in 1946 thousands of refugees from China poured into the colony, providing cheap labor for the many new factories. With a strong determination to succeed, the local people and immigrants from China began to make fortunes with savvy management styles and shrewd investments. Mainland China was stagnant and chaotic under central-planning mismanagement. The people of Hong Kong seized business as a way of life, gradually taking financial dominance, but not ultimate political power, from foreign and colonial capitalists.

Early Hong Kong advertising was closely linked with painting and fine arts. Companies hired artists who practiced the traditional style of painting. Most of the artists where brought to Hong Kong from Guangdong province in the PRC. Calendars, matchbox covers, newspapers, magazines and painted signs and posters reflected the adaptation of traditional Chinese painting to product promotion. Many of the painters who are prominent in Hong Kong art history enhanced advertising creativity in the early days.

Along with establishment of local agencies in the late 1920s, one multinational agency, D'Arcy Masius Benton & Bowles (DMB&B), began operation in Hong Kong in 1927 (Euromonitor 1993). Throughout the 1930s small agencies and freelance artists provided advertising support for companies. Although radio began in 1928, no advertising was allowed until the start of commercial radio in 1959. Commercial television broadcasting began in 1967 (Everest 1978). Two multinational agencies were established in the 1940s and 1950s, four more in the 1960s, and most of the remainder of the multinational agencies operating today began in Hong Kong in the 1970s (Euromonitor 1993; Dun & Bradstreet 1993).

The leap into financial world-class status was stimulated by Deng Xiaoping's "Open Door" policies in 1978. Hong Kong was naturally suited to provide the business skills China desperately needed, and the port handled southern China's exports. Guangdong Province provided investments and cheap labor. Hong Kong entrepreneurs zealously moved into the China market. Industrial jobs moved to the mainland, with Hong Kong providing the financial, transportation and marketing services. Western companies set up business headquarters in Hong Kong for easy access to China because of the long history of commerce and the use of English as the language of business.

Under a 1984 joint declaration between China and Britain, sovereignty of Hong Kong returns to the PRC in 1997 when the 99-year lease expires. The agreement was favorable to Hong Kong, stipulating that Hong Kong's "capital-ist system, and lifestyle will remain unchanged for 50 years." Hong Kong will retain its separate currency, and no tax money will go to China. The PRC will be responsible for the defense of Hong Kong. The "one country, two systems" al-lows Hong Kong to maintain its economic system—but, without doubt the polit-ical system will be brought into alignment with sovereignty.

Although some people in Hong Kong are concerned about whether China will live up to the promise of "one country, two systems," many believe that the PRC will not upset Hong Kong's strong economy. China needs hard currency and Hong Kong can supply it. The belief is that Hong Kong will continue to sail along without interference in its free-market system.

Hong Kong continues to sit at the hub of a huge economic powerhouse called "Greater China," which includes the combined economic resources of China, Taiwan, Hong Kong, Singapore, Macao and other overseas Chinese com-munities in Southeast Asia. Greater China transcends geopolitical borders and is bound together by a common cultural tradition. As Greater China further devel-ops, it will be an economic bloc as powerful, if not more powerful, than North America, Europe or Japan. Without dispute, Hong Kong is the capital of Greater China.

Economy

Overall indicators point to Hong Kong's economic strength. With the gross domestic product (GDP) growing in 1994 (by 5.5 percent at constant 1990 mar-ket prices and 12.3 percent at current market prices) and per capita income of US$15,316, Hong Kong has kept inflation under double digits at 8.6 percent.

Hong Kong's financial secretary estimated 1995 GNP growth equal to 1994 at 5.5 percent and inflation constant at 8.5 percent. Although the overall GDP is strong, the growth has been showing a slight slowdown after years of gathering strength. Economists are predicting a slight downturn from the peak of growth. While the economy is fundamentally strong, the slowdown is because of the property and financial markets. What is called the "wealth effect" (property ap-preciation/speculation and stock market growth), which powered expenditures in recent years, is gone. Reverses in the property and stock markets hit Hong Kong consumers, causing private consumption to slow down.

Regardless, whether there is a "negative wealth effect" slowdown, the Hong Kong GDP shows a powerful economy. The figures are correct when they show a high standard of living for Hong Kong residents. The 1993 World Bank's an-nual survey of the world's rich and poor placed Hong Kong in the top 10. Switzerland is the top, followed by United Arab Emirates and Qatar with billions of barrels of oil and very few citizens. Following Hong Kong in the "top 10" are Japan, Germany and Singapore.

However, real-life experience demonstrates that the average citizen is not in the same bracket as the other "top 10" countries of Switzerland and Germany in either terms of income or wealth.

The composition of Hong Kong's GDP points out why. Hong Kong is a trading entrepot—a conduit for China's foreign trade. The value of exports plus imports is well over twice the size of the GDP, with less of the money ending up with the wage earner. The difference between Hong Kong and a European industrial country is seen in the share of the GDP in private consumption. In Hong Kong it is 57 percent of the GDP. In Europe private consumption is customarily 66 percent.

The interesting question is what happens after 1997, with two systems but not two countries. Incomes in Hong Kong and Guangdong province eventually must come together, as water finds its own level. Hong Kong is hoping that it will be accomplished by Guangdong leveling up with Hong Kong, not Hong Kong leveling down (Last 1994–95, 32).

While inflation has been constantly driving prices higher in Hong Kong, the rate has been fairly stable and controllable. The average annual rate of inflation over the past 10 years is about 7.5 percent. The Consumer Price Index (CPI), in constant dollars, does show a high level of price increase putting pressure on wage earners in the territory, with 1993 CPI up 188.8 percent against the 1984–85 index.

The Hong Kong dollar is pegged to the U.S. dollar, keeping the currency very stable against world currency leaders (Daryanani 1994, 457).

Consumers

POPULATION

The population of Hong Kong passed six million for the first time in 1993 (Daryanani 1994, 410). According to government figures from the 1991 population census, approximately 60 percent of the population was born in Hong Kong and 34 percent in China. The 10-year population growth (1983–1993) is 11.9 percent, reflecting an annual growth rate of 1.1 percent. Despite a decrease in the number of births during the past 5 years, the population grew at about the same rate because of a larger net inflow of persons into the territory. The rate of natural increase dropped steadily during the last 10 years—from 11 to 6.8 per 1,000 people—with births dropping from 16 per 1,000 people in 1983 to 12 per 1,000 people in 1993, and a stable death rate of 5 per 1,000 people (Daryanani 1994, 410).

During the same period, emigration, the so-called "brain drain," increased—especially after 1989. The number of persons leaving Hong Kong increased from 20,000 a year in the early 1980s to 66,000 in 1992. The increase has been attributed to many factors, including concern about Hong Kong's future after the 1997 change of sovereignty and emigration opportunities in popular countries like Canada, Australia, New Zealand, the United States and Britain. In 1993, the number of emigrants dropped to about 54,000 because of the economic downturn and reduced intake of some countries (Daryanani 1994, 412).

While many were leaving for foreign countries, others immigrated to the fertile business environs of the territory. The net change was an inflow. Additionally, since 1993 a "reverse brain drain" has been occurring, with Hong Kong Chinese who have obtained a foreign passport, often in countries still suffering from the tail-end of the world-wide recession, returning to the prosperous economy of Hong Kong. The government estimates that at least 12 percent of persons who emigrated between 1982 and 1992 have returned to Hong Kong (Daryanani 1994, 412).

The projections of Hong Kong's annual growth rate is to slow down to eight-tenths of a percent (0.8 percent) for the period of 1991–2000. This is down from 1.1 percent for the period 1983 to 1993, and 2.4 percent annual growth from 1970 to 1980 (Genzberger et al. 1994, 141). The projections do not take into account possible large-scale movement of mainland workers to Hong Kong following 1997.

LEGAL AND ILLEGAL IMMIGRANTS FROM CHINA

The number of legal and illegal immigrants (IIs) from China continues to increase. During 1993, 32,900 residents of China settled in Hong Kong, 89 percent for the stated purpose of "family reunion." In November 1993 an agreement was reached with the Chinese government to increase the daily quota from 75 to 105 a day—38,000 a year. Although there is no specific measure of illegal immigrants, an indication of the increase comes from government reports of a 5 percent increase in arrests of Chinese IIs from 1992 to 1993. The daily arrest figure is 103—more daily arrests of illegal immigrants than the daily legal immigration quota. Most IIs come to Hong Kong for higher-wage jobs, especially construction and factory work. It is expected that the flow of illegal immigrants from China will increase during the run up to 1997.

MARKET SEGMENTATION

Hong Kong is a diverse society, with the 98 percent Chinese residents reflecting a wide range of attitudes, lifestyles and behaviors. With its distinctiveness, the marketing challenge in Hong Kong is to classify the population into meaningful groups of consumers. Market segmentation, in essence, lays the foundation on which a group will be targeted in an advertising or more general marketing effort (Martin 1995, 12–13). Many attributes can be used to divide a population into segments. Historically in Hong Kong, as well as in much of the rest of the world, demographics (age, sex, race, income, education) and geographics (areas of residence) have been the building blocks for defining market segmentation. More recently, psychographics (lifestyle and value segmentation) have been added to the mix. The following discussion describes the segmentation of the Hong Kong population based on geographics and demographics and psychographics.

DENSITY

With a land area of only 1,078 square kilometers and over six million people, Hong Kong is one of the most densely populated places in the world. The proportion of the population is 21.7 percent on Hong Kong Island, 33.5 percent in Kowloon and 44.5 percent in the New Territories (Daryanani 1994, 411). In 1991, 94 percent of the total population were was (Genzberger et al. 1994, 141).

GENDER

In 1993, Hong Kong had 3,058,300 males and 2,961,600 females. The ratio of males to females in the population has declined during the past 10 years (Daryanani 1994, 411).

RACE

Approximately 98 percent of Hong Kong residents are Chinese. Non-Chinese include, in order of proportions in the population, Filipino, Thai, American, British, Australian, Indonesian, Canadian and many others.

AGE

The consumers of Hong Kong are "aging." Although, compared with most Western markets, Hong Kong is a "youth" market; the demographic skew has changed over the past 10 years. In 1993, the proportion of the population under 15 years of age was 20.0 percent—down from 24.1 in 1983. At the other end of the age spectrum, the proportion of people aged 65 and above rose from 7 percent in 1983 to 9.2 percent in 1993 (Daryanani 1994, 411).

The projected age structure of the Hong Kong population continues to show "aging." By the year 2025, 15.4 percent will be under 15 years of age, 61.4 percent will be 15–64 years old, and a significant 23.2 percent will be over 64 years of age, compared with only 9.1 percent in 1991 (Genzberger et al. 1994, 141).

EDUCATION

To maintain a strong economic position in Asia, education has been a priority of the Hong Kong government. About one-fifth of Hong Kong's residents are studying full-time. All children between the ages of 6 and 15 are required by law to be in full-time education, or to complete Secondary 3. After Secondary 3, most stay on for a 2-year senior secondary course, leading to the first public examination. Others enroll full-time in vocational training, and a small number leave formal education.

The educational level in Hong Kong is rising. A substantial increase in those completing secondary education has occurred—from 43 percent in 1987 to 53 percent in 1992. Tertiary education has remained fairly constant at about 12 percent (Ogilvy & Mather 1993, 8).

LITERACY

Ninety-three percent of the population of Hong Kong is literate. The official languages are Chinese (Cantonese) and English. Forty-one percent are literate in Chinese only, 3 percent in English only, 49 percent in both Chinese and English, and 7 percent are illiterate (Ogilvy & Mather 1993, 11).

It must be noted, however, that literacy is not the same as fluency. Although English is a mandatory subject of study throughout school years, most schools utilize Cantonese as the language of tuition. The proportion of Chinese Hong Kong residents who are fluent English/Cantonese bilinguals may be as low as 7 to 10 percent.

INCOME

The average per capita earnings (GDP per capita in 1991) was US$13,430. The average annual growth rate between 1980 and 1991 was 5.6 percent (Genzberger et al. 1994, 143). With inflation, the pressure on family income is great.

Wage rates for all employees, including hourly and salaried workers, increased 10.4 percent in money (or 2.4 percent in real terms) between September 1992 and September 1993. The average monthly wage for services sector was $8,579, and for the manufacturing sector $6,780 (Daryanani 1994, 112). Because of differences in jobs and the traditional wage differential between men and women in manufacturing, women received an average of 68 percent of the male wages in manufacturing wages (Genzberger et al. 1994, 142).

Hong Kong is a community of contrasts in everything, including income distribution. Almost one-third of all income is earned by 10 percent of the population. In other words, one out of 10 people control 1 out of 3 of the dollars.

The income stratification in 1991 in Hong Kong dollars is shown in Table 3.1.

Table 3.1.   Hong Kong Monthly Income, 1991

Monthly Income (HK$)	%
Under $4,000	12.1
$4,000–5,999	12.8
$6,000–7,999	13.8
$8,000–9,999	11.5
$10,000–14,999	19.9
$15,000–19,999	11.1
$20,000–29,999	9.9
$30,000–39,999	3.8
$40,000 and over	5.1

HOUSEHOLD EXPENDITURES

Hong Kong consumers on average spend a large proportion of their income on food (35 percent) and housing (24 percent). It should be noted that about 1 dollar out of every 5 spent is to eat out at restaurants in Hong Kong (Daryanani 1994, 468–69).

The pattern of household expenditures has changed dramatically since 1985 when only 12 percent was spent on food (compared with 35 percent in 1993), and only 15 percent for housing, utilities and fuel, as compared with 27 percent in 1993 (Genzberger et al. 1994, 143). This is an indication of increased standard of living, a higher proportion of home ownership, and dramatic increases in property prices.

HOUSING

Hong Kong continues to have expensive housing. The government has a public housing program to subsidize those in need. About three million people, half the population, live in subsidized public housing in 874,000 flats in 286 estates throughout Hong Kong (Daryanani 1994, 187). The government auctions land for the private sector to sustain a high level of private flats. The government plan is that by 1997, nearly 55 percent of families in Hong Kong will own their own homes (Daryanani 1994, 187). This is highly unlikely given the current price of flats, the large cash down payment and the number of people who would need to make purchases.

EMPLOYMENT

Hong Kong employment in 1993 is 2.8 million, with unemployment at 2 percent and underemployment at 1.3 percent. The service and manufacturing sectors accounted for the largest percentage, followed by transportation, storage and communication services, financing, insurance, real estate and business services, and community, social and personal services (Daryanani 1994, 111).

A number of Hong Kong residents—52,400 in a recent survey—work across the border in China (Daryanani 1994, 111). Even a larger number spend 1 or more days a week in Guangdong Province on business.

Over the past years, the number of manufacturing jobs in Hong Kong has diminished, with manufacturing shifting first to Guangdong Province and now spreading farther into the mainland. Service establishments now employ three times as many workers as manufacturing. Within the services sector, the import and export trade is the largest group, followed by retail, restaurants and business services. Within manufacturing, the clothing industry remains the largest, followed by electronics and textiles.

OTHER POPULATION INDICATORS

A number of other population indicators and projects shed light on the demographic composition of Hong Kong. Marriage rates have remained stable and divorce rates are low. For the population as a whole, 37 percent are single, 57 percent married and 5 percent separated, divorced or widowed (Ogilvy & Mather 1993, 7).

Average household size has declined in the past 10 years, down to 3.4 persons in 1991. The number of women of childbearing age has increased; however, the fertility rate has declined. The fertility rate is projected to be stable (1.5 percent) at least until the year 2000. Life expectancy at birth has increased to 78 years of age in 1990, compared with 64 years of age in 1960.

INDIVIDUAL MODERNITY AND WESTERN ORIENTATION

In the wake of modernization and Western influence in Hong Kong, psychographic segmentation utilizing these dimensions is useful for dividing the world of consumers for a variety of products.

Despite the modern, deceptively Western look of the Hong Kong society, the ethnic Hong Kong Chinese have maintained a strong cultural identity (Bond et. al. 1985). In summarizing previous findings in the field, Bond (1991) and Yang (1986) contend that individual traditional and modern attitudes do not necessarily exist in opposition to each other, especially when mediated with Chinese values. In studies in North America, Taiwan, Hong Kong and China, "Modern Chinese" is a person who retains the essential Chinese virtues (especially families, achievement and moderation) in a creative amalgam with Western technical mastery. A "traditional Chinese" maintains valued traditional characteristics like filial piety and thrift as well as traits of noncompetitiveness, superstition and authoritarianism (Bond 1991).

To summarize findings from the literature dealing with the Chinese personality, individuals who consider themselves modern tend to develop a greater concern with self-expression, self-assertion, independence, personal achievement, dominance, tolerance, as well as less inhibition in associating with the opposite sex. They also develop less concern with conforming to customs, achieving organization and orderliness, blaming and belittling self, helping or giving sympathy to others, persevering in a task or activity until finished, seeking approval or admiration from others or society, and striving to achieve goals set by others or society (Martin 1995).

A continuing series of research studies on Chinese market segmentation have been conducted. Martin et al. (1993, 1994a and b), Martin and Wilson (1993), and Martin and Tsui (1993) found the combined concepts of individual modernity/traditionalism and Chinese/Western value orientation are desirous in segmenting the Hong Kong Chinese population with its very diverse backgrounds, status and life experiences.

Five clusters are identified to segment the Hong Kong population. The "Middle-Middle" cluster is largest, with 51.4 percent; "Modern-Western" cluster is second largest with 20.9 percent; "Traditional-Chinese" is third largest with 13.9 percent; "Modern-Chinese" has 7.9 percent; and "Traditional-Middle" is smallest with 5.9 percent (Martin et al. 1994a).

The demographics of the clusters indicate a significant age skew with Modern-Western being youngest, Modern-Chinese, Middle-Middle, Traditional-Middle progressively older, and Traditional-Chinese with the oldest age skew. The educational attainment of the respondents within clusters is highest among Modern-Western, Middle-Middle and Modern-Chinese clusters, and lowest among Traditional-Chinese and Traditional-Middle clusters. Family income demographics indicate that the Modern-Western cluster is more affluent than the Traditional-Chinese cluster.

Media usage also varies for each cluster. Television usage is heaviest among the Traditional-Chinese and Traditional-Middle segments, with Modern-Western and Modern-Chinese segments being the lightest TV viewers. Newspaper usage is heaviest for the Middle-Middle segment. The Modern-Chinese segment respondents are the lightest newspaper readers. Radio usage is heaviest among the Traditional-Middle cluster. Magazine usage is heaviest for Modern-Western and lightest for Traditional-Chinese.

In their attitudes toward advertising, Hong Kong respondents are generally supportive. The Modern-Western and Modern-Chinese segments give the greatest support, whereas the Traditional-Chinese segment is most critical (Martin et al. 1994a).

IMPACT OF CULTURE ON HONG KONG CONSUMERS

In its very broadest meaning, culture refers to the way of life of a group of people that is passed on from one generation to another. Terpstra and David (1985) define culture as a learned, shared and compelling interrelated set of symbols that provides a set of orientations for a society.

History, including the collective memory of colonialism, imperialism and the motherland, has shaped contemporary Hong Kong attitudes. Religions and ethical/philosophical traditions are also significant. Buddhism, Taoism and Confucianism (and the fusion) contribute to the cultural tapestry of Hong Kong.

Important in impacting advertising and marketing communication in Hong Kong is the notion of relationship. Martin (1995) has proposed a model of the communication process in an Asian context that has, as its base, a "relationship fulcrum" with concepts of social harmony and structural harmony. The concepts of social and structural harmony are resultant from inner goodness and coupled to exterior grace and social decorum (Redding 1990).

SOCIAL HARMONY

Social harmony can generally be called Virtuous Behavior (*Ren/Li*). *Ren* is, in general, human-heartiness in which the person can only be considered fully human when she or he takes proper account of others and acts toward them as she or he would want to be acted toward (Westwood 1992a). *Li* are rules (or more accurately, cultivation of an awareness) of propriety or proper behavior in any given situation. It serves to structure social relationships and to maintain order in hierarchical situations. The key elements of the *Ren/Li* social harmony is collectivism/relationship-centeredness with related concepts of (a) reciprocity, (b) *guanxi,* the status and intensity of relationships, and (c) face and shame. There are differences among Asian societies in the degree that collectivism/relationship-centeredness is present. Meindl et al. (1989) propose that collectivism can be present at different levels. The United States belongs to high-individualism (low-collectivism) category, whereas China belongs to high-collectivism (low-individualism). Hong Kong is in the moderate-collectivism category as a society with individual variations.

The sense of self is not the Western idea of a separate ego, but is based on sets of relationships (Tu 1984). In Asia people are very group oriented, with strong attachments formed to significant groups. The chief Chinese collective is family—the extended family and kinship groups. Family relationships are strong, persistent and tightly structured, with roles clearly defined and implicit rules for appropriate behavior. The key is filial piety—respecting and obeying one's father.

Reciprocity means that a favor given by someone must be returned. Yang (1970) says that when a Chinese acts, he normally anticipates a response or return. Westwood (1992a) calls it "social investments." Gifts and favors lead to feelings of trust, reciprocity and obligation.

An additional element of relationship-centeredness is *guanxi,* the status and intensity of an ongoing relationship between two parties. People seek to build the relationship up, to intensify the bonds, and to build on reciprocation. The quality of *guanxi* governs how one should behave within it, with implicit rules governing the behavior (Westwood 1992a).

"Face" for the Chinese is a major mechanism governing social relationships and providing the strongest social sanctions. Gaining and giving "face" is within the context of particular relationships. Bond and Hwang (1986) identify six forms of "face" behavior: enhancing one's own face; giving face to another; losing one's own face; damaging another's face; saving one's own face; saving the face of another. Face is closely tied to status and social structures and, in Hong Kong and most Chinese cultures, is the ultimate social sanction (Hsu 1971).

Several Chinese and Asian cultures, including Hong Kong, are cultures of "shame" as opposed to the Western "guilt" cultures. In a collectivist and relationship-centered culture, if a person breaks the norms, he or she is judged by peers. The person will know that she or he acted improperly and will feel shame. In a guilt culture, a person will refer to an internalized set of moral standards and will feel guilty if she or he breaks them (Westwood 1992a).

STRUCTURAL HARMONY

Structural harmony is hierarchical and is based on the Confucianism principle of *Wu Lun.* The key relationships in this hierarchy are related to concepts of (a) authority, (b) patriarchy, (c) trust and (d) personalism.

The firm hierarchical relationships, identified in Confucianism in the *Wu Lun,* are unequal relationships with reciprocal obligations and duties between prince and minister, father and son, husband and wife, older brother and younger brother, friend and friend. Clear role positions are represented, and role behavior is guided by *li* (Westwood 1992a). Hong Kong Chinese children are socialized to internalize the values and behavior patterns accompanying acceptance of the role positions (Bond 1991). These hierarchical and paternalistic structures have been reported in research throughout Asia, including Hong Kong (Redding 1977; Redding and Wong 1986).

Respect for authority is an essential element of hierarchical role positions. Several research studies have shown that Chinese are quite deferential toward whomever or whatever they consider to be an authority. Chu (1967), in studying persuasibility or change of opinion among Chinese populations, found submission to the authority of age, status and tradition. Hiniker (1969) experimented with a forced-compliance paradigm for attitude change in Hong Kong and found it easy to induce compliance with authority, although compliance did not necessarily indicate private acceptance. Yang (1970) found role behaviors of acquiescence, subordination and dependency in equal-power role pairs, suggesting that for Chinese the best policy is to behave like a subordinate and treat the other as authority, unless he or she is clearly the authority in a role relationship.

Patriarchy, classically referred to by Weber (1951) in Chinese social order, is defined as that power held and expressed personally by the male head, regardless of the structural arrangements. This is contrasted with the formal bureaucratic Western systems with emphasis on impersonal and abstract rule systems. Relationships have mutual obligations. As long as the power of the head is accepted and legitimized and everyone stays within their respective roles and abides by the implicit rules of behavior, order is assured, with relations remaining personal (Westwood 1992b).

All aspects of hierarchy, including patriarchy, operate with the concept of personalism—that is, it is the quality of relationships between people that matters and determines what happens, not aspects of a formal and impersonal system (Westwood 1992a).

Although today references to Confucian texts are not explicit, the socialization of children and the lessons in proper behavior and proper structures are still passed on to Chinese children (Westwood 1992a; Bond 1991). Coming from Confucian principles, Bond and Hofstede (1989) showed a partial causal relationship between the cultural values in "Confucian Work Dynamism" and economic growth. Hui (1992) argues that people favoring Confucian values including interpersonal harmony, hierarchy, family integrity, kinship affiliation and individual responsibility are characterized by a strong entrepreneurial spirit and desire for success, and that a society that adopts such values has a high growth potential.

ESTEEM FOR POWER AND STATUS HIERARCHY

Asian cultures, including Hong Kong, specially revere status and power and accept the hierarchical structure of society (Kao and Young 1992). In Hong Kong the upward mobility of people in the lower social and power hierarchy is also accepted. A vast body of research, with classic literature typified by Earle (1969), Meade and Whittaker (1967), and Singh et al. (1962), indicates the significant importance of the acceptance of power in the Asian personality. Yang (1986) contends that Chinese are conspicuously deferential toward anyone or anything considered an authority (person, situation, or institution).

TENDENCY TOWARD CONFORMITY

Related to the power and status hierarchy is the tendency for conforming behavior with submission to authority, status and tradition. Conformity to superiors in the hierarchy, however, is done subtly and with circumspection (Bond and Lee 1981) and may not be related to private belief (Bond and Hui 1982; Leung and Bond 1984; Bond and Hwang 1986).

TRUST

In most Western communication situations, the assumption of trust is the start and then it is tested over and over. In Hong Kong, with a different cultural derivative, trust—outside of a close circle of family and friends—must be earned, with proof provided. Chua (1992), in summarizing trust and self-disclosure in Asia and the West, points out that a healthy level of trust between parties develops through frequent interaction and shared experience.

PRACTICAL ETHICS

The underlying core of what a person says and how a person acts in a communication situation is based on the underlying ethical system. Ethics are the values that have been instilled through socialization, either knowingly or unknowingly. Some observers describe a Hong Kong notion of "practical" or situational ethics. Whereas one kind of behavior is appropriate in one setting, it is natural that another kind of behavior is appropriate in another setting. This observation has also been made in some other Asian countries (Holstein 1990). Hampden-Turner and Trompenaars (1993) contend that the moral core of "the good" in Asian society is an elegant pattern and fine arrangement at different levels of intimacy, rather than a single ethical value. In other words it depends on the situation and the relationship between the parties in the communication.

MOTIVATION

There are a large number of human needs. The hierarchy of human needs of Maslow (1954) is one of the dominant Western theories. According to Maslow, the basic—and the most important—are physiological needs like hunger and thirst. Second are safety needs and third are the needs for social relationships, belonging, love and affection. The next set is esteem needs, including both self-respect and the respect of others. The highest level is self-actualization: to realize one's potential and to experience a sense of self-growth and development.

Maslow proposes that most humans have these five needs, and when not satisfied they provide the motivating mechanism for all actions.

Hofstede (1980) argues that motivation theories, including Maslow's hierarchy of human needs, reflect American cultural values of high individualism, weak uncertainty avoidance and lower power distance. Redding (1977) questions the strong emphasis on individual-oriented needs like self-actualization. Redding and Martyn-Johns (1979), based their research on Hong Kong, Thailand, Malaysia, Indonesia, Vietnam and the Philippines, and they also argue that culture affects basic thought processes and leads to different motivations.

Taken as a whole, the results of research studies in Hong Kong (an most of Asia) throw doubt on a rigid hierarchy of needs applicable in the West and Asia. They do, however, suggest that certain needs are significant and that there are some similarities across cultures about what people consider important (Westwood 1992c; Martin 1995).

As an alternative view of motivation applicable to Hong Kong consumers, Hsu (1971) identifies three basic needs in Chinese cultures: sociability, security and status. Importantly, these needs are satisfied through interpersonal interaction, especially an "in group" composed of family and close friends. The theory is built on the principle that basic needs and motivation are a relational, social phenomena, rather than the Western conception of individual, independent motivation. Satisfaction of basic needs depends on being able to bring behavior in line with social norms and expectations. A key motivating force is avoidance of social disapproval and social shame (Yang 1981). In summary the social aspects of motivation are of high significance in marketing communication situations in Hong Kong.

Advertising Industry

The advertising industry in Hong Kong is sophisticated, fast-paced and money-driven. The intense competition is unrivaled anywhere in the region—indeed, anywhere in the world. Advertisers are demanding and cut-throat business maneuvering among competitive agencies is common.

There are 787 advertising agencies in Hong Kong, employing approximately 6,000 people (Genzberger et al. 1994, 149). There are more advertising agencies listed in Hong Kong telephone directories than in New York City (TVB 1991, 23).

Advertising expenditures soared to HK$14 billion in 1994, a huge increase of 29 percent over 1993. The average annual growth rate since 1986 is almost 20 percent (Table 3.2).

STRUCTURE OF THE INDUSTRY

Most of the major international (predominately U.S.) advertising agencies

Table 3.2.   Advertising Expenditure, 1993

Year	Ad Volume (HK $000)	Approximate % Increase
1986	3,376	—
1987	3,899	+15
1988	4,711	+21
1989	5,541	+18
1990	6,719	+21
1991	7,569	+13
1992	9,261	+22
1993	11,029	+19
1994E	14,186	+29
1995E	16,989	+20

Source: Ogilvy & Mather, 1993, 13; *ADEX,* 1994; *Media,* 1994e, 3.

are in Hong Kong, either as wholly owned, majority owned or joint-venture arrangements with local companies.

The agencies are divided into the "4A's" membership, which is limited to the larger multinational agencies, and the "2A's" composed primarily of smaller, Chinese-owned agencies. Over 80 percent of total advertising billings are generally placed by the 4A agencies (TVB 1991, 23). In 1993, the top 10 in billings were large multinational agencies, alone accounting for an over 70 percent market share (Genzberger et al. 1994, 149) (Table 3.3).

Table 3.3.   Top Hong Kong Advertising Agency Billings

	1993 (million US$)	Rank
J. Walter Thompson	111.95	1
DDB Needham	85.81	2
Ogilvy & Mather	74.29	3
Leo Burnett	70.92	4
McCann-Erickson	64.58	5
Grey Hong Kong	61.22	6
Backer Spielvogel Bates	59.01	7
Ball Euro RSCG	51.90	8
Bozell	49.31	9
Dentsu, Young & Rubicam	44.78	10

Source: *Media,* 1994f, 1.

In addition to the advertising agencies themselves, the infrastructure for advertising is as complete as anywhere in the world, with a massive selection of graphic and photographic services, film/video production houses, and translation and other services.

Direct response agencies have expanded rapidly during the past few years to offer integrated promotion techniques to clients. There are several dozen available; many, like J. Walter Thompson Direct, Ogilvy & Mather Direct, Adcom BBDO HK, and others, springing out of full service agencies.

Another group of service companies provides sales promotion specialty, over a hundred companies provide public relations consultancy, and at least two dozen companies provide market research services at an international standard.

Weekly TV ratings (sample of 100+, 4 years of age and older) use people meters. Radio listening habits (sample of 1,400, 12 years of age and older) use a diary. An annual media index of demographics and media habits (sample of 8,000+, 9 years of age and older) is conducted with personal interviews.

In the past 10 years Hong Kong has made a quantum leap in both the quantity and quality of production and creative services, to bring the communications and advertising industries on par with other international centers.

ADVERTISING AGENCY RATE STRUCTURE

Hong Kong agencies generally follow international standards for compensation for services. Agencies charge a 15 percent commission on media space and time, production work is billed at cost plus 17.65 percent, and artwork fees were US$96 per hour in 1992 (Genzberger et al. 1994, 149).

"MUSICAL CHAIRS" IN AGENCIES

In recent years the "brain drain," coupled with a very competitive business environment and the expansion of ventures in the China market, has created a "musical chairs" situation among personnel in Hong Kong agencies. Advertising executives have been moving among agencies at an alarming rate. Since the latter half of 1994, a temporary stability has been restored with a "reverse brain drain" as experienced Hong Kong advertising personnel have returned to Hong Kong (having successfully gained foreign passports).

Agency employment in Hong Kong, like the rest of the world, generally parallels the billings and number of clients (Table 3.4).

Hong Kong's employee distribution is 31 percent in management and client services, 17 percent in creative, 45 percent in production, and 7 percent in media and research. Salaries of agency personnel continue to be some of the highest in Asia (Table 3.5).

IMPORTANCE OF CHINA

Advertising in Hong Kong is dramatically impacted by China. China is responsible for an increasing share of advertising spending. In 1992, it was estimated to account for 10 percent of all Hong Kong agency advertising (Genzberger et al. 1994, 147). Sources estimate China business accounted for twice that amount in 1993. China billing for 4As agencies surpassed HK$1 billion in 1993 (*Media* 1994a, 1). With 1 out of 6 advertising dollars dependent on China, the fate of Hong Kong advertising extends far beyond its borders.

HONG KONG ADVERTISING EXPENDITURES BY MEDIUM

Television in Hong Kong provides the interaction of sight, sound, motion

Table 3.4.   Number of Employees in Top Hong Kong Advertising Agencies, 1993

	Rank	No. of Employees
J. Walter Thompson	1	253
DDB Needham	2	226
Ogilvy & Mather	3	195
Leo Burnett	4	201
McCann-Erickson	5	136
Grey Hong Kong	6	138
Backer Spielvogel Bates	7	124
Ball Euro RSCG	8	120
Bozell	9	112
Dentsu, Young & Rubicam	10	133
Saatchi & Saatchi	11	83
BBDO	12	86
DMB&B	13	71
Lintas: Hong Kong	14	53
Live Communications	15	49
Foote, Cone & Belding	16	54
Fortune	17	50
Lee Davis Ayer	18	54
Compu-Ad	19	28
CCAA PAW Int.	20	22

Source: *Media*, 1994f, 1.

Table 3.5.   Hong Kong Agency Salaries

Job Nature	Salary Range (US$ per Month Total Package, 1994)
Director of Client Services	9,480–12,880
Account Director	4,430–10,750
Account Manager	1,850– 3,940
Account Executive	1,230– 1,850
Media Director	4,690– 9,300
Media Manager/Group Head	2,340– 4,070
Media Planner/Buyer	1,230– 1,850
Head of Creative	7,890–28,670
Creative Director	6,280–10,750
Creative Group Head	4,430– 8,620
English Copywriter	2,340– 7,150
Chinese Copywriter	1,720– 4,070
Art Director	2,340– 7,890

Source: *Media*, 1994e, 7.

and emotion—with choices of language or combinations of languages. Two commercial operators, Television Broadcasts Limited (TVB) and Asia Television Limited (ATV), each operate one Cantonese channel and one predominately English channel. Radio Television Hong Kong (RTHK) shares the use of all four channels for program presentation at various times.

Television remains the medium with the highest advertising expenditure. Forty-four percent of expenditures go to television, 35 percent to newspaper, 12 percent to magazines, 6 percent to radio, 2 percent to Mass Transit Railway (MTR) and 1 percent to other (*ADEX* 1994).

Cost of space and time has risen dramatically in Hong Kong. From 1986 to 1992, the average media cost index (base of 100 in 1986) has risen to 372 for radio (average annual increase of 26 percent), 205 for TV (average annual increase of 13 percent), 197 for newspaper (average annual increase of 11 percent) and 172 for magazine—an average annual increase of 10 percent (Ogilvy & Mather 1993, 15).

ADVERTISING EXPENDITURES FOR PRODUCT CATEGORIES

Leisure, real estate and retail account for over a third of the advertising expenditures in Hong Kong. The major growth category is real estate (Table 3.6).

Table 3.6.   Advertising Expenditure by Category

	1993 (HK $000)	% Increase over 1992	Rank in 1993
Leisure	1,614	11	1
Real Estate	1,598	45	2
Retail	954	11	3
Toiletries	672	12	4
Personal Items	644	10	5
Foodstuffs	640	16	6
Industrial/Office Equipment	609	28	7
Electrical Appliances	581	5	8
Finance/Bank	572	40	9
Miscellaneous	487	49	10

Source: Ogilvy & Mather, 1993, 14; *Media*, 1994g, 4.

In Hong Kong the recall of brands in various product categories generally parallels the amount of money spent on advertising. However, creativity and memorability sometimes bring high recall without as large a budget. In Hong Kong recall research is continuously done. In addition a guide of "value for money" (index of brand advertising spent, average advertising spent and recall result) often shows the general correlation with money spent, but not without the other factor of advertising creativity. In 1994, Coca-Cola was the top of the recall and "value for money," but spent substantially less than some other advertisers (Table 3.7).

Hong Kong Media

The media in Hong Kong include 77 daily newspapers, 619 periodicals, two private television companies programming four channels, a subscription television service, an Asian regional satellite television service with five channels, one government radio-television station with seven radio channels and shared usage of all four TV channels, two commercial radio stations with six channels, a radio

Table 3.7. Hong Kong TV Recall, Spending, and "Value for Money," 1994

Brand Name	Ad (HK$)	Recall Rank	"Value"
Coke	13.2	1	16.67
HI-C	8.6	5	15.29
Vitasoy	13.2	3	13.33
Sifone	18.2	2	10.88
Park 'n Shop	7.4	9	5.92
Rejoice	20.0	6	5.50
Tin Dey Seen	23.5	7	3.74
Pantene	24.7	8	2.68
McDonald's	66.2	4	2.33
San Miguel	25.0	10	0.88

Source: *Media*, 1995b, 4.

station for the British armed forces with two channels, and 190 cinemas (Daryanani 1994, 315–333).

COVERAGE BY THE MEDIA

The circulation of media in Hong Kong indicates that television has the highest coverage (96 percent), with Chinese-language channels dominating. It should be noted that the English channels telecast recent movies in English and Cantonese with Near Instantaneously Compounded Audio Multiplex (NICAM) (11 percent penetration). Radio has high coverage (47 percent) compared with the proportion of advertising dollars spent on radio (6 percent). Newspaper circulation is also high (79 percent), and dominated by the Chinese press. Weekly magazines achieve a 30 percent coverage. Hong Kong's urban underground—the MTR, which operates in Hong Kong Island, Kowloon and the western New Territories—has coverage of 51 percent, and the train—the Kowloon-Canton Railway (KCR), which operates in Kowloon and New Territories—has a 12 percent coverage. Cinema has coverage of 6 percent of the population and Star TV approximately 1 percent (Table 3.8).

TELEVISION

Television viewing is the most popular leisure time activity, with more than 98 percent of households owning one or more television sets. Ninety-six percent tune in during any 24-hour period. The average person (aged 9 years and older) watched 3.4 hours of television per day in 1992, somewhat down from the peak of 4 hours a day in 1990 (Ogilvy & Mather 1993, 21). The decline continues with an SRG Research Services (SRG) estimate of 3.1 hours watched per day in 1994 (*Media* 1994b, 37).

Each of the private television broadcasters, Television Broadcasts Limited (TVB) and Asia Television Limited (ATV), provides one Chinese- and one English-language channel. Because of the terrain, there are a total of 24 transponder

Table 3.8. Coverage of Hong Kong Media, 1992

	%*
Any TV	96
Any Chinese TV	93
Any English TV	17
Any Radio	47
Any Newspaper	79
Any Chinese Newspaper	76
Any English Newspaper	5
Any Weekly Magazine	30
Any Monthly Magazine	7
Any Fortnightly Magazine	4
MTR	51
KCR	12
Cinema	6
Star TV	1

Source: Ogilvy & Mather, 1993, 16-18.
*Percentage of adults aged 15 and older.

stations to provide a high-quality over-the-air signal in all parts of the territory. Together, on average, the stations transmitted over 580 hours per week in 1993, a slight increase of about 3 percent compared with 1992 (Daryanani 1994, 326).

Competition is high, with each trying to strengthen their audience share by diversifying and enriching program content. A variety of movies, variety shows, continuing comedies and dramas, magazine shows, sports and horse racing, and news programs are aired. On the Chinese channels, locally produced serialized dramas (and some from Taiwan dubbed into Cantonese) remain the programming cornerstone with romance, human conflict, police, martial arts, ghost and costume period shows as the pivotal plots. Feature films continue to maintain strong popularity. Game/contest shows, beauty pageants, musical specials and fundraising charity musical variety programs are also prevalent.

TVB Jade dominates the Chinese TV station share with slightly over three-fourths of the viewers. ATV Home, the competing Cantonese channel, has increased from its lowly 10 percent share several years ago (Ogilvy & Mather 1993, 21). ATV Home's increase is dramatic in one-day cumulative measurement. TVB Jade leads with 90 percent, a cumulative figure they have maintained for several years. By 1992, ATV Home had a one-day cumulative audience of 47 percent, up from 20 percent in 1988 (Ogilvy & Mather 1993, 21). By 1994, in some measures of reach, parity is close. SRG, in May 1994, estimated TVB Jade's daily Monday–Friday reach in Hong Kong at 3,789,000, and ATV Home at 3,009,000 (*Media* 1994c, 16). In ratings, TVB Jade prime time slipped to 27 in 1994 from 29 in 1993 (71 share in 1994 compared with 72 share in 1993), while ATV Home stayed constant with a 9 rating—share was up to 29 in 1994 compared with 28 in 1993 (*Media* 1995a, 3).

On the English channels, feature films, imported comedies and drama, nature programming, documentaries, sports and cartoons remain strong programming elements. TVB Pearl generally has significantly higher ratings than ATV World, but for specific feature films, ATV World at times surpasses TVB Pearl. The viewership of the English channels is much more fragmented, without the loyal "single channel" partisans enjoyed by TVB Jade.

News and information programs are an important part of the programming on all channels. *Putonghua* (the official language throughout the PRC) news and financial reports have been introduced, as well as overnight foreign language newscasts from Japan, Taiwan and early morning live carriage of the *CBS Evening News.*

Broadcasting in bilingual format, with the use of multichannel sound with NICAM, has increased with feature films, documentaries, nature programs, sports programs and some foreign news programs. This has enabled the English services to attract more Cantonese-speaking viewers and Cantonese programs to be enjoyed by *Putonghua* speakers. At this time NICAM is used for programming but rarely used for commercials, a situation that probably will change soon.

The majority of Hong Kong television programs are locally produced on TVB Jade and ATV Home. Ninety-three percent of the top 100 programs are local. The 7 percent foreign programs (predominately from Taiwan and Japan), accounting for 11.8 percent of the total air time of the top 100 programs, account for 18.6 percent of the audience share. In short, although fewer in number, the average foreign program is longer and generates higher average ratings (*Media* 1994b, 37).

SATELLITE TELEVISION

Star TV is a satellite television service from Hong Kong to the Asian region. Five channels providing sports, music, entertainment and Chinese programs are broadcast throughout the region. The service in Hong Kong is predominantly English and *Putonghua* programming.

At the end of 1993 over 325,000 homes in Hong Kong received Star TV's signal through Satellite Master Antenna Television systems (SMATV) (Daryanani 1994, 326). Although a small percentage of households receive Star TV, among those who have access to the service, 32 percent watch some Star TV programming each day (*Media* 1994d, 14).

CABLE TELEVISION

Cable or subscription television was introduced in Hong Kong with the franchise award in June 1993. The license was initially for a 12-year period. The PRC has indicated that the franchise will be allowed to transcend the change of sovereignty in 1997.

On October 31, 1993, Wharf Cable Limited launched the service, initially delivered by microwave. Eight channels include a 24-hour Cantonese news service produced in Hong Kong, movies, sports, children's programs and entertainment programs. The microwave system is being replaced by an optical fiber network, with capacity increased to a maximum of 39 channels (Daryanini 1994, 327).

RADIO TELEVISION HONG KONG (TV)

Radio Television Hong Kong (RTHK) produces 10 hours of public affairs television programs, each generally half an hour in duration. Five of the hours are broadcast during prime time on TVB Jade and ATV Home. The programs are current affairs, drama, information and community services, variety and quiz shows, children's programs and general educational programs. The average viewer size of RTHK programs during prime time was 1,273,000 on TVB and 330,000 on ATV in 1993 (Daryanani 1994, 327).

TELEVISION VIEWERSHIP

Viewer composition is fairly balanced across all services, with the exception of English TV and Star having a younger, more affluent and more white collar skew (Table 3.9).

Cost per thousands (CPM) are in the following ranges: Morning 7:00 a.m.–12:00 noon (26 TVB Jade, 11 ATV Home); Daytime 12:30 noon–5:35 p.m. (21 TVB Jade, 22 ATV Home); Early Shoulder Prime 5:45–6:45 p.m. (50 TVB Jade, 17 ATV Home); Prime Time 6:55–10:55 p.m. (43 TVB Jade, 38 ATV Home); Late Shoulder Prime 11:00 p.m.–12:30 a.m. (43 TVB Jade, 33 ATV Home) (Ogilvy & Mather 1993, 22).

The prime time 30-second spot rates are HK$56,680 for TVB Jade and HK$16,420 for ATV Home (*Media* 1994c, 16).

RADIO

Fifteen radio channels broadcast in Hong Kong, including seven for RTHK; three by Hong Kong Commercial Broadcasting Company (Commercial Radio); three by Metro Broadcast corporation (Metro); and two by the British Forces Broadcasting Service. Advertising is accepted on all Commercial Radio and Metro Broadcast channels. Program sponsorships are accepted on RTHK.

COMMERCIAL RADIO AND METRO RADIO

Commercial Radio operates two Chinese services (CR1 and CR2) on FM and one English service on AM (AM 864) on a 24-hour basis.

After a 32-year monopoly on commercial radio in Hong Kong by Commercial Radio, Metro Broadcast began in July 1991. Metro operates three channels of formatted radio (FM Select and Hit Radio on FM and Metro Plus on AM).

The identities of the stations are the following:

CR1—Provides news and current affairs programs in Chinese

Table 3.9. Hong Kong Viewer Composition Profile (TV and Star TV), 1992

Population	Total TV	Any Chinese TV	Any English TV	Any Jade TV	TVB Home	ATV Pearl	TVB World	ATV	Star TV
				(%)					
Gender									
Male	51	51	51	54	51	52	54	56	56
Female	49	49	49	46	49	48	46	44	44
Race									
Chinese	97	98	100	94	100	100	94	85	94
Non-Chinese	3	2	—	6	—	—	6	15	6
Age									
9–14	10	10	10	10	10	10	10	10	16
15–19	9	9	9	13	9	9	13	9	9
20–29	20	21	19	28	19	19	28	25	23
30–39	25	23	25	30	25	26	30	33	29
40–54	18	16	18	13	17	17	13	19	15
55+	20	20	20	6	20	19	6	4	10
Income (HK$)									
Under $6,000	7	8	7	2	7	6	2	3	0
$6,000–7,999	9	12	9	6	9	9	6	5	2
$8,000–9,999	13	16	13	11	13	13	11	9	4
$10,000–14,999	34	36	34	33	43	35	33	30	19
$15,000–19,999	20	14	20	23	20	20	23	20	43
$20,000–29,999	11	8	11	14	11	11	14	18	15
$30,000+	6	6	5	9	5	5	9	12	17
Occupation									
Prof./Mgr./Exec.	4	4	3	7	3	4	7	11	7
Trader/Proprietor	3	3	2	4	2	3	4	5	8
Office Skilled	11	10	11	16	11	11	16	17	17
Office Unskilled	4	5	4	5	4	4	5	5	6
Factory/Shop Skilled	11	13	11	13	11	12	13	13	12
Factory/Shop Unskilled	17	15	17	12	17	16	11	10	9
Student	19	18	19	24	19	20	24	20	24
Housewife	23	24	24	17	24	24	17	16	14
Retired/Unemployed	9	8	9	3	9	8	3	3	4

Source: Ogilvy & Mather, 1993, 23, 26.

CR2—Appeals to students and youth with popular Cantonese music ("Canto-pop")

AM 864—Programs an all music format

FM Select—Bilingual programming with oldies, targeted at 25- to 49-year-olds

Hit Radio—Contemporary hit radio format with Cantonese and Western top hits and oldies

Metro Plus—originally "Metro News," the station is a bilingual service with 5 hours of English news with Cantonese and Western music

RADIO TELEVISION HONG KONG (RADIO)

As a publicly funded station, RTHK is to provide balanced and objective broadcasting services that inform, educate and entertain the listeners of Hong

Kong. RTHK broadcasts 1,148 hours a week with Radio 1 (Chinese) and Radio 3 (English) operating 24 hours a day. Each of the seven channels has established an identity as follows:

Radio 1—Main news and information channels in Chinese

Radio 2—Programs in Chinese ranging from civic education to entertainment

Radio 3—English language service with current affairs and news, interviews on controversial issues, international telephone calls, documentaries, specialist music

Radio 4—Bilingual cultural channel for music and fine arts

Radio 5—Programs educational, cultural and minority interest programs

Radio 6—BBC World Service on a 24-hour basis

Radio 7—Programs middle-of-the-road music with news summaries every quarter-hour during the week (every half-hour on weekends)

LISTENERSHIP COMPOSITIONAL PROFILE
Audience composition for each station in Hong Kong tends to follow its programming format and identity (Table 3.10).

NEWSPAPER
With 77 newspapers in Hong Kong, intense competition is evident. There is a great deal of niche positioning among the newspapers, with the general categories being the English-language newspapers, Chinese-language broad-appeal newspapers. and many Chinese-language specialty newspapers (mostly gossip oriented). Hong Kong newspapers include 41 Chinese-language dailies and seven English-language dailies (Daryanani 1994, 316). Of the Chinese language dailies, 33 cover mostly general local and overseas news, three are primarily financial news and the remainder cover entertainment and gossip, especially movie and TV personalities. The larger papers are distributed to overseas Chinese communities, with some having editions printed in the United States, Canada, the United Kingdom and Australia (Daryanani 1994, 316).

Readership levels are high, with 77 percent of the population reading a newspaper on an average day (74 percent Chinese paper and 5 percent English paper). The overall daily newspaper readership level has not changed substantially for the past 5 years (Ogilvy & Mather 1993, 31).

The leading Chinese-language newspapers are the *Oriental Daily News, Sing Pao, Tin Tin Daily News, Ming Pao, Hong Kong Daily News, Sing Tao Daily, Express* and *Hong Kong Economic Journal.* The three English-language newspapers are the *South China Morning Post, The Hong Kong Standard* and *Eastern Express.*

Recently Hong Kong has begun research into readership of different newspaper sections to provide a basis for negotiations. Variations are great for differ-

Table 3.10.   Hong Kong Listener Composition Profile, 1992

	Total Population	Any Radio	CR1	CR2	HIT	FM
			(%)			
Gender						
Male	51	51	56	56	62	63
Female	49	49	44	44	38	37
Race						
Chinese	97	98	100	100	100	78
Non-Chinese	3	2	—	—	—	22
Age						
9–14	10	9	8	10	13	6
15–19	9	11	7	15	24	17
20–29	20	22	19	25	33	33
30–39	25	27	27	25	20	29
40–54	18	17	20	14	12	12
55+	20	15	20	11	3	4
Income (HK$)						
Under $6,000	7	5	7	5	2	1
$6,000–7,999	9	8	8	6	4	1
$8,000–9,999	13	12	14	12	9	5
$10,000–14,999	34	33	34	36	38	28
$15,000–19,999	20	22	22	23	26	27
$20,000–29,999	11	13	11	12	15	19
$30,000+	6	7	4	5	4	19
Occupation						
Prof./ Mgr./ Exec.	4	5	4	3	4	14
Trader/Proprietor	3	3	3	3	2	7
Office Skilled	11	12	10	12	14	17
Office Unskilled	4	4	3	6	6	5
Factory/Shop Skilled	11	13	15	16	16	15
Factory/Shop Unskilled	17	16	18	15	13	9
Student	19	19	15	24	37	24
Housewife	23	20	22	15	7	7
Retired/Unemployed	9	6	9	6	2	2

Source: Ogilvy & Mather, 1993, 29.
Note: CR1 and Cr2 represent the two Chinese services operated by Commercial Radio on FM.

ent papers. For example, for financial news page "usually read," the *South China Morning Post* has 41 percent, followed by *Ming Pao* (39 percent), *Sing Tao* (31 percent), *Tin Tin Daily News* (29 percent), and *Oriental Daily News* (26 percent) (*Media* 1994e, 6).

Readership composition for various newspapers in Hong Kong are shown in Table 3.11, with the younger, more affluent and professional readership concentrating with *Ming Pao* and *South China Morning Post*.

MAGAZINES

The 619 periodical titles provide Hong Kong magazines for every taste. The coverage of weekly magazines is highest (30 percent coverage of the market), with monthly (7 percent coverage) and biweekly (4 percent coverage) also contributing.

Table 3.11.   Hong Kong Newspaper Readership Composition Profile, 1992

	Total Popula-tion	Any Chinese Paper	Any English Paper	ODN	SP	TTDN	MP	SCMP
			(%)					
Gender								
Male	51	55	57	55	55	62	51	57
Female	49	45	42	45	45	38	49	43
Race								
Chinese	97	100	62	100	100	100	100	60
Non-Chinese	3	—	38	—	—	—	—	40
Age								
9–14	10	8	5	8	4	5	5	5
15–19	9	10	20	10	7	8	13	19
20–29	20	21	25	24	22	23	21	34
30–39	25	28	24	28	29	37	26	25
40–54	18	19	11	18	21	19	20	12
55+	20	15	7	12	17	8	15	5
Income (HK $)								
Under $6,000	7	4	1	4	5	3	2	1
$6000–7,999	9	8	1	8	7	8	6	1
$8000–9,999	13	12	5	12	12	18	7	5
$10,000–14,999	34	36	18	38	32	38	28	17
$15,000–19,999	20	21	18	22	24	20	25	18
$20,000–29,999	11	12	24	11	14	9	18	24
$30,000+	5	5	31	6	4	3	13	33
Occupation								
Prof./ Mgr./ Exec.	4	4	20	3	4	2	12	21
Trader/Proprietor	3	3	10	3	4	2	4	10
Office Skilled	17	11	13	17	12	15	10	18
Office Unskilled	4	4	4	5	5	3	6	3
Factory/Shop Skilled	11	14	7	14	15	21	10	7
Factory/Shop Unskilled	17	18	1	19	15	25	8	1
Student	19	17	31	18	13	14	20	29
Housewife	24	20	8	19	21	18	19	8
Retired/Unemployed	8	7	3	7	8	5	4	3

Source: Ogilvy & Mather, 1993, 33–34.
Note: ODN, *Oriental Daily News;* SP, *Sing Pao;* TTDN, *Tin Tin Daily News;* MP, *Ming Pao;* SCMP, *South China Morning Post.*

General-interest magazines include weeklies of *Ming Pao Weekly, Oriental Sunday, Next Magazine, East Week Magazine, Metropolitan Weekly, Fresh Weekly* and biweeklies of *Young Generation* and *Sister's Pictorial.* Business/finance weeklies include *Economic Digest, Window* and *China Times Weekly,* with monthlies including *Capital, Hong Kong Business, The Executive, The Securities Journal, Hong Kong Economic Journal Monthly,* and *Ming Pao Monthly.* Hong Kong editions of business and regional magazines include weeklies of *Yazhou Zhoukan, Time, Newsweek, Asiaweek, Feer* and monthlies of *Reader's Digest* and *Asian Business.* Women's monthly magazines include *Elegance, Cosmopolitan, Bazaar, Elle, Marie Claire, Eve, Style, Mode* and *Ryuko Tsushin.* Leisure weekly magazines include *Sunday Magazine,* with monthlies including *Penthouse, Play-*

boy, City Magazine, Golden Age, Esquire, Hong Kong Tatler, B-International, Epicure and *Peak.* There are also a range of auto, sports, *TV Guides,* electronics, computer, hi-fi, photography, interior design, club and trade magazines. Magazine readership composition for weekly, biweekly and monthly is shown in Table 3.12.

Table 3.12. Hong Kong Magazine Readership Composition Profile, 1992

	Total Population	Any Weekly	Any Fortnightly	Any Monthly
		(%)		
Gender				
Male	51	45	16	56
Female	49	55	84	44
Race				
Chinese	97	98	100	95
Non-Chinese	3	2	—	5
Age				
9–14	10	11	9	8
15–19	9	13	22	12
20–29	20	30	35	34
30–39	25	28	22	27
40–54	18	10	9	16
55+	20	9	2	4
Income (HK$)				
Under $6,000	7	2	1	1
$6,000–7,999	9	6	6	5
$8,000–9,999	13	11	13	12
$10,000–14,999	34	34	38	30
$15,000–19,999	20	25	24	25
$20,000–29,999	11	14	14	16
$30,000+	6	7	4	11
Occupation				
Prof./ Mgr./ Exec.	4	4	1	12
Trader/Proprietor	3	3	2	6
Office Skilled	11	15	16	18
Office Unskilled	4	7	10	6
Factory/Shop Skilled	11	12	6	17
Factory/Shop Unskilled	17	13	8	9
Student	19	24	30	21
Housewife	23	19	24	10
Retired/Unemployed	9	3	3	1

Source: Ogilvy & Mather, 1993, 39.

The 1995 rate cards show many increases, but rates are beginning to drop with *Next* magazine leading the way (Table 3.13).

CINEMA

With 190 theaters, with capacity from 300–1,900 seats, and high cinema attendance, three contractors in Hong Kong place 30- and 60-second advertisements in cinemas. Cinema attendance is high, with 49 percent of residents at-

Table 3.13.   Hong Kong Magazine Rate Card

Title	Circulation 1993	Circulation 1994	1995 Rate	% Change
The Economist	54,119	58,725	US $ 7,029	+ 6.5
Window	21,683	23,000	HK $18,000	–
Newsweek	234,055	237,860	US $35,625	+ 5.0
Asian Business	91,882	101,832	US $12,490	+ 5.0
Asia, Inc.	42,086	63,317	US $11,000	+ 4.5
Business Week	36,119	37,745	US $ 9,200	+ 7.0
Asiaweek	96,917	96,826	US $16,708	+ 7.0
Yazhou Zhoukan	95,415	94,971	US $11,800	+12.0
Time	313,851	306,956	US $40,690	+ 6.0
Fortune	57,148	60,575	US $ 8,810	–
Next Magazine	135,006	152,188	HK $28,000	–17.0
Eastweek	150,000	170,000	HK $26,000	+ 9.2
Oriental Sunday	125,000	130,000	HK $27,500	+10.0

Source: *Media,* 1994b, 4.

tending the cinema during the past 3 months, 25 percent during the past month and 6 percent in the past week (Ogilvy & Mather 1993, 43). Theaters are well distributed for convenience with 24 percent on Hong Kong Island, 40 percent in Kowloon and 36 percent in the New Territories.

A cinema attendance profile is shown in Table 3.14.

MASS TRANSIT RAILWAY AND KOWLOON-CANTON RAILWAY

Hong Kong has a very complete and well-used rail public transportation system. The MTR and KCR provide additional advertising coverage for Hong Kong commuters.

The MTR operates a three-line system in the urban area. The 43-kilometer route has 38 stations, with a fleet of 671 cars structured into eight-car trains. The system began operation in 1979. The MTR carries 2.13 million passengers a day (Daryanani 1994, 242). On a cumulative basis, 86% percent of Hong Kong consumers use the MTR in an average month, 49 percent in an average week and 23 percent in an average day.

The KCR began operation in 1910 and was electrified and double tracked in the early 1980s. The 34-kilometer railway provides suburban service to the new towns and northeastern New Territories and a freight service to China. The fleet of 351 cars is structured into 12-car trains. With 13 stations, the KCR carries 569,500 passengers a day. Cumulatively, 32 percent of Hong Kong consumers use the KCR during an average month, 12 percent during the past week and 5 percent on an average day.

The KCR also owns and operates a 31-kilometer light rail transit (LRT) in the northwest New Territories with almost 300,000 passengers feeding bus terminals in the territory.

The composition of passengers on the KCR and MTR reflects the skew toward males, 20- to 39-year-olds, middle income and skilled workers.

Table 3.14.   Hong Kong Cinema Attendance Composition Profile, 1992

	Total Population	Past Month
	(%)	
Gender		
Male	51	56
Female	49	44
Race		
Chinese	97	95
Non-Chinese	3	5
Age		
9–14	10	10
15–19	9	17
20–29	20	41
30–39	25	22
40–54	18	8
55+	20	2
Income (HK$)		
Under $6,000	7	1
$6,000–7,999	9	5
$8,000–9,999	13	8
$10,000–14,999	34	31
$15,000–19,999	20	26
$20,000–29,999	11	17
$30,000+	6	10
Occupation		
Prof./ Mgr./ Exec	4	6
Trader/Proprietor	3	4
Office Skilled	11	17
Office Unskilled	4	7
Factory/Shop Skilled	11	16
Factory/Shop Unskilled	17	13
Student	19	26
Retired/Unemployed	9	2

Source: Ogilvy & Mather, 1993, 45.

OTHER TRANSPORTATION AND OUTDOOR

In addition to the rail services, four franchised bus services carry 3.4 million passengers a day on a network of 469 routes (Daryanani 1994, 242). The Kowloon Motor Bus Company (KMB), China Motor Bus Company (CMB) and Citybus Limited (Citybus) are the major carriers, with New Lantao Bus Company (NLB) operating on an outlying island. Each bus company provides advertising availability, including whole bus painting.

Hong Kong minibuses carry 16 passengers. There were 6,904 private light buses in operation in 1993, offering advertisers side panels and seat back availability (Daryanani 1994, 244).

Taxis (almost 18,000 in 1993) offer limited advertising availability.

Outdoor panels and neon are evident throughout Hong Kong. Panels popular with advertisers include the Star Ferry, Wilson Car Park locations, Pacific

Place, Airport, electronic display board at Causeway Bay and the Cross Harbor Tunnel, Tsim Sha Tsui and telephone booths.

ADVERTISING INDUSTRY REGULATION

Unlike most Asian governments, Hong Kong has a *laissez-faire* approach to the advertising industry. The specific prohibitions are the following:

1. Direct comparison advertising is prohibited.
2. Any claims of "number one" must be substantiated.
3. Doctors and lawyers cannot advertise on the mass media.
4. Prescription medicines cannot be advertised.
5. Advertising of tobacco products are prohibited in broadcast.

The Complaints Committee of the Broadcasting Authority investigates complaints about advertising and programs. In 1993, 637 complaints were investigated and 14 warnings were issued to TV stations, one to a radio station. Fines were imposed on three TV stations and one radio station (Daryanani 1994, 325).

In addition authority is granted to the Consumer Council to investigate false advertising.

The Broadcasting Authority regulates commercial television, radio broadcasting and satellite broadcasting. The television and radio codes of practice on program, advertising and technical standards provide guidelines for broadcast and satellite stations.

FUTURE OF HONG KONG IN REGION

The future of Hong Kong as an Asian advertising powerhouse is generally secure against rising costs, political uncertainty, and international competition (Parton 1994, 1). Not only is Hong Kong a strong local market, it is traditionally the regional center of Asia. However, during the past 2 years a number of multinational clients and senior advertising staff have relocated, predominately to Singapore. Chris Jaques, regional managing director of Bates, notes that more businesses are setting up in Hong Kong than Singapore.

> Those moving to Hong Kong are moving for business reasons. Those relocating to Singapore are moving primarily for cost reasons. Advertising agencies tend to run on smaller margins than most businesses and so all agencies have been considering Singapore as an option. The costs of operating in Hong Kong are ridiculously high for a business which runs as tightly as ours. However, all the biggest consumer markets are currently in North Asia and Hong Kong will remain Asia's business center for the foreseeable future.
>
> (Parton 1994, 1)

In the survey, all agency heads agreed that there are likely to be agency headquarters in many different Asian countries after 1997, with Hong Kong's importance hinging on the development of Greater China. Of the 16 agencies listing regional headquarters in *Media's All-Asia Ad Agency Guide,* only one gave a Singapore address, two gave split addresses, and some others gave Chicago and New York City as Asia headquarters (*Media,* 1995b, 4).

Bibliography

ADEX (Advertising Index). 1994. Hong Kong: SRG Research Services.

Bartos, R. 1976. *Marketing to Women Around the World.* Boston: Harvard Business School Press.

Bauer, R.A. and S.A. Greyser. 1968. *Advertising in America: The Consumer View.* Cambridge, MA: Harvard Business School.

Bond, M.H. 1991. *Beyond the Chinese Face: Insights from Psychology.* Hong Kong: Oxford University Press.

Bond, M.H. and G. Hofstede. 1989. The Cash Value of Confucian Values. *Human Systems Management,* 8: 195–200.

Bond, M.H. and H.C.C. Hui. 1982. Rater Competitiveness and the Experimenter's Influence on Ratings of a Future Opponent. *Psychologia* 25: 91–99.

Bond, M.H. and K.K. Hwang. 1986. The Social Psychology of the Chinese People. In: Bond, M.H., ed. *The Psychology of the Chinese People.* Hong Kong: Oxford University Press.

Bond, M.H. and P.W.L. Lee. 1981. Face-Saving in Chinese Culture: A Discussion and Experimental Study of Hong Kong Students. In: King, A.Y.C. and R.P.L. Lee, eds. *Social Life and Development in Hong Kong.* Hong Kong: Chinese University Press.

Bond, M.H., K.C. Wan, K. Leung, and R. Giacalone. 1985. How Are Responses to Verbal Insult Related to Cultural Collectivism and Power Distance?" *Journal of Cross-Cultural Psychology* 16: 111–127.

Chu, G.C. 1967. Sex Differences in Persuasibility Factors Among Chinese. *International Journal of Psychology* 2: 283–288.

Chua, B.L. 1992. The Communication Process. In: Westwood, R.I., ed. *Organizational Behavior: Southeast Asian Perspectives.* Hong Kong: Longman.

Daryanani, R., ed. *Hong Kong 1994.* 1994. Hong Kong: Government Printing Department.

Dun & Bradstreet. 1993. *Dun's Guide to Hong Kong Businesses 1993.* Hong Kong: Dun & Bradstreet Information Services.

Earle, M.J. 1969. A Cross-Cultural and Cross-Language Comparison on Dogmatism Scores. *Journal of Social Psychology,* 79: 19–24.

Euromonitor. 1993. *The World Directory of Advertising Agencies 1993.* Chicago: Euromonitor.

Everest F.A. 1978. Hong Kong. In: Lent, J.A., ed. *Broadcasting in Asia and the Pacific: A Continental Survey of Radio and Television.* Philadelphia: Temple University Press.

Genzberger, C.A., E.G. Hinkelman, D.E. Horovitz, W.T. LeGro, J.W. Libbey, C.S. Mills, J.L. Nolan, S.S. Padrick, K.C. Shippey, K.X. Wang, C.B. Wedemeyer, and A. Woznick. 1994. *Hong Kong Business*. San Rafael, California: World Trade Press.

Hampden-Turner, C. and A. Trompenaars. 1993. *The Seven Cultures of Capitalism*. New York: Currency Doubleday.

Hiniker, P.J. 1969. Chinese Reactions to Forced Compliance: Dissonance Reduction or National Character?" *Journal of Social Psychology* 77: 157–176.

Ho, S.C. and Y.M. Sin. 1986. *Advertising in China: Looking Back at Looking Forward*. Hong Kong: Chinese University of Hong Kong Faculty of Business Administration.

Hofstede, G. 1980. *Culture's Consequences: International Differences in Work-Related Values*. Beverly Hills, CA: Sage.

Holstein, W.J. 1990. *The Japanese Power Game: What It Means for Americans*. New York: Charles Scribner and Sons.

Hsu, F.L.K. 1971. Psychological Homeostasis and Jen: Conceptual Tools of Advancing Psychological Anthropology. *American Anthropologist*, 73: 23–44.

Hui, C.H. 1992. Values and Attitudes. In: Westwood, R.I., ed. *Organizational Behavior: Southeast Asian Perspectives*. Hong Kong: Longman.

Kao, H. and L. Young. 1992. The individual and the Organization. In: Westwood, R.I., ed. *Organizational Behavior: Southeast Asian Perspectives*. Hong Kong: Longman.

Last, D. 1994–95. The Dragon Enters the League of the Fat Cat. *Eastern Express*, December 31, 1994–January 1, 1995, p. 32.

Leung, K. and M.H. Bond. 1984. How Americans and Chinese Reward Task-Related Contributions: A Preliminary Study. *Psychologia* 25: 2–9.

Martin, E.F., Jr. 1995. The Interviewing Process in Communicating Change: An Asian Perspective. In: Cushman, D.P., ed. *Communicating Organizational Change*. Albany: SUNY Press.

Martin, E.F., Jr. and Y.W. Tsui. 1993. Hong Kong Chinese Opinions Toward the Portrayal of Women in Advertising. Paper Presented at the University Women of Asia (UWA) Triennial Conference, Hong Kong. November. [Also published in Chinese in *Xinwen Yanjiu Ziliao* 1994, vol. 2, pp. 33–38. Beijing: China Social Sciences Publication House.]

Martin, E.F., Jr. and G.B. Wilson. 1993. Hong Kong Chinese Individual Modernity and Western Orientation Related to Job and Educational Expectations: A Preliminary Study. Paper Presented at the 4th International Intercultural Conference, San Antonio, TX, March.

Martin, E.F., Jr., Y.M. Cheng, G.B. Wilson, and Y.W. Tsui. 1993. Advertising Images Among Hong Kong Chinese: A Preliminary Study of Individual Modernity and Western Orientation. Paper Presented at Asian Mass Communication Information Centre Conference on Communication, Technology and Development: Alternatives for Asia, Kuala Lumpur, June.

Martin, E.F., Jr., Y.M. Cheng, G.B. Wilson, and Y.W. Tsui. 1994a. Advertising Images Among Hong Kong Chinese: Use of Individual Modernity and Western Orientation Clusters in Determining Market Segmentation. *Asian Journal of Communication*, 4 (1): 12–32.

Martin, E.F., Jr., G.B. Wilson and Y.M. Cheng. 1994b. Attitudes Toward Media Freedoms in Hong Kong: A Prelude to 1997. *Gazette: The International Journal of Mass Communication Research*, 54 (2): 103–120. [An earlier paper presented at International

Communication Division of the International Association for Mass Communication Research. Seoul, July 1994.]

Maslow, A. 1954. *Motivation and Personality.* New York: Harper and Row.

Meade, R.D. and J.O. Whittaker. 1967. A Cross-Cultural Study of Authoritarianism. *Journal of Social Psychology,* 72: 3–7.

Media. 1994a. China Figures to Stay Undisclosed Over Tax Queries. May 13, p. 1.

Media. 1994b. A-P Spend Set to Increase Share. December 16, p. 37.

Media. 1994c. Battle Heats Up Between HK Rivals for TV Audience Share in Pearl River Delta Region, October 14, p. 16.

Media. 1994d. Star "Surprised" as Survey Shows 42.1 Million Households, February 4, p. 14.

Media. 1994e. Advertising Expenditure Estimates and Forecasts, September 30, p. 3.

Media. 1994f. 4A's Agencies Ranking Summary: 1993 vs 1992, May 13, p. 1.

Media. 1994g. HK Adspend Leaps, February 18, p. 4.

Media. 1994h. SRG Introduces Research to Indicate Popularity of Newspaper Sections, September 30, p. 6.

Media. 1995a. ATV Boosts Ratings in '94 Despite Overall Downward TV Trend, February 17, p. 3.

Media. 1995b. Coke Tops '94 TVC Recall, January 20, p. 4.

Meindl, J.R., R.G. Hunt, and W. Lee. 1989. Individualism: Collectivism and Work Values: Data from the United States, China, Taiwan, Korea and Hong Kong. *Research in Personnel and Human Resources Management,* Supp. 1, pp. 59–77.

Michman, R.D. 1991. *Lifestyle Market Segmentation.* New York: Praeger.

Nelson, T. 1966. *Ethics in Speech Communication.* Indianapolis: Bobbs-Merrill.

Ogilvy & Mather. 1993. *Pocket Guide To Media 1993.* Hong Kong: Ogilvy & Mather.

Parton, A. 1994. Hong Kong Holds on in Regional Realignment. *Media,* July 22, 1994, pp. 1, 4.

Redding, S.G. 1977. Some Perceptions of Psychological Needs Among Managers in Southeast Asia. In: Poortinga, Y.H., ed. *Basic Problems in Cross-Cultural Psychology.* Amsterdam: Swets and Zeitlinger.

Redding, S.G. 1990. *The Spirit of Chinese Capitalism.* New York: Walter de Gruyter.

Redding, S.G. and T.A. Martyn-Johns. 1979. Paradigm Differences and Their Relation to Management, With Reference to Southeast Asia. In: England, G.W., A.R. Negandhi, and B. Wilpert, eds. *Organizational Functioning in a Cross-Cultural Perspective.* Kent, OH: Kent State University Press.

Redding, S.G. and G.Y.Y. Wong. 1986. The Psychology of Chinese Organizational Behavior. In: M.H. Bond, ed. *The Psychology of the Chinese People.* Hong Kong: Oxford University Press.

Sin, Y.M. Leo and Danny W.L. Cheng. 1984. *Advertising in Hong Kong: The Consumer View.* Hong Kong: Chinese University of Hong Kong Faculty of Business Administration.

Singh, P.N., S. Huang, and G.C. Thompson. 1962. A Comparative Study of Selected Attitudes, Values and Personality Characteristics of American, Chinese, and Indian Students. *Journal of Social Psychology,* 57: 123–132.

Terpstra, V. and K. David. 1985. *The Cultural Environment of International Business.* Cincinnati, OH: South-Western Publishing.

Tu, W.M. 1984. *Confucian Ethics Today.* Singapore: Federal Publishing.

TVB. 1991. *The Advertisers' Guide to Hong Kong.* Hong Kong: Television Broadcasts Limited.

Weber, M. 1951. *The Religion of China.* Glencoe, IL: The Free Press.

Westwood, R.I. 1992a. On Motivation and Work. In: Westwood, R.I., ed. *Organizational Behavior: Southeast Asian Perspectives.* Hong Kong: Longman.

Westwood, R.I. 1992b. Organizational Rationale and Structure. In: Westwood, R.I., ed. *Organizational Behavior: Southeast Asian Perspectives.* Hong Kong: Longman.

Westwood, R.I. 1992c. Culture, Cultural Differences, and Organizational Behavior. In: Westwood, R.I., ed. *Organizational Behavior: Southeast Asian Perspectives.* Hong Kong: Longman.

Yang, K.S. 1981. Social Orientation and Individual Modernity Amongst Chinese Students in Taiwan. *Journal of Social Psychology,* 113: 159–170.

Yang, K.S. 1970. Authoritarianism and Evaluation of Appropriateness of Role Behavior. *Journal of Social Psychology,* 80: 171–181.

Yang, K.S. 1986. Chinese Personality and Its Change. In: Bond, M.H., ed. *The Psychology of the Chinese People.* Hong Kong: Oxford University Press.

4

Advertising in China: A Socialist Experiment

HONG CHENG

Introduction

Today advertisements are ubiquitous in China—on billboards, on public buses, in shopping centers, in sports venues and, above all, in magazines and newspapers and on radio and television. This might be taken for granted in Western countries, but for China, a nation that claims to stick to socialism, this is really unusual and extremely meaningful, as advertising was regarded as "a capitalist tool" during the Cultural Revolution from 1966 to 1976.

GEOGRAPHIC SETTING

China, located in East Asia, is the most populous nation in the world, having a population of 1.2 billion. With an area of 9.6 million square kilometers (about 3.7 million square miles), China is much larger than Western Europe (*Academic American Encyclopedia* 1993). It shares a border with 14 countries: North Korea, Russia, Mongolia, Kazakhstan, Kyrgyzstan, Tajikistan, Afghanistan, Pakistan, India, Nepal, Bhutan, Burma, Laos and Vietnam.

Eastern China is densely inhabited by Chinese-speaking people, who belong to the Han nationality, and western China is scattered with ethnic minorities. While minority nationalities take up 6 percent of China's population, they are spread throughout 50 to 60 percent of the country's area (Hook and Twitchett 1991).

RECENT HISTORY

When the Chinese Communist Party came to power in 1949, its leaders' fundamental long-range goals were to transform China into a modern, powerful, socialist nation. As the years passed the leadership continued to subscribe to these goals, but the economic policies formulated to achieve them were dramatically altered on several occasions in response to major changes in the economy, internal politics, and international political and economic situations (Worden et al. 1988).

During the Communist Party's early years in power, economic policy was primarily concerned with implementing land reform and controlling inflation. In 1953, the party launched its First Five-Year Plan, which marked the beginning of its long-term goal to industrialize China. The policy of concentrating resources on heavy industry at the expense of light industry and agriculture created a strain on the economy and people's living standards. In an attempt to speed up development in 1955, Mao Zedong called for a High Tide of Socialism. This led to the swift collectivization of agriculture followed by the socialization of industry and handicrafts. Dissatisfaction with the outcome of these campaigns led to the adoption of the Great Leap Forward strategy in 1958. This called for even more extreme socialist measures, including the creation of the people's communes. Bad policies, bad weather and the withdrawal of Soviet aid combined to bring the economy to the verge of collapse in 1960.

At this point China adopted a strategy that emphasized more intersectoral balance and a slower rate of growth. The planning priorities of the previous decade were reversed. Agriculture and light industry took precedence over heavy industry in growth. However, once the emergency period was over, political goals began to displace the pragmatic economic strategy. In 1962, Mao launched the Socialist Education Campaign, which finally led to the Cultural Revolution, bringing much disruption to the Chinese economy.

In the late 1970s Deng Xiaoping introduced a new economic strategy, which has remained until the present. The basis of Deng's strategy is a rejection of central planning as the major means of allocating resources. Deng has emphasized the need to secure balanced growth of both modern industry and modern agriculture. The growth is supported by foreign trade, the import of foreign technology and the gradual buildup of foreign investment. Under Deng, China has moved from being a centrally planned economy to one in which prices and markets play an increasingly important role. This shift has been accompanied by an enormous decentralization of powers to enterprises, institutions and peasant households. Consumer demand has become the main signal for the evolving structure of the Chinese economy. Since 1979, rural and urban incomes have risen much faster than in the preceding 30 years, and this has been reflected in better food consumption and housing, and in the availability of basic consumer goods (Hook and Twitchett 1991).

History of Advertising in China

Advertising in China is both old and new. It is old because it has a very long history; it is new because it did not reappear until the year 1979. If advertising could be defined, in a loose sense, as any human communication that is intended to persuade or influence buyers in their purchase decisions, commercial advertising in China, as studies have suggested, dates back to the Western Zhou Dynasty (11th century-771 B.C.) when daytime trade fairs began to appear. Ware displays and street hawking were the major forms of advertising then (Sun 1991; Xu 1989).

Other advertising forms like shop banners and shop signboards started to appear during the Spring and Autumn Period (770–476 B.C.) (Sun 1991). Those who used the banners most often in ancient China were wine shop owners (Xu 1989). Wooden signboards first appeared during the Spring and Autumn Period and became popular during the Tang Dynasty (618–907). Since then, wooden signboards have been a very popular traditional form of advertising in China (Sun 1991).

By the Song Dynasty (960–1279), popular advertising media included high-flying wine banners, lanterns, pictures, signboards, decorated structures, and wrappers (Liu and Chen 1989; Sun 1991; Xu 1989). Printed advertisements also came into existence in China in that period. The Shanghai Museum displays a bronze plaque from the Song Dynasty, which was used by a Liu family's needle shop in Jinan, Shandong Province, to print wrappers for advertising its products.

Among various ancient advertising media, antithetical couplets written in scrolls were widely used for commercial advertising. For example, "When birds smell the mellowness of my wine, they become phoenixes; when fish eat the dregs of my wine, they turn into dragons." This antithetical couplet was for a wine shop (Li and Li 1993).

EMERGENCE OF MODERN ADVERTISING

Although primitive forms of advertising existed in China for over 2,000 years, the notion of modern advertising was entirely foreign to the Chinese. Here, *modern advertising* refers to the "paid nonpersonal communication from an identified sponsor using mass media to persuade or influence an audience" (Wells et al. 1992, 10). Just as Thomas Gorman and Jeffery Muir of the China Consultants International observed,

> Although advertising was practiced in a variety of forms around the turn of the century by both international and local Chinese companies in China, the concept of advertising per se was foreign, introduced only in recent Chinese history; and first popularized by foreign tobacco and petroleum companies.
>
> (Rotzoll 1986, 9)

As a matter of fact, the foreign idea of advertising was put into practice in China in the middle of the 19th century. The first modern media that carried advertisements in the country were three British-run English-language newspapers in Hong Kong: the *Friend of China and Hongkong Gazette* (1842–59), the *Hongkong Register* (1844–59) and the *China Mail* (1845–1911) (King and Clarke 1965).

In the second half of the 19th century more than 300 foreign-run newspapers and magazines were circulated in China, with most of them published in Shanghai (Chang 1989), the commercial center of the country. Many of these publications were in Chinese, which became the major modern mass media for advertising in the country. The first Chinese-language newspapers carrying advertisements were *Zhongwai Xinbao* (*Chinese and Foreign New Paper*) founded in Hong Kong in 1858, and *Shanghai Xinbao* (*Shanghai New Paper*) launched in Shanghai in 1861 (Xu 1989).

The first Chinese magazine carrying advertisements was the British-run *Xia'er Guanzhen* (*Chinese Serial*) (1853–56) in Hong Kong. The magazines that carried most advertisements in early 20th-century China were *Dongfang Zhazhi* (*Eastern Miscellany*) (1901–41), *Funu Zhazhi* (*Women's Magazine*) (1915–45), and *Kuaile Jiating* (*Happy Home*) (1935–45), all published in Shanghai (Ding et al. 1985; Xu 1989).

Modern advertising media practices and skills, introduced by the Westerners, were well received by the Chinese. Even *Zhengzhi Guanbao* (*Political Official Gazette*), the first newspaper established by the government of the Qing Dynasty in 1907, carried advertisements (Liu and Chen 1989). The competing *Shen Bao* (*Shanghai Gazette*) and *Xinwen Bao* (*News Gazette*), which eventually became Chinese owned, were the most successful and longest-running newspapers, and both carried advertisements in the early 20th century (Liu and Chen 1989; Xu 1989).

The 1930s was the golden age for China's modern advertising prior to the Communist revolution. In addition to newspapers, magazines, billboards, posters, neon signs, streetcars, booklets and calendars, the list of advertising media at that time also included radio broadcasting (Xu 1990).

Radio broadcasting in China dates back to 1922. By 1936, Shanghai had 36 privately owned Chinese stations, four foreign-run stations, one station run by the municipal government, and one run by the Ministry of Communications. Advertisers purchased spots and program time on nearly every station. The U.S.–owned Henningsen Produce Company even ran newspaper advertisements that announced the air times of their radio commercials for Hazelwood Ice Cream, boosting sales immediately (Xu 1990).

The most important benchmark in the growth of the modern advertising industry in China was the emergence of advertising agencies in the early 20th century. Again introduced from the West, Chinese advertising agencies evolved from media brokers. Toward the 1930s there were around 20 agencies in Shanghai.

The first modern agency was the China Commercial Advertising Agency (CCAA), founded in 1926 by C.P. Ling, the U.S.–educated "father of Chinese advertising." Together with Ling's agency, Carl Crow, Inc. from the United States, Millington Ltd. from Britain and the Consolidated National Advertising Company—another Chinese-run agency—became the dominant "Big Four" in Shanghai during 1930s. Before 1949 when the People's Republic was founded, around 100 advertising agencies were in operation in Shanghai, with a few others in Beijing, Chongqing and Guangzhou. All these agencies added luster to the golden age of advertising in China. But this age was short-lived, truncated by World War II and the civil war of the 1940s (Xu 1990).

During World War II many newspapers were moved to Chongqing, Sichuan Province, where the Nationalist government was temporarily located. All the major newspapers published there carried advertisements (Sun 1991).

Meanwhile the major newspapers run by the Communist Party of China, which seemed to have no serious ideological objections to advertising at that time, also started to carry advertisements (Liu and Chen 1989). What the communist newspapers only accepted, however, were "decent and honest" advertisements (Rotzoll 1986).

But on the whole, the infant modern advertising industry, just like the economy in the entire country, suffered from World War II. For instance, when Shanghai was under Japanese occupation, all the major advertising agencies there were forced to cease operation. A few lingering agencies were operated only to promote Japanese products (Sun 1991).

With the defeat of their common enemy, the Japanese, in 1945 came an immediate renewal of internal hostilities between the Communists and Nationalists in China. This led to the "Third Civil War" from 1945 to 1949, which drained the national economy and left the advertising industry in the country at a low tide. In 1949, the Communists came to power.

ADVERTISING IN THE THREE POST-LIBERATION DECADES

During the first few years after 1949 the Chinese government allowed advertising to exist, though foreign participation was virtually ended (Seligman 1984). After January 1956 all the remaining advertising agencies in China became completely state owned. The 108 agencies in Shanghai, for instance, were merged into the state-run Shanghai Advertising Corporation (Xu 1990).

In December 1957 the first Conference of Advertising Workers in Socialist Countries was held in Prague, Czech Republic. Dominated by the theme that "socialism needs advertising," this conference was attended by representatives from 13 socialist countries. It gave an impetus to China's advertising (Baudot 1989).

Advertising business boomed for a while in China, slumped during the hard time around the early 1960s, and then picked up again. In 1962, for example, the former Shanghai Advertising Corporation was changed into the Shanghai Advertising and Packaging Corporation, and "kept busy promoting national products, and advertising on the packaging of products for exports" (Howkins 1982, 107).

It is evident that advertising was never officially banned during the postrevolution years until the Cultural Revolution. Instead it was "encouraged" occasionally. Nevertheless, the seedbed for advertising during this period was more barren than fertile, which made any significant growth of the industry impossible.

The hardest and final blows to advertising in China came from the Cultural Revolution. In addition to the vigorous centrally planned economy, the blows were mainly ideological. Judged by Mao's policy, advertising was a societal waste, not adding any value to commodities.

When the Cultural Revolution began, neon signs were first smashed by "red guards." Advertisements disappeared from newspapers, except those showing and staging the eight "model dramas." All shop windows were pasted with "big character posters" and all shop names were changed. There were only political slogans on billboards. Agencies that had managed to hang on during the early 1960s were reduced to producing political posters, and finally closed. Not until 1979 did the first local agency reopen for business.

RECURRENCE OF ADVERTISING. The renaissance of advertising in China was preluded by a few articles published in the nation's leading newspapers and magazines. On January 14, 1979, an editorial appeared in the Shanghai-based *Wenhui Daily*, calling for "restoring the good name of advertising" (Ding 1979, 3). Seeing advertising as a "means of promoting trade, earning foreign exchange, and broadening the masses' horizons," the editorial encouraged China's mass media to carry foreign as well as domestic advertisements. This viewpoint was really a breakthrough in the late 1970s. The editorial, actually the first call for the return of advertising after a 10-year absence in China, was immediately supported by other articles published in official publications.

On January 14, 1979, the *Tianjin Daily* ran an advertisement for the Tianjin Toothpaste Factory. This was the first advertisement in China since the Cultural Revolution. But the renaissance of the advertising industry in China largely began in Shanghai, the focal point of the golden age of China's advertising in the 1930s.

On January 28, 1979, the *Liberation Daily*, another Shanghai-based newspaper, carried advertisements for several domestic products. On the same day, the Shanghai Television Station showed a commercial for a Chinese-made tonic wine, the first time ever in the history of China's television. On March 5, 1979, the Shanghai Broadcasting Station broadcast a radio commercial for a local photo studio. On the 15th of the same month, the *Wenhui Daily* carried an advertisement for the Swiss-made Rado watch, the first foreign advertisement that appeared in China after the Cultural Revolution.

As the mass media opened up to advertising, advertising agencies began to reopen in China. The Shanghai Advertising Corporation, the last company to cease operation when advertising was banned during the Cultural Revolution, first reopened in late 1978. In 1979, only 10 advertising agencies operated in a few major cities. Today advertising agencies are spread all over the country, although most of them are still concentrated in urban areas.

SOCIAL CHANGES IN THE EARLY POST-MAO YEARS

The dramatic revival of the Chinese advertising industry was by no means accidental. Instead it was an inevitable consequence of the social changes in China. Just as the political swing to the extreme left meant the demise of the advertising industry, a swing back to the right led to its reoccurrence.

The death of Mao Zedong (on September 9, 1976) was a turning point in China's politics. Mao, the late chairman of the Communist Party of China, had been the most powerful political figure in the People's Republic, affecting decisively the policies regarding China's political, economic and social life. He died at a time when China was suffering from political instability and economic stagnation. Within months of his death, the "Gang of Four," the leading force behind the Cultural Revolution, was overthrown. As the driving force for the post-Mao reform, Deng Xiaoping encouraged people to "emancipate the mind" and to "seek truth from facts" so as to break away from the politics characterized by the Cultural Revolution (Deng 1984).

ECONOMIC REFORMS. In the late 1970s the post-Mao Chinese leadership declared for the first time that a socialist economy is a commodity economy planned on the basis of public ownership. It must pay due attention to the important functions of economic levers and market mechanism. This view was based on the argument that "the commodity economy is an unavoidable state in the development of a socialist economy" (James 1989, 485).

Thus, central planning and market mechanism are believed to be the "two sides of the same coin under socialist conditions" (Minami 1994, 20). This combination of central planning and market mechanism is what "socialism with Chinese characteristics" actually means. As Deng once explained, "we need both a planned economy and a market economy" (*China Daily* 1993a, 4).

As a result of the emphasis on the role of market mechanism in economic development, advertising—an integral "institution *within* the master institution of the market" (Rotzoll et al. 1976, 15) and a catalyst in a market-driven economy (Azrry and Wilson 1981, 1)—naturally and easily came back to life in China. Since the late 1970s, advertising, which was treated as a "capitalist tool" during the Cultural Revolution, has been officially called "an accelerator for the economic development in China" (Wang 1991, 2).

GROWTH OF ADVERTISING INDUSTRY

Since 1979 the advertising industry in China has experienced consistent growth. The annual business volumes rose at an average rate of over 40 percent between 1981 and 1992, far faster than the increase in the gross national product (GNP) of the country. Table 4.1 highlights the growth of China's advertising industry during those 12 years.

The Chinese government, which owned 12,181 of the country's 16,683 advertising units in 1992, declared that "China's advertising industry is witnessing its fastest growth ever" (Parsons 1993, 18). In 1986, the business volume of Chinese advertising only ranked 34th in the world (Xu 1989), but in 1993 it had climbed to the 15th (*Zhongguo Daobao* 1994). In fact, 1993 was named the "Ad-

Table 4.1.   China's Advertising Industry Growth (1981–1992)

Year	Business Volume (million yuan)	Advertising Expenditure in the GNP (%)	Per Capita Spending on Advertising (yuan)	Advertising Units*	Advertising Employees (persons)	Per Capita Business Volume by Advertising Employees (yuan)
1981	118.000	0.024	0.117	1,160	16,160	7,302
1982	150.000	0.028	0.147	1,500	18,000	8,333
1983	234.074	0.040	0.227	2,340	34,853	6,716
1984	365.278	0.052	0.350	4,077	47,259	7,929
1985	605.225	0.070	0.571	6,052	63,819	9,483
1986	844.777	0.087	0.786	6,944	81,130	10,412
1987	1,112.003	0.098	1.017	8,225	92,279	12,050
1988	1,492.939	0.107	1.345	10,677	112,139	13,313
1989	1,998.998	0.127	1.774	11,142	128,203	15,592
1990	2,501.726	0.144	2.188	11,123	131,970	18,957
1991	3,508.926	0.171	3.030	11,769	134,506	26,008
1992	6,786.754	0.283	5.792	16,683	185,428	36,600

Source: *Guoji Guanggao,* 1993, 42.

*Advertising units include advertising agencies, advertising departments in the media, and advertising suppliers.

vertising Year of China" because of the unprecedented growth of the advertising industry in the country (Fan 1994). In that year Chinese advertising's turnover soared to 13.4 billion yuan (about US$1.9 billion), a rise of 43 percent over the previous year (*Baokan Guanggao Wenzhai,* 1994b). At the same time, the number of advertising units reached 31,770, which was almost double that of 1992, and advertising employees in China totaled 310,638, a 66 percent increase over 1992 (*Baokan Guanggao Wenzhai* 1994a). The rapid growth of the Chinese advertising industry is expected to continue. It is estimated that the annual advertising spending in the country will hit US$4.8 billion by the year 2000 (*Wall Street Journal* 1993; Yuan 1993).

Structure of the Advertising Industry

The practice of advertising is very much constrained in China by the socialist framework within which it operates. The current Constitution of the People's Republic of China stipulates the four cardinal principles as the national ideology, namely, adherence to the socialist road, to the people's democratic dictatorship, to leadership by the Communist Party of China, and to Marxism-Leninism and Mao Zedong thought. The constitution stipulates explicitly:

> The basic task of the nation in the years to come is to concentrate its effort on socialist modernization. . . . The Chinese people of all nationalities will continue . . . to modernize industry, agriculture, national defense and science and

technology step by step to turn China into a socialist country with a high level of culture and democracy.

(James 1989, 386)

Although advertising was welcomed back into China in the late 1970s after the Cultural Revolution, it was not allowed a free rein. What the Chinese government permitted was "socialist commercial advertising" (Liu 1986, 3). The official position held that because socialist and capitalist commodity economies differ in nature, socialist advertising—the offspring of a socialist commodity economy—should also differ from the advertising in capitalist countries. This position was clearly stated in the Beijing-based *Guangming Daily,*

> Socialist advertising requires that consideration be given to the social benefits of the theme, wording and visuals of the advertisements concerned, and that its essence be healthy. However, the basic aim of advertising is to introduce certain commodities to consumers, and it is necessary to correctly link advertising commodities with political propaganda. Advertising should introduce commodities to consumers and display political ideology.
>
> (Liu 1986, 3)

This conviction that advertising must promote the appropriate political ideology while serving as a marketing tool distinctly marks the Chinese government's attitude toward advertising.

The creation of a hierarchical industry structure with supervisory functions at many levels was one of the first overt official attempts to exercise some central control on advertising. Since the late 1970s China's advertising industry has developed mainly along three lines: (a) through advertising agencies, (b) through advertising suppliers, and (c) through advertising media. All three of these are called advertising "units" by the government.

ADVERTISING AGENCIES
The growth of Chinese advertising agencies since 1949 has gone through three phases: (a) the advertising workshops before the mid-1950s; (b) the art and designing companies from the mid-1950s to mid-1960s; and (c) the professional advertising corporations since the 1980s. In the early 1980s the business of advertising companies mainly involved design and manufacture of product catalogs, media buying, and indoor and outdoor decorating for department stores and sales exhibitions. Since 1986 a greater priority has been given to advertising creation, media planning, market research, and consulting services (*Zhongguo Guanggao Nianjian* 1988).

Chinese advertising agencies, often identifying themselves as companies or corporations, fall into two major groups: one affiliated with the Ministry of Foreign Economic Relations and Trade (MOFERT), the other attached to various non-MOFERT departments. While bounded by government regulations for advertising, all the agencies are subject to the management by departments to which they are affiliated.

Under the aegis of the MOFERT, the China International Advertising Corporation handles national foreign trade advertising and coordinates local foreign trade advertising agencies. The foreign trade advertising agencies in all provinces and major cities undertake foreign advertising as well as advertising for export products on a regional or local basis. Nowadays some of them have also started to handle domestic advertising business, and to operate in joint ventureship with foreign agencies.

In addition to the main foreign trade advertising agency in each province or major city, there are numerous other smaller corporations mainly handling domestic advertising. In fact, many of them have also been licensed to handle foreign advertising business. The affiliation of these agencies varies greatly.

Authorized by the State Administration for Industry and Commerce (SAIC), and containing 73 member companies in 1991, the Beijing-based China National United Advertising Corporation coordinates and oversees the major local domestic advertising agencies (*Agency Brochure* 1991).

In 1994, advertising agencies in China were for the first time officially ranked, based on their 1992 business volumes. Table 4.2 lists the top 10 agencies.

Table 4.2.   Top 10 Advertising Agencies in China (by Business Volumes, 1992)

Agencies	Business Volume (million yuan)
Oriental Advertising Corporation, Ltd. (Zhuhai Special Economic Zone)	96.00
Great Wall International Film and Television Advertising Corporation, Ltd.	91.82
China National United Advertising Corporation	86.05
Shanghai Advertising Corporation	84.84
Shanghai Advertising and Decorating Corporation	78.40
Guangdong Advertising Corporation	75.00
Dentsu, Young & Rubincam China	62.23
Golden Horse Advertising Corporation, Ltd. (Hainan Province)	60.34
Beijing Advertising Corporation	50.00
Beijing Guo'an Advertising Corporation	47.70

Source: *Baokan Guanggao Wenzhai*, 1994d, 59.

Currently foreign advertising agencies are doing a limited but growing business in China. For example, in 1986 and 1992, foreign advertising accounted for US$15 million and US$75 million in billing respectively—both about 6 percent of China's total advertising spending in those 2 years (Baudot 1989; Keobke and Woo 1992). In 1993, foreign advertising business volume reached US$133 million, taking up 7 percent of the national turnover (*Zhongguo Daobao* 1994). The billings of foreign advertising were mainly generated by a dozen transnational agencies and thirty-odd Hong Kong–based companies (Keobke and Woo 1992). The leading foreign agencies operating in China from 1992 through 1993 are listed in Table 4.3.

The world's major advertising agencies rushed into the Chinese market during the last 10 years and are now recording annual billing growth of up to 400 percent (Table 4.3). Dentsu, Young & Rubicam was the first transnational advertising agency starting offices in Beijing and Shanghai soon after advertising was resumed in 1979 (Matsuda 1981; Parsons 1993). Leo Burnett has made the development of China "the highest priority of any new market in the world" (Miao 1993a, 14). In 1993, Saatchi & Saatchi turned out to be the most successful foreign advertising agency in the Chinese market (Table 4.3).

Table 4.3.   Top Foreign Advertising Agencies in China

Agency	Billing (thousand US$)		Approximate % Increase
	1992	1993	
Saatchi & Saatchi, Beijing/Guangzhou	5,476	28,002	411
Dentsu, Young & Rubicam China, Beijing	13,860	23,889	72
Ogilvy & Mather, Beijing	NA	20,408	NA
J. Walter Thompson China, Beijing/Shanghai	11,428	19,358	69
McCann-Erickson Guangming, Guangzhou	7,862	17,140	118
Grey China, Beijing	5,853	9,067	55
D'Arcy Masius Benton & Bowles, Guangzhou	4,027	8,687	116
Leo Burnett Ltd., Guangzhou	1,633	8,325	410
BBDO/CNUAC, Beijing	1,921	5,636	193
Lintas China, Shanghai	NA	5,527	NA
Euro RSCG Ball Partnership China, Beijing	NA	5,501	NA

Source: *Advertising Age,* 1993, 28; *Advertising Age,* 1994, 26.
Note: NA, not applicable.

Some foreign agencies have chosen to locate in Hong Kong, as their client bases are there. Many other agencies, however, prefer to go into joint ventureship, which has become a popular way to enter the Chinese market. By 1993, 79 advertising ventures had been set up in 16 provinces and municipalities in China, with 31 of them located in Beijing, 11 in Shanghai, nine in Jiangsu Province, and six in Guangdong Province (Wang 1993).

ADVERTISING SUPPLIERS
Since the late 1980s the increasingly diversified advertising forms in China have turned many suppliers of advertising products into independent entrepreneurs in the industry. Their business services range from designing and printing posters and product catalogs to manufacturing neon lights, light boxes and electronic displays. Their clients include advertisers as well as advertising agencies and the media. Their business volumes during the 1980s varied from nearly 20 percent to less than 10 percent of China's total advertising billings (*Zhongguo Guanggao Nianjian* 1988).

Advertising Media

In China the mass media are either state owned or collectively owned. Today the major mass media institutions engaged in advertising there are newspapers, magazines, and broadcasting and television stations. Some of the media institutions have set up subsidiary companies to handle their advertising business; however, most of the media institutions only have advertising departments or sections.

In China, media institutions have historically produced advertisements for their clients by using the traditional agency–client structure that is so familiar in the West. Until recently, direct expenditure to the media was still the main method of advertising. In 1991, for instance, although direct placements of advertisements with newspapers, television, magazines and radio added up to 62.7 percent of total billings, advertising agencies received only 19.7 percent. The remaining 17.5 percent mainly came from advertising suppliers (*Zhongguo Guanggao Nianjian* 1992).

The SAIC, however, initiated steps to eliminate the direct placement of advertising by clients into the media, and to ban the media from acting as agencies for other media. As a result, in 1992, the volume of agencies' business increased to 27.5 percent of total billings, the highest rate since 1985 (Lu 1993).

NEWSPAPERS

In 1993, there were 2,054 newspapers carrying advertisements in China (*Baokan Guanggao Wenzhai* 1994c). Before 1990 the average annual business volume of newspaper advertising accounted for more than 50 percent of the total generated by all advertising media in China. Table 4.4 lists China's top 10 newspapers in advertising.

Table 4.4. Top 10 Newspapers in Advertising in China, 1992 (by Business Volume)

Newspapers	Business Volume (million yuan)
Liberation Daily	81.38
Guangzhou Daily	81.00
Yangcheng Evening Paper	68.00
Xinmin Evening Paper	66.10
Shenzhen Special Zone Paper	60.05
Wenhui Daily	50.90
People's Daily	50.00
Nanjing Daily	49.68
Beijing Daily	41.74
Changjiang Daily	27.00

Source: *Baokan Guanggao Wenzhai*, 1994c, 61.

As demonstrated in Table 4.5, the media rates in some cases are based on the "prestige" rather than the actual circulation of newspapers.

MAGAZINES

The number of magazines in China has significantly increased since the late 1970s. In 1978, only 930 magazines were published in the country. But in 1993 the number increased to 6,810 (*Beijing Review* 1994), 3,324 of which carried ad-

Table 4.5.　Media Rates for Major Daily Newspapers in China, 1992

Newspapers	Circulation (million)	Distribution	Rate per Column cm		
			Local Enterprise	Joint Venture	Foreign Enterprise
People's Daily	4.50	Nationwide	Y220	Y275	US $130
Economic Daily	1.00	Nationwide	Y90	Y90	US $60
Beijing Daily	0.70	Beijing and vicinity	Y76	Y114	US $50
Wenhui Bao	0.97	Shanghai and vicinity	Y150	Y150	US $50
Guangzhou Daily	0.51	Guangzhou and vicinity	Y125	Y150	HK $380
China Daily	0.15	Nationwide	Y50	US$26	US $26

Source: Friske, 1993, 280.
Note: Y = yuan.

vertisements, an increase of 23 percent from 1992 (*Baokan Guanggao Wenzhai* 1994c). Since the early 1980s the average annual business volume of magazine advertising has been below 10 percent of the total generated by all advertising media in China. Table 4.6 lists China's top 10 magazines in advertising.

Table 4.6.　Top 10 Magazines in Advertising in China, 1992 (by Business Volume)

Magazine	Business Volume (million yuan)
China Telephone Directory	4.20
Far East Economic Pictorial	1.28
Shanghai Industry and Business	0.99
Practical Chinese Medications	0.80
Guangxi Press Photos Pictorial	0.78
Family	0.67
World of Electricity	0.60
International Exchange	0.60
Democracy and Legal System	0.56
Shanghai Pictorial	0.44

Source: *Baokan Guanggao Wenzhai*, 1994c, 61.

BROADCASTING STATIONS

China's broadcasting system, through its 983 wireless and more than 2,000 wired stations in 1993, covered all cities and most villages (*Beijing Review* 1994). In the same year 834 of the wireless and 40 percent of the wired broadcasting stations were handling advertising business (*Baokan Guanggao Wenzhai* 1994c). Although their annual business volume in the total advertising media billings declined from more than 15 percent in the early 1980s to less than 10 percent in the early 1990s, radio advertising still covers 75.6 percent of the population in China. With over 300 million radio sets and radio-cassettes in Chinese households, 53.7 percent of Chinese people listen to radio frequently today (*Zhongguo Guangbo Dianshi Nianjian* 1993). Table 4.7 lists China's top 10 broadcasting stations in advertising.

Table 4.7.   Top 10 Broadcasting Stations in Advertising in China, 1992 (by Business Volume)

Station	Business Volume (million yuan)
Central People's Broadcasting Station	25.75
Guangdong People's Broadcasting Station	16.33
Shanghai People's Broadcasting Station	13.00
Guangzhou People's Broadcasting Station	8.44
Beijing People's Broadcasting Station	6.50
Foshan People's Broadcasting Station	6.00
Jiangsu People's Broadcasting Station	5.27
Shenzhen People's Broadcasting Station	4.80
Shandong People's Broadcasting Station	3.96
Nanjing People's Broadcasting Station	3.57

Source: *Baokan Guanggao Wenzhai,* 1994c, 61.

The media rate for broadcasting advertising varies greatly from station to station, which is illustrated in Table 4.8.

Table 4.8.   Media Rates for Selected Radio Stations in China, 1992

		Rate for 30 Seconds		
Station	Broadcast Area	Local Enterprise	Joint Venture	Foreign Enterprise (US$)
The Central People's Broadcasting Station	Nationwide	Y600	Y690	$400
Beijing Radio	Beijing and vicinity	Y250	Y325	$238
Shanghai Radio	Shanghai and vicinity	Y400	Y400	$140
Guangzhou Radio	Guangzhou and vicinity	Y115	Y115	$102

Source: Friske, 1993, 280.

Note: Y = yuan.

TELEVISION STATIONS

China's first television commercial was produced by the Shanghai Television Station in 1979, 2 decades after the occurrence of China's first television program service in Beijing. In 1992, television broadcasting covered 81.3 percent of the total population, even higher than the coverage of radio broadcasting (*Zhongguo Guangbo Dianshi Nianjian* 1993).

Since the early 1980s television has been the fastest-growing advertising medium in China, with its annual increasing rate above 45 percent. Its average annual business volume has increased from about 10 percent in the early 1980s to more than 40 percent in the early 1990s in the total billings generated by all advertising media in the country. In 1991 and 1992, television surpassed newspapers in advertising business volume for the first time, and became the largest advertising medium in China. But in 1993 it lost the crown to newspapers (*Baokan Guanggao Wenzhai* 1994c).

In 1993, one out of every five Chinese owned at least one television set, compared with one out of every 400 people only 15 years ago. Over 800 million Chinese watch television, nearly 200 million more than the figure in the late 1980s (*China Daily* 1993b). By 1993, the television stations handling advertising business had totaled 1,606, including about 1,000 cable television stations (Fan 1994). Table 4.9 lists China's top 10 television stations in advertising.

Table 4.9. Top 10 Television Stations in Advertising in China (by Business Volume, 1992)

Station	Business Volume (million yuan)
China Central Television Station	490.45
Shanghai Television Station	146.75
Guangdong Television Station	114.00
Beijing Television Station	80.00
Sichuan Television Station	80.00
Tianjin Television Station	54.60
Guangzhou Television Station	53.20
Fujian Television Station	45.46
Zhejiang Television Station	42.35
Shaanxi Television Station	33.00

Source: *Baokan Guanggao Wenzhai*, 1994c, 61.

The differences in media rates are even sharper for television advertising than for radio advertising in China, which is quite evident from Table 4.10.

Table 4.10. Media Rates for Selected Television Stations in China in 1992

Station	Broadcast Area	Day	Rate for 30 Seconds		
			Local Enterprise	Joint Venture	Foreign Enterprise
CCTV2	Nationwide	Mon–Fri	Y4,000–10,000	Y6,000–13,000	US $4,000–8,000
		Sat–Sun	Y5,000–11,000	Y7,500–14,000	US $5,000–9,000
CCTV8	Beijing	Mon–Sun	Y4,000	Y5,500	US $3,000
BTV6	Beijing and vicinity	Mon–Fri	Y4,500	Y4,500	US $1,600
BTV21	Beijing and vicinity	Mon–Sun	Y1,500	Y1,500	US $1,000
STV8 and STV20	Shanghai and vicinity	Mon–Fri	Y1,200–3,000	Y1,800–4,500	US $500–1,800
		Sat–Sun	Y1,400–3,500	Y1,800–5,250	US $500–2,160
GDTV14 (Cantonese)	Guangdong	Mon–Fri	Y300–2,200	Y450–3,300	HK $1,800–12,900
		Sat–Sun	Y350–2,500	Y520–3,800	HK $1,800–16,770
GDTV2 (Mandarin)	Guangdong	Mon–Fri	Y500–1,000	Y750–1,500	HK $1,800–9,100
		Sat–Sun	Y800–1,150	Y870–1,730	HK $1,800–11,830

Source: Friske, 1993, 280.
Note: Y = yuan. CCTV2, China Central Television Channel 2; CCTV8, China Central Television Channel 8; BTV6, Beijing Television Channel 6; BTV21, Beijing Television Channel 21; STV8, Shanghai Television Channel 8; STV20, Shanghai Television Channel 20; GDTV14, Guangdong Television Channel 14; GDTV2, Guangdong Television Channel 2.

The media rates in China have been firming up for two reasons. First, in the early 1990s overall advertising spending was up by more than 60 percent, but there was no corresponding growth in media outlets (Miao 1993b). So the media equation is simply that demand outstrips supply. The tone of the media rate increase in this seller's market is usually set by the China Central Television (CCTV) and the *People's Daily,* the largest and most influential institutions in China's electronic and print media, respectively.

In 1993, the CCTV hiked its average 30-second prime time slot for joint-venture advertisers from 16,900 to 35,200 yuan (US$6,175), a jump of 108 percent (Geddes 1993b; Miao 1993b). Similar increases were slated for local stations in major cities like Beijing, Shanghai and Guangdong, which showed increases ranging from 45 percent to 100 percent. This compared with rate-card inflation rates in newspapers from as low as 20 percent to as high as 100 percent (Geddes 1993b; Miao 1993b). For instance, the rate for less than a half page, the largest space available in the *People's Daily,* was US$30,000 in 1993 (Geddes 1993b). Even so, advertising space in China's newspapers is so heavily booked that clients sometimes have to wait up to 6 months to place an advertisement (Shuang 1992).

In the meantime the flood of advertising by joint-venture companies has helped push the increase of media rates in the country (Geddes 1993a). The inconsistent media rates are now described as the "biggest hurdle to overcome" in the development of the advertising industry in China (Miao 1993c).

Despite the jump in rates, however, foreign advertising executives still see the rates as a tremendous bargain compared with other markets. As Lyric Hughes, president of Chicago-based T.L.I., admitted,

> Historically, rates have been very low. For example, on the Super Bowl [in the US] you pay more than half a million dollars. In China, a 30-second spot on the Super Bowl, [which could reach] 400 million viewers, has been $10,000.
> (Geddes 1993b, I-3)

Although the increase in rates caused "some short-term pain" for advertisers, it has led foreign advertisers to demand "improved programming standards," and is believed to "stimulate a more professional media and make new media outlets more viable (Geddes 1993b). Many executives of foreign advertising agencies "would rather pay more in rates than have to bribe" (Karp 1993, 53). Nevertheless, it was reported in 1994 that competition among television stations in major Chinese cities, and an expected slowing of economic growth, have slowed down the rate increases (Parton 1994).

Television and newspapers have assumed more and more of companies' advertising budgets, and are now the two most popular advertising media in China. And television has proved to be more powerful and cost-effective than print or radio, with its penetration in urban areas estimated at an average of at least 90 percent—close to saturation in 1992 (Keobke and Woo 1992).

In addition there are still many other options for advertisers in China. For instance, major urban centers are the best places for a company to introduce its name to the Chinese consumers. The heavy traffic and bustling crowds typical of most major cities guarantee a large audience for outdoor advertisements, which include billboards, bus shelters, bus and trolley bodies, and light boxes. As a matter of fact, these advertising media are quite popular in Chinese urban areas today. In November 1994 a giant color LED audio-video screen, the largest in the world, was put into operation in Tianjin. The 36-million-yuan screen (about US$4.2 million) is 15 meters tall and 40 meters long, offering visual displays 20 hours a day on the banks of the Haihe River (Li 1994). Table 4.11 presents some outdoor advertising rates in China.

Table 4.11. Chinese Outdoor Advertising Rates (US$, 1992)

Type	Rate	Minimum Rental Period
Billboards	$35–80/sq m per month	6 months
Neon signs	$60–80/sq m per month	3 years
Bus shelter*	$7,000 per shelter	1 year
Trolleys*	$10,000 for three trolleys	6 months
Light boxes	Negotiable	Negotiable

Source: Friske, 1993, 281.
*Shanghai only.

Direct mail advertising is still a novelty in China, so the people are found to read and consider direct mail more carefully than Westerners (Xu 1992). While mass advertising is used to establish product awareness, targeted public relations efforts are used to enhance a company's image. Since the mid-1980s, public relations firms have been channeling advertisers to a variety of promotions in China (Seligman 1986).

ADVERTISING ASSOCIATIONS

There are two national advertising associations in China. One is the China Advertising Association (CAA), established in December 1983, which had 8,875 corporate members from government administrative bodies, advertising companies or agencies, media, and advertisers in 1992. The CAA coordinates and gives guidance to the local advertising associations that have been set up in 27 provinces and 14 major cities. The CAA has five affiliated committees: newspaper, television, radio, advertising agency, and research committees.

The other association is the China National Advertising Association for Foreign Economic Relations and Trade (CFAA), set up in August 1981. Its more than 100 members include foreign trade advertising corporations, newspapers, magazines and publishing houses under the MOFERT. The CFAA participates in international activities on behalf of China's foreign economic relations and trade sector. It cosponsored with the *South* magazine the Third World Advertising Congress held in Beijing from June 16 to 20, 1987.

The China Chapter of the New York–based International Advertising Association was officially set up in Beijing in May 1987. The new IAA Chapter has 32 members from 13 cities, each prominent in China's advertising industry (Xu 1990).

Advertising Regulation and Policy Issues

The highest administrative body in charge of advertising in China is the SAIC, which is authorized by the State Council to supervise and provide guidance to all advertising agencies, advertising media, and advertisers in China. In turn, administrations for industry and commerce of local governments at various levels all have advertising departments or sections.

While implementing the general regulations for advertising promulgated by the State Council, the Advertising Office of the SAIC drafts detailed rules governing advertising in China. It inspects and registers units engaged in advertising business; issues advertising business licenses; examines and supervises advertising activities; solves disputes in advertising business; encourages the disclosure of deception and other illegal behavior in advertising; and gives guidance to advertising associations.

Units that intend to be engaged in advertising business nationally apply to the Advertising Office of the SAIC for business licenses. Those preferring to do local advertising business apply for licenses through corresponding local administrations for industry and commerce.

Foreign advertising agencies intending to open offices in China first apply to the Advertising Office of the SAIC for approval, and then register at all local administrations for industry and commerce in the areas where their offices are to be set up. Foreign enterprises intending to start advertising companies or joint ventures on a national scale apply to the MOFERT for approval, and then report to the SAIC for business licenses. If the proposed companies or joint ventures are local in scope, applications are sent for review to both local government departments of foreign economic relations and trade, and local advertising departments of the administration for industry and commerce. The applications are then forwarded to the Advertising Office of the SAIC for approval. Once an application is approved, a local advertising department will issue the business license (Swanson 1990).

Between 1949 when the People's Republic of China was founded and 1966 when the Cultural Revolution started, there was no national advertising regulation in China. All the regulations regarding advertising were made by some local governments. During the Cultural Revolution all those local regulations disappeared along with the entire advertising industry in the country.

The first national regulation for advertising was the *Interim Regulations for Advertising Management,* promulgated by the State Council in February 1982. It went into effect on May 1 of the same year. The 5 years following the implementation of the *Interim Regulations* had proved that a more detailed set of regulations was needed. In December 1987 the *Regulations for Advertising Management* superseded the *Interim Regulations.*

Although the 1982 and 1987 regulations were similar in substance, some noticeable changes were made in the newer regulations. First, the 1987 regulations were less ideological in formulation than the earlier text. The 1982 regulations set a stronger ideological tone in the statement of purpose, stressing that the establishment of an effective control over the industry was to ensure that advertising "effectively serve the needs of socialist construction and promote socialist moral standards" (*Zhongguo Guanggao Nianjian* 1988, 48).

In the 1982 regulations all of the five items contained in a list of forbidden advertising content in Article 8 were ideology oriented (*Zhongguo Guanggao Nianjian* 1988). In the 1987 regulations, which had six such items, however, the number of ideology-oriented rules dropped to three (*Zhongguo Guanggao Nianjian* 1988). The two items not mentioned in the new regulations were "libelous propaganda" and "state secrets." This change was in line with the social trend in the post-Mao China—the ideological and political coloring has, on the whole, faded away little by little, while economic development has become a dominant national theme.

The second major change in the 1987 regulations was that self-employed individuals may engage in advertising business so long as they hold business licenses. This was absolutely not allowed in the earlier regulations. This change was by no means a unique innovation in advertising regulations. Rather, it was only part of the social changes taking place in China. As a result of the ideological changes and the pragmatic policies in the post-Mao era, private businesses and enterprises have become legally accepted in the socialist China since the mid-1980s (Kraus 1991).

Another major change in the 1987 advertising regulations regarded advertising rates. According to Article 11 of the 1982 regulations, rates were set by industry and commerce administrations. In the 1987 regulations rates were allowed to be "decided by those engaged in advertising business" (Article 14). This change indicated a higher degree of decentralized supervision, part of the Chinese government's efforts to help market mechanisms function properly in the country.

Although the two sets of advertising regulations revealed the initial good intentions of the Chinese government to ensure the proper development of advertising in the country, they were still far from being satisfactory. There were two major problems concerning those advertising regulations. The first one was the simplicity of the regulations. There was a widespread doubt that only a few pages of regulations were capable of governing the entire advertising business in such a huge country (Yu 1991). In some cases the rules of advertising were vague and unclear. For instance, Article 10 of the 1987 regulations reads:

> Advertisements for cigarettes are forbidden on broadcasting, television, and newspapers. Famous and high-quality liquors which have been awarded national, ministerial, or provincial prizes can be advertised with the permission of the administrations for industry and commerce.
>
> *(Zhongguo Guanggao Nianjian* 1992, 48)

There are several loopholes in this rule. It only states that cigarette advertisements are forbidden on broadcasting, television and newspapers. But how about other media such as magazines, cinemas and billboards? If these unmentioned media are permitted to accept cigarette advertisements, what is the rationale for such a distinction here? Furthermore, the rule does not address the controversy over cigarette companies' sponsorship on sports events. Similarly, what is the demarcation line between "famous and high-quality liquors" and nonfamous and non-high-quality ones?

The vagueness of the advertising regulations leaves too much room for personal interpretations, which has become a headache for foreign advertisers in China. As Baudot (1989) mentioned,

> Although the Chinese consider the substance of their laws self-evident, for foreigners, there is uncertainty regarding the spirit and application of the law. To them official interpretations of laws appear to differ from what is written in the official text. And in unpredictable circumstances, administrative authorities may cite internal rules that deviate from the explicit formulation of promulgated laws and regulations. Moreover, such international laws may not have been published.
>
> *(Id.* 1989, 198)

The other major problem concerning the 1982 and 1987 advertising regulations was their weak enforcement. As a well-known Chinese jurist once commented,

> The problem we are facing now doesn't lie in the allegation that we have not law to abide, but in the fact that we have not abided by the law.
>
> *(Beijing Review* 1985, 8)

The weak enforcement of those advertising regulations in China was partly revealed by the sharp increase in the number of complaint letters on deceptive advertisements the Chinese Consumer Association (CCA) received in the late 1980s and the early 1990s. From 1987 through 1988, the CCA received about 1,000 such letters (Yu 1991). However, the number in only the first half of 1990 jumped to 6,162 (Wang 1991).

These figures might also suggest a rapid growth of consumerism in China—the average Chinese consumers have become more "mature" and learned how to protect their own rights within a comparatively short period of time. Neverthe-less, the weak enforcement of advertising regulations cannot be denied. A survey on advertising in Shanghai revealed that the majority of the 1,285 respondents found advertising's credibility low, and only one-third showed "limited confi-dence and welcome" (Yu 1991, 25). Although the making of advertising regula-tions involves the central authority, the enforcement requires coordination from all government departments, and the reinforcement of the legal system in the whole country.

Empowered by the State Council, the SAIC promulgated detailed rules in June 1982 and January 1988, respectively, to explain the 1882 and 1987 regula-tions for advertising. Since 1987 the SAIC has also jointly issued about 20 sets of additional rules and circulars with other government departments under the State Council to deal with the problems and malpractices in advertising.

In order to conform with international practices, China introduced a number of reforms for its advertising industry in 1993. For instance, the requirement that all advertisements must be sanctioned before being displayed by the media was abolished in selected cities such as Beijing, Shanghai, Guangzhou and Fujian. However, content of radio and television commercials as well as print advertise-ments still require approval in certain categories, including household appli-ances, drugs, foods, alcoholic beverages and cosmetics (Miao 1993d). Those consumer product categories represent the lion's share of the products advertised in China (Cheng 1994), so controlling them virtually means a control over most advertising activities in the market.

On October 27, 1994, the *Advertising Law of People's Republic of China*, the first of its kind in China's history, was passed by the People's National Con-gress and promulgated by State Chairmen Jiang Zemin (*Guangming Daily* 1994). It came into effect on February 1, 1995 to replace the *Regulations for Advertis-ing Management* of 1987.

As a continued effort to standardize advertising activities across the coun-try, the new law contains all the major improvements in the previous govern-mental regulations and rules for advertising. But instead of providing many new stipulations, it mainly synthesizes and upgrades those advertising regulations and rules formulated after 1987 to a national law.

Nevertheless, when compared with its predecessor, the new law has four major new features. First, it is much less ideology oriented than the 1987 regu-lations. Although the word "socialism" is used twice in the new law (Articles 1 and 3) (*Guangming Daily* 1994, 8) those more aggressive political terms such as "the dignity of the Chinese nation," and "reactionary," which were still used in the 1987 regulations (Article 8) (*Zhongguo Guanggao Nianjian* 1992, 48), do not occur in the new law.

Second, the new law is more consumer oriented. As stated in the beginning of the law, it is formulated to protect consumers' legal rights (Article 1). The new law includes special items on advertisements for medications, medical equipment (Articles 15 and 16), pesticides (Article 17), foods, alcohol and cosmetics (Article 19) (*Guangming Daily* 1994). All are products closely related with consumer health and safety.

Third, the ban on cigarette advertising in the new law is extended from radio, television and newspapers in the 1987 regulations to magazines and such public arenas as waiting rooms in airports and railway stations, cinemas and theaters, and sports venues (Article 18) (*Guangming Daily* 1994).

The most outstanding feature of the new advertising law is that it stipulates more severe punishments for malpractice than the 1987 regulations. In the *Detailed Rules of Regulations for Advertising Management* promulgated by the SAIC in January 1988 to supplement the 1987 regulations, the maximum fine for malpractice in advertising was 10,000 yuan (about US$2,700) (*Zhongguo Guanggao Nianjian* 1992). But this amount has become the minimum fine in the new law, and the maximum fine can be either 100,000 yuan (about US$11,500) or five times the advertising fee involved (Articles 37–44) (*Guangming Daily* 1994).

Consumer Behavior

The years from 1978 to now are unprecedented in Chinese history. During this period of time the consumption ethic has been reintroduced into Chinese society. In what is currently called "socialist market economy," consumers have been encouraged as well as allowed to want things that would have been entirely unthinkable years ago. Until the late 1970s China had followed a 3-decade policy of income leveling, guaranteed work, subsidized necessities, and discouraging consumption gratification. There was an emphasis in the media on selfless dedication and self-sacrifice as well as a willingness to forgo private material gain and personal comfort (Wang 1983). In addition to these impediments to a consumer culture, China's per capita GNP in 1979 was US$253, ranking it 101st of 150 countries and territories in the world (Berney 1981).

But since the late 1970s China has followed Deng Xiaoping's new slogan, "To Get Rich Is Glorious." The wealthy were touted as virtuous successes rather than "capitalist roaders" across the country (Schell 1984). Such dramatic ideological and policy changes have made a great impact on Chinese consumers' material desires. During the Cultural Revolution the "three bigs" in Chinese consumption aspirations were a bicycle, a wristwatch and a manual sewing machine; however, by the early 1980s half of all Chinese households owned at least one of these former "three bigs" (Weil 1982), and by the mid-1980s a "new big three" (a refrigerator, a washing machine, and a television set) had been developed (Church 1986). Meanwhile, a "new big six" that added cassette recorders, electric fans, and motorcycles (Jones et al. 1985) and the "eight new things" that changed black-and-white television sets to color sets and added cameras and video recorders to the set of consumption aspirations (Reiss 1986). As Belk and Zhou (1987) summarized, the Chinese people had learned to "want things" (478), and as Pollay et al. (1990) suggested, "China is in the midst of another cultural revolution, an eager adoption of consumption materialism" (83).

Since 1978 real per capita material consumption in China has risen at an average annual rate of 7 percent and more than doubled the living standard of the average citizen. The shares of most basic necessities such as food, clothing and fuel in total household expenditures were significantly reduced, whereas those of mostly nonbasic goods rose (Chai 1992).

Marketers say that once an economy breaks through an annual per capita income barrier of roughly US$1,000, consumers move beyond buying staples and begin shopping for durables such as television sets, nonessential processed foods like ice cream, and packaged goods, including brand name vanities (Tanzer 1993). But how can China be a lucrative consumer market, as the current per capita income in the country is merely around US$400 a year? Part of the answer is that the remnants of the socialist state still shower urban workers with huge subsidies. So most of their income gains go right to disposable income. For instance, Chinese families spend less than 5 percent of household income on housing, health care, education and transportation combined, compared with 30 to 40 percent in other Asian countries. A typical Chinese urban worker spends US$1 or $2 a month on housing, but eight times as much on cigarettes and liquors (Tanzer 1993). A recent study reckons that the average purchasing power in China is almost 30 percent higher than published figures indicate. This gives China 60 million people with an annual income above the magic threshold of US$1,000. The figure could well rise to 200 million by the year 2000 (*The Economist* 1993). True visionaries reckon that the thing to watch will be the emergence early next century of millions of Chinese above the US$4,000 threshold. That is when people begin buying cars (Tanzer 1993).

Presently Chinese consumers do not only have a strong passion for consumption, but also have a strong preference for Western brands. *Forbes* has described the newly opened Shanghai Orient Shopping Center as follows:

> Opened this past spring, it could be in Hong Kong or Seattle. A piano tinkles in the lobby. On the first floor, fashionably dressed Shanghai women shop for Christian Dior cosmetics, Rado watches and gold jewelry. Downstairs, shoppers stock up on Unilever's Lux shampoo, Heinz infant cereal, Nestle powdered milk and other Western brands. In the electric appliance section, newly married couples look over $1,000 Toshiba refrigerators and Panasonic color TV sets and $1,500 Pioneer stereo systems.
>
> (Tanzer 1993, 58)

Other popular Western brands for Chinese consumers today at least include Coca-Cola, which had sales of 2.2 billion cans in 1994 (Crovitz 1995), Kentucky

Fried Chicken, Band-Aids by Johnson & Johnson, Contac cold capsules by SmithKline Beecham, hair care products by Procter & Gamble, contact lenses by Bausch & Lomb, and Avon ladies (Tanzer 1993).

IMPACT OF CONSUMER ISSUES ON PUBLIC POLICY

After a decade of rapid growth the Chinese government began to admit in the late 1980s that economic development and reform faced a new set of difficulties and problems. Inflation was the most outstanding. One of its major causes, as suggested in the Chinese media, has been "excessive demand created by the rise in individual and group purchasing powers" (Zhang 1989, 27). Overall demand still outstrips overall supply. In 1989, for example, the purchasing power was 20 billion yuan more than the value of available commodities. Some commodities vital to the national economy and people's livelihood were still in serious short supply. Because of the imbalance between overall supply and demand, the inflation rate averaged as high as 17.8 percent that year (Ma and Wu 1990). Today while many Asian governments are delighted at the rapid economic growth, Beijing worries about the risks of growth because the national inflation rate averaged more than 27 percent in 1994 (Crovitz 1995).

In the last few years the Chinese government has been trying to cool down the overheating consumption across the country. For instance, it intended to stop the widening of income gaps by levying a personal income tax regulation and by maintaining strict supervision and examination of income sources (Ma and Wu 1990). It cut group purchasing powers by reducing expenditures on everyday commodities by 20 percent from 1990 through 1991. And it redirected individual purchasing power through measures such as privatizing housing and establishing contributory welfare and health care systems (Zhang 1989).

The government has also tried to restructure the consumption pattern in the country. For instance, owing to the shortage of cotton and fur resources, it encourages the use of synthetic and blended fabrics for garments, reducing pure cotton cloth and other valuable materials to a secondary position. With the growth of new houses built by farmers in rural areas, and the implementation of commercial housing in urban areas, the government has increased people's percentage expenditure on housing. Although the government encourages energy production, it restricts household air-conditioning equipment because of power shortage (Ding 1988).

The rise in personal income and the shift from an agrarian-based country to a newly industrialized nation has created tremendous cultural changes in China. In 1987, the Chinese Culture Connection, an international network of behavioral scientists, developed a measure of values that would reflect indigenous themes and concerns of Chinese culture. They identified 40 traditional Chinese cultural values as shown in Table 4.12.

In *The Great Wall in Ruins,* Chu and Ju (1993) presented a recent survey of rural and urban Chinese. The authors discovered that the Chinese people no

Table 4.12.   Traditional Chinese Cultural Values

1. Filial piety (obedience to parents, respect for parents, honoring of ancestors, financial support of parents)
2. Industry (working hard)
3. Tolerance of others
4. Harmony with others
5. Humbleness
6. Loyalty to superiors
7. Observation of rites and social rituals
8. Reciprocation of greetings, favors, and gifts
9. Kindness (forgiveness, compassion)
10. Knowledge (education)
11. Solidarity with others
12. Moderation, following the middle way
13. Self-cultivation
14. Ordering relationships by status and observing this order
15. Sense of righteousness
16. Benevolent authority
17. Noncompetitiveness
18. Personal steadiness and stability
19. Resistance to corruption
20. Patriotism
21. Sincerity
22. Keeping oneself disinterested and pure
23. Thrift
24. Persistence (perseverance)
25. Patience
26. Repayment of the good or the evil that another person has caused you
27. A sense of cultural superiority
28. Adaptability
29. Prudence (carefulness)
30. Trustworthiness
31. Having a sense of shame
32. Courtesy
33. Contentedness with one's position in life
34. Being conservative
35. Protecting your "face"
36. Being a close, intimate friend
37. Chastity in woman
38. Having few desires
39. Respect for tradition
40. Wealth

Source: The Chinese Culture Connection, 1987, 147–148.

longer endorse the Confucian precepts of harmony and tolerance, nor do they submit compliantly to authority as previous generations did. They now demonstrate, in an environment of rising aspirations and mounting frustration, a new assertiveness.

Chu and Ju collected their data in the late 1980s by presenting their respondents with 18 traditional values. They asked: "Of these elements of traditional Chinese culture, in your opinion which ones do you feel proud of, which ones should be discarded, and which ones are you not sure of?" The values were presented in a random order so that the way the respondents answered one question would have a minimum effect on the way they answered others. As a first step of data analysis, Chu and Ju used the percentage who were proud of a value, minus the percentage who said it should be discarded, to construct an index of endorsement for each of the 18 values. The indices ranged from a positive 89.7 percent to a negative 64.0 percent. They presented the traditional values and indices in the descending order as shown in Table 4.13.

Table 4.13.   Endorsement and Rejection of Traditional Chinese Values

Traditional Chinese Values	Positive Endorsement Indices (%)	Traditional Chinese Values	Negative Endorsement Indices (%)
Long historical heritage	89.7	Chastity for women	−13.5
Diligence and frugality	86.2	Glory to ancestors	−23.8
Loyalty and devotion to state	67.5	A house full of sons and grandsons	−35.5
Benevolent father, filial son	48.0	Farmers high, merchants low	−43.3
Generosity and virtues	39.8	Pleasing superiors	−48.9
Respect for traditions	38.5	Discretion for self-preservation	−55.9
Submission to authority	33.2	Differentation between men and women	−59.2
Preciousness of harmony	29.5	Way of golden mean	−59.6
Tolerance, propriety, deference	25.3	Three obediences and four virtues	−64.0

Source: Chu and Ju, 1993, 222.

Chu and Ju's data reveal how much revolution and modernization have changed the face of China. They believed that "if a similar survey had been conducted half a century ago, one would expect high and positive ratings on nearly all these traditional values" (Chu and Ju 1993, 245).

Conclusion

The rapid growth of advertising in China since 1979 is both socially and culturally unusual. Socially, China is one of the few communist countries in the world experimenting with advertising. This is a new phenomenon for a socialist environment that had previously been extremely hostile to this marketing tool. This experiment began when market mechanism was ideologically justified by the government in the late 1970s as a means to speed up the economic development. The introduction of market mechanism has completely changed the Chinese leadership from deeming advertising as "a capitalist tool" to an "accelerator" in the ongoing "Four Modernizations" drive. The newly adopted advertising law and all the previous advertising regulations are just part of the government's efforts to experiment advertising in a socialist environment—encouraging it, but keeping it "in conformity with the criteria for socialist spiritual civilization" (*Guangming Daily* 1994, 8).

The rapid growth of advertising in China over the last decade also indicates a dramatic cultural change across the country. Under the influence of Confucianism, the dominant philosophical thinking for most of Chinese history, there was a longstanding contempt for commerce. In the ideal Confucian scheme of social stratification, scholars were at the top of the line, followed by farmers, then by artisans, with merchants in the last place (Worden et al. 1988). In Confucians' thinking, there was a distinction between what were called "root" and the "branch." The "root" referred to agriculture and the "branch" to commerce. This distinction was based on the rationale that agriculture was concerned with production, whereas commerce was merely concerned with exchange. In an agrarian country like China, agriculture was the major form of production. Therefore, throughout Chinese history, social and economic theories, together with government policies, all attempted "to emphasize the root and slight the branch" (Fung 1968, 18).

So, the positive attitude the Chinese leadership currently holds toward advertising and the new views the average Chinese people have toward commerce, together with their increasing inspiration for consumption, are a sharp U-turn in Chinese culture.

Both the unique social reform and the dramatic cultural change in China entail further growth of advertising in the future. However, the current "unprecedented" growth rate of advertising in China has, in fact, encountered many problems, such as poor quality of advertisements, deceptive advertising, inadequate research, and lack of well-trained advertising professionals, to mention but a few. These problems may greatly reduce the effectiveness of advertising in this booming market. So, for further growth of advertising in China, the market mechanism in the economic system is the prerequisite; effective advertising laws and regulations are important measures; and education and research are the key.

Bibliography

Academic American Encyclopedia, vol. 4. 1993. Danbury, CT: Grolier.

Advertising Age. 1993. Annual Report, April 14, p. 28.

Advertising Age. 1994. Annual Report, April 13, p. 26.

Agency Brochure. 1991. China National United Advertising Corporation.

Azrry, P.T. and R.D. Wilson, eds. 1981. *Advertising in Canada: Its Theory and Practice*. Toronto and Montreal: McGraw-Hill Ryerson.

Baokan Guanggao Wenzhai [Advertising Digest from the Press]. 1994a. Advertising Units and Employees in China, 1990–1993, (5): 57.

Baokan Guanggao Wenzhai [Advertising Digest from the Press]. 1994b. China's Advertising Business Volume Increased Sharply, (5): 1.

Baokan Guanggao Wenzhai [Advertising Digest from the Press]. 1994c. China's Advertising Media, 1990–1993, (5): 57.

Baokan Guanggao Wenzhai [Advertising Digest from the Press]. 1994d. First Ranking for Advertising Agencies in China, (5): 59.

Baudot, B.S. 1989. *International Advertising Handbook: A User's Guide to Rules and Regulations*. Lexington, MA, and Toronto: Lexington Books.

Beijing Review. 1994. Economic and Social Development in China. October 17, p. 18.

Beijing Review. 1985. False Advertising Angers Consumers. July 29, pp. 8–9.

Belk, R.W. and N. Zhou. 1987. Learning to Want Things. In: Wallendorf, M. and P. Anderson, eds. *Advances in Consumer Research.* Provo, UT: ACR, pp. 478–481.

Berney, K. 1981. China's Growing Consumer Market. *The China Business Review,* 8 (4): 18.

Chai, J.C.H. 1992. Consumption and Living Standards in China. *The China Quarterly,* September, pp. 748–749.

Chang, W.H. 1989. *Mass Media in China: The History and the Future.* Ames, IA: Iowa State University Press.

Cheng, H. 1994. Reflections of Cultural Values: A Content Analysis of Chinese Magazine Advertisements from 1982 and 1992. *International Journal of Advertising,* 13: (2): 167–183.

China Daily (Beijing). 1993a. A Pioneering Path to Economic Reform, November 15, p. 4.

China Daily (Beijing). 1993b. China's TVs Tune in to Prime Time, August 30, p. 3.

Chinese Culture Connection, The. 1987. Chinese Values and the Search for Culture-Free Dimensions of Culture. *Journal of Cross-Cultural Psychology,* 18 (2): 143–164.

Chu, G.C. and Y.A. Ju. 1993. *The Great Wall in Ruins: Communication and Cultural Change in China.* Albany, NY: State University of New York Press.

Church, G.J. 1986. China: Deng Xiaoping Leads a Far-Reaching Audacious But Risky Second Revolution. *Time,* January 6, p. 24.

Crovitz, L.G. 1995. '94 Free Trade: Key Asian Value. *Far Eastern Economic Review,* January 5, pp. 26–27.

Deng, X.P. 1984. *Selected Works of Deng Xiaoping.* Beijing: Foreign Languages Press.

Ding, G.L., G.R. Ma, W. Wu, Z.H. Hu, G.G. Gao, S.D. Qin and Y.M. Zhang. 1985. *Jianming Zhongguo Xinwen Shi* [A Concise History of Chinese Press]. Fuzhou, Fujian: Fujian People's Publishing House.

Ding, S.P. 1988. Projected Changes in Chinese Consumption. *Beijing Review,* October 3, p. 25.

Ding, Y.P. 1979. Restoring the Good Name for Advertising in China. *Wenhui Daily* (Shanghai), January 14, p. 3.

The Economist. 1993. Chinese Consumers, Next in Line. January 23, pp. 66–77.

Fan, L.B. 1994. *Baokan Guanggao Wenzhai* [Advertising Digest for the Press]. 1993—the Advertising Year of China, (5): 56.

Friske, J.D., ed. 1993. *China Facts and Figures Annual Handbook.* Gulf Breeze, FL: Academic International Press.

Fung, Y.L. 1948. Reprint 1968. *A Short History of Chinese Philosophy.* Bodde, D., ed. New York: The Free Press.

Geddes, A. 1993a. China Plans New Ad Rules: Changes Come with Western Shops' Increasing Presence. *Advertising Age International,* June 21, p. I-6.

Geddes, A. 1993b. China TV Ad Rates Soar, Though Still a Bargain. *Advertising Age International,* January 18, p. I-3.

Guangming Daily (Beijing). 1994. Advertising Law of the People's Republic of China. October 28, p. 8.

Guoji Guanggao [International Advertising]. 1993. China's Advertising Industry Growth, 1981–1992, (4) : 42.

Hook, B. and D. Twitchett, eds. 1991. *The Cambridge Encyclopedia of China,* 2nd ed. Cambridge and New York: Cambridge University Press.

Howkins, J. 1982. *Mass Communication in China*. New York and London: Longman.
James, C.V., ed. 1989. *Information China, the Complete and Authoritative Reference Source of New China*, vol. 2. Oxford and New York: Pergamon Press.
Jones, D.E., D. Elliot, E. Terry, C. A. Robbins, C. Gaffney and B. Nussbaum. 1985. Capitalism in China. *Business Week*, January 14, p. 53.
Karp, J. 1993. China's Ad Boom. *Far Eastern Economic Review*, February 25, p. 53.
Keobke, K. and J. Woo. 1992. China. *Asian Advertising and Marketing*, April, p. 26.
King, F.H.H. and P. Clarke. 1965. *A Research Guide to China-Coast Newspapers, 1822–1911*. Cambridge, MA: East Asian Research Center, Harvard University.
Kraus, W. 1991. *Private Business in China: Revival Between Ideology and Pragmatism*. [Translated by Erich Holz.] Honolulu: University of Hawaii Press.
Li, N. 1994. World's Largest LED Screen in Operation. *Beijing Review*, November 21, p. 28.
Li, Y. and Li Qingbo. 1993. Antithetical Couples in Wine Advertising. *Baokan Guanggao Wenzhai* [Advertising Digest from the Press], (6): 2–3.
Liu, L.Q. and J.X. Chen. 1989. *Guanggao Guanli* [Advertising Management]. Beijing: China Finance and Economics Press.
Liu W.Z. 1986. The Characteristics of Socialist Commercial Advertising. *Guangming Daily* (Beijing), February 15, p. 3.
Lu, B. 1993. Chinese Advertising in 1992. *Zhongguo Guanggao* [China Advertising], (3): 4.
Ma, Z.P. and Z.P. Wu. 1990. Consumerism Loses Its Appeal. *Beijing Review*, May 21, p. 32.
Matsuda, M. 1981. Dentsu Eases Through Open Door. *Advertising Age*, December 14, p. S–9.
Miao, S. 1993a. Burnett Looks to Build in China. *Adweek*, May 3, p. 14.
Miao, S. 1993b. Chinese Advertisers Face Rate Hikes: Media Costs Skyrocket at TV Stations, Newspapers. *Adweek*, January 4, p. 32B.
Miao, S. 1993c. China: the Final Frontier. *Campaign London*, September 24, p. 25.
Miao, S. 1993d. China Loosens Ad Guidelines in Cities: New Regulations for Direct Advertising in Certain Product Categories. *Adweek*, April 19, p. 16.
Minami, R. 1994. *The Economic Development of China: A Comparison with the Japanese Experience*. [Translated by Wenran Jiang and Tanya Jiang.] New York: St. Martin's Press.
Parsons, P. 1993. Marketing Revolution Hits Staid Giants . . . While in China, Advertising Blooms like a Hundred Flowers. *Advertising Age*, July 19, p. 18.
Parton, A. 1994. Television Ad Rates on Rise in China. *Adweek*, January 17, p. 16.
Pollay, R.W., D.K. Tse, and Z.Y. Wang. 1990. Advertising, Propaganda, and Value Change in Economic Development: The New Cultural Revolution in China and Attitudes Toward Advertising. *Journal of Business Research*, 20 (2); pp. 83–95.
Reiss, S. 1986. Deng's Drive. *Newsweek*, September 8, p. 9.
Rotzoll, K.B. 1986. Advertising in China. Working Paper. Urbana-Champaign: Department of Advertising, University of Illinois.
Rotzoll, K.B., J.E. Haefner, and C.H. Sandage. 1976. *Advertising in Contemporary Society: Perspective Toward Understanding*. Columbus, OH: Copyright Grid, Inc.
Schell, O. 1984. *To Get Rich is Glorious: China in the 80s*. New York: Pantheon Books.
Seligman, S.D. 1984. China's Fledgling Advertising Industry. *The China Business Review*, 11 January/February 1:12.

Seligman, S.D. 1986. Corporate and Product Promotion. *The China Business Review,* 13 (May/June): 8–13.

Shuang, J. 1992. Ads Lead China into Consumers' Era. *Beijing Review,* February 24, p. 11.

Sun, Y.W. 1991. *Guanggao Xue* [Advertising]. Beijing: World Affairs Press.

Swanson, L.A. 1990. Advertising in China: Viability and Structure. *European Journal of Marketing,* 24 (10): 19–31.

Tanzer, A. 1993. This Time It's for Real. *Forbes,* August 2, pp. 58–60.

Wall Street Journal. 1993. China Expects to Boom. November 8, p. A10.

Wang, D.M. 1993. The Current Situation and a Complete Roster of the Advertising Joint Ventures in China. *Guoji Guanggao* [International Advertising], (4): 6–7.

Wang, J.C.F. 1983. Values of the Cultural Revolutions. *Journal of Communication,* 27 (3): 41–46.

Wang, Y. H. 1991. Advertising: An Accelerator for the Economic Development in China. *Economic Information Daily.* Beijing, September 8, p. 2.

Weil, M. 1982. China's Consuming Interest. *The China Business Review,* 9 (January/February): 19.

Wells, W., J. Burnett, and S. Moriarty. 1992. *Advertising Principles and Practice,* 2nd ed. Englewood Cliffs, NJ: Prentice Hall.

Worden, R.L., A.M. Savada, and R.E. Dolan 1988. *China, a Country Study.* Washington, DC: Federal Research Division, Library of Congress.

Xu, B.Y. 1989. The Role of Advertising in China. Working Paper. Urbana-Champaign: Department of Advertising, University of Illinois.

Xu, B.Y. 1990. *Marketing to China: One Billion New Customers*: Lincolnwood, IL: NTC Business Books.

Xu, B.Y. 1992. Reaching the Chinese Consumer. *The China Business Review,* 19 (November/December): 36–42.

Yu, X.J. 1991. Government Policies Toward Advertising in China (1979–1989). *Gazette: The International Journal for Mass Communication Studies,* 48 (1): 17–30.

Yuan, L. 1993. Annual Ad Bills to Hit $4.8b. *China Daily.* Beijing, November 8, p. 2.

Zhang, Z.B. 1989. The Struggle with Inflation: Cutting Back Consumption. *Beijing Review,* February 6, p. 27.

Zhongguo Daobao [China Guide] 1994. Chinese Advertising Industry: A Vigorous Dragon Crossing the River. Los Angeles, June 2, p. 2.

Zhongguo Guangbo Dianshi Nianjian [China Broadcasting and Television Yearbook]. 1993. Beijing: Beijing Broadcasting Institute Press.

Zhongguo Guanggao Nianjian [China Advertising Yearbook]. 1988. Beijing: Xinhua Publishing House.

Zhongguo Guanggao Nianjian [China Advertising Yearbook]. 1992. Beijing: Xinhua Publishing House.

5

Advertising in Taiwan: Sociopolitical Changes and Multinational Impact

JAMES TSAO

Introduction

The advertising industry was established in Taiwan over 40 years ago. However, it was not until the mid-1980s that the industry began to experience unprecedented changes and dramatic growth (Goldstein 1989). These changes have enabled advertising to play a dynamic role in a transitional period during which the island country of 21 million people has been progressively moving from a developing to a newly industrial stage. With a strong economic environment and international affiliations as backup, it is expected that the advertising industry in Taiwan may play an even more significant role in the future. As one senior advertising executive put it, "advertising fields are developing at different rates in Taiwan, Hong Kong, and mainland China, but they are gradually merging into one "Greater China" market with Taiwan at the center of the action ..." (Hwang 1993a, 21).

A number of factors have contributed to these changing scenarios in a country that is not even as large in size as the state of New Jersey. Improved living standards, deregulated media policy, Western marketing concepts, internationalized trading relations, dynamic cultural values and sophisticated consumer markets are just a few of the phenomena that have been identified as factors pushing the advertising industry to the forefront. Some of these factors will be discussed later in this chapter. However, first, the background of the political, social and economic history of Taiwan is reviewed.

Political-Economic Development of Taiwan

POLITICAL DEVELOPMENT

To many developing nations Taiwan is a model country that has successfully transformed its authoritarian structure to a democratic system over the past

4 decades. This transformation has been praised as the pioneering experiment for democracy in Chinese history (Lee 1993). The process, however, has been painstaking both domestically and internationally. Domestically, the ruling party, Kuomintang (KMT)/Nationalist, has long been concerned that a fully open and democratic political system could open the gate for Chinese Communists to foment a revolt against the government. On the other hand, Taiwan has continually been pressured by its ally, the United States, to reform the political system and adopt Western-style democracy.

Though Taiwan has historically been part of China, the struggle between the Chinese Nationalists and Communists did not take place until 1949 when the Nationalist/KMT government in China was ousted by the Communists. The Nationalists moved to Taiwan and have remained in power, still claiming to be the only legitimate government representing China (that is, the Republic of China). In 1975, diplomatic activities were severed with Taiwan when the Republic of China lost the legitimate seat in the United Nations to the People's Republic of China. Since then, most countries have refused to maintain formal relations with this island country (Chang and Holt 1991). In particular, a major blow struck in 1979 when the United States, a long-time supporter of Taiwan, normalized its relationship with China while cutting off diplomatic ties with Taiwan. Because of China's power, many attempts made by Taiwan to break through the international isolation have failed (Tien 1989).

Although international activities have been severely limited, internal political/democratic developments in Taiwan have gradually progressed, especially in the last 10 years. Between 1949 and 1987 the political development of Taiwan remained at the political-tutelage stage, which was one of three phases designed by the Republic of China's founding father, Dr. Sun Yet-sen. During the political-tutelage stage the Nationalist government of Chiang Kai-shek was responsible for educating the public about the elements of democracy and government. On the other hand, political and press freedom was severely suppressed in this stage because the KMT implemented martial law to close any channels that might invite communist penetration (Rampal 1994).

President Chiang Kai-shek died in 1975, yet the political-tutelage stage was continued by the administration of his son, President Chiang Ching-kuo, who was more open-minded toward democracy than was his father (Rampal 1994). In 1987, Chiang Ching-kuo decided to lift the martial law. The move ended the political-tutelage stage and set the tone for the next stage, the constitutional phase. The lifting of martial law and the abolishment of the "Temporary Provisions" gave opportunities to Chiang's successor, Lee Teng-hui, to carry on political reforms that would allow a multiparty system and press freedom to exist (Rampal 1994).

ECONOMIC GROWTH

The political developments in Taiwan may not be as impressive when com-

pared with Western standards, yet the growth of Taiwan's economy can be regarded as nothing short of miraculous. Taiwan's exports in 1960 totaled US$3.03
billion, yet reached US$121.9 billion by 1990 (*The Europa World Yearbook,*
1991). The 1960s were a period of prosperity during which Taiwan's economy
began to take off. While potential threats were eliminated domestically in the
1960s, the KMT skillfully funneled public concerns away from expectations of
political reforms to the concerns of economic growth. As Lee (1993) observed,

> Taiwan's gross national product was to rise annually at a rate of 10 percent
> [in the 1960s]. The growth of advertising in this decade—averaging 21 percent
> annually—was even more striking; the total size of advertising revenues was es-
> timated at $27 million (in U.S. dollars) in 1969, half of which were claimed by
> newspapers.
>
> (Lee 1993, 13)

In the middle of the 1970s Chiang Kai-shek's death and the second oil embargo temporarily set back Taiwan's economic development. However, the situation was quickly turned around by a national development plan involving 10
massive construction projects initiated by Chiang Ching-kuo (Lee 1993). These
projects are aimed at increasing Taiwan's trading competitiveness and upgrading
the infrastructure system.

Political constraints were relaxed in the middle of the 1980s and the economic structure was becoming internationalized. During the 1980s the Taiwan
government lifted its restrictions on the number of print media, and allowed foreign investment in service industries including advertising agencies (Goldstein
1989). Moreover, restraints to transactions of foreign exchange were lifted,
which in turn encouraged the public to travel abroad (Li 1989). Another significant move stimulating economic development was that the banking industry began to relax its policy on credit cards in 1989, which made the use of credit cards
quite popular to the general public (Hwang 1995). On the average, users of credit
cards in Taiwan spend 12 times as much as the amount of U.S. card holders
(Yuan 1993). Domestic markets in this period were rapidly growing as a result of
changing consumer behaviors. In brief the 1980s was a golden age of economic
prosperity characterized by high productivity and growing consumption in Taiwan.

The 1980s was also a period when the advertising industry began to experience dramatic changes, especially in the business structure and annual advertising revenues. When restrictions on foreign investment in service industries
were deregulated, a number of foreign advertising agencies quickly opened in
Taiwan. In addition to local agencies, these foreign firms played an active role in
stimulating economic growth. The total advertising expenditures in Taiwan in
1989 reached US$17 billion, a 40 percent increase over that of 1979 expenditures
(Goldstein 1989).

Sociocultural Changes in Taiwan

As Taiwan has undergone political and economic changes, the cultural environment has also faced unprecedented challenges. In fact the dramatic shift in cultural values may have had a more complex and subtle impact on modern Taiwan society than has political and economic development. Two phenomena, "accommodation" and "displacement," characterize the cultural changes in Taiwan (Smith 1992).

On the one hand, traditional Chinese life is *accommodating* to Western cultures. As a result, a new and modern lifestyle is discernible in almost every aspect of consumption and communication behaviors. In Taiwan, on the other hand, as the country moves into a developed stage, many traditional Chinese cultural values have been *displaced* by the Western lifestyle. Both phenomena have had a profound impact on the social structure in Taiwan. In particular, family structure, women's role, teen behaviors, eating habits and time usage are some of the cultural phenomena that have been deeply influenced by Westernization. Advertising and the mass media have played a vital role in facilitating the changes (Smith 1992).

FAMILY STRUCTURE

The function of the family in Chinese society is different from its counterpart in the West. Following the Chinese tradition, the family in Taiwan is treated as the main source of economic support, educational assistance, social connections, cultural heritage and recreational gathering (Fairbank et al. 1973). However, the role of the family is being seriously challenged by urbanization. Today because of urbanization, more and more nuclear families have replaced the traditional extended family in Taiwan society. More than half of the households in Taiwan are nuclear families, whereas only one-fourth are two-generation households (Smith 1992). And more importantly, because many parents in nuclear families are full-time employees, time spent with their families has been sharply reduced. As a result, these parents tend to buy expensive goods for their family members in order to compensate for emotional guilt. Advertisements therefore frequently use images of family life as a theme to evoke emotional responses in these parents (Fu 1994).

Nuclear families are not the only byproduct of social changes from industrialization. DINK, meaning "double income no kids," is a new family structure now appealing to many young married couples. In such families both husband and wife tend to be busy pursuing their careers and developing their social life. Time spent for communication between the husband and wife is becoming rare. As a result DINK marriages tend to be short-lived. This is one of the reasons that the divorce rate in Taiwan has continued to grow in recent years. In fact Taiwan now has the highest divorce rate in Asia, 1.51 per 1,000 population. Although the figure is considered low when compared with the rates of Western nations, it is quite alarming given that one out of every five married couples in Taiwan becomes divorced (Pun 1995). Interestingly, as the divorce rate has increased, advertising has begun to show more images of individualism, such as personal success, freedom and the types of enjoyment that are especially appealing to the DINK families (Fu 1994).

WOMEN'S ROLE

The traditional role of women has been dramatically challenged by socioeconomic development. Traditionally, the role of a Chinese woman in an agricultural society was that of a servant to her husband and in-laws. In the past 3 decades, however, as educational opportunities have risen, the employment rate for women has dramatically increased. Today 45 percent of women in Taiwan have entered the work force. In addition urbanization often leaves women no other choice but to consider family economy as their primary concern. Leaving their kitchens and entering the labor force has become the only option for women wanting to survive in modern Taiwan society (Lin 1994).

Accommodating such dramatic role shifts, modern women show patterns of consumption needs quite different from those of their more traditional counterparts. For instance, among modern women, searching for a style of self-expression is not only a desire, but a routine necessary to maintain status. According to the Chinese-language version of *Elle* magazine, the average woman in Taiwan spends US$978 on cosmetics yearly. In 1993, women spent US$755 million on perfumes. The cosmetic industry in Taiwan is so lucrative that some major companies including Lancôme, Elizabeth Arden and Christian Dior are enjoying 100 percent revenue increases lately (Her 1994).

TEEN BEHAVIORS

While the role of women has been dramatically changed, so has the image of teens. Teenagers used to be stereotyped as self-disciplined, conservative, dependent and timid. However, teens in modern Taiwan have been coined the "new new youth" meaning today's teen generation is very different from the youth of 2 decades ago. They are brash, fashionable, individualistic and liberal. This changing image is evidenced by a study showing that the number of teenagers considering themselves "self-disciplined" is sharply declining; in the meantime, the number of trend-seeking youngsters is increasing (Chan 1994b).

Economic prosperity has contributed to the changing behavior of teens. In 1993, the average income of Taiwan households was US$30,270, nearly 15 percent higher than that of 1992. The rapid growth of household income in the middle class enables families to pour over two-thirds of their income into improving their living quality (Chan 1994a). Certainly today's teenagers receive more financial support from their parents than in previous generations.

Twenty years ago youngsters worked hard and saved money to share the financial burden of their households. However, the "new new youth" today make money only if they can spend it (Chan 1994b). A recent study found that there are approximately 330,000 teenagers having part-time jobs, and another 180,000 teens are irregular part-timers. A governmental report states that the average monthly income of a teenage part-timer is US$575. This statistical figure demonstrates a strong consuming power. Take the following figures for an example: 18 percent of the population are teenagers who generate 20 percent of department store sales and 80 percent of compact disc sales. In Taipei, the capital city, youngsters purchase some 20,000 bottles of perfume each month. In total these youth contribute US$154 million pocket money to the consumer market each year. With such zestful consuming behaviors, it is no wonder that advertisers go after youth through every possible medium. As a result, advertising has helped create a new generation characterized by a unique image-consciousness and different communication behaviors (Chan 1994c; Kuo and Tsia 1994). Their hairstyles, clothes, dialogues, material pursuit and attitude toward life are dramatically different from previous generations (Chan 1994b).

EATING HABITS

Just as the role of women and behavior of teens are being challenged by modernization, eating habits of Taiwan residents are also undergoing some revolutionary changes. Taiwan and other Chinese regions were considered the last frontier for Western fast foods because these markets are so accustomed to the unique cooking style and taste of Chinese cuisine. However, ever since McDonald's first branch restaurant was opened in Taipei in 1984, the Taiwanese eating behaviors have been diversified. This is especially true for the age group who are under 30. The younger generation who grew up under the golden arches prefer the clean environment and quick service of fast-food chains to the traditional Chinese restaurants (Shen 1994).

Today McDonald's has set up 81 chain stores in Taiwan. Following McDonald's expansion, Wendy's, Hardee's, Kentucky Fried Chicken, Pizza Hut, Burger King and several other Western fast-food chains have also mushroomed in Taiwan. As expected, Westernized eating behaviors have stimulated fierce competition between Chinese restaurants and fast-food chains. Advertising, therefore, has been heavily used by the restaurant business to survive (Shen 1994).

LEISURE BEHAVIOR AND TIME ORIENTATION

While young people prefer hamburgers to egg rolls, adults pursue a different taste for their social gathering. Besides frequenting karaokes, yuppies are fond of gathering in pubs for socializing after their long stress-filled work day. Because of its Western implication, the word "pub" has often been used as a fashionable and magnetic word to attract customers to restaurants. Differing from karaokes and regular restaurants, pubs offer yuppies a quiet and relaxing atmosphere to eat Western foods, as well as a place for chat and entertainment (Wong 1994).

The leisure behavior of adults is also related to another cultural value, time orientation. Time in Chinese culture was traditionally considered to be "polychronic." Countries with a polychronic orientation are less likely to relate to time as a tangible, discrete and linear entity. Instead time conception in traditional Chinese culture was viewed as something interacting with events spontaneously and simultaneously (Kim 1985, 403). An empirical study supports this point of view. Levine (1988) found that the perception of people in Taiwan with respect to time accuracy, walking speed and postal speed were different or slower than that of people in more-developed nations, such as Japan and the United States. Advertising, accordingly, seems to reflect the shift of time concern. An empirical study shows that there is a sharp contrast on the reflection of time perspectives in the advertising of two different periods (1981–1985 and 1986–1990). This contrast is marked by the social and economic changes of Taiwan during the given years (Tsao 1994).

As Taiwan is opening the door to revitalize its political-economic system and sociocultural values, the market is getting segmented and consumers are becoming more demanding. The changing face of the new socioeconomic system forces private businesses to be market driven and consumer oriented. At this time, the advertising industry has begun to play a dynamic role in the facilitation of market communication. Though the media industry may have fallen a few steps behind the advertising industry, it is catching up and heading for a more diversified future under deregulation.

Overview of Major Media Industries

Interference from the government has historically played a powerful role that has set back the progress of the media system in Taiwan for many years. For example, in 1949 the government issued a martial law restricting the number of print and broadcast media that could be established. All newspapers were standardized and limited to only two and a half pages per day. Press freedom was severely controlled. In the name of anticommunism the government imposed these rigid guidelines for 38 years (Lee 1993). One immediate result of deregulation is that the media industry has entered into a state of *laissez-faire*. The press has earned unprecedented freedom of news coverage and business management. Fierce competition has forced newspapers to expand the number of news pages to increase circulation and advertising revenues (Clifford 1993).

At present there are more than 300 newspapers, 2,600 magazines, three commercial television networks, and 46 radio stations throughout Taiwan (Baum 1993a; Tien 1989). In addition 42 satellite and cable television channels recently have joined the media market, drawing a large segment of audience away from the commercial networks. The liberal climate has obviously helped deregulate the media industry, but it is based on advertising that Taiwan's media "prosper or perish" (Clifford 1993).

NEWSPAPERS

Historically, the newspaper market has been dominated by two newspaper groups, the United Daily News and the China Times News. Both groups have strong financial and political footholds. Each paper claims to have more than a million in circulation (Baum 1993a). The United Daily News Group owns five newspapers: the *United Daily News, United Evening News, Economic Daily News, Ming Sheng Pao,* and a weekly paper, *Business Taiwan.* The China Times News Group, on the other hand, publishes three titles including the *China Times, Commercial Times,* and *China Times Evening News* (Lee 1993). Recently the *Liberty Times,* a new kid on the block, has joined the news publishing business. The *Liberty Times,* with its populist editorial viewpoints and aggressive promotional campaigns, has reached 700,000 readers within a short period of time (Baum 1993a).

Though many newspapers have rapidly emerged since the end of martial law in 1987, most new entries are financially in the red (Baum 1993a). Barely surviving are newspapers with small circulations and the government/party-owned dailies. The *Central Daily News,* a party organ of the Kuomintang, for example, has continually lost circulation and revenues over the years. However, it is able to sustain its losses because the KMT subsidizes the *Central Daily News* with a long-term investment (Tien 1989). Small and private newspapers are not so lucky as the *Central Daily News.* Poor editorials, insufficient advertising revenues and intense competition have made it hard for the small newspapers to survive. A study shows that though many newspapers have joined the media market, the percentages of newspaper pages devoted to advertisements have not increased since the 1988 media deregulation (Lay and Schweitzer 1990).

As the media market has become saturated in Taiwan, some newspapers have begun to expand their publishing business overseas. For instance, the *World Journal,* a daily paper and subsidiary of the United Daily News Group, is published in the United States for Chinese readers living in North America. Although it is a long shot for the time being, some newspapers in Taiwan are even attempting to negotiate with dailies in China for cooperative publishing opportunities (Clifford 1993).

MAGAZINES

The magazine business in Taiwan runs a different path from its newspaper counterpart. The martial law was not rigidly applied to magazines (except for political magazines) because the government did not consider them a major threat to national stability (Lee 1993). Though government intervention has been minimal, the survival rate of magazines in Taiwan has always been low. Small circulations, insufficient advertising revenues and intense competition are the common factors that make magazines difficult to be managed. As a result, only a handful of magazines enjoys steady circulation and advertising support, although new publications appear each year.

The *Commonwealth* (Tien Hsia), *Reader's Digest* (Chinese edition), *Crown,* and *Woman* (Fu Nui) are the few weekly and leading magazines that show steady support from readers and advertisers. *Commonwealth* is a prestigious financial magazine, which has a circulation of 84,000. It is mainly read by the middle class, particularly business professionals (Ying 1993). The media and advertising industries regarded the debut of *Commonwealth* in 1981 as one of the major cultural events of the decade (Li 1989). *Woman,* on the other hand, is a popular magazine targeted at the female professional and the housewives in Taiwan. Media observers rated *Woman* as one of the pioneering magazines in Taiwan for upgraded editorial quality and sustained readers' interests. *Reader's Digest* (Chinese edition) is published in Hong Kong. It is unique in that this magazine has traditionally relied mainly on subscribers, instead of advertisers, for support. *Crown* is a popular tabloid-format magazine targeted at young, working female readers. The content of *Crown* is focused on fictional articles with romantic and legendary themes.

As more information channels have been made available to the public since media deregulation, the magazine industry has faced unprecedented challenges. In order to survive the competition, some magazines have chosen to upgrade their editorial quality by making agreements with foreign publications, such as *People* and *Cosmopolitan,* for exclusive rights to publish the Chinese editions. As consumer markets become segmented, the editorial formats of many magazines have become specialized. Many magazines are targeted at certain demographic groups and focused on special fields such as computers, gardening, architecture, automobiles, religion and tourism. Some of these magazines, including the *New Women* and *P.C. World* (Chinese edition) have gained steady subscriptions, whereas other magazines including the *U.S. News and World Report* (Chinese edition) failed in this market (Lin 1991).

RADIO

Before the martial law was lifted Taiwan had 33 FM and AM radio stations, with 21 of them private. Half of the advertising revenues was shared by the state-run and Kuomintang-owned stations, and the other half was picked up by private stations. By the end of 1994, 13 new FM stations had been approved. In 1995, the government opened more radio frequencies to private operators. More than 40 applicants have been granted licenses to found low-power community stations (Pun and Yu 1994).

Prior to 1995, radio was strictly controlled by the government for national security reasons. Most of the radio frequencies were reserved for the Ministry of National Defense to jam radio propaganda transmitted from the mainland. In order to fulfill the jamming purpose, the KMT, Ministry of National Defense and police administration were all assigned to establish radio stations that offered homogenous programs and accepted commercials (Tien 1989). Today, the Broadcasting Corporation of China, owned by the KMT, holds the dominant position with eight national radio networks of which four are AM networks and four are FM. The Cheng-Sheng Broadcast Network, a private and pro-government radio operator, is considered the second largest moneymaker in the radio industry. International Community Radio of Taipei (ICRT), a dark horse in the radio industry, is an English-language station that has been quite popular with younger audiences. Most advertisers on ICRT are transnational companies doing businesses in Taiwan (Wong 1991; Yu 1994).

Deregulation of the radio industry has resulted in more diversified programming. In particular the advent of new radio stations has made the industry more dynamic and diversified. In fact the opening up of radio to ownership other than government has resulted in more diversified programming. For instance, ownership of the "Voice of Taipei" is composed of journalists, musicians, dancers, writers, television producers and business professionals. While programs of the "Voice of Taipei" are more news and cultural oriented, another new station, the "All People's Station," has focused on political programs, especially activities of the Democratic Progressive Party, which is a rising opponent to the ruling party (Yu 1994).

The different programs and viewpoints brought by the new stations certainly have had an impact on the radio industry, but more than anything else, it has been the 50 or so underground, low-budget stations that have led the shift to radical and controversial changes in program formats. For example, uncensored call-ins have become a popular format after the illegal stations used these shows to mobilize political demonstrations. Most of the underground stations are associated with the Democratic Progressive Party (DPP). Breaking the broadcast monopoly of the Kuomintang and disseminating information of an antiauthority nature have become the primary missions of these underground stations. However, it is predicted that these underground stations will have a short life span because their program quality is too unprofessional to compete for listener support with well-established stations. More importantly, advertisers are likely to shy away from these underground stations because of their one-sided views of the DPP (Yu 1994).

TELEVISION

Taiwan has three commercial television stations, the Taiwan Television Corporation (TTV), China Television Corporation (CTV), and Chinese Television Services (CTS). They are all affiliated or controlled by the government/Kuomintang, though some stocks are shared by private investors. The broadcast monopoly has lasted for over 30 years since the founding of the TTV in 1962. Facing competition from a number of cable and satellite television channels in the early 1990s, the monopoly formed by the three major television stations has gradually collapsed.

The cartel shaped by these three stations has severely limited information flow and created a natural oligopoly for advertising time slots. According to survey research, watching television, especially TV news, is a major passtime for Taiwan's viewers (Shen 1995). However, because of the political affiliation with the KMT, news content offered by the stations has been strongly criticized for being biased. Responding to pressure from the opposition parties, the government decided to open air frequency to the private sectors in 1994 (Baum 1993b). The fourth terrestrial television station is scheduled to be set up by a group of private investors in the middle of the 1990s. Further, the Cable Television Act, passed in the early 1990s, has legalized a number of cable operations that are now able to compete with the three television stations (Dikenson 1995; Kao 1991).

Though the monopoly is gradually fading out, advertisers still have to pay a high price for a package of programs that may not be their first choice. Advertising professionals have criticized this type of business practice because it fails to consider the advertiser's interest. It is predicted, however, these oligarchic policies will soon be changed because satellite television channels are taking away some audience segments from the three government-owned stations (Kao 1991). For example, Star TV, the pan-Asian satellite network owned by Rupert Murdoch, launched in its first pay channel to Taiwan audiences in 1992. Within 1 year, Star TV had already been able to reach 198 million subscribers, 41 percent of the TV households in Taiwan. Star TV is not the only satellite channel available. Recently, TVB (a Hong Kong–based rival) and Sky TV have also joined the marketing battle, which makes the competition more intense and diversified (Staff 1993; Dikenson 1995).

AUDIENCE BEHAVIORS AND ADVERTISING INVESTMENT

According to the surveys conducted by the *United Daily News* and the *Survey Research Taiwan,* of the four major types of mass media, television is the most powerful. It reaches 85 percent of all households in Taiwan. In fact watching television, especially network news, is the most popular leisure time activity in Taiwan. Newspaper reading was listed as the second most popular information channel by respondents (83 percent). Public exposure to magazines and radio dropped sharply, compared with those figures of TV and newspapers. About 55 percent of the surveyed residents regularly read a magazine, whereas only one-third of the people tune in to radio programs every day (Shen 1995; Yuan 1993).

The distribution of advertising expenditures shows a slightly different pattern than the audience ratings of the four major media channels. Between 1981 and 1991, expenditures on newspaper advertising were higher than those of television, while advertising expenditures on radio and magazines fell far behind the top two media. It is expected that television and newspaper will retain the dominant positions in terms of advertising expenditures through the mid-1990s (Wang 1993; Yuan 1993). Nontraditional media advertising has maintained between 15 and 17 percent of the overall advertising expenditures over the years, and expenditures on sales promotion and direct mail are still slight (Huang 1991).

Growth of the Advertising Industry

HISTORICAL REVIEW

The 40-year history of the advertising industry in Taiwan can be classified into five chronological stages: the beginning period of the 1950s, the intermediate period of the 1960s, the developing period of the 1970s, the international period of the 1980s, and the stable period of the 1990s (Lee and Leu 1992). The year 1985 represented a turning point in the advertising history of Taiwan. Mirroring the features of the indigenous economy before 1985, most advertising agencies were small scale and owner operated. However, since 1985 the influx of multinational advertising agencies into Taiwan has dramatically changed the standard of advertising practice (Li 1989). By 1989, the advertising industry in Taiwan had been totally transformed from the underdeveloped stage into the international level. At present over 20 transnational advertising agencies have established affiliations with local agencies or set up their branch offices in Taiwan (Lee and Leu 1992). In addition there are about 500 small agencies scattered all over the island to handle smaller accounts (Tseng 1993).

There are four different kinds of advertising agencies in Taiwan, varying in their types of financial investment: joint ventures, foreign branches, local agencies having cooperation contracts with international agencies, and local companies without any affiliations with foreign agencies. The first international advertising agency arriving in Taiwan was the U.S.–based Ogilvy & Mather (O&M). In 1984, the government approved a policy of joint ventures in service industries, including advertising agencies. The next year O&M and its local partner set up the first joint venture in Taiwan's advertising industry. Shortly after, several other U.S. players, such as Grey, McCann-Erickson, BBDO, Lintas, and DDB Needham followed by either expanding their earlier cooperative agreements or simply teaming up with local agencies for joint ventures. By 1988, after the government made the service sector available for fully owned foreign firms to set up local branches, the advertising industry in Taiwan changed dramatically. Saatchi & Saatchi, J. Walter Thompson and Backer Spielvogel Bates were three of a handful of transnational latecomers who opened their shops at that time (Chen and Sun 1989). Table 5.1 shows the billings of top 10 advertising agencies of Taiwan.

IMPACT OF TRANSNATIONAL ADVERTISING AGENCIES

It did not take long for these foreign-owned or joint ventures to dominate the advertising industry in Taiwan. In 1992, O&M topped the list of foreign-owned agencies, with advertising revenues around US$55 million. In addition to O&M, four of the top six firms are currently foreign owned or a joint partnership. The revenues earned by all of these agencies near US$300 million. During the late 1980s these agencies enjoyed an average growth rate of nearly 18 percent in advertising revenues. In contrast, local agencies lost a great amount of their business. This was due to consolidation of agencies at the request of their multinational clients and a high turnover rate of top employees. For example, the multinational account of Max Factor was switched from Target, a local advertising

Table 5.1.   Top 10 Advertising Agencies in Taiwan, 1992 and 1993

Agency	Billings (millions US$) 1992	1993	Foreign Capital	Foreign Affiliates
United Advertising	55.00	65.90	No	Dentsu, Toei CM, JEMCO, Orion SP, Nippon, etc.
J. Walter Thompson	48.50	57.70	Yes	J.W.T.
Ogilvy & Mather	54.70	52.70	Yes	O&M
Hwa Wei & Grey	43.40	50.40	Yes	Grey
McCann-Erickson	46.40	51.20	Yes	McCann-Erickson
H & Y Communications	41.30	48.00	Yes	Hakubodo (Japan)
Taiwan Advertising	46.80	45.80	No	Dentsu
Saatchi & Saatchi	21.60	36.20	Yes	Saatchi & Saatchi
Kuo Hua Advertising	24.90	30.00	No	Dentsu, AMC (Malaysia)
Eastern Advertising	29.00	29.50	No	Tokyo Agency, Standard, CFK (Germany)

Source: Lee, W-N. and Y-F.J. Leu, 1992; *Asian Advertising and Marketing,* 1994.

agency, to Leo Burnett, the agency of the parent company Proctor & Gamble. The higher pay and better management of transnational agencies also lured experienced advertising professionals from local firms. As a result, the local agencies had a hard time trying to survive in the business (Yuan 1993).

Relying on tremendous support from their parent agencies in areas such as advanced training and professional experience, the joint ventures and foreign branches have quickly dominated the advertising industry. Today they control 60 percent of the market share (Lee and Leu 1992). However, one area in which they lack control is in local business connections. Given that advertising is still a localized industry in Taiwan, establishing local connections has become a major challenge for foreign agencies (Chard 1993). In contrast, having been in business for quite a long time, some local advertising agencies are able to use their local connections to survive. The United Advertising Agency is a typical example. United, a 100 percent locally owned advertising agency, is the largest advertising firm in terms of hiring of employees (220 staff members) and it ranked first in billings in both 1992 and 1993. In the early 1990s, as a part of their efforts to secure local clients, United tried a new management strategy, the "reverse brain drain," to lure well-trained employees aggressively from foreign agencies. Later other local agencies followed the same move as United and as a result, the gap in professional standards between foreign and local agencies has been substantially narrowed in recent years (Yuan 1993).

EVOLUTIONARY CHANGES OF THE ADVERTISING INDUSTRY

The narrowed gap can be seen in three different areas: advertising creativity, market research and agency structure. Prior to the mid-1980s, both print and television advertisements were criticized as "reminiscent of the U.S. advertisements in the 1950s" (Yuan 1993, 7). While hard/direct sale was the main strategy used in advertisements, product availability was the major information conveyed to the audience. In other words "creativity" was not a term highly recognized and fully understood by advertising professionals during the "innocent" period when advertising creativity was unexplored. In the mid-1980s creative development entered into a "wild west" period. Because of deregulated media channels, reduced tariffs on imported goods and higher standards of living, consumers had a tremendous desire for foreign information and products. "Foreign production" or "imported goods" were buzz words used in advertising copy to guarantee the sales of products. Consequently, applying a standardized strategy to creative styles and copying messages of Western advertisements was a popular practice (Yuan 1993; Yu-Chin 1988).

By the end of the 1980s, professional standards were upgraded to a stage where Western concepts were blended with traditional values in advertising performance. At that time, new concepts such as product image and brand equity were recognized. Advertising professionals began to realize that creating an advertising campaign was a more sophisticated process than simply dubbing Western commercials. On the other hand, advertising professionals grew confident about developing their own styles, and sent out their entries for competitions. Two prominent outlets for advertising competition are the Times Advertising Award established by the China Times in 1978 and the Creativity Award of 4 A's (The Association of Accredited Advertising Agents) held since 1993. In addition several advertising magazines, such as *Brain Marketing & Communication, Ad Pros, Ad Age* (Chinese edition), *Advertising & Life Style* and some in-house publications of advertising agencies have helped improve advertising quality. A result of the conceptual merge between the East and West is that a unique style has been created. As one advertising professional put it, the style is very much "Chinese," though Western concepts are discernible everywhere in the advertising industry (Huang 1993; Hwang 1993a; Tsao 1994).

Before the arrival of multinational advertising agencies, "market research" used to be treated as the least important job of the advertising industry. At present, however, most full-service advertising agencies, especially joint ventures and foreign branches, have their own research departments. In addition some local advertising agencies, such as United, Union and several other sister agencies, have formed a research center to share market resources for cost reduction (Smith 1988). As well, there are about 20 independent companies that concentrate on market or advertising research. These include some well-known research firms, such as Burke, Survey Research Inc. and the Gallup (Chiu 1993).

Perhaps the most striking feature of the advertising industry today as compared with the old days is agency structure. Family business or one-person operations were the typical style of management in the advertising industry prior to the mid-1980s. In those days one person might play different positions, including general manager, copywriter and account executive, for the same account. Replacing the old system, transnational agencies brought in two management concepts, teamwork and specialization. The result is that efficiency has been dramatically improved. In return, more young professionals select advertising as their job career because advertising is regarded as a specialized and glamorous profession (Yuan 1993; Yu-Chin 1988).

CURRENT PROBLEMS OF THE ADVERTISING INDUSTRY
The recent growth of the advertising industry does not mean that there are no problems. The problems can be summarized as inadequate support from other businesses, shortage of higher-level managers and high turnover rate of entry-level professionals (Herendeen 1993; Hwang 1993a). For example, development of media planning is handicapped because the Audit Bureau of Circulation (ABC) system is yet to be established. Further, the unreasonable rate structure of television stations forces advertisers to hesitate to use it effectively for their marketing communications (Hwang 1993a).

Duties of upper-level managers used to be quite straightforward, as long as they took good care of the relations between client and agency. As market demand has changed and the number of international clients has increased, strong marketing expertise and foreign language skills are now required for high-level managers to cope with daily routines. However, a person with both skills is still hard to come by mainly because Taiwan is not yet as fully internationalized as Hong Kong and Singapore (Chard 1993).

Although upper-level managers are still a rare commodity, entry-level staff enjoy the job-hopping trend. The turnover rate reached a climax in the late 1980s when transnational agencies entered the market. The job-hopping trend continues today, though it is fading out. The advertising industry has paid a high price for internationalization, such as inflated titles, higher overhead, wasted cost on training and client confusion (Herendeen 1993).

The Regulatory and Self-Screening Environment of Advertising

Advertising in Taiwan is a regulated industry and there are several laws and codes that have been used to monitor the practice of advertising. Table 5.2 shows major legislation and codes that have been used by the government and industry to protect consumer interest. The Governmental Information Office (GIO), Fair Trade Commission (FTC), Department of Health (DOH), Environmental Protection Administration, Ministry of Transportation, and Department of Construction Management are the governmental agencies that share responsibility for the enforcement of advertising regulation. On the other hand, the 4A's and the Press Council are major industrial groups involved in the self-regulation of advertising. In addition there are some public interest groups, such as the Consumer Cultural and Educational Foundation and the Awakening Foundation, which are constantly reviewing controversial advertisements. Although government and self-regulation of advertising is well established, the enforcement of the laws and regulations still needs to be improved (Tseng 1993).

GOVERNMENTAL AGENCIES AND ADVERTISING LAWS
The most powerful regulatory body for advertising is the GIO, a Cabinet-

Table 5.2. Advertising Laws and Self-Regulation in Taiwan

Law/Code	Governmental/Self-Regulatory Agency	Legal/Self-Screening Scope Related to Advertising
Radio-TV law	Governmental Information Office (GIO)	Regulate radio-TV commercials regarding content, frequency and production
Publication law	Governmental Information Office (GIO)	Regulate print ads regarding violations on accuracy, taste, honesty and legality
Fair trade law	Fair Trade Commission (FTC)	Eliminate unfair trade practices, including false and misleading advertising claims
Outdoor and transit ad law	Ministry of Transportation, Environmental Protection Administration, and Department of Construction Management	Maintain clean scenery, public safety and traffic order
Pharmaceutical affairs law	Department of Public Health (DPH)	Penalize media carrying false ads of medical/drug products
Code of advertising practice	Association of Accredited Advertising Agents (4A's)	Self-screen advertising claims regarding legality, decency, honesty and accuracy
Code of press council	Press Council	Conduct symposiums on ethical issues related to advertising content

level agency. The GIO enforces two types of legislation, the Radio-TV Law and the Publication Law. The former is applied to broadcast commercials, and the latter was developed for print advertisements. Checking false claims in both broadcast and print advertisements is just one of GIO's major responsibilities. In addition the GIO censors other controversial content such as those issues that are politically sensitive, of a sexual nature, of concern for public safety or children's health, as well as copy infringements (Liu 1991; Tseng 1993).

For television commercials, all visual and verbal materials except slides must be submitted to the GIO for review before they are approved to air. For radio advertisements, stations must file all commercial tapes and scripts for 15 days before they are broadcast. Violators receive different levels of penalty ranging from verbatim warnings to suspensions of media licenses (Liu 1991). The screening process has received mixed reviews from the advertising industry. On the one hand, advertising professionals feel that the GIO is doing a fine job in implementing advertising standards to protect consumer interest. The guidelines enforced by the GIO are considered reasonable and necessary. On the other hand, GIO's rules have also been criticized as being outdated. Some practitioners believe that the legislation used by the GIO is not precise enough to regulate the constantly changing world of advertisements. They feel that the rules should be relaxed to foster a more liberal environment for advertising creativity (Tseng 1993).

The Fair Trade Law and the Pharmaceutical Affairs Law are two new regulations approved in the early 1990s to address the gray areas that the GIO has been missing (Tseng 1993). The FTC is the governmental agency enforcing the Fair Trade Law. The law protects both advertiser and consumer interests by eliminating false and deceptive advertisements. Consequently it assures that trade and promotion of products can be practiced in a fair and honest manner. Within a year after its enactment, 69 advertisers had been penalized for presenting false claims. Violators were required to run corrective advertisements and pay a maximum fine of US$40,000. As advertising agencies and mass media are both liable for damages due to false and deceptive claims, they are taking a more cautious approach when designing and running advertisements (Tseng 1993).

The Pharmaceutical Affairs Law is enforced by the DOH to penalize any mass media that carries advertisements with false claims for food, drugs, medical equipment or cosmetics. The law is complementary to the Fair Trade Law. Before the Pharmaceutical Affairs Law was promulgated, the legal position of the DOH was quite weak because its only authority was to advise violators to run corrective claims. At that time, no penalties could be issued to the media for carrying false and deceptive advertisements. With the Pharmaceutical Affairs Law as its powerful arm, however, the DOH now screens every medical advertisement. Further, media violators can receive a fine ranging from US$400 to US$2,000 for running false advertisements (Tseng 1993).

TRADE GROUPS AND SELF-REGULATIONS

In addition to the governmental agencies regulating advertising performance, some trade groups self-screen advertisements and attempt to improve the standards of advertising. The groups actively involved in self-regulation are the 4A's and the Press Council. The 4A's was inaugurated in July 1987 as a formal organization representing the advertising industry. It now has 29 members. Qualifications to be a member of the 4A's are quite strict. Membership criteria require that an agency be a full-service operation with an annual billing of at least US$4 million. In addition the agency must service at least 10 clients and have established business contacts with the major media channels. The Press Council was organized by the Newspaper Association of Taipei in 1963, and was expanded in 1974 to include several other press associations as members. Because both organizations are trade groups, instead of governmental agencies, their authority to sanction violators effectively is limited (Liu 1991; *Standard Operations Handbook of the Association of Accredited Advertising Agents* 1990).

The Code of Advertising Practice of the 4A's requires members to develop advertisements following the principles of "legality, decency, honesty, and accuracy" (*Standard Operations Handbook of the Association of Accredited Advertising Agents* 1990, 78). The 4A's claims to take responsibility for investigating "all complaints of untruthful or otherwise unacceptable advertising" (78). Further, members who violate these propositions are subject to punishment. However, the Code does not explain what types of punishment will be given if members violate the rules. Although the 4A's has only limited power to take legal actions against its members who violate the Code, the 4A's' contributions to the improvement of advertising quality should not be overlooked. For examples, the 4A's and academic institutions often cosponsor workshops to train entry-level employees in the professionalism of advertising (Tseng 1993). The annual Advertising Creativity Award sponsored by the 4A's also shows its efforts and determination to improve advertising performance (Staff 1993).

The Press Council is composed of eight press associations, all of which are related to newspapers, news agencies, radio stations and television networks. Twelve social and academic elites are invited to be neutral counselors of the organization. They investigate complaints and conduct symposiums for different issues related to advertising ethics. The Council has no legal authority to sanction violators. However, recommendations made by the counselors are published and sent to accused media for future reference (Liu 1991). Not all of the suggestions are implemented by the media institutions, but the ongoing efforts made by the Council to bring up issues of advertising ethics have been highly praised.

CONSUMER INTEREST GROUPS

As society becomes more liberal and consumer oriented, some nonprofit organizations representing certain interest groups have begun to play the role of watchdog in monitoring advertising performance. To name just a few, for example, the Cultural and Educational Foundation for Consumers, Awakening Foundation, and the John Tung Foundation are some active groups that constantly challenge advertisements that they feel may be damaging to consumer interests.

The Cultural and Educational Foundation for Consumers (CEFC) was established in 1987 (Li 1989). One of its functions is to investigate consumer complaints about advertising. For example, since the ban on imported cigarettes was lifted in 1987, the CEFC has actively protested the promotion of cigarettes targeted at youth as well as advertisements that do not carry a health hazards message. Over the years the CEFC has handled many cases, but like other consumer interest groups, it lacks a legitimate power to sanction advertisers. The CEFC has, however, established strong grass-roots support in Taiwan.

The Awakening Foundation focuses on investigation of activities related to women's rights. It is particularly concerned about the issue of sex in advertising. After an advertisement is identified as one that demeans women, the foundation will file a complaint directly to advertisers and request improvement. If advertisers ignore their viewpoints, persuading the public to boycott the offending companies becomes the next move for the foundation. The foundation's focus on attacking sexism has earned it strong support from women (Kirby 1989).

The John Tung Foundation is a nonprofit antismoking group. Instead of organizing public demonstrations against controversial cigarettes advertisements, the Tung Foundation uses advertising campaigns to express their antismoking concerns. The approach has been shown to be quite successful and, in turn, has led several other nonprofit organizations to use public service announcements to promote their causes (Liu 1993).

Advertising regulation, self-screening activities and consumers' scrutiny in the past decade all have had a positive impact on the improvement of advertising. A recent survey of consumers found that nearly three out of five feel that television commercials are more acceptable and enjoyable to watch than those advertisements aired several years ago. Even drug commercials, which used to be the target of criticism, are considered to be more believable. It is also interesting to note that some people would rather watch television commercials than view regular programs. However, the public still takes a cynical attitude toward whether advertising can be positively used as a tool for accessing market information (Wang 1991; Yu-Chin 1988).

Conclusions

As socioeconomic development in Taiwan has reached the developed stage, the advertising industry is entering a more stable period. The second half of the 1990s will be an interesting time to observe how the industry can adapt to new developments in society and upgrade itself to reach a more mature stage. Following are some factors that may determine whether the industry can still play a vital role in market communication.

Factor 1: A more liberalized media system is forming, which will increase media selections for the advertising industry.

Regulations of all of the major media industries, including newspapers, magazines, radio, television and cable TV have been relaxed. Soon, the satellite television system will be deregulated as well. A liberalized media system presents advertisers with more channels for marketing communication.

Factor 2: Developing Taiwan as an Asia-Pacific Regional Operations Center may simultaneously raise advertising quality and increase advertising revenues.

As Hong Kong prepares to be returned to China in 1997, Taiwan is ambitiously planning to develop itself as a regional operations center and to attempt to replace the trading position of Hong Kong in the Pacific Rim area. The center will provide financial, media, marketing and telecommunication bases for Western manufacturers and marketers who wish to oversee their operations in the Asia-Pacific region (Flannery 1994). Establishment of the center may have a strong impact on the advertising industry in terms of upgrading its level of professionalism.

Factor 3: Cultivating the mainland market may represent another opportunity for the advertising industry in Taiwan.

In recent years the political and military hostility between China and Taiwan has been relaxed. As both sides begin to communicate, the advertising industry is in an ideal position to facilitate the bridging of the two nations. Both countries share the same characteristics, including cultural traits, consumer needs and media markets. Some advertising agencies, including J. Walter Thompson, Ogilvy & Mather, and Lintas, have set up their branches in China to explore market opportunities. Setting up operations in China is still a high-cost and risk-taking move, but the payoff may be far beyond what can currently be measured (Hwang 1993b).

Factor 4: A more efficient system for enforcing advertising regulations is needed in order to maintain a fair and responsible advertising environment.

The regulatory environment at Taiwan has been well established. However, all of the enforcement agencies share the same problem, the shortage of personnel to enforce the laws (Tseng 1993). As a result, some guidelines become showcases, which have never been enforced. For example, sexual images and questionable claims for quack drugs regularly appear in newspaper advertisements. Given that most of the questionable advertisements are created by hundreds of small advertising agencies, which are not members of the 4A's, developing an effective strategy to encourage and enforce more ethical practice in the advertising industry seems to be an urgent priority.

Bibliography

Asian Advertising and Marketing. 1994. A Regional Ranking of Ad Spend in 1992 and 1993. April 22.

Baum, J. 1993a. Media: Golden Gambit. *Far Eastern Economic Review,* June 24, pp. 65–66.

Baum, J. 1993b. Media: Taiwan's Air War. *Far Eastern Economic Review,* December 9, p. 65.

Chan, V. 1994a. Studies Examine Quality of Life. *The Free China Journal,* November 18, p. 4.

Chan, V. 1994b. Taipei Princes and Princesses of Sidewalk Fashions. *The Free China Journal,* December 16, p. 4.

Chan, V. 1994c. Image-Conscious Teens Work Part Time for Pocket Money. *The Free China Journal,* August 12, p. 4.

Chang, H.C. and G.R. Holt 1991. Tourism as Consciousness of Struggle: Cultural Representations of Taiwan. *Critical Studies in Mass Communication,* 8: 102–118.

Chard, D. 1993. Taiwan Communicators Growing in Status. *Communication World,* June/July, p. 43.

Chen, S.C. and Sun, H.P. 1989. Development of International Advertising and Taiwan's Ad Industry. In: Chu, D.K., ed. *A Ten-Year Review on Advertising: 1978–1987.* Taipei, Taiwan: The China Times Publishing Co., pp. 62–68.

Chiu, K.S. 1993. The Application of Market and Consumer Research in Advertising Practices. *The Journal of Advertising Research [Kwang-Kao Hshei Yein Choi],* 1: 119–155.

Clifford, M. 1993. Media: Read and In the Block. *Far Eastern Economic Review,* June 24, pp. 62–63.

"Debates on 4A's Advertising Creativity Award of 1993." 1993. *Brain,* 206 (June): 16–23.

Dikenson, N. 1995. TV Boom Fuels Media Chaos. *Campaign.* January 27, pp. 81–82.

The Europa World Yearbook. 1991. London: Europa Publication Limited.

Fairbank, J.K., E.O. Reischauer, and A.M. Craig. 1973. *East Asia: Tradition and Transformation.* NY: Houghton and Mifflin Co.

Flannery, R. 1994. Taking the Tiger by the Tail. *Asian Business.* December, pp. 32–35.

Fu, H-P. 1994. Neo Consumerism in the Uncertain Period. *Cho-Yueh [Outstanding],* January 20, p. 24.

Goldstein, C. 1989. The Selling of Asia. *Far Economist Review,* June 29, *61–63.*

Her, K. 1994. Cosmetics Market in Boom Period. *The Free China Journal,* August 12, p. 8.

Herendeen, J.W. 1993. A View of the Advertising Situation in Taiwan. *Brain,* 206 (June): 120–121.

Huang, C.C. 1991. Sales Promotion Media Situation in 1990. In: Liu, Y.C., ed. *ROC Advertising Yearbook 1990–1991.* Taipei, Taiwan: Association of Taipei Advertising Agencies, pp. 8–82.

Huang, J-H. 1993. Color in U.S. and Taiwanese Industrial Advertising. *Industrial Marketing Management,* 22: 195–198.

Hwang, J. 1993a. Integrate and Refine, Then Sell. *Free China Review,* April, pp. 20–21.

Hwang, J. 1993b. Advertisers Head to a New Wild West. *Free China Review,* April, pp. 22–23.

Hwang, J. 1995. In Cash We Trust. *Free China Review,* March, pp. 35–39.

Kao, T.S. 1991. Changes and Impact of Media Environment in Taiwan. *Viewpoint By, For and About Ogilvy & Mather,* November, pp. 19–21.

Kim, Y.Y. 1985. Intercultural Personhood: An Integration of Eastern and Western Perspectives. In: Samovar, L.A. and R.E. Porter, eds. *Intercultural Communication: A Reader.* Belmont, CA: Wadsworth Publishing Co., pp. 400–409.

Kirby, J. 1989. Sex Sells. *Free China Review,* October, pp. 57–61.

Kuo, C. and Tsia, M. 1994. *Investigating the Compulsive Buying Behaviors Among the Chinese Youths: An Integrated Model.* Paper Presented at the 1994 Association for Education in Journalism and Mass Communication Annual Conference, Atlanta, GA.

Lay, Y.J. and Schweitzer, J.C. 1990. Advertising in Taiwan Newspapers Since the Lifting of the Bans. *Journalism Quarterly,* 67 (1): 201–206.

Lee, C.C. 1993. Sparking a Fire. *Journalism Monograph,* Vol. 138 (April), p. 13.

Lee, W-N. and Leu, Y-F.J. 1992. Development of the Advertising Industry in Taiwan. *International Communication Bulletin,* 27 (1–2): 11–16.

Levine, R.V. 1988. The Pace of Life Across Cultures. In: McGrath, M.E., ed. *The Social Psychology of Time: New Perspectives.* Newbury, CA: Sage Publications, Inc., pp. 39–60.

Li, T.M. 1989. Advertising and Economy in the Past Ten Years. In: Chu, D.K., ed. *A Ten-Year Review on Advertising: 1978–1987.* Taipei, Taiwan: The China Times Publishing Co., pp. 30–33.

Lin, D. 1994. Out of Kitchen, Into the Economy. *The Free China Journal,* November 11, p. 7.

Lin, S.M. 1991. Look Back at ROC Magazine Advertising Evolution in Past 45 years. In: Liu, Y.C., ed. *ROC Advertising Yearbook 1990–1991.* Taipei, Taiwan: Association of Taipei Advertising Agencies, pp. 62–68.

Liu, P. 1993. Commercials with a Conscience. *Free China Review,* April, pp. 24–29.

Liu, Y.C., ed. 1991. *ROC Advertising Yearbook 1990–1991*. Taipei, Taiwan: Association of Taipei Advertising Agencies.

Pun, A. 1995. Taiwan's Steadily Rising Divorce Rate Considered to Be the Highest in Asia. *The Free China Journal*, February 10, 4.

Pun, A. and Yu, S. 1994. Approval Granted to Open 46 Private Radio Stations. *The Free China Journal*, December 30, p. 4.

Rampal, K.R. 1994. Press and Political Liberalization in Taiwan. *Journalism Quarterly*, 71 (3): 637–651.

Shen, D. 1994. Fast-Food Chains Drawing Up Major Expansion Plans. *The Free China Journal*, September 24, p. 8.

Shen, D. 1995. TV News Top Broadcast Format. *The Free China Journal*, January 7, p. 4.

Smith, D.C. 1992. *The Chinese Family in Transition: Implications for Education and Society in Modern Taiwan*. Paper Presented at the Comparative Education Association/World Bank Seminar, Annapolis, MD.

Smith, G. 1988. Cultivating a Consumer Society. *Free China Review*, September, pp. 48–53.

Standard Operations Handbook of the Association of Accredited Advertising Agents. 1990. Taipei, Taiwan: The Association of Accredited Advertising Agents of Taiwan R.O.C.

Tien, H-M. 1989. *The Great Transition: Political and Social Change in the Republic of China*. Stanford, CA: Hoover Institution Press.

Tsao, J.C. 1994. Advertising and Cultural Values: A Content Analysis of Advertising in Taiwan. *Gazette*, 53: 93–110.

Tseng, O. 1993. False Ads Draw Heavy Flak. *Free China Review*, April, pp. 30–34.

Wang, S-F.S. 1991. Content Analysis of ROC Newspaper Ads Readership. In: Liu, Y.C., ed. *ROC Advertising Yearbook 1990–1991*. Taipei, Taiwan: Association of Taipei Advertising Agencies, pp. 107–117.

Wang, S-F.S. 1993. An Analysis of the Development of Advertising Investment in the 1980s in Taiwan Area: A Ten-Year Review. *The Journal of Advertising Research [Kwang-Kao Hshei Yein Choi]*, 1: 3–32.

Wong, C.W. 1991. ROC Radio Advertising: Its Present Situation and Future Prospect. In: Liu, Y.C., ed. *ROC Advertising Yearbook 1990–1991*. Taipei, Taiwan: Association of Taipei Advertising Agencies, pp. 69–77.

Wong, V. 1994. Taipei Unwinds With a Refreshing Mug of "Atmosphere." *The Free China Journal*, July 1, p. 5.

Ying, D. 1993. A Magazine Publisher Committed to Taiwan. *Far Eastern Economic Review*, April 1, p. 90.

Yu, S. 1994. Government Offers More TV Channels to Private Owners. *The Free China Journal*, August 26, p. 2.

Yuan, Y. 1993. Masters of the Marketplace. *Free China Review*, April, pp. 4–17.

Yu-Chin, Y. 1988. Young Image Makers. *Free China Review*, September, pp. 54–57.

6

Advertising in Korea: International Challenges and Politics

KWANGMI KO KIM

Introduction

As one of Asia's newly industrializing countries (NICs), Korea has experienced rapid economic growth and change in its major sectors including the economy, culture, mass media and advertising (Balassa 1981 and Evans 1979). Reflecting such development, the Korean advertising industry has evolved its own unique structure. This chapter describes the dynamics of the Korean advertising industry by analyzing the environmental factors surrounding the industry and by examining its major characteristics such as organization, regulation and relationship with the media.

The Economic Context

As an economic and cultural institution, the Korean advertising industry has developed within the unique political, cultural and social context of Korea. A discussion of its growth and practices, therefore, needs to be placed in the broader context of Korea's economic development in which national and foreign factors are intertwined.

Korea's development process can be traced back to the early 1900s when Korea was subject to the dominance of Japan (Amsden 1989). However, it is the past 30 years that have been the greatest period of economic growth in the country. By the early 1960s, Korea had completed the "easy" stage of domestic production of nondurable goods through import substitution and begun to experience a slower growth of output (Kim 1991). In 1965, President Park Chung Hee, who had seized power with a coup d'état in May 1961, announced a major industrial economic policy change from import substitution to export promotion. By utilizing foreign capital, imported raw materials and imported capital goods, the main industrialization strategy focused on the export of manufactured goods

125

to international markets. This strategy relied on developing labor-intensive, light industries in the 1960s and the early 1970s, and then shifted to promotion of capital-intensive, heavy industries in the late 1970s. Between 1961 and 1979 Korea achieved an uninterrupted economic growth rate averaging about 9.2 percent per annum.

In the industrializing process the Korean state has adopted a "growth first, then redistribution or equality later" approach and directly made major decisions regarding the production process. For example, government officials from Korea's Economic Planning Board would target a specific industry for development and then work with other government agencies and financial institutions (which were controlled by the government) to give a variety of benefits (for example, subsidiaries, tax and tariff exemptions, and favorable financing terms). As Cumings (1987) calls it, the Korean state was a series of "bureaucratic-authoritarian industrializing regimes" (71).

Such government policy favored local capitalists rather than the transnational corporations (TNCs), giving special incentives to the local capitalist industries oriented toward exports. Eventually this policy yielded to a concentration of private capital by a handful of conglomerates, the so-called *chaebol.* In Korean *chaebol* refers to large industrial conglomerates, generally run by family members. As a result of the state's support throughout the industrialization period, the *chaebol* have rapidly grown and have dominated the domestic market in a wide range of diverse industries. Table 6.1 shows the 10 largest business groups, or *chaebol* in Korea.

Table 6.1.   The 10 Largest Business Groups (*Chaebol*) in Korea

Rank	*Chaebol* Group	Total Sales (billion US$)
1	Samsung	34.3
2	Hyundai	32.5
3	Lucky-Goldstar	23.1
4	Daewoo	18.1
5	Sunkyong	9.4
6	Saangyong	7.5
7	Hyosung	5.2
8	Hanjin	4.8
9	Korea Explosives	4.6
10	Kia	4.4

By the mid-1980s, the top 10 *chaebol* accounted for almost 70 percent of Korea's gross national product (GNP). In 1990, the combined sales of the 30 largest conglomerates accounted for about $231 billion or approximately 90 percent of Korea's GNP (*Wall Street Journal* 1991). The top *chaebol* received 70 percent of the total bank loans available, making money tighter for small businesses trying to start up or to strengthen their market positions (Amsden 1989).

As is discussed later in this chapter, the concentrated economic structure dominated by *chaebol* has affected the shape of the advertising industry in Korea, yielding to a structure dominated by the large in-house agencies of these large *chaebol*.

The significant power of the Korean state and its nationalistic policy have been possible because of Korea's unique geopolitical situation. During the Cold War Korea's incorporation into the international capitalist system was largely motivated by U.S. security interests in Northeast Asia. In order to maintain stability and an anti-Communist sentiment in this region, the United States gave massive economic and military aid to Korea. After the Korean War in 1953, Korea was able to rebuild the nation mainly based on U.S. capital and support. This made Korea dependent in various ways on the United States, both in terms of domestic and international affairs. For example, to support its containment policy in Asia the United States played a major role in making the military one of the dominant institutions in Korea. The United States also intervened in the establishment of the right-wing Rhee regime in 1948 right after the end of the World War II, and pressured the Park regime to normalize diplomatic relations with Japan in 1965. Since the late 1940s the United States has been a strong guardian for Korea in the international economic and political arena. In other words due to the security issue in the region, the United States had let Korea pursue its nationalistic economic policies without asking it to open up to U.S. products, at least, until the early 1980s.

The relationship between Korea and the United States, however, has changed since the 1980s. As the tension of the Cold War era disappeared, the economic interest of the United States in Korea became more apparent. The growth of the Korean economy and the relatively stable political situation have made Korea one of the most important markets in the Asia/Pacific region. In addition the huge trade deficits between the United States and Korea have had an impact on U.S. economic policy toward Korea. These changes have led to pressure for Korea to open up its industries. In particular, in the 1980s, the United States began to pressure Korea to open up its advertising industry to foreign agencies. Finally in 1987, Korea liberalized its advertising industry.

The Political Context

The dual ideologies of economic development and anticommunism have been an effective means for Korean administrations to control and repress the Korean people and social institutions. After the assassination of President Park in 1979, the administration of Chun Doo Whan took power. This administration decided to reorganize the TV broadcasting system from a commercial system to a public broadcasting system in the name of "public interest." Two private TV networks, Tongyang Broadcasting Corporation (TBC-TV) and Munwha Broadcasting Corporation (MBC-TV), were put under the control of the state. TBC-TV—owned by the Samsung Group, one of the large conglomerates—was completely merged with Korean Broadcasting System (KBS-TV), and MBC-TV was placed under the substantial ownership (79 percent) of KBS (Yoon 1994).

In the face of massive and prolonged antigovernment demonstrations in June 1987, Roh Tae Woo, then chairman of the ruling party and President-appointed, announced the Declaration of June 29, which promised political reforms and the freedom of the press. This announcement became a watershed in recent Korean history in terms of political liberalization. Various restrictions have been abolished in favor of a "free press." Through the Roh administration (1987–1993), which functioned as a bridge transferring the power center from the military to the civilian sector, Korea was able to establish a new civilian government in 1994 led by President Kim Young Sam, the first nonmilitary leader to be elected by the Korean people in more than 4 decades.

The Cultural Context

Korea does not have any specific religious ideology; rather, Confucianism and Buddhism have become the philosophical foundations for the Korean value system. These two philosophies have shaped the ideas of the Korean people on how to consume and have contributed to shaping hierarchical social structures. Buddhism has taught the Korean people about the relationship between the mind and worldly desires. The saying that, "the most important thing is controlling the mind since it is the center of the universe" reflects this philosophy. Within this context the possession of material things and other secular desires are considered temporary and trivial.

Confucianism has introduced the philosophy of human nature and defined proper human relationships as the basis for a just society. As Confucianism was the official philosophy of the Yi Dynasty (1832–1910) in Korea, it has been thoroughly institutionalized and systematically diffused to the Korean people (Yum 1987). The implications of Confucianism are also visible in the Korean advertising world. First, people tend not to perceive advertising as a serious and professional occupation. For Confucian cultures, sales activities are considered as second-rate jobs and so the selling of products or services is not regarded as a proper professional activity. Advertising has been regarded as a necessary evil, rather than a useful marketing tool (*Far Eastern Economic Review* 1984). Therefore, working in advertising has not been perceived as a "good" or respectable occupation. This is, however, rapidly changing as traditional beliefs are challenged by the modern values. Advertising has become one of the more popular jobs since early 1990s. Second, Confucianism structures the relationship between advertisers and advertising professionals to resemble the master/servant relationship. This is not an equally sharing relationship, but a vertical and servicing one.

Third, the Confucian ethic puts a damper on creativity, as hierarchy is emphasized. This type of social order between juniors and seniors makes it hard for junior employees to stand up for their ideas in the face of opposition from their elders or bosses. This inhibits the development of new marketing concepts and means that often the "best ideas" are those that come from the top executives. Finally, Confucianism values the concept of *Ury-ri,* or collectivism, rather than individualism. It also emphasizes the value of cooperation, rather than competition. These underlying philosophies influence the Korean mind and the practices of advertising business. For example, advertisers tend to find their agencies more likely based on personal bonds such as friendships forged in high school or coming from the same hometown neighborhood. Professional expertise in the area of advertising for specific products or companies is ranked lower in value than these personal or social bonds.

As Korean society develops and modernizes, new values challenge these traditional beliefs and practices. Western values such as competition, freedom, professionalism and individualism are challenging the less-effective and less-efficient traditions. The advertising industry in particular is struggling to improve its way of doing business, especially among young professionals (Choi 1994).

The Growth of the Korean Advertising Industry

THE EARLY HISTORY: 1960 TO 1970

The history of the advertising industry in Korea is relatively short. The first modern Korean advertisement appeared in 1886 in the *Hansong Chunbo,* the first Korean newspaper. However, it was not until the mid-1970s that the Korean advertising industry began to grow and take its current shape.

In the late 1950s after the Korean War ended, the advertising agency business had to start from scratch because the few Japanese agencies operating in Korea during its occupation between 1910 and 1945 left Korea after World War II (Shin 1989). The introduction of television broadcasting greatly facilitated the growth of advertising. Television broadcasting in Korea was initiated by the American corporation RCA, not by the Korean government, and was set up at a time when even radio broadcasting was not yet fully developed. In the mid-1950s, at the request of KBS, a Korean representative of KORCAD (the Korean branch of RCA) made a trip to the United States to order radio broadcasting technology from RCA, and instead came back with some basic TV broadcasting equipment. Therefore, RCA's international marketing strategy to sell more TV sets to developing countries directly contributed to the emergence of TV broadcasting in Korea (Yoon 1994). Here, KORCAD (HLKZ-TV) was a major actor in bringing the U.S. commercial broadcasting model into Korea.

Since the early 1960s, Korea's TV broadcasting has quantitatively and qualitatively expanded. Although DBC-TV, the first TV station in Korea (the old

HLKZ-TV), was closed down due to fire, the state-owned KBS started KBS-TV in 1961, and two other commercial TV stations, TBC-TV and MBC-TV, opened in 1964 and in 1969, respectively. With the opening of the electronic age and the rapid dissemination of domestically manufactured television sets, the advertising industry was able to grow and expand. By the end of the 1970s, TV sets had spread to rural areas and accelerated the dissemination of a television culture (Shin 1989 and Yoon 1994).

Along with the influence of the United States on Korean TV broadcasting, the establishment of advertising agencies was initiated by foreign professionals at this early stage. In 1962, a media representative company named Impact, which was managed by Michael O'Sammon, started its operation as an advertising agency (Shin 1989). Impact was later bought out by MBC-TV and became Union Advertising. John C. Sticker, an American who worked for Impact, established his own agency, called S/K Associates, in 1965. Another agency, Hapdong Advertising Bureau, was established in 1967 as the in-house department of Hapdong News, Korea's first news agency. However, it was Manbosa Advertising, established in 1969, that played a major role in shaping the agency recognition and commission system (Shin 1989). The birth of Manbosa was directly attributable to the market entry by Coke and Pepsi, both of which came into Korea in the late 1960s. By 1974, there were 11 advertising agencies. Of these only two remain today, Korea First Advertising (later renamed Cheil Communications) and Union Advertising. Manbosa and Hapdong merged in 1975 to form Oricom Advertising. The early history of agency development and the television broadcasting industry in Korea reveals that the United States had played a role in providing technologies and shaping certain aspects of the advertising and broadcasting industry.

Since the 1970s, Korean agencies have had technical assistance agreements or affiliations with U.S. and Japanese agencies. McCann-Erickson established its presence in 1975 through its Coca-Cola and Nestlé accounts with Oricom Advertising, an in-house agency of the Doosan Group. Hence Coca-Cola, Pepsi-Cola, Pan Am Airlines, Northwest Airlines, Kodak, Japanese Airlines and Pfizer were among the earliest transnational advertisers in Korea.

THE ERA OF THE 1980S: INTERNATIONAL CHALLENGES THROUGH MARKET LIBERALIZATION

During the 1980s the local Korean advertising industry was experiencing the dual burdens of trying to improve business practices while having to cope with challenges caused by market liberalization. Liberalization of the Korean advertising industry was stimulated by two major factors. The first came from the United States, which had been experiencing a growing trade deficit with many of its trading partners and had lost its competitive advantage in many manufacturing sectors. Because the U.S. service industries wished to capture a competitive advantage over their other trading partners, American trade policy was set to promote liberalization. One major target of the U.S. policy was the Korean advertising industry.

The other factor driving liberalization of the Korean advertising industry was the rapid growth of the market itself. In 1987, advertising expenditures reached US$1.2 billion, surpassing 1 percent of the GNP. From 1980 to 1990 this industry has averaged an annual growth rate of 22.3 percent. After Japan, Korea had the highest advertising expenditures of any Asian country (Table 6.2).

Table 6.2. Advertising Expenditures by Asian Countries, 1988

Country	Total Advertising Expenditure (million US$)	GNP (billion US$)	Adversity as a % of GNP
Japan	34,471.3	2,576.6	1.3
Korea	1,747.9	150.3	1.1
Taiwan*	1,091.7	—	—
Hong Kong	629.6	52.4	1.2
China	430.4	356.5	0.2
Malaysia	212.1	31.7	0.7
Philippines	138.0	37.8	0.4
Indonesia	123.1	76.0	0.2

Source: *Twenty-third Survey of World Advertising Expenditures: A Survey of World Advertising Expenditures in 1988*, 1989.
Note: GNP, gross national product.
*Data for Taiwan's GNP and ad expenditures as a % of GNP were not available.

The number of advertising agencies "fully recognized" by the Korean Broadcasting Advertising Corporation (KOBACO) increased from four in 1981 to 85 in 1991 (Korean Federation of Advertising Associations 1992). However, despite its growing market size, Korea was one of only three Asian advertising markets that prohibited foreign investment in this industry. The United States estimated the 1985 value of Korean advertising at about US$800 million with a 10 to 20 percent annual growth rate. It also estimated that without investment restrictions, U.S. advertising firms could capture about 20 percent share of this market (Office of the U.S. Trade Representative 1987).

Once the goal of market liberalization was set, the United States began to address this issue through various channels. A 1984 editorial in *Advertising Age* argued the unfairness of Korea's closed market. During the 1985 U.S.–Korean Economic Consultations, liberalization of the Korean advertising industry first emerged as a trade issue. In the bilateral trade talks, U.S. delegations asked Korea to open up its service sectors including insurance, banking, motion picture distribution and advertising (Office of the U.S. Trade Representative 1987). Specifically they urged the Korean government to permit foreign investment in advertising and, as an interim measure, to approve U.S. applications to open branch offices in Korea.

In September 1985 the American Chamber of Commerce (ACC) in Korea joined a rally by the U.S. industry, and distributed a position paper to the Korean government and the mass media publicly demanding opening of the Korean advertising market (American Chamber of Commerce in Korea 1985). One month later the National Advertising Council of Korea (NACK), the only industry organization in Korea at that time, challenged the ACC arguments, urging the Korean government to delay liberalization until local agencies achieved "a higher state of maturity." The NACK advocated a gradual liberalization plan for the industry only after other sectors of the economy were liberalized (Shin 1989).

In 1986, U.S. trade representatives became more aggressive and their requests for liberalization became much more detailed. The United States pressed Korea during the Generalized System of Preferences (GSP) Consultations held in Washington, D.C., on August 14, 1986. The GSP is a special tax system to give U.S. trading partners, especially developing countries, the means to increase their exports to the United States. By reducing import duties, the United States seeks to give the exports of these developing countries a competitive advantage over other, more developed countries. Therefore, GSP not only benefits the exporting countries, but also becomes a means by which the United States is able to leverage its vulnerable trading partners. The United States threatened Korea that if it did not open its advertising market, it would face a reduction in the GSP benefits that Korea was receiving for some of its exports to the United States (Kim 1987). The United States actually used the leverage of GSP benefits to reduce Korea's trade barriers in several areas covering intellectual property rights, motion pictures, cigarettes and insurance. After several threats, the United States finally stopped GSP benefits for Korea in January 1988 (Embassy of the Republic of Korea 1986; Chanda 1988).

In June 1987, 3 years after *Advertising Age*'s first editorial and after 2.5 years of negotiation and pressure from the United States, the Korean government finally relaxed this "barrier" by moving advertising from the "negative" list to the "restricted" list under the Foreign Capital Inducement Law. This measure opened the way to equity ventures between U.S. and Korean agencies by enabling foreign companies to invest in and own up to a 49 percent interest in Korean agencies. Following the new policy the Korean government tried to resist U.S. pressure for a complete opening of the market by maintaining the position that it would not immediately allow the operations of wholly owned subsidiaries of foreign advertising agencies in Korea. This position did not last long, however. In the end, in October 1988, during the ninth U.S.–Korean Economic Consultations and U.S.–Korean Trade Subgroup Talks, Korea announced that it would allow majority foreign-owned joint ventures in 1990 and wholly owned subsidiaries in 1991 (Kim 1990). As in the cases of intellectual property rights and motion picture distribution, Korea was forced to open its advertising market under the threat of Section 301 investigations. This decision ushered in a new era for the Korean advertising industry.

The whole process of market liberalization reveals the changed and rede-fined relationship between the United States and Korea in the post–Cold War era in terms of economic interests. The United States considered foreign investment restrictions on advertising a nontariff trade (or service) barrier. Thus, the United States dealt with the opening of the Korean advertising market as part of trade negotiation pacts. A bilateral trade negotiation allowed the United States to use its global economic and political power to leverage Korea unilaterally to open up and restructure its markets for exploitation by U.S.–based transnational advertising agencies (TNAAs). In particular, the United States obtained its goal by utilizing GSP benefits and the Section 301 provision. This U.S. commercial victory over Korea is a typical example of its continuous dominant position vis-à-vis Korea. However, while Korea was forced to open its doors to transnational advertising agencies, the structure of the Korean economy and the advertising industry—dominated in large part by the *chaebol*—created challenges for the foreign agencies. These are described next.

The Structure of the Korean Advertising Industry

THE DOMINANCE OF LARGE IN-HOUSE AGENCIES

The Korean advertising industry is characterized by many full-service, in-house advertising agencies. As the Korean economy was expanding in the 1970s, large conglomerates—the *chaebol*—needed to advertise their products and thus created their own in-house agencies. The *chaebol* could save money and maintain control over the campaign development by using the in-house agency. This meant that the advertising industry in Korea was dominated by the in-house agencies within the *chaebol*.

As Table 6.3 shows, among the top 10 agencies, the eight largest are in-house agencies (Union Advertising failed to respond to the survey by Korean Federation of Advertising Associations and was omitted from the Table). Only one agency among the top 10 agencies, Seoul D'Arcy Masius Benton & Bowles (DMB&B), is an independent agency. A handful of *chaebol* controls the Korean economy in general; and as a subgroup, the in-house agencies of these *chaebol* dominate the advertising industry.

The relative strength of these in-house agencies results from their relationships with their parent companies, which consistently have been the top 10 advertisers in Korea (see Table 6.4). The Samsung Group, which includes Samsung Electronics and Cheil Sugar, controls Cheil Communications—the largest advertising agency in Korea. Lucky-Goldstar controls LGAd. Pacific Chemical controls Dongbang Ad. The Lotte Group, which includes Lotte Confectionery and Lotte Chilsung, controls Daehong Advertising; and the Hyundai Group, which manufactures Hyundai Auto, controls Diamond Advertising. Among the major industrial conglomerates, only the Daewoo Group does not have its own in-house agency.

Table 6.3.   The Top 10 Agencies and Their Group Affiliations and Percent of Billings from Group Affiliations in Korea, 1991*

Rank	Agency	Type of Agency	Group Affiliations (*chaebols*)	Total Billings (million won)	% Billings from the Group
1	Cheil Comm.	IH	Samsung	217,403	63.2
2	LGAd	IH	Lucky-Goldstar	133,771	65.4
3	Daehong	IH	Lotte	128,052	58.1
4	Oricom	IH	Doosan	108,003	21.1
5	Korad Ogilvy & Mather	IH	Haitai	95,827	29.6
6	Samhee Comm.	IH	Korea Explosive	85,199	36.5
7	Diamond Ad	IH	Hyundai	82,146	58.6
8	Dongbang Ad	IH	Pacific Chemical	66,669	43.1
9	Seoul DMB&B	ID	—	40,200	—
10	Geoson	ID	—	24,847	—

Source: Korean Federation of Advertising Associations, *Kwangkogye Donghyang Bunsuk Bogosuh*, vol. 19, 1992, 159.
Note: IH, in-house agency; ID, independent agency.
*Union Advertising did not respond to the survey conducted by the Korean Federation of Advertising Associations (KFAA) and was therefore not included in the statistics. However, the estimates of Union Ad's 1991 total billings might put Union Ad in ninth position after Dongbang.

Table 6.4.   The Top 10 Advertisers by Brand in Korea, 1991 and 1992

Rank	Top 10 Advertisers in 1991	Group Affiliations (*chaebols*)	Top 10 Advertisers in 1992	Group Affiliations (*chaebols*)
1	Samsung (electronics)	Samsung	Samsung (electronics)	Samsung
2	Lucky (detergent, chemicals and cosmetics)	Lucky-Goldstar	Lucky (detergent, chemicals and cosmetics)	Lucky-Goldstar
3	Goldstar (electronics)	Lucky-Goldstar	Pacific Chemical (detergent and cosmetics)	Pacific Chemical
4	Pacific Chemical (detergent and cosmetics)	Pacific Chemical	Goldstar (electronics)	Lucky-Goldstar
5	Daewoo (electronics)	Daewoo	Daewoo (electronics)	Daewoo
6	Lotte (confectionery)	Lotte	Lotte (confectionery)	Lotte
7	Lotte Chilsung (soft drinks)	Lotte	Cheil Sugar (food)	Samsung
8	Cheil Sugar (food)	Samsung	Hyundai Auto	Hyundai
9	Daewoong (pharmaceutical)	Daewoong	Daewoo Auto	Daewoo
10	Ildong (pharmaceutical)	Ildong	Lotte Chilsung (soft drinks)	Lotte

Source: Cheil Communications, 1993, *Advertising Year Book 1992*, 645.

These large in-house agencies handle outside accounts as well as inside accounts, but their major financial strength comes from their parent corporation. As Table 6.3 indicates, among these "major" in-house agencies, LGAd is the agency most dependent upon the parent company in terms of its billings (65.4 percent of its total billings were generated from the group), followed by Cheil Communications (63.2 percent) and Diamond Ad (58.6 percent). On the other hand, Oricom and Korad Ogilvy & Mather have a relatively small portion of group billings, 21.1 percent and 29.6 percent, respectively.

The dependence of in-house agencies on the parent corporation has various implications. The biggest advantage of in-house agencies is their stability in terms of their clients. Internal clients associated with their parent company become automatically guaranteed accounts for in-house agencies. Hence, in-house agencies are less vulnerable to external factors such as economic recession and can receive financial support from their group. Another advantage is that in-house agencies are able to receive detailed information on marketing strategies from their inside clients.

In terms of efficiency, however, in-house agencies have several disadvantages. Due to the hierarchy within any group, these agencies tend to be bureaucratic, which slows down the process of operations and creates difficulties in planning and executing advertising campaigns. According to a survey of Korean advertising professionals, 36.5 percent of respondents pointed out that in-house agencies were influenced by the parent company in various ways that restricted prompt servicing (Cho 1989).

Another disadvantage of in-house agencies is their close relationship with the clients. Normally, advertising agencies work in an equal partnership with their client; however, most in-house agencies in hierarchical Korean society satisfy their clients by following the directives of their clients. Most expatriates working in Korea consider this relationship the most unique aspect of the Korean advertising culture (*Kwangko Chongbo* 1992). Also, the bureaucratic and administrative practices and structures of in-house agencies inhibit the mobility of advertising professionals, as most important management positions tend to be awarded for years of service to the corporation without regard to advertising experience.

The economic power of the advertising industry is also concentrated in large in-house agencies. In 1990, the 10 largest agencies accounted for 45.3 percent of total advertising expenditures. In 1991, their market share was 42.2 percent. Although the market share of the top 10 agencies decreased slightly due to the liberalization of the market and the loss of international clients to transnational agencies, the largest Korean agencies still maintained a dominant position in the market. The economic power of the top 10 agencies is even greater when we examine their billings in broadcast advertising. As Table 6.5 indicates, in 1990 the 10 largest agencies controlled 75 percent of total broadcasting expenditures spent by the 64 "accredited" broadcast advertising agencies. In 1991, the top 10 agencies accounted for 67.4 percent of total broadcasting expenditures spent by 85 advertising agencies; and in 1992 their market share was 66.5 percent of total broadcasting expenditures by 95 advertising agencies. Even with the increased number of advertising agencies, the market share of the top 10 agencies in broadcast media is highly oligopolistic. Considering the limited availability of broadcast advertising time in Korea, the dominant power of the top 10 agencies in broadcast media amounts to significant leverage over other mid-sized and small agencies, and inhibits growth of these agencies into the broadcast advertising market.

Table 6.5. Broadcast Advertising Expenditures of the Top 10 Agencies and Market Share of Total Broadcast Advertising Expenditures in Korea 1990–92 (million won)

Rank	Agency	1990	1991	1992
		(% Market Share)		
1	Cheil Comm.	85,926 (13.0%)	89,267 (12.2%)	123,295 (13.3%)
2	Daehong	75,080 (11.4%)	77,213 (10.5%)	92,697 (10.0%)
3	LGAd	67,891 (10.3%)	68,102 (9.3%)	89,822 (9.7%)
4	Korad Ogilvy & Mather	52,439 (7.9%)	57,866 (7.9%)	73,634 (7.9%)
5	Dongbang	38,177 (5.8%)	39,753 (5.4%)	50,819 (5.5%)
6	Oricom	46,535 (7.1%)	37,525 (5.1%)	49,924 (5.4%)
7	Samhee Comm.	36,040 (5.5%)	36,598 (5.0%)	39,694 (4.3%)
8	Diamond Ad	28,998 (4.4%)	33,417 (4.6%)	39,187 (4.1%)
9	Union	39,238 (5.9%)	31,976 (4.3%)	36,071 (3.9%)
10	Seoul DMB&B	24,783 (3.7%)	22,806 (3.1%)	22,426 (2.4%)
	Total Broadcasting Expenditures of the Top 10 Agencies	495,107 (75%)	494,523 (67.4%)	617,569 (66.5%)
	Total Broadcasting Expenditures of All Accredited Agencies	659,844	733,768	928,006
	Number of All Accredited Agencies for Broadcast Media	64	85	95

Source: Cheil Communications, 1994a, *Advertising Year Book 1993*, Tables 12 and 13, 266–267; Cheil Communications, 1993, *Advertising Year Book 1992*, Tables 7 and 10, 284 and 286.

THE DIFFICULTIES ENCOUNTERED BY INDEPENDENT ADVERTISING AGENCIES

In an industry dominated by large in-house agencies, independent advertising agencies have struggled to survive in the market. They have neither the resources nor the high-profile accounts to attract the best talent. Because their client base is unstable and relatively weak, these agencies are vulnerable to cash flow problems.

The increased number of newly established in-house agencies, together with the opening of the market to transnational advertising agencies, led 34 independent agencies to form their own association in 1990, named the Korean Association of Independent Advertising Agencies. This new association represents an alternative to the Korean Association of Advertising Agencies—an association dominated by in-house advertising agencies. The major objectives of this new association are to address members' problems, raise the voice of independent agencies in the industry and seek better ways to cope with the rapidly changing market environment (*Hankook Ilbo* 1990).

Owing to relaxed accreditation requirements for advertising agencies in the late 1980s and in the early 1990s, the number of advertising agencies increased from 12 in 1988 to 95 in 1992. It would seem that the market reflects healthy competition among many advertising agencies. However, what this really means is that although the number of advertising agencies increased, the slice of the advertising market pie for each independent agency decreased, because more independent agencies had to compete with one another for the same small portion of the market remaining after the major in-house agencies had taken the lion's share.

When external factors such as economic recession hit the industry, independent agencies became more vulnerable than major in-house agencies. While major in-house agencies continued to grow or experienced slower growth, large and mid-sized independent agencies experienced negative growth from 1990 to 1991. The total billings of the three largest independent agencies, Seoul DMB&B, Geoson, and Nara, dropped in 1991 (see Table 6.6). Among these three, Nara Advertising experienced severe reduction in its total billings mainly due to its loss of major transnational advertisers to TNAAs (Kim 1990).

By comparison, under the same economic circumstance, due to their structural strength and financial power, large in-house advertising agencies were more able to endure the recession. Among large in-house agencies only Daehong Advertising showed negative growth in 1991; LGAd, Dongbang and Oricom had slow growth. Despite the economic recession, Cheil Communications, Samhee and Diamond Advertising enjoyed a growth rate of more than 15 percent in 1991.

ALLIANCE OF LARGE IN-HOUSE AGENCIES AND TRANSNATIONAL ADVERTISING AGENCIES

When the Korean advertising market was liberalized, it was the large in-house agencies that immediately developed relationships with TNAAs. Paradoxically, they had been the main outspoken opponents against market liberalization. By and large, U.S. TNAAs entered the Korean market in one of three ways: by purchasing either a minority or a majority stake in an existing Korean agency; by establishing a new agency with Korean partners as a joint-venture company; or

Table 6.6.   The Growth Rate of Large In-House Agencies and Independent Agencies in Korea, 1990–91

Type of Agency	Agency	Total Billings (million won)		Approximate % Growth Rate
		1990	1991	
In-House Agencies	Cheil Comm.	184,770	217,403	17.6
	LGAd	128,052	133,771	4.4
	Daehong	128,838	128,052	−0.006
	Oricom	105,338	108,003	2.5
	Korad Ogilvy & Mather	86,768	95,827	10.4
	Samhee	68,195	85,199	24.9
	Diamond	66,505	82,146	23.5
	Dongbang	66,145	67,669	2.3
Independent Agencies	Seoul DMB&B	44,778	40,200	−10.2
	Geoson	26,802	24,847	−7.3
	Nara	19,829	15,000*	−24.4

Source: *Korean Federation of Advertising Agencies*, vol. 19, 1992.
*For the 1991 total billings of Nara, "Dokrip kwangkohoesa Uryuum manha [Independent Advertising Agencies Undergo Hard Times]," *Maeil Kyungje Sinmun* [*The Economic Daily*], February 20, 1992.

by developing an affiliate relationship with a Korean agency without any equity involvement. Two powerful transnational agencies, J. Walter Thompson and Mc-Cann-Erickson took a majority holding in existing Korean agencies. Others including Ogilvy & Mather, Backer & Spielvogel Bates Worldwide and DMB&B purchased a minority stake in Korean agencies. Without management control in the purchased agencies, these three TNAAs offer their worldwide clients to their Korean partners.

Four transnational advertising agencies, Cheil Bozell, Dentsu, Young & Rubicam Korea, DDB Needham Dai-Ichi Kikaku Korea and Leo Burnett Sonyon formed joint venture agreements. Although these four agencies are "transnational," Korean partners, mostly large Korean in-house agencies, hold the majority stake and management control of these agencies.

The last method was for TNAAs to develop affiliate relationships without any equity involvement in Korean agencies, as they had during the pre-liberalization period. BBDO, Grey, Ketchum International, FCB, and Saatchi & Saatchi Advertising are in such a relationship with Korean agencies (Table 6.7). TNAAs tend to choose this strategy when they need time to research the market or when they do not have strong international clients in the market. Under these agreements, most Korean agencies have a division within their organizations that serves the needs of transnational corporations for their affiliated foreign partners. Alliances between large Korean in-house agencies and TNAAs were based on mutual interests. While foreign capital needed stable and profitable Korean partners for their establishment in the new market, the Korean partners needed global clients and the advertising skills of TNAAs for the maintenance of their dominance in the market. In addition alliances were mainly determined by the finan-

Table 6.7. TNAAs in Korean Market, Their Form of Investment and Their Korean Partners as of 1994

Type of Relationship	Foreign Agencies	Korean Agencies	Title of New Agencies	Year of Establishment
Majority foreign-owned agencies	McCann-Erickson (51%)	Creworld	McCann-Erickson (Korea)	1989
	J. Walter Thompson (100%)	Business World Services	J. Walter Thompson, Korea	1989 [a]
Minority foreign-owned agencies	Ogilvy & Mather (30%)	Korad, International	Korad, Ogilvy & Mather	1988
	DMB&B (20%)	Seoul Ad.	Seoul DMB&B	1990
	BSBW (10%)	Diamond	Diamond	1988
Joint ventures of U.S. and Korean agencies	Bozell (30%)	Cheil Comm.	Cheil Bozell	1989
	Dentsu, Young & Rubicam (49%)	Oricom	DYR Korea[b]	1989
	DDB Needham (24.5%)	Daehong	DDK	1991
	Dai-Ichi Kikaku (24.5%)			
	Leo Burnett (40%)	Sonyon	Leo Burnett Sonyon	1991
Affiliations or associations	BBDO	LGAd	LGAd	1985
	Lintas	Samhee	Samhee:Lintas[c]	1984–1992
	Grey	Geoson	Geoson Grey	1990
	FCB (Daiko)	Union	Union FCB	1992
	Saatchi & Saatchi	IMC	IMC Saatchi & Saatchi	1989

Note: TNAA, transnational advertising agency.
[a] This date is for the establishment of Business World Service (BWS). The contract of JWT and BWS was made in August, 1990.
[b] DYR Korea is a new name for HDM Korea, as Havas left a joint venture partnership from HDM in 1990 and HDM (Havas, Dentsu, and Y & R Marsteller) was changed into DYR (Dentsu and Y & R).
[c] Lintas: Worldwide had an associate relationship with Samhee since 1984, but it broke with Samhee in September 1992 in order to establish its own office in Korea.

cial interests of both parties: whether Korean agencies were willing to share their equity with Tnaas; or whether TNAAs had large and stable transnational clients in Korea that enabled them to negotiate their partnership with Korean agencies.

The Korean Advertising Industry after Market Liberalization

ACCOUNT TRANSFER AND TURNOVER OF PERSONNEL

The consequences of the entry of transnational agencies into the Korean marketplace has been twofold. First, most transnational advertisers have moved their accounts from their old Korean agencies to foreign advertising agencies. This has resulted in a dual structure in the Korean advertising industry whereby transnational agencies serve transnational clients and Korean agencies handle domestic clients.

A second factor in the emergence of a dual industry was the cultural and communication barriers between transnational clients and Korean advertising personnel. The differences of culture, language and ways of doing business have made it difficult for both parties to develop successful business relationships. It is hard for transnational advertisers to communicate with Korean professionals and to understand the Korean style of business. Korean professionals, on the other hand, tend to be reluctant to communicate directly with foreigners, as they are often uncomfortable with foreign clients and because these clients demand more-sophisticated services (for example, detailed market segment analyses and media research) from agencies than do domestic clients.

The rapid growth of the Korean advertising industry and the establishment of new agencies in the 1980s caused a shortage of qualified advertising personnel and resulted in rapid turnover rates. When the market opened, most transnational advertising agencies recruited well-trained and experienced personnel from local agencies with offers of higher salaries and better benefits. Thus, market liberalization further accelerated the shortage of qualified labor by stimulating a migration of qualified workers to transnational advertising agencies. This recruiting practice invoked many concerns among Korean advertising professionals, as TNAAs took the few personnel specializing in international accounts from domestic agencies. Moreover, most Korean employees who joined TNAAs often did not hold important managerial positions. Expatriates held supervisory positions and directed all the detailed and practical aspects of the advertising business.

Korean employees working in foreign-owned or -operated agencies have slowly begun to feel the power inequalities in their companies, as a senior Korean account executive reflects:

McCann-Erickson is an ideal place for Korean advertising professionals who want to have intensive experiences in international advertising. However, there are some problems here. Korean employees have less power and their influences on the agency work are insignificant and limited. We cannot join the important meetings where major decisions are made. If we do, we mostly do many simple tasks such as writing a report about the meeting. As simple followers, Korean employees are often isolated from the company's operations. This working condition discourages most of my colleagues in foreign agencies, and many have left their "ideal agencies" and gone back to Korean agencies.

(Kim 1994, 307)

Against the TNAAs' claim that they value and guarantee equal relationships among their employees, an invisible wall exists between Korean employees and expatriates working in Korea.

EFFORTS TO MODERNIZE ADVERTISING PRACTICES

For over 30 years the need for an independent auditing bureau in Korea has been raised but, due to the publishers' reluctance to make public their circulation figures and due to the small scale of the domestic advertising industry itself, an auditing bureau was never established. The opening of the Korean advertising industry to foreign companies, however, prompted the establishment of an audit bureau of circulation and the development of television ratings services, both long awaited by the Korean advertising industry. In addition it pushed local advertising agencies to turn to market research and audience studies.

In May 1989 the Korea Audit Bureau of Circulation (KABC) was finally established to organize circulation audits of print media. The KABC is a tripartite organization of advertisers, advertising agencies and publishers. By 1992, 23 out of Korea's 85 dailies had become members of the KABC, which accounted for nearly 95 percent of total newspaper circulation (Chun 1992). Though it has finally been established, KABC is still experiencing difficulties in performing its role. For example, it planned to present circulation figures of the major Korean dailies and other print media to the public by July 1992, but failed because the media refused to provide circulation figures. Along with an effort to make print advertising "scientific," the advertising industry also prompted the need for a television ratings system. By 1992, two media-rating companies were operating: Media Services Korea (MSK; established 1991) and Korea Survey Gallup Polls (KSG; established in 1990).

In addition many local advertising agencies are making efforts to develop the science of advertising, build research centers for consumer studies, and develop effective marketing models. Since Cheil Communications established the first marketing research institute among domestic agencies in November 1991, other major large agencies such as Daehong, Korad, LGAd and Seoul DMB&B have followed suit.

INCREASE OF BROADCAST ADVERTISING TIME

Since the market liberalization, foreign advertising companies have tried to increase their access to audiences and consumers. Their major concern has been the lack of advertising air time in the media. U.S. advertising agencies have specifically requested several changes during talks between the ACC and Korean government officials: to have daytime broadcasting, to raise prices for advertising time/space in media, to establish new private television stations, and to increase the amount of advertising time from 8 percent of total broadcasting air time to 10 percent. In addition the Chamber asked the government to change advertising formats in broadcasting from before and after programs and to allow for commercials in the middle of programs as is done in the United States (Kim 1990).

Although all these requests had also been made by Korean counterparts for many years, the voices of foreign companies exert strong pressure on the Korean government. Although the government has not yet responded to all of their requests, it has allowed for the establishment of a new broadcasting network—the Seoul Broadcasting System (SBS), a private television/radio station that first aired in 1990. The opening of SBS is seen by advertising professionals as a major step toward solving the problem of the lack of advertising air time. In April 1994 the Korean government further announced that it would increase advertising time in broadcast media from 8 percent of total broadcasting air time to 10 percent (*Chosun-Ilbo* 1994a).

THE USE OF FOREIGN MODELS AND FOREIGN LANGUAGE IN ADVERTISEMENTS

Since market liberalization, foreign models appear more frequently in television and magazine advertisements, and the use of foreign language in advertisements has intensified. Previously Korea did not allow the use of foreign models in television advertisements; however, when the Korean Broadcasting Commission began to preview all broadcast advertisements in 1989, the commission lifted this restriction. Since then, foreign movie stars and singers such as Sofia Mars, Brook Shields and Kenny Rogers gradually have begun to appear on Korean television. Besides television, magazines have become a popular medium for advertisements using foreign models. This largely results from the tendency of TNCs to use global campaigns to reduce production costs.

Regardless of their effectiveness, Korean and transnational advertisers pay a premium to attract foreign stars and celebrities. According to Wan Yang Choi, who compared the effectiveness of appeals between foreign models and Korean models, there was a slight difference in brand recall, but no difference in terms of effectiveness between advertisements using foreign models and those using local models (Choi 1990). Beyond the economic implications, this use of foreign models may erode traditional cultural values and promote the Western consumer ideology. In an analysis of Korean advertisements from 1965 to 1989, Gee Hyun Chung (1990) showed that Western consumer ideology has been intrinsically embedded in Korean advertisements from the time when modern advertising emerged in the 1960s, and that it has been greatly increasing. In addition to promoting foreign brand names, the advertisements for these products have emphasized a more Westernized consumer ideology than before (Chung 1990).

According to a study by the Korean Federation of Consumer Protection Associations, in 1991, 58.5 percent of the advertisements in the sample used "improper" language (for example, incorrect use of words and meaning and mix of English and Korean letters in the same sentence), an increase from 32.1 percent since 1990. The category in which foreign language is most used is fashion advertisements, and foreign language is now even used for advertisements aimed at children (Lee 1992).

During June 1992, Korea's Department of Information and Culture analyzed 4,056 advertisements of consumer products from four television channels, seven radio channels, 28 daily newspapers and 28 magazines. It revealed that 36.7 percent of its sample advertisements (1,488 advertisements) had foreign language in them. Among 1,488 advertisements with foreign language, fashion advertisements used the greatest amount of foreign language (a total of 367 advertisements), followed by 245 food and beverage advertisements and 231 drug advertisements (Ko 1992). Chung (1990) also revealed that after the adoption of foreign brand names, the advertisements for these brands used more Westernized forms, especially foreign words in headline, subline and copy. Thus the market liberalization paved the way toward intensifying the reproduction of Western consumer ideology in Korean advertisements, partly through the mechanisms of foreign models and language.

Advertising Regulation and Public Policy Issues

According to a survey by the Department of Information, there are about 190 rules and regulations regarding advertising in Korea (Korean Federation of Advertising Associations 1991). This figure reflects the complexity of advertising regulations in Korea. There have been continuous conflicts between the advertising industry and advertising critics. The industry complains that many "unnecessary" rules and regulations inhibit the development of creativity of advertising. Advertising critics, particularly the consumer associations, argue that these rules are not carried out in advertising practices, and hence ask for more-detailed rules and clearer applications.

Unlike in the United States, the freedom of "commercial speech" for advertising is not fully recognized in the Korean constitution. Advertising is viewed as a profit-seeking business and, therefore, Korea excludes the "right to advertise" from the protection of the freedom of expression. Because of this, a branch of the Korean government had been previewing all broadcast advertising since 1976 (Korean Federation of Advertising Associations 1991).

When the Chun Doo Whan administration took power in Korea in 1980, it passed the Korean Broadcasting Advertising Corporation Law (KBACOL) on December 31, 1980, and established the KOBACO as a government agency on January 22, 1981. The Korean Broadcasting Advertising Corporation serves as the intermediary between the broadcast media and advertising agencies (and advertisers). Under the KBACOL the broadcast media have to make a deal with advertising agencies through KOBACO, which has come to serve as the only sales agent for all broadcast time.

KOBACO's major functions were to recognize advertising agencies, to sell advertising time on the broadcast media and to preview all the TV and radio commercials before they aired through the Broadcasting Advertising Preview Committee (BAPS). However, since the Korean Broadcasting Commission began to preview all broadcast advertisements in 1989, KOBACO has ceased to perform the second function and focused on accrediting advertising agencies and selling advertising time.

Today every advertisement for television and radio has to be previewed by the BAPS of the Korean Broadcasting Commission. If the advertisements do not violate any restrictions, the BAPS issues a certificate of approval to agencies. Agencies are required to submit a final, previewed advertisement with the certificate of approval to KOBACO for distribution to each TV station. When commercials are submitted, agencies are not yet sure of in which time slots their advertisements will appear, and hence submit the spot in three types, 15-, 20-, and 30-second formats, for possible time slots. When advertisements are rejected by the BAPS, agencies have to make changes based on the recommendations of the BAPS committee and then resubmit them for a second preview (Figure 6.1).

KOBACO collects a 20 percent commission on advertising revenues from the broadcast media and allocates 10 percent of that commission to a "public service fund," which aims to improve and develop the mass communications industry and arts and culture. KOBACO then returns approximately 9 percent of the commission to the advertising agencies and keeps about 1 to 1.5 percent for operational expenses (Cho 1991). Nonaccredited agencies can place advertisements in broadcasting media for their clients, but they cannot receive a commission from KOBACO.

THE REGULATION OF PRINT ADVERTISING

Print advertising is regulated by a review rather than by government-controlled censorship. The Korean Federation of Consumer Protection Associations (KFCPA) reviews all newspapers and magazines advertisements. If this regulatory body finds deceptiveness or untruthfulness in advertisements, the advertiser and their advertising agency are asked to correct the advertisements or withdraw them from the media. In order to avoid conflicts with interest groups and consumers that might lead to product boycotts or bad publicity, most advertisers follow the recommendations of KFCPA.

Overall the regulations and rules for print advertising are less stringent than those for broadcast advertising. For example, television advertisements for ciga-

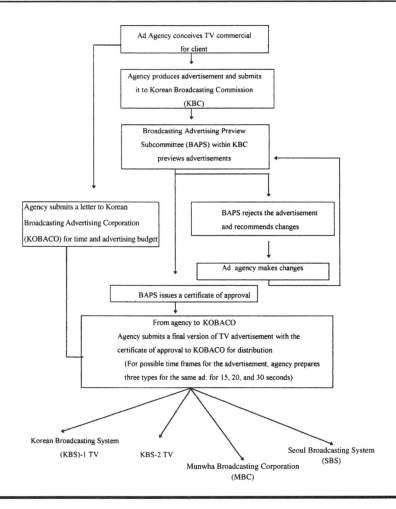

Fig. 6.1. Korean TV commercial production, distribution and previewing process.

rettes are not permitted in Korea, but cigarettes advertisements are on the increase in magazines, billboards and through sponsorships. A single brand of cigarettes is permitted to be advertised 120 times a year in magazines circulated in Korea.

THE REGULATION OF BROADCAST ADVERTISING
The Broadcast Act specifies general rules for broadcast advertising in Korea. First, advertising cannot harm traditional culture and cultural values or arouse national emotions. Second, advertising cannot solely address market-oriented characteristics and must consider its social accountability. Third, advertis-

ing time on television is restricted to 10 percent of total broadcasting air time. Advertising is allowed only in a block format (for example, before and after programs) except sports-game broadcasts, thus allowing viewers to avoid commercial messages if they wish. Fourth, unlike in the United States, comparative advertising is not allowed in Korea, as criticizing or attacking other competitors through advertisements—even with correct information—is considered "unethical" in the Korean value system. Fifth, advertising cannot use children directly to promote product sales, and children cannot even read or sing in commercials except for advertisements promoting children's health and good behavior. Advertising should not confuse children by presenting material with content that is indistinguishable from programs. To prevent this confusion, advertisements that used child models or cartoon characters from specific programs must be broadcast at different times during the day. Sixth, mostly as a result of Confucian conservatism, advertisements for feminine hygiene products, contraceptives, superstition and gambling are banned from television. For underwear advertisements, the close-up shots of specific parts of the body are not allowed. Advertisements for alcoholic beverages or adult underwear have to be broadcast in limited time slots, mostly after 10:00 p.m.

These Korean regulations are not perfect, however. Women's groups, in particular, point out that Korea has no rules or regulations restricting sexually discriminating advertisements that perpetuate sex-role bias. Hence, they suggest that the government add certain mandatory clauses, related to the use of women in advertisements, to the current regulations (Korean Council of Women's Organizations 1991).

The industry itself also attempts to improve ethical standards of advertising through self-regulation. Major advertising associations such as the Korean Advertisers Association, the Korean Association of Advertising Agencies, and the Korean Federation of Advertising Associations have developed codes of ethics to achieve these goals. The Korean Press Ethics Commission also deals with ethical aspects of advertising through monitoring and discussions with advertisers.

Consumer Issues Related to Advertising

THE RISE OF MIDDLE-CLASS CONSUMERS AND CHANGING CONSUMPTION CULTURE

The rise of the middle class and its growing buying power are some of the major reasons why Asia has become an important world market. For example, Star TV often claims that as a regional medium it can deliver the "right" consumers to global advertisers who want to reach Asia's rising middle class. According to the *Direction des Relations Economiques Exterieurs* (Foreign Economic Relations section of the French Finance Ministry), almost 40 percent of French quality clothing, perfume, cosmetics and spirits exports are consumed in

Asia (*Far Eastern Economic Review* 1993). The Korean middle class forms one of these prosperous Asian markets.

As Korea becomes transformed from a "traditional" society to an industrial and consumer society, the value of material possessions has come to signify social status. The booming phenomenon of "my car" [*mai k'a* in Korean] is one fascinating artifact of middle class consumption behavior. Koreans refer to "my car" as their private vehicle. Emerging in the middle of the 1980s and becoming popular in the late 1980s and early 1990s, this phenomenon became popular even among young college students. Although Korea has a well-developed mass transportation system, owning a passenger car has become an imperative for the middle class. Previously, owning a house was the most significant accomplishment for the working middle class. However, due to the skyrocketing prices of houses, the "my car" boom spread. Now, the desire to own a car has displaced the desire to own a house, especially among young adults. According to a survey by Korea Gallup and *Chosun Ilbo,* 35.5 percent of all respondents had their own cars and 44 percent of respondents living in Seoul owned cars. Approximately 75 percent of respondents answered that a car is one of the necessities of life (Kim 1994).

Such emerging consumption behaviors among the growing middle class make Korea an increasingly profitable market for transnational marketers. Furthermore, the growing middle class is largely made up of younger (under 40 years old) consumers who did not experience the Korean war or the poverty of the past. As these new generations form their families, their buying power and family lifestyles are becoming similar to those of the West. For example, the ritual birthday party held for children and young adults is changing from simply giving presents to throwing a U.S.-style party with family and friends with birthday hats, balloons and whistles. As the birthday-party ritual changes among younger generations, various party products such as cups, plates, invitation cards, napkins and table covers are introduced and aggressively marketed in department stores in Korea (Kang 1993).

Teenagers, often called "Generation X," represent a distinct segment within the emerging Korean middle class. They think that they can better define themselves by purchasing brand-name products. Their preference and loyalties toward famous brand names differentiate them from the older, more traditional generations in Korea (Deval 1992).

Another example of the shifting lifestyles of middle class people is in the changing consumption patterns of young married couples. In Korea the wedding culture is so developed that there are many complex things to be done for a "proper" marriage. One of them is the giving of wedding presents by the bride's family to the bridegroom's parents and their families. To show off their social status and save "face" to others, most people tend to give presents as special and as expensive as their financial resources permit (indeed some people even borrow money to purchase them). Since imports of foreign consumer products were liberalized, foreign luxury imports became "basic and popular items" for wedding presents among the middle class. Until the late 1980s these foreign imports were limited to the upper class, but since then they have become widespread among the middle class across the country. In 1994, the imports of foreign cars increased to 358 percent over the previous year and luxurious furniture increased by 80.8 percent (Kim 1994). Such consumption behaviors are encouraging to transnational marketers, who take advantage of this trend to cultivate the needs for their products among the middle class.

These consumption patterns, however, are of concern to consumer groups and other social organizations who argue that these growing consumption behaviors do not support traditional Korean cultural values. Rather than emphasizing thrift, saving, social integration and sharing, these behaviors tend to promote the values of consumption and make people without access to these goods feel relatively deprived. Critics point out that Korean spirit and morals that used to support and integrate the nation are rapidly disappearing.

Addressing these concerns, several consumer groups have focused on the representation in advertising. They have analyzed various aspects of advertising from truthfulness to sexism in advertisements. The promotion of consumption through advertising, particularly of luxury goods, has recently become highly controversial. The Young Women's Christian Association (YWCA) has its own group monitoring advertising and regularly reviewing TV and print advertisements. This group tries to raise consciousness about "problematic ads" among media and advertising professionals by publishing and distributing its review. The Korean Council of Women's Organizations is also actively involved in monitoring advertising. In 1991, its mass communication monitoring club mainly focused on three areas: sexually oriented advertisements, sexist advertisements, and advertisements promoting the consumption of luxury goods. Based on their research, they exhibited a collection of "problematic ads" with commentary as to why these advertisements were unethical or problematic. Besides publishing research reports, they also have held a public seminar for making "healthy advertising culture" (Korean Council of Women's Organizations 1991). All these efforts from women's and consumers' groups have contributed to informing and educating consumers about the flood of advertisements surrounding them.

The Future of the Mass Media and Advertising

The democratization movement in the late 1980s, liberalization of the economy, and the increased economic power and diversified interests of consumers have together brought about greater diversity of media in Korea, ranging from foreign-owned and -operated magazines to satellite television. Between 1987 and 1990, the number of print media outlets doubled and the number of weekly newspapers increased about fivefold. Along with this increase, each daily newspaper published more pages than before; the total number of pages for a daily newspaper was 16 pages in 1988, increased to 24 pages in 1990 and to 32 in 1993. The total pages of the four major daily newspapers—*Dong A, Chosun, Jung-Ang* (Central), *Hankook* (Korea)—increased 40.7 percent between 1989 and 1990 and further increased by 61.5 percent from 1989 to 1992. Advertising space in newspapers also increased 5.8 percent between 1991 and 1992 and its ratio to total newspaper space increased to 48.7 percent in 1992 from 47.9 percent in 1991 (Cheil Communications 1994a). Among the media, newspapers became the leading vehicle for advertising expenditures.

The number of magazine publications also has increased and become more specialized. In particular, foreign fashion magazines such as *Elle,* a French fashion magazine, *Vogue,* a U.S. fashion magazine, and *Nonno,* a Japanese magazine, now publish Korean editions. With diversified layout and multipage photo advertisements, these foreign magazines are shifting the format of magazines in Korea from being "reading magazines" to being "picture- and photo-oriented magazines." They attract many foreign fashion advertisers and have become an important vehicle for major foreign fashion brands to introduce global fashion trends, especially to young Korean adults (Cheil Communications 1994b).

Broadcast media outlets are also increasing in number. Since the SBS, a private broadcast network, opened in December 1991, satellite television from Japan (Japanese Satellite Television) and Hong Kong (Hutch Vision's Satellite Television Asian Region Television, known as Star TV) emerged as new media channels and now reach affluent Korean viewers. According to domestic receiver manufacturers' estimates in 1992, about 10,000 households watched Star TV and about 200,000 households watched Japanese Satellite Television's three channels—NHK 1 and NHK 2, the Japanese public broadcasting channels, and WOWOW, a commercial channel (Won 1993).

The liberalization of imports has lowered the cost of satellite receivers and further broadened the availability of Star TV to larger audiences. The demand for receiver dishes increased 10 to 20 percent per month in 1990. Many middle-class Korean households have set up their own dishes on the balconies of their apartments or large dishes on top of apartment buildings to share with other households (Kim 1990). It is now common to see many antennas standing above apartments located in Korea's affluent residential areas, especially in the Kangnam area of Seoul.

Another huge potential medium for advertising space and time is cable television. Korea began experimenting with cable TV in 10,000 households in July 1991 with a system of 13 channels (seven TV channels, three FM radio channels, and three information service channels) designed and operated by Korea Telecom. CATV was initially planning to start operating in 1992, but actually began service in March 1995. According to the Korea Cable Communications Commission (KCC), CATV initially operates 15 to 20 channels, with plans for 40 available within the next 5 years. Thus, the coming era of CATV in the late 1990s will provide further opportunities for advertisers and the advertising industry.

Most importantly, advertising on cable television is not controlled by KOBACO or by any other institution. The Presidential Decree of the 1991 Cable Act puts advertising on cable television in the hands of program providers, leaving cable television entirely to the whims of the market (Chun 1993 and Han 1994). Under this government policy, there will be no limits on hours or advertising time or content. Advertising rates and distribution methods will be decided by market forces, mainly through negotiation between program providers and system operators.

Such a "liberalized" policy for CATV raises several problems; among them are questions of whether the local production industry has the capability to produce local programming to meet the increased demand, and how 15 to 20 channels are to be supplied with programs. Considering the possibility of domination by foreign programming on CATV, the Korean government has limited foreign-made programs on cable television to 30 percent of total programming time.

In a seminar held in Korea, Dan Schiller, an American communications scholar, argued that the United States and Japan are seeking to capture the emerging information markets of the Asian region and convert them to huge commercial markets for their products and technologies (Park 1992). According to Schiller, U.S. companies increased their investment in the mass communication area in Korea from $0.7 billion in 1986 to $2 billion in 1990 and Japanese companies increased their outlays from $3 billion in 1988 to $4 billion in 1990. Increasing media outlets in Korea will provide golden opportunities for the United States and Japan who want to penetrate this regional market. It means the increase of imports of their programs into Korea and an increase of advertising space and time available to transnational, as well as domestic, advertisers.

Bibliography

Advertising Age. 1984. A "No" Vote for Korea's "No" List. Editorial, August 6, p. 14.
The American Chamber of Commerce in Korea. 1985. Opening the Korean Advertising Market to U.S. Agencies. Unpublished Manuscript, September 3.
Amsden, Alice H. 1989. *Asia's Next Giant: South Korea and Late Industrialization.* New York: Oxford University Press.
Asian Advertising Review 86/87. 1987. *Asian Advertising & Marketing,* April, pp. 18–39.
Asian Advertising Review 89/90. 1990. *Asian Advertising & Marketing,* April, pp. 52–95.
Balassa, Bela. 1981. *The Newly Industrializing Countries in the World Economy.* New York: Pergamon.
Chanda, Nayan. 1988. Concession Bending: The U.S. Cuts Trade Benefits for Four Asian Exporters. *Far Eastern Economic Review,* February 11, p. 68.
Cheil Communications. 1993. *Advertising Year Book 1992.* Seoul.
Cheil Communications. 1994a. *Advertising Year Book 1993.* Seoul.
Cheil Communications. 1994b. *Kwangko Yonkam '93 Pyolch'aek: Kwangkokwanryon-*

popkyuchip [Supplement to Advertising Yearbook 1993: Advertising Regulations]. Seoul.

Cho, B.R. 1989. Urinara kwangkotaehaengsanopui t'uksong mich' palchon panghyange kwanhan yonku [A Study for the Characteristics and Improvement of Korean Advertising Agencies Operations]. *Kwangko Yonku [Advertising Research]*, Winter, pp. 183–215.

Cho, S.Y. 1991. Korea's Nouveaux Riches Light-Up. *Business Korea*, January, pp. 34–36.

Choi, J.K. 1994. Suippumman "OK" ... Olppachin pumodul [The Wedding Culture: Only Imports "OK" ... Foolish Parents]. *Chosun Ilbo*, April 15, p. 13.

Choi, W.Y. 1990. Oekukin modelui kwangkohyokwae kwanhan yonku [A Study on Advertising Effectiveness of Foreign Models]. *Kwangko Chongbo*, February, pp. 73–76.

Chosun Ilbo. 1994a. TV kwangko nulrindanunte [The Increase of TV Advertising] (Editorial) April 12, p. 26.

Chosun Ilbo. 1994b. Foreign Luxury Consumer Imports. December 27, p. 6.

Chun, S. 1992. The Big Lie. *Business Korea*, September, pp. 58–59.

Chun, S. 1993. Lucrative Market Heightens Competition. *Business Korea*, August, pp. 33–34.

Chung, G.H. 1990. Transnationalization of Korean Advertising: A Qualitative and Quantitative Analysis. Dissertation. The University of Minnesota.

Cumings, B. 1987. The Origins and Development of the Northeast Asian Political Economy: Industrial Sectors, Product Cycles, and Political Consequences. In: Deyo, F.C., ed. *Political Economy of the New Asian Industrialism*. Ithaca and London: Cornell University Press.

Deval, A.W. 1992. Asia: A Young Hungry Marketplace. *Advertising Age*, September 7, p. S20.

Embassy of the Republic of Korea. 1986. Korean Position on Proposed GSP Modifications Submitted to the Finance Committee of the U.S. Senate. *Generalized System of Preferences*. Washington: GPO, July 10, pp. 65–74.

Evans, P. 1979. *Dependent Development: The Alliance of Multinational, State, and Local Capital in Brazil*. Princeton, NJ: Princeton University Press.

Executive Office of the President of the U.S. 1986. *Annual Report on National Trade Estimates 1985*. Washington: GPO.

Far Eastern Economic Review. 1984. Necessary Evil Rather Than Useful Marketing Tool, July 19, pp. 53–54.

Far Eastern Economic Review. 1993. French Quality Still Means *Savoir-Vivre*, October 21, p. 52.

Han, Gwang-jub. 1994. Promises and Myths of Cable Television and Telecommunications Infrastructure in Korea. In: Kim, C-W. and Kim, J-W., eds. *Elite Media Amidst Mass Culture: A Critical Look at Mass Communication in Korea*. Seoul: Nanam Publishing House.

The Hankook Ilbo. 1990. Inmul: hankuktokripkwangkohoesayon ch'otaehoechang Chung Daekilssi [Profile: Interview with Mr. Chung, Daekil, First President of the Korean Association of Independent Advertising Agencies], December 13, p. 13.

Kang, B.W. 1993. Sokusik p'at'i kuknaesangryuk inki [Western-style Party Popular]. *Chosun Ilbo*, U.S. Edition, December 15, p. 6.

Kim, C.H. 1990. Takukchok kwangkotaehaengsa hankukur molryuwa [Rush of Transnational Advertising Agencies into the Korean Advertising Industry]. *Kwangko Chongbo*, December, pp. 60–65.

Kim, H.G. 1990, December. Takukchok kwangko taehaengsa [Transnational Advertising Agencies]. *Wal Kan Ad Chu Nal*, pp. 90–95.

Kim, H.S. 1994. [Car: Seoul Area 44% Owns 'My Car']. *Chosun Ilbo*, May 14.

Kim, J.H. 1990. Takukchok kwangkohoesaui chinch'ulroswi [Rush of Transnational Advertising Agencies into the Korean Industry]. *Kwangko Chongbo*, December, pp. 59–63.

Kim, K.K. 1994. The Globalization of the Korean Advertising Industry: History of Early Penetration of TNAAs and Their Effects on Korean Society. Doctoral Dissertation. State College: The Pennsylvania State University.

Kim, K.S. 1991. The 1964–65 Exchange Rate Reform, Export-Promotion Measures, and Import-Liberalization Program. In: Cho, L-J and Kim, Y.H., eds. *Economic Development in the Republic of Korea: A Policy Perspective*. Honolulu: The East-West Center, pp. 101–134.

Kim, S.S. 1987. Olbarn kaebang sikiya bumui jal koryohaeya [Better Consider a Right Time and Range for Opening]. *Kwangko Chongbo*, March, pp. 39–40.

Ko, Jin Ha. 1992. Saenghwalyongpum 37% kukchokopsnun kwangko [37 Percent of Consumer Products Uses Advertisements Without Any National Identity]. *Dong A Ilbo*, September 4, p. 11.

Korean Council of Women's Organizations. 1991. *Reports on the Research about Print Advertising in Korea*. Seoul. December.

Korean Federation of Advertising Associations. 1992. Kihoek—'91 Pangsong kwangkohoesa ch'wikupko [Feature: '91 Billings of Broadcast Advertising Agencies]. *Kwangkogye Donghyang*, March 3, pp. 4–11.

Korean Federation of Advertising Associations 1992. Pangsongkwangko taehaenginchungjokon mich' ch'wokupkko ch'ui [The Trend of Recognition Regulations for Advertising Agencies]. *Kwangkogye Donghyang*, March, pp. 13–14.

Korean Federation of Advertising Associations. 1991. Yongop 1 nyonjjae machnun oekukkye kwangkohoesa hyonhwang [The First Anniversary of Foreign Advertising Agencies in Korea]. *Kwangkogye Donghyang*, June, pp. 6–7.

Kwangko Chongbo. 1992. T'uchip I: kwangkosichang kaebang 1 nyon [Special Feature: The First Anniversary of Advertising Market Opening]. KOBACO, March, pp. 39–61.

Lee, Ku Kyung. 1992. Saenghwalyongpumkwangko "oekuko ch'umch'unda" [Foreign Language in Advertisements for Consumer Products]. *Kyunghyang Sinmun*. May 12.

National Advertising Council of Korea. 1985. Hankukkwangkosichang kaebange kwanhan konuiso [Recommendations on the Liberalization of the Korean Advertising Industry]. Unpublished Manuscript, October.

The Office of the U.S. Trade Representative. 1987. *1987 National Trade Estimate Report on Foreign Trade Barriers*. Washington: GPO.

Park, S.J. 1992. Sonjinkuk "chonpach'imryak" simkakhada ["Broadcasting Invasion" by Advanced Countries is Serious]. *Kyunghyang Sinmun*, April 15.

Shin, I.S. 1989 *Advertising in Korea*. Seoul: Si-sa-yong-o-sa, Inc.

Shin, I.S. 1991. *Advertising in Korea*. Supplement to *Advertising in Korea*, 1989 edition. April.

Twenty-Third Survey of World Advertising Expenditures: A Survey of World Advertising Expenditures in 1988. 1989. Mamaroneck, NY: Starch Inra Hooper Inc. and IAA.

Wall Street Journal. 1990. Foreign Advertisers Face Hurdles Getting Air Time on Korean TV. August 14, p. B3.

Wall Street Journal. 1991. South Korea is Seeking to Hone Giant Firms' Competitive Edge. April 30, p. A10.

Won, W-H. 1993. The Social and Cultural Impact of Satellite Broadcasting in Korea. *Media Asia,* 20 (1): 15–20.

Yoon, Y. 1994. Political Economy of Television Broadcasting in South Korea. In: Kim, C-W. and Lee, J-W., eds. *Elite Media Amidst Mass Culture: A Critical Look at Mass Communication in Korea.* Seoul: Nanam Publishing House, pp. 191–213.

Yum, J-O. 1987. Korean Philosophy and Communication, and The Practice of *Uye-Ri* in Interpersonal Relationships. In: Kincaid, D.L., ed. *Communication Theory: Eastern and Western Perspectives.* New York: Academic Press, Inc.

7
Advertising in India: The Winds of Change

SUBIR SENGUPTA and KARTIK PASHUPATI

The purpose of the chapter is twofold. First, a historical perspective is provided in order to acquaint the reader with the culture, government, economic policies and media environment in India. This sets the stage for the second part, which provides an overview of Indian advertising and consumer-related issues.

Background

India, a nation of about 900 million people, is bordered by the Himalayan ranges in the north, and extends as a huge wedge-shaped peninsula more than 1,000 miles long. To its south lies the Indian Ocean, to the west the Arabian Sea and to the east the Bay of Bengal. The remarkable location of India with its natural land barriers, however, was not able to isolate it from frequent invasions through the mountain passes of the north. Some of these invaders left after pillaging India, while others stayed behind. These periodic migrations, and later the colonization by the British, have had a strong influence on Indian culture and its sociopolitical institutions (Reddi 1989).

THE ARYAN INFLUENCE

The original inhabitants of India were Dravidians who were a pastoral people. Historians believe that around 1500 B.C., Aryan tribes migrated from what is now southern Russia to the northwestern part of India. The Aryans practiced a polytheistic religion that strongly influenced Hinduism, the dominant religion of

Both authors have contributed equally to the preparation of this chapter.

The authors thank Mr. Vivek Basrur, Director, DIREM Marketing Services Private Limited, Bombay, and Mr. Swaminathan S. Anklesaria-Aiyar, Editor, *The Economic Times*, New Delhi, for providing valuable resource materials without which this chapter would not have been possible. The authors are also indebted to Mr. K. Kurian, Radeus Advertising Private Limited, Bombay, for his insightful comments on an earlier draft of this chapter.

155

India (Nehru 1989). Aryan Brahmanism, the precursor of Hinduism, made its first incursion into Punjab, the northwestern part of India, in about 1500 B.C. and later moved to other parts of the subcontinent. The sects of Vaishnavism (devotees of Vishnu) and Saivism (devotees of Shiva) are the two main divisions of Hinduism that have existed all over India since the sixth century B.C. (Basham 1970). Hindus presently constitute over 80 percent of India's population (Weiner 1989).

Another legacy of the Aryan society is the strong belief in family as the basic unit of society (Basham 1959). In the last 3,000 years little has changed, except that due to increased urbanization extended families are slowly disappearing. Gender and age continue to be the main ordering principles in family hierarchy; a younger male sibling is still expected to have greater influence and formal authority over family matters than his older sister. To this day, the spheres of activity within and outside the family continue to be sharply divided between men and women (Reddi 1989).

ISLAMIC AND BRITISH INFLUENCE

In 712 A.D. the Arabs invaded and occupied parts of northwestern India. Between that time and the Mughal invasion of India in 1526 A.D., there were numerous invasions by Afghans and Turks. These invasions, however, had very little influence on the lives of ordinary people. On the other hand, the Mughals, who came from northern Afghanistan, brought freshness and life to art, architecture and other cultural patterns and popularized the use of Hindi, the national language of modern India. During their reign the Mughals built many excellent structures, most notably, the Taj Mahal. These beautiful edifices represent the zenith of Mughal imperial splendor (Nehru 1989). Although some Muslim rulers were tolerant toward the Hindus, others were not. The bigots among them used repressive measures to force many Hindus to accept Islam. Today, it is estimated that about 75.5 million Indians follow Islam (Weiner 1989), which makes India a nation with one of the largest Muslim populations in the world (Oommen 1990).

The waning power of the Mughal rulers made it easy for the Europeans to gain a foothold in India. The British, Portuguese, Dutch and French came at first to trade, but were slowly able to carve out their own territories within the Indian subcontinent. The British were the most successful among them. Operated by the East India company, which was based in London, British ships carried bullion, wool and metal to India and shipped back spices, cotton, indigo, jute, tea and coffee to Europe. In the Indian polities and culture within which the British traders operated, there was a consistent interweaving of political authority and commercial enterprise. Gradually by 1757, the British were able to get a firm control over parts of India, and by 1857, they virtually controlled the entire country (Nehru 1989).

Almost 200 years of British rule over the Indians had a lasting influence on all spheres of Indian society. As early as 1813 the British parliament publicly recognized that it was the duty of the East India Company to better the "moral condition" of its Indian subjects. Christian missionaries as a group were small and insignificant in the beginning of the 19th century, and they were permitted to work in British Indian territories under a system of licensing. They challenged Hinduism and Islam, questioning the authority and authenticity of scriptures, beliefs and the relationship of reason to belief and practice. Although their initial success at conversions was encouraging, they were not able to sustain it except among the lower classes (Brown 1994). Today, with 2.4 percent of India's population, Christians comprise the third largest religious group (Weiner 1989).

Although the British had little impact on religion in India, they proved to be much more successful in reforming the system of education. In 1835 Macaulay, then President of the Committee of Public Instruction, drew up the *Minute on Education* in which he noted that "a single shelf of European library was worth the whole native literature of India and Arabia." He believed that English education would bring light to "the children of darkness" and would bring up a class that would be "Indian in blood and color but English in taste, in opinions, in morals, and in intellect" (Brown 1994). Thereafter, a system of education similar to those experienced by students in England was introduced. A number of schools run by missionaries were opened all across India, and in 1857, the first universities were established in Calcutta, Bombay and Madras. The newly introduced system of education, along with books and journals, made it possible to transmit modern as well as traditional knowledge to the masses, rather than to just a privileged few, as had been the case under the old system.

English education resulted in a large pool of middle-class Indians who were able to meet the low-level administrative requirements of British India (Frankel 1988). This new education was to have some unexpected social and political implications. Exposed to Western literature and thought, an elite group of Indians became committed to social and political reforms, thinking—perhaps for the first time—about a new society that would transcend old barriers of caste, creed and region (Brown 1994). However, the racial discrimination practiced by the British in all walks of life, coupled with the slow pace of political reforms, disillusioned this group. That disillusionment ultimately provided the impetus for a nationalist movement led by Mahatma Gandhi, Jawaharlal Nehru and others, culminating in India's independence in 1947.

Government

When India achieved independence, it was faced with the daunting task of drawing up the blueprint of the type of government that would best suit the country's needs. Indian leaders acquainted themselves with the unwritten constitution of the British, and studied the American, French and Russian constitutions. The newly formed Indian union comprised 27 states and was federal in setup, although considerable power was concentrated at the center. For example, the central and state governments were to have concurrent power over economic and social planning, commerce, social security, health and education. The central government was to have sole authority over foreign policy, defense, internal security and revenue. Additionally, all the residual powers not specified in the constitution were to be under the purview of the center.

The Indian parliamentary system was modeled largely after the British system, with the elected representatives of the Lok Sabha (House of the People) comparable to the British House of Commons. The other house, the Rajya Sabha (Council of States), was to comprise members elected by the state legislatures (modeled after the French system) and a few members, distinguished in various fields, were to be nominated by the President. But as in Britain, real power rests with the Prime Minister, who must have majority support in the parliament (Brown 1994).

The Economy

India became independent in 1947 after almost 200 years of British rule. At independence, India had inherited an economy with serious market imperfections. The internal market mechanisms were so damaged that effective resource allocations became impossible (Tomlinson 1993). To shore up the economy, Jawaharlal Nehru, the first Prime Minister of independent India, set up the Planning Commission. The 5-year plans produced by this body were to be guidelines only, and were not designed to have any force of law. But with the Prime Minister as the ex-officio chairman, the commission had a prominent position.

The ideological predilections of Nehru and some of his close associates, who were influenced heavily by the ideals of Fabian Socialism, made them more prone to adopt a socialistic framework of economic policy (Chakravarty 1987). The Indian leaders chose to follow a mixed economy, which combines private enterprise with government planning, including overall direction and control as well as investments by the government in infrastructure areas of power, transport and communication.

In the early years a simple two-sector model of Soviet planning was adopted: investment goods (like steel and machinery) and consumption goods. The disadvantage of this strategy was the commitment of a major portion of the budget to heavy industries, which would yield low returns. Moreover, this investment would generate buying power, which would not be absorbed due to an insufficient supply of consumption goods.

These prospects did not seem to deter the Indian leaders. They believed that given the country's limited resources of capital, technical skills and foreign currency, the production of "unnecessary" consumer goods would be detrimental to the economy in the long run (Dean 1959). The Indians leaders were also conscious of the social effects of excessive consumption. As these leaders were mentored by Mahatma Gandhi during the struggle for independence, most of them considered themselves to be Gandhians, that is, followers of Gandhi's philosophy. Gandhi strongly believed that acquisitiveness breeds social inequality, exploitation and domination (Roy 1988).

Up until 1964–65, considered a high period of growth, the gross national product grew at an average annual rate of 4.2 percent and per capita net national product grew at an average rate of 1.9 percent. However, during this period there was a marked difference in the way different industries progressed. Heavy industries, of which steel industry was the top priority for investment, grew rapidly, but the production of mass consumption goods faltered.

After the mid-1960s India's economic growth began to decelerate. In 1965, India fought a war with Pakistan, which resulted in greater commitment to defense expenditure, and a reduction in the flow of foreign aid. Also, in 1965 and 1966, India suffered severe droughts. Pressured by the World Bank the Indian currency was devalued by about 50 percent in 1966. These forces pushed up consumer price index (CPI) from a base of 100 in 1960 to 167 in 1967. Another war with Pakistan in 1971, bad harvests in 1972 and 1974, and hikes in world prices for crude oil in 1974 and 1979 pushed the CPI to 420. In other words prices had increased more than four times in 20 years. Food prices were on the rise and two-thirds of the average household income continued to be spent on food, causing a crippling effect on the demand for consumer goods (Rothermund 1993).

The situation was further exacerbated by a series of acts passed during the regime of Prime Minister Indira Gandhi (no relation of Mahatma Gandhi) who moved further to the left on industrial policy. In 1969, the Monopolies and Restrictive Trade Practices (MRTP) Act was passed, enabling the government to place restrictions on new licenses for larger firms. She nationalized banks, insurance and the coal industry. In 1973, the Foreign Exchange Regulation Act (FERA) was passed solely for the purpose of restricting foreign investment. It is worth noting here that most of Mrs. Gandhi's advisors were sympathetic to the left position, and even some "conservative" bureaucrats supported the expansion of government control because it would mean enhancing their powers as grantors of industrial licenses (Weiner 1989).

The word "socialism" found its way into the Indian constitution in 1976, although it must be noted that the Indian brand of socialism is different in theory and practice from socialism elsewhere. Although it recognizes the "evils" of concentration of economic resources, socialism in India does not attempt collectivization of private property, but only to limit it; the legitimacy of private property is not questioned, but the cautious restriction of private property appears to be the sole aim (Oommen 1990). Toward that end, extremely high rates of direct taxation were imposed on upper income brackets, and indirect taxes on certain commodities termed "luxury" goods were raised to very high levels. In a country where a large portion of the population does not receive adequate nourishment in terms of caloric intake, these moves were clearly popular with the Indian voters but did not bode well for the economy in general nor for the demand for consumer goods in particular.

In order to come to grips with an economy that was rigid and faltering, Rajiv Gandhi, who became the Prime Minister in 1985, decided to adopt a new view of the state and the economy. Unencumbered by the socialistic principles espoused by his grandfather (Nehru) and mother (Indira Gandhi), Rajiv Gandhi surrounded himself with young advisors who had previously held high-level executive positions in multinational companies, and set the country on a course that was revolutionary by Indian standards.

His new strategy of liberalized imports, greater sensitivity to market signals, and liberalized rules of entry and growth for the industry, implied that the government would not shield any industry, public or private, from competition. These liberalization policies were aimed primarily at upgrading technology, reducing cost and modernizing plant and equipment. In addition the Fourth Pay Commission in 1986 more than doubled the salaries of government employees. This proved to be a tremendous boost to the purchasing power and to the explosive growth of the middle class in India (Dubey 1992).

Although the going was good during his first year in office, Rajiv Gandhi faced stiff opposition from Indian industrialists and left-leaning economists, resulting in some loss of momentum with which the new economic policies were implemented in subsequent years. Nonetheless, modest gains were made. For example, during the 1980s gross domestic product (GDP) reached an average of 5.3 percent, and per capita income increased by 40 percent. The new economic policies and the rising disposable income of the 150 million–strong middle class also had far-reaching consequences on consumption patterns. Between 1980–81 and 1990–91 the sale of room air conditioners increased 64.7 percent; refrigerators, 361.5 percent; cars, 472.3 percent; motor scooters, 1102.8 percent; and wrist watches 145.4 percent (Khatkhate 1992).

The assassination of Rajiv Gandhi in 1989 was initially seen as a setback for economic liberalization. However, Prime Minister P.V. Narasimha Rao, who assumed office in 1990, vowed to follow in the lines of his predecessor. He introduced economic policies that promised to stimulate the economy by way of easing restraints on large companies, implementing easier procedures for investment, making availability of term loans and bank finance easier, introducing hire-purchase and home financing, lowering taxes, making travel abroad easier, and stimulating the stock market (Dubey 1992). Furthermore, in an attempt to lure multinational companies to invest in India, in May 1990 the government made a policy announcement proposing to approve automatically foreign investments of up to 40 percent of common stock. Higher foreign equity would be allowed depending on the nature of the business. For example, for a wholly export-oriented business, the government would even allow 100 percent foreign equity (Price Waterhouse 1990).

According to Jalan (1990), the major beneficiary of these policies is the Indian middle class, which is currently estimated to be around 150 million, representing one of the largest consumer markets in the free world. This number is expected to grow to around 300 million by the turn of the century, surpassing the population of the United States (Dubey 1992). This group of educated Indians, with a large disposable income and exposure to the influences of the world outside, has shown a growing interest in the consumption of luxury goods (Khatkhate 1992).

The Media Environment

PRINT

The ownership of newspapers and magazines is in private hands, and the press in India has operated largely without any fear of censorship. The *Bombay Samachar,* first published in 1822, is the oldest existing daily newspaper in India. The total number of newspapers and periodicals at the end of 1989 was estimated at 27,054, including 42 that have been around for more than 100 years. As of 1987, the total circulation of newspapers was 22.6 million, with at least 136 newspapers reporting a circulation of over 75,000. The circulation figures for individual newspapers might seem low by international standards, but the reader should bear in mind that newspaper readership in India is limited by two major factors: (1) a low literacy rate, and (2) the proliferation of many languages (India has 13 constitutionally recognized "regional" languages, in addition to Hindi, the national language, and English, which is the major language of commerce and business). The rate of literacy varies widely from one state to another and this is also reflected in the differential circulation of newspapers and magazines. The newspapers and magazines with the greatest circulation are published in the states of Kerala and West Bengal, both of which have relatively higher rates of literacy than the rest of the country. In terms of prestige and political influence, however, the English-language newspapers and newsmagazines probably have the greatest impact. In recent years newspapers that are published in Hindi and other Indian languages have also become increasingly influential.

Although newspapers are by nature a regional medium, several English and Hindi newspapers have attempted to establish a national presence by publishing editions in more than one major metropolitan center. For example, *The Times of India,* an English daily, publishes not only in its original hometown of Bombay, but also in New Delhi and Bangalore. Another English daily, *The Indian Express,* is published from several cities, including Bombay, New Delhi, Madras, Hyderabad and Madurai. The presence of such multiple editions makes it easier for advertisers to use newspapers as a medium of national coverage. Likewise, several regional language newspaper chains have multiple editions within individual states.

RADIO

Radio broadcasting is a state monopoly in India. In 1930, the government of India took over two privately owned transmitters in Bombay and Calcutta and started operating them as the Indian Broadcasting Service, under the aegis of the Posts and Telegraphs Department (Mehta 1980). The name was changed to All India Radio (AIR) in 1936, and subsequently to Akashvani in 1957 (Xavier and Eashwer 1993). During the 1960s the introduction of transistor radio speeded the diffusion of radios in India. It would have grown at a faster rate if the Government of India had not treated it as a luxury item, levying a heavy import duty and collecting an annual fee from all radio owners. Gradually these policies were changed when the government realized the potential of the medium to bring about social change. As of 1991, AIR's network operated 106 stations and broadcast through 192 transmitters covering 95 percent of the population (Xavier and Eashwer 1993). Roughly 24 percent of the Indian households own a radio, and they receive about 17,000 program hours per day in 18 languages and 126 dialects (Singhal and Rogers 1989). Recently, commercial broadcasting has received a boost in the major metropolitan cities, with the franchising of several radio programs (mainly in the FM band) to private program producers.

TELEVISION

Television was introduced in Delhi in 1959 on an experimental basis with transmissions limited to 3 days a week. Regular service in Delhi began in 1965, and up until 1982 it was confined to only the major Indian cities (Mehta 1980). In 1975–76, NASA loaned India the Application Technology Satellite (ATS-6) to conduct Satellite Instructional Television Experiment (SITE) in 2,400 Indian villages (Singhal and Rogers 1989).

The first Indian satellite, INSAT-1A, was launched by NASA in 1982. During this time, coinciding with the Asian games held in Delhi, color broadcasting was introduced for the first time, resulting in an extraordinary boost to the diffusion of television in India (Singhal and Rogers 1989). In 1983, another satellite, INSAT-1B, was launched. Since then transmitters have been set up at an amazing rate. From 46 transmitters in 1984, covering 30 percent of the population, the number of transmitters in 1991 increased to 519, covering 76 percent of the population (Dubey 1992).

In 1984, Doordarshan, the state-run Indian television network, set up a second channel in Delhi, followed by Bombay, Calcutta, and Madras. And by the end of 1997, a second channel will be introduced in 16 other state capitals. The number of television sets in use in India climbed from a mere 3.63 million in 1984 to a whopping 32 million by the end of 1991, an increase of nearly nine-fold in 7 years (Xavier and Eashwer 1993).

Television in India received a tremendous boost when Hong Kong–based Satellite Television Asian Region (STAR) started beaming a variety of advertiser-supported television programs to 38 Asian nations, including India, that fall under the footprint of the broadcasting satellite, ASIA SAT-I. As STAR TV programs are not encrypted, the signals can be picked up by cable operators with one or two dishes and then transmitted to TV homes by overhead wires or underground cables. In India an estimated 17 percent of TV homes have access to STAR TV, for which they are charged a nominal monthly subscription fee that is the equivalent of about 2 to 3 U.S. dollars (Kishore 1994).

The four primary channels offered by STAR TV in India are Prime Sports, BBC World Service, Starplus (a mix of popular American and British shows) and MTV Asia. These four channels are obtained through contractual suppliers or the international market. In addition ZEE TV, a Hindi general entertainment channel affiliated with STAR TV, is available to Indian viewers (Chan 1994). According to a study conducted in 1994 by the Indian Market Research Bureau (IMRB), over 7 million homes across India have access to ZEE TV. Of these, 51.1% are in the western part of the country, 25.9% are in the north, 13.5% are in the south and 9.5% are in the east (Rediffusion Precision Media 1994). The penetration of this channel is expected to improve in the north, but further growth in the south could be limited by the fact that all of ZEE TV's programming is in Hindi, which is not very widely understood in many parts of southern India, although it is officially the country's national language.

The enormous popularity of STAR TV and its immense growth, especially in India, China, Taiwan and Israel, have sparked interest in the launching of other regional commercial satellites (Kishore 1994). Although currently there are about 2,000 dish antennae in India, this number is expected to increase very rapidly with the planned access to Malaysia's RTM and TV 3, the Philippines' ABS-CBN, Indonesia's RCTI, France's Canal Television International, Japan's NHK, Hong Kong Taiwan Business News Network and a channel from Pakistan (Xavier and Eashwer 1993). In addition an American satellite company, PanAmSat, is planning to launch its satellite PAS-4 over India for a "direct-to-home" retail service primarily dedicated to Indian viewers through its 120 channels. Viewers will need a dish and a decoder box to tune in.

The rapid proliferation of satellite broadcasts has created formidable challenges for national broadcasters, who are not in a position to satisfy the appetite of audiences who have developed a taste for sophisticated programming after having been exposed to transnational broadcasts. Consequently international broadcasters have been able to lure away audiences, and with them, advertising revenues (Khushu 1993). But in spite of that, since 1976 when the first commercials were aired on Doordarshan, its annual earnings from advertising revenues increased from $0.6 million to about $300 million in 1990 (Singhal and Rogers 1989).

The Advertising Industry

EARLY DAYS

The history of advertising in India is almost as old as the history of modern print media in the country. According to Banerjee (1981), the first newspaper in India was the *Bengal Gazette,* or *Calcutta General Advertiser,* published by a Britisher, James Augustus Hickey, on January 29, 1780. The title of the newspaper did not refer to advertising in its modern sense; the verb "to advertise" was used in its archaic sense of "to inform." However, the paper did carry a few advertisements in its first issue. Other newspapers published during the same decade also carried advertisements. During the 19th century most of the commercial advertisers in India were British business houses. The industrial revolution in Great Britain had resulted in the creation of mass-produced goods, many of which were imported by these trading companies for the Indian market. However, advertising agencies did not exist in India at that time (Banerjee 1981).

Advertising agencies began emerging in the country in the early part of the 20th century. The first recognized advertising agency in the country was B. Dattaram and Company, which was founded in 1905 (Shiva Ramu 1991). The Ind-Advertising Agency was established in Bombay in 1907, followed by the Calcutta Advertising Agency in 1909. Some leading newspapers also set up studios to provide assistance to advertisers in copywriting and illustration (Banerjee 1981).

Within the next 2 decades, a few multinational agencies had begun to establish a presence on the Indian advertising scene. A British agency, S.H. Benson, commenced operations in India in 1928. Subsequently this agency was acquired by Ogilvy and Mather, to form Ogilvy, Benson and Mather. The Indian affiliate of Ogilvy and Mather continued to be known as Ogilvy, Benson and Mather (India) Private Limited (or OBM), right until the mid-1980s, when its name was changed to Ogilvy and Mather. The J. Walter Thompson Company (JWT) commenced operations in India in 1929. JWT's Indian associate, known as Hindustan Thompson Associates (HTA), is presently the largest advertising agency in the country. Lintas India Limited was founded in 1939. Lintas was initially the house agency for Lever Brothers (operating in India as Hindustan Lever), but was later spun off by Lever into an independent company. (Lintas is an abbreviation for "Lever International Advertising Services.") Another large multinational agency, McCann-Erickson, formed an alliance with Calcutta-based Clarion Advertising in 1956. A few smaller multinational agencies also operated in India, such as the now-defunct Grant, Kenyon and Eckhardt (India) Private Limited.

In the late 1960s and early 1970s the fortunes of multinational enterprises in various sectors were adversely affected by the political climate of the country. With the objective of promoting domestic business enterprises, the Government of India began to impose restrictions on foreign ownership of equity in companies that were not involved in "core sector" activities. The most visible manifestation of this was in the strict enforcement of the FERA, by which companies not operating in the "core sector" were required to dilute their overseas equity holding to one-third (or less) of the total capital. Several multinational enterprises, notably Coca-Cola and IBM, closed their doors after being required to dilute their shareholding.

One cannot directly link the implementation of FERA with developments in the advertising industry, but there is little doubt that the socialist policies of successive governments in the 1960s and 1970s—such as the disallowance of advertising expenditures for income tax purposes—had a dampening effect on the industry and provided little incentive for new multinational entrants into the field. In the 1960s JWT divested its equity stake in HTA, which became a wholly employee-owned company. Lintas India Limited was also "Indianized" in 1969 (Shiva Ramu 1991). In overall terms, however, the industry experienced record growth during this decade, despite all the setbacks. The number of advertising agencies registered with the Indian Newspaper Society during this period grew by 58.5 percent, from 106 agencies in 1969 to 168 agencies in 1979.

Although the 1970s were not very good times for transnational advertising agencies in India, this decade did give birth to several new home-grown agencies. Some of these have become significant players in the industry today. Of the top 10 Indian advertising agencies ranked by *Advertising and Marketing* magazine (India's leading trade publication in the field) in its 1993–94 annual review, two were established in the 1960s, three in the 1970s, and two in the 1980s. The remaining three agencies in the top 10 list are transnational affiliates—HTA, Lintas and O&M—which were established several decades earlier (*Advertising and Marketing* 1994).

Today the shares in almost all the advertising agencies in India are privately held, mostly by the promoters of these enterprises. Most advertising agencies are set up under Indian corporate law as "private limited companies," which means that they are not required to trade their shares publicly. Even the major multinational subsidiaries in India—HTA, O&M and Lintas—are primarily employee-owned companies. This pattern of shareholding suggests that (a) the capital cost of entry into the advertising agency business is seldom large enough to necessitate a public offering of equity, and (b) most agency promoters are unwilling to go public and render themselves vulnerable to external financial controls and the possibility of hostile takeovers.

PERIOD OF GROWTH

In the mid-1980s the Government of India began to change its industrial policies with the objective of inviting greater overseas investment in the economy. Two policy changes that have had a direct impact on the advertising industry are (a) easing restrictions on foreign investments in various industries, including consumer products, and (b) permitting multinational companies to operate under their own names (Shiva Ramu 1991).

Almost as if the advertising industry anticipated the liberalization of the economy, a number of home-grown agencies began forming new partnerships with transnational agencies. One of the earliest alliances in this genre was a partnership in the early 1980s between Bombay-based Rediffusion Advertising and New York–based Ted Bates Advertising (which was later acquired by Saatchi and Saatchi). Neither party had a financial stake in the partnership. The stated purpose of the alliance was primarily to provide uniform servicing standards for some of Rediffusion's existing multinational clients, most notably Union Carbide, which was then marketing Eveready batteries worldwide. (Due to subsequent developments Rediffusion broke its links with Ted Bates, and is now affiliated with DY&R—Dentsu, Young & Rubicam.)

Even in the absence of a financial stake (in the form of stockholding), it soon became apparent to both Indian and multinational agencies that such partnerships could be mutually beneficial. The benefits for the multinational agencies are (a) access to expertise in the Indian market, (b) absence of the start-up costs that would be involved if they opened their own office, and (c) ability to acquire and retain multinational accounts on the basis of the claim that they can provide global coverage (and, presumably, uniform standards of creative and client services). The benefits for the Indian agencies are (a) the possibility of growth due to business from new multinationals entering the Indian market, (b) the acquisition of business from multinationals already operating in India, on the basis of affiliating with the agencies servicing their parent companies, (c) the prestige associated with multinational affiliations, (d) the access to overseas market information, and (e) the access to the research and training methodology of multinational agencies.

Shortly after the signing of the agreement between Rediffusion and Ted Bates, Saatchi & Saatchi was reported to have acquired a minority shareholding in the Bombay-based Everest Advertising. Several other indigenous agencies jumped onto the bandwagon of acquiring multinational partners. Madras-based R K Swamy Advertising Associates entered into an agreement with BBDO in 1988. Mrs. Tara Sinha, the CEO of Calcutta-based Clarion Advertising, broke away in 1985 to start her own agency (now known as Tara Sinha McCann-Erickson), taking with her not only Clarion's major clients, but also its multinational partner, McCann-Erickson. (Mrs. Tara Sinha later left the agency that she founded.) Shortly thereafter, Clarion entered into a partnership with the U.S.–based D'Arcy Masius Benton & Bowles (DMB&B), which was subsequently terminated in 1990.

The liberalization of the Indian economy in the mid-1980s and early 1990s has had several important repercussions for advertising agency affiliations. First, the number of alliances with multinational agencies has increased. Second, multinational agencies have sought to strengthen their financial control over their Indian associates through the acquisition of stock. Even transnational agencies that had earlier divested themselves of equity holdings in their Indian affiliates are seeking their way back. For example, JWT bought back a 49 percent stake in

HTA in 1993–94, reportedly at the rather high price of Rs.5,400 (US$170–180) per share (D'Souza 1994). The importance of both of these developments is underscored by the fact that 11 of the top 20 Indian advertising agencies in 1992–93 had affiliations with multinational agencies (see Table 7.1). Nine of these 10 reportedly involved some form of stock ownership by the multinational (*Advertising and Marketing* 1993a). This is a departure from the closely held pattern of stockholding that characterized Indian agencies up until the 1990s. The willingness of Indian advertising agencies to let their multinational partners acquire stock probably signals a perceived need for a larger capital base to cope with the changing structure of the industry in the coming decade.

It is probably too early to assess the true impact of the new wave of adver-

Table 7.1.   Largest Advertising Agencies in India

Agency	Capitalized Billings 1993–94 (million rupees)	Growth over Previous Year (%)	Ranking 1992–93	Ranking 1993–94	Multinational Affiliate
Hindustan Thompson Associates (HTA)	2928.38	40.6	1	1	J. Walter Thompson (JWT)
Lintas India	2443.82	21.4	2	2	Lintas Worldwide
Mudra Communications	1600.00	39.1	3	3	DDB Needham Worldwide
Ogilvy & Mather (O&M)	1217.56	30.4	4	4	Ogilvy & Mather
Ulka Advertising	1100.00	36.7	5	5	None
R K Swamy/ BBDO	695.09	37.7	7	6	BBDO
Clea Advertising & Marketing	672.41	56.8	13	7	None
Trikaya Grey Advertising	657.00	28.7	6	8	Grey Advertising
Contract Advertising	632.60	33.6	8	9	JWT
Rediffusion Advertising	624.00	44.0	12	10	DYR
MAA Communications Bozell	602.40	29.5	9	11	Bozell
Chaitra Leo Burnett	570.01	24.4	12	11	Leo Burnett
Clarion Advertising Services	420.00	68.0	NA	13	None
Enterprise Advertising	410.00	23.0	14	14	None
Concept Communications	404.91	324.6	NA	15	None
Everest Advertising	401.76	33.3	NA	16	None
Tara Sinha McCann-Erickson	332.77	21.3	16	17	McCann-Erickson
Triton Communications	312.70	60.8	18	18	None
Advertising Avenues	265.00	26.0	19	NA	None
daCunha Associates	250.13	15.7	20	17	None
Total (Top 20)	16,540.72				
Total (132 Agencies)	22,200.62				
Concentration ratio (Top 10)			42.3%	56.6%	
Concentration ratio (Top 20)			55.7%	74.5%	

Source: *Advertising and Marketing*, Agency Report (1993, 1994).
Note: NA, not available; at current exchange rates, US$1 = 35 rupees, approximately.

tising agency tie-ups. According to a report in *The Times of India,* some major multinational advertisers operating in India have indeed changed agencies in keeping with the norms dictated by their parent companies. For example, when Lufthansa decided to shift from McCann-Erickson to Dentsu, Young & Rubicam (DY&R) globally, the airline's Indian business went to DY&R affiliate Rediffusion Advertising (D'Souza, 1994). Similarly, R K Swamy/BBDO acquired the Visa International and Delta Airlines accounts on the basis of their transnational affiliation. However, transnational affiliations may not always be the determining criterion in an advertiser's selection of an advertising agency, as shown by the case of Pepsi-Cola Co. In view of Pepsi's longstanding relationship with BBDO in the United States, when Pepsi was launched in India the account was expected to go to R K Swamy/BBDO. Instead Pepsi elected to place its advertising in India with HTA.

In the near future it is expected that even medium-sized Indian agencies will seek multinational affiliation, as such an affiliation may be the price of entry in a highly competitive marketplace. This strategy might work with multinational advertisers who follow a policy of global alignment of agencies, such as Procter & Gamble (P&G) and Unilever. However, astute domestic agencies can still differentiate themselves on the basis of their expertise in specific markets. For example, Citibank (a large U.S. multinational) uses several medium-sized agencies such as Madras-based Fountainhead Communications, in addition to Lintas, its main agency of record.

LARGEST ADVERTISING AGENCIES

Indian advertising agencies were uncertain about their future at the beginning of the 1990s. Following a cash crunch in 1991, the industry was bracing itself for a recession. In 1992, the chief executive of India's largest advertising agency forecast a growth rate of 12 to 14 percent over the next 3 years—an estimate that was considered too optimistic by some others in the industry (Sen 1992). Defying these initial gloomy forecasts, advertising expenditures in India have grown at a phenomenal rate in subsequent years. According to the annual advertising agency reports compiled by *Advertising and Marketing* magazine, the capitalized billings of 131 advertising agencies were up 37.4 percent in 1993–94 over the previous year. ("Capitalized billing" is a term used to refer to media and nonmedia billings). This figure came on top of growth rates of 36.5 percent in 1992–93, 25.2 percent in 1991–92, and 17.1 percent in 1990–91 (*Advertising and Marketing* 1994). Some industry observers have urged caution in the interpretation of this data. They feel that the apparent boom in Indian advertising is partly accounted for by the steep increase in media costs during these years and does not represent a true increase in advertising volume (Kurian 1995).

In the aggregate, the 131 agencies included in the *Advertising and Marketing* Agency Report for 1993–94 reported a capitalized billing of Rs.22.2 billion, and a gross income of Rs.3.33 billion. A limitation of the report compiled by *Ad-*

vertising and Marketing magazine is that it is based on self-reported statistics volunteered by agencies that agreed to participate in the annual survey. Thus while the Indian Newspaper Society (the major accrediting body) reported the existence of 460 advertising agencies in 1988 (Shiva Ramu 1991), the 1993–94 *Advertising and Marketing* Agency Report includes data from only 131 agencies. Nevertheless this report does represent most of the larger agencies in the country (with the exception of a few that chose not to participate in the survey).

An analysis of the advertising industry data contained in the *Advertising and Marketing* Agency Report shows that the 10 largest agencies in 1993–94 accounted for 56.6 percent of capitalized billings, and the top 20 agencies together accounted for 74.5 percent of capitalized billings (see Table 7.1). These data suggest a concentration of revenues among the big players in the agency business. In the near future, too, one can expect the larger agencies to reap the greatest benefits from the entry of an increasing number of multinational brands into the Indian market. Multinational advertisers are likely to prefer agencies with transnational alliances, or at least those with a "national presence," a condition that will preclude many smaller agencies from the race.

Despite the concentration of billings among the top agencies, the *Advertising and Marketing* Agency Report for 1993–94 notes that the benefits of the rapid growth in the Indian advertising industry have not been confined to a few large advertising agencies. Of the 131 advertising agencies surveyed by the magazine in 1993–94 as well as 1992–93, only 12 registered negative growth in 1993–94. Twenty of the 131 agencies surveyed in both years reported a growth in billings of 0–20 percent, 43 reported a growth of 20–40 percent, and 56 agencies reported a growth of more than 40 percent in 1993–94, compared with the previous financial year.

SUBSIDIARY ADVERTISING AGENCIES

Advertising agencies in India, in keeping with the tradition of their counterparts in the United States, usually do not solicit new business from advertisers whose interests may conflict directly with those of the agency's existing clients. An obvious drawback of this policy from the agency's viewpoint is that it places limits on agency growth. Some large advertising agencies have managed to get around this restriction by establishing allegedly independent subsidiary or affiliate agencies that can pitch for new business without being accused of creating a conflict with existing clients. One of the earliest and most successful examples of this type of agency is Contract Advertising, which was established in 1969 as a subsidiary of HTA. In 1993–94, Contract was the ninth largest Indian agency in terms of capitalized billings. Sixty percent of its shares are owned by HTA and the rest are held by HTA's parent company, JWT. Other successful subsidiary agencies are Karishma Advertising (wholly owned by Lintas India), Hansavision (owned by R K Swamy/BBDO), Interact-Vision (owned by Mudra Communications) and The Edge Communications (owned by Everest Advertising).

FINANCIAL ADVERTISING AGENCIES

The strict implementation of the FERA by the Government of India in the late 1970s and early 1980s forced several multinational companies operating in India to dilute their foreign ownership and to offer shares to the Indian public. The Indian investor was suddenly confronted with the opportunity to own blue-chip stocks at a relatively moderate price. This resulted in a sudden and unprecedented interest in stocks and shares by middle-class investors who had hitherto preferred more-conservative savings options, such as bank deposits. Following closely on the offerings of the blue-chip multinational stocks, many Indian companies cashed in on the public's newfound enthusiasm for the stock market by making public offerings of their shares. Soon the growing multitude of corporations seeking to get the attention of investors gave rise to a very specialized organization—the financial advertising agency.

These advertising agencies have little involvement in corporate or brand advertising for their clients, but they derive a major portion of their business from publicizing stock, share and bond issues. Financial agencies differentiated themselves from the competition by undertaking nonadvertising activities that traditional agencies were initially reluctant to handle, such as arranging stockbroker conferences and handling press relations (Chiravuri 1992). In the process such agencies have created an attractive niche market, which is estimated to range from 20 to 40 million rupees.

The oldest and best-known financial advertising agency is Calcutta-based Pressman Advertising and Marketing, which ranked 10th in capitalized billings among all agencies in 1992–93 (*Advertising and Marketing* 1993a). Other prominent financial advertising agencies are Concept Communications, Sobhayga Advertising, Clea Advertising and Imageads, all of which are based in Bombay. Most of these were relatively unknown traditional advertising agencies prior to the stock market boom. Their success can be attributed to their ability to recognize and fulfill a distinct market need. Many of the larger advertising agencies (including the multinationals) have now realized the potential of the financial advertising segment, and are trying to cash in on the opportunity by setting up special financial advertising divisions. Some advertising agencies (including the transnationals) have formed special partnerships for this purpose. For example, Trikaya Grey's financial communications division (Options) has formed an affiliation with the U.K.–based financial agency Dewe Rogerson (*Advertising and Marketing* 1993a; Chiravuri 1992).

Critics of the financial advertising agencies have alleged that their work tends to be in the nature of "tombstone advertising," a mere statement of the highlight of the stock offering, with no evidence of real creative effort. This scenario is expected to change as the Indian investment market stabilizes, and companies making stock offerings have to compete actively for the scarce rupees of the Indian investor. Only time will tell if the mainstream agencies will make major inroads into this specialized segment on the strength of their superior creative capabilities.

OTHER SPECIALIZED AGENCIES

In addition to financial advertising, agencies have begun to extend their service offerings to cover nonadvertising aspects of the marketing communication mix such as sales promotion and database marketing. Some transnational agency affiliates have set up specialty divisions, such as Ogilvy and Mather Direct and Trikaya Grey Direct, that provide direct marketing services. In addition to the multinationals, several specialist domestic agencies have sprung up to seize the newly emerging opportunities in database marketing and sales promotion.

Largest National Advertisers

Critics of advertising in less-developed countries have alleged that advertising promotes demand for products that are not relevant to the immediate needs of the local economy (see, for example, Tansey and Hyman 1994; Vilanilam 1989). Regardless of whether one agrees with this viewpoint, it is relevant to bear it in mind while examining the patterns of advertising expenditures by corporations in India across diverse product categories. The 10 most advertised product categories (in terms of total mass media expenditure) are listed in Table 7.2. As might be expected, nine of the 10 most advertised products are consumer nondurables. Bath soaps and laundry detergents together account for 36.7 percent of advertising expenditure across the top 10 categories. If all forms of laundry detergent—liquid, powder and bars—are consolidated into a single category, this product comes in second only to bath soaps, and accounts for 18.9 percent of advertising spending in the top 10 categories.

Of the 10 most advertised product categories in India, the one with which Western readers are probably least familiar is "suitings and textiles." Although ready-to-wear garments are steadily making inroads in India, the majority of middle- and upper-class Indian men and women still have their clothes custom tailored. Typically consumers buy fabric for blouses, dresses, shirts and trousers

Table 7.2. Most Advertised Product Categories— 1992

Category	Expenditure (million rupees)
Bath soaps	505
Soft drinks	333
Laundry detergent liquids and powders	295
Toothpastes and tooth powders	257
Suitings (Textiles)	232
Tires	220
Chocolates	211
Cigarettes	200
Tea	199
Laundry detergent bars	159

Source: *Advertising Club of Bombay Diary,* 1994 (Lintas estimates).

by the meter, and then hand it over to a tailor of their choice for stitching. Marketers of textiles advertise directly to consumers, with a view to building a preference for their brand of suiting (this term includes fabrics used for trousers), shirt cloth, and dress material. An important secondary target audience for advertising in this product category is the trade channel, which consists of at least two levels—the wholesaler and the retailer.

In 1992, the top 10 advertisers in descending order were Hindustan Lever, Tatas, Godrej, P&G, Parle, Colgate, Palmolive, Nestlé, ITC, Bajaj Auto, and Philips (Advertising Club of Bombay Diary 1994). Given that soaps and detergents account for a substantial portion of total advertising spending in India, it should come as little surprise that the top four advertisers in the country are involved—to a greater or lesser extent—in the marketing of these products. It is interesting to note that six of the top 10 advertisers in 1992, Hindustan Lever, P&G, Colgate Palmolive, Nestlé, ITC and Philips are affiliates of multinational corporations.

Three major developments since 1992 involving these 10 advertisers signal a strengthening presence for multinationals in Indian advertising and marketing. The first development is the acquisition of TOMCO (Tata Oil Mills Company—a single enterprise within the Tata group of companies), one of the larger indigenous soaps and detergents companies, by Hindustan Lever, Unilever's Indian company. The second development is the forging of a strategic alliance between Godrej Soaps, the leading indigenous manufacturer of soaps and detergents and P&G. Procter & Gamble entered India relatively late—in the mid-1980s—through its acquisition of Richardson Vicks. At the time of its acquisition by P&G, Richardson Hindustan (Richardson Vicks' Indian subsidiary) was a high-profile, medium-sized marketing company, marketing mostly over-the-counter pharmaceuticals, such as Vicks and Clearasil. Under its new ownership, the company, now renamed Procter & Gamble (India) Limited, has launched a number of soaps and detergents, including the highly successful Ariel, and made its presence felt in the marketplace in no uncertain manner. The third development is the acquisition of Parle, India's largest soft drink company, by Coca-Cola, which reentered the Indian market in 1993 after a voluntary exile of 16 years. These developments, in conjunction with the increasing presence of multinational corporations in various other sectors, have led some people to speculate whether indigenous brands will survive in the face of multinational competition (*Advertising and Marketing* 1993b).

RECENT DEVELOPMENT IN MEDIA BUYING

A study conducted by the Center for Monitoring the Indian Economy (CMIE) in 1989 indicated that the amount of concentration in the Indian marketplace was on the decline compared with a similar study conducted 3 years earlier (Shiva Ramu 1991). In the advertising arena, however, the recent availability of more broadcast media options for advertisers has led to a strengthening of the bargaining power of some large advertisers. This is probably best exemplified by the media-buying strategy of the Unilever companies in India. Over the last 2 decades, Unilever has consolidated its presence in the packaged goods market in India (and elsewhere in the world) through a series of corporate acquisitions. Today Unilever's companies in India include four major consumer products companies—the flagship Hindustan Lever, Brooke Bond-Lipton India (a tea, coffee and packaged foods giant formed through the acquisition and merger of former rivals Brooke Bond and Lipton), Pond's (primarily known as a cosmetics company) and TOMCO.

The Unilever companies have a combined turnover of 50 billion rupees and a combined advertising budget of 1.4 billion rupees. Using their gigantic marketing presence, the Unilever companies have managed to capture the sponsorship of "almost every popular program on almost every television channel in the country" (Carvalho 1994). They have also created a specialized media cell that has been entrusted with the tasks of identifying producers of new television programs and negotiating with the media. According to Carvalho (1994), even the officials at Doordarshan (India's government-owned television network) are willing to listen to ideas from Unilever's media cell. In February 1994 Unilever's media specialists made a presentation to 16 senior Doordarshan officials, explaining how the network could earn more revenue from its programs. Even a few years ago it is unlikely that Doordarshan's bureaucratic officials would have been receptive to such a presentation from an advertiser.

The overwhelming media-buying clout of Unilever has caused some chagrin among rival advertisers and agencies alike. Even other large multinationals in India, like P&G and Colgate-Palmolive (with estimated 1993–94 advertising budgets of 300 million rupees and 200 million rupees, respectively), have had to settle for the sponsorship of television programs with lower audience ratings. As a countermeasure, seven advertising agencies—Rediffusion (which handles Colgate-Palmolive's brands), Madison (which has the P&G account), Nexus Equity, DaCunha Associates, Sista's, Ambience and Advertising Avenues—have formed their own media-buying club, named Stratagem Media. Their intended strategy is to pool together the resources of their clients to rival Unilever's buying power (Carvalho 1994).

One of the factors contributing to the success of the Unilever group's strategies is its ability to finance TV program producers with substantial cash advances (Carvalho 1994). According to a recent report, this kind of direct advertiser involvement with media buying and programming is on the rise (Nagarajan 1994). As a consequence advertising agencies feel alienated, as their role in the media planning-and-buying process is threatened. This is a vital issue for advertising agencies in India, the majority of which are still compensated through media commissions (typically, the traditional 15 percent). The Advertising Agencies Association of India (AAAI) has requested clients and television producers to refrain from practices that might alienate advertising agencies. However, some agency executives feel that in view of similar developments in Europe and elsewhere, the eventual unbundling of creative and media services is inevitable (Nagarajan 1994). If this is true, agencies will need to seek some alternative form of compensation when the media commissions stop rolling in.

Advertising Organizations

According to a framework proposed by Aaker and Myers (1987), advertising involves communication between the advertiser (source) and the consumer (receiver). This communication process is made possible by a variety of "facilitating institutions," such as advertising agencies, the media, market research suppliers and suppliers of other services including photographers, television and film producers, and printers. It is also governed by a number of "control institutions," such as government, competition, consumer groups and trade association. This framework is useful in examining some of the organizations that have an impact on the advertising industry in India.

ADVERTISER ORGANIZATIONS
Indian Society of Advertisers: The Indian Society of Advertisers (ISA), which is based in Bombay, is the main organization representing advertisers. The ISA publishes a newsletter to inform its members of significant developments.

MEDIA ORGANIZATIONS
Indian Newspaper Society: One of the oldest and most influential organizations affecting the advertising business in India is the Indian Newspaper Society (INS), formerly known as the Indian and Eastern Newspaper Society (IENS). Membership of the INS is comprised of the publishers of most major newspapers and magazines in India. The importance of the INS stems from the fact that it is responsible for conferring accreditation to advertising agencies. It has also laid down rules and regulations, and a code of advertising ethics, that have had a significant influence on the functioning of the Indian advertising industry.

Accreditation from the INS entitles agencies to a 60-day grace period in the payment of print media bills. In the absence of accreditation, the amount of credit allowed to an agency depends on the agency's relationship with individual media vehicles. As stated in the Preamble to the Society's Accreditation Rules, the objectives of the accreditation process are: "(1) to ensure that recognition is awarded only to such agencies which can carry on business observing the ethics of maintaining high professional standards; (2) ensuring that all advertising agencies conduct their business in conformity with principles laid down by the Society; and (3) ensuring that member newspapers do not suffer on account of sudden insolvency and/or liquidation of advertising agencies" (Shiva Ramu 1991).

The Rules and Regulations of the INS also contain important provisions pertaining to agency compensation and commissions. Accredited advertising agencies are entitled to receive from member publications, "the minimum and maximum commission of 15 percent." Provisionally accredited agencies are entitled to a 10 percent commission. Accredited agencies are enjoined not to share or split this commission with other agencies or with their clients (Shiva Ramu 1991).

AGENCY ORGANIZATIONS

Advertising Agencies Association of India: The Advertising Agencies Association of India (AAAI) was formed in September 1945 and now has 120 members on its roster. These 120 agencies are said to account for nearly 75 percent of the advertising business in India. The AAAI is actively involved in protecting the interests of member agencies. For instance, when the Government of India tried to impose a tax (deductible at source) on the standard 15 percent commission received by agencies, the Association filed a petition on behalf of its members.

The AAAI does occasionally participate in the resolution of conflicts, although such intervention is usually restricted to conflicts involving interagency relationships, or client–agency relationships that are likely to have an impact on the industry as a whole. When necessary the Association also takes punitive actions in the collective interests of its members. For example, the Association barred Tara Sinha McCann-Erickson (TSME) from its fold when the agency took over a disputed client from another agency (Oke 1994).

OTHER ORGANIZATIONS

Advertising Standards Council of India: The Advertising Standards Council of India (ASCI) was incorporated in October 1985, as a nonprofit body. The promoters of the council include executives from major advertisers, agencies and print media. The primary objectives of the ASCI are to administer a code of ethical practices in advertising and to encourage self-regulation (Shiva Ramu 1991). The code of ethics has been drawn up to ensure the truthfulness of claims made in advertisements, to safeguard against misleading advertising, and to ensure that advertisements are not offensive to generally accepted standards of public decency (Oke 1994).

The ASCI has limited legal powers to compel manufacturers and agencies to adhere to its code of conduct. The Council itself does not evaluate advertisements; rather, it serves as a channel for others' complaints against advertisements. On receipt of a complaint, the Council asks for the advertiser or agency to comment. If there is no reply, the Council decides on the course of investigation during its biweekly meeting. If the complaint is upheld on the basis of the ASCI's code of ethics, the advertiser is asked to withdraw the advertisement. If the advertiser fails to respond, the Council approaches the advertising agency or media to drop the advertising (Shiva Ramu 1991).

Advertising Regulation

LEGAL REGULATIONS

The advertising industry in India is obviously affected by all the laws governing various mass media, as well as marketing practices. In addition there are certain laws, or parts of legislative enactments, that are directed specifically at the industry, which determine both the broad framework within which the industry is allowed to operate, as well as the content of its output (Venkateswaran 1993).

FREEDOM OF SPEECH AND ADVERTISING

The Indian Constitution, one of the world's longest, has several provisions that have a bearing on the freedom of the mass media. The most important of these is Article 19(1)(a), which states: "All citizens shall have the right to freedom of speech and expression." This right is qualified by Article 19(2), which provides that the state can impose reasonable restrictions on its exercise "in the interests of the sovereignty and integrity of India, the security of the State, friendly relations with foreign States, public order, decency or morality, or in relation to contempt of court, defamation or incitement to an offense." Although the press or mass media are not specifically mentioned in Article 19(1)(a), various judicial decisions have affirmed that this constitutional provision is wide enough to include freedom of the press and, implicitly, the freedom of other mass media (Venkateswaran 1993, 30).

Within this constitutional framework, advertising is accorded less protection than political speech. In 1960, the Supreme Court of India ruled (in the case of *Hamdard Dawakhana [Wakf] Lal Kuan v. Union of India*) that there was a distinction between commercial advertising and advertising concerned with the expression and propagation of ideas. According to the court, only the latter form of advertising could claim the full protection of Article 19(1)(a) of the Constitution (Venkateswaran 1993, 60).

LAWS REGULATING ADVERTISING

There are four laws that directly affect advertising practices in India. The 1969 Monopolies and Restrictive Trade Practices (MRTP) Act includes misleading advertisements under its definition of "unfair trade practices." The Act defines an "unfair trade practice" very widely to cover several acts aimed at promoting the sale, use or supply of any goods or services that cause loss or injury to the consumers of these goods or services. Apart from prohibiting factual misrepresentations with respect to price and quality, the Act also forbids "bait and switch" practices. A Commission (the Monopolies and Restrictive Trade Practices Commission, or MRTPC) established under the Act has powers to adjudicate upon receipt of complaints and to issue injunctions (Venkateswaran 1993, 61). Recently, the MRTPC has dealt with complaints that comparative advertisements constitute an unfair trade practice. In one such dispute, the MRTP Commissioner declared that he cannot initiate action against an advertiser making comparative claims unless the aggrieved party can provide evidence of "specific damage" caused by the advertisement (Chakraborty 1994).

The Drugs and Magic Remedies (Objectionable Advertisements) Act of 1954 contains provisions that forbid the publication of advertisements concerning drugs that may be used for certain prohibited purposes, for example, to procure miscarriages or prevent conception in women, to improve sexual pleasure, to correct menstrual disorders, or to diagnose, prevent or treat certain specified diseases. The Act also prohibits the publication of advertisements for a drug if the advertisement gives a false impression about the true character of the drug, or makes false claims for the drug (Venkateswaran 1993, 44).

The Indecent Representation of Women (Prohibition) Act of 1986 was introduced in response to growing demands, especially from women's organizations, to curb the exploitation of women by the media. The Act makes it an offense for any publication or advertisement to depict a woman, or her body, in an indecent or derogatory manner. Offenses are punishable with imprisonment and/or fines (Venkateswaran 1993, 61).

The Emblems and Names (Prevention of Improper Use) Act of 1950 imposes restrictions on the use by anyone, including the media, of certain emblems and names. For example, one cannot use the Indian national flag, the name, emblem or official seal of the United Nations, the official seal of the Government of India, or of any state governments, except under such conditions as may be authorized by the government (Venkateswaran 1993, 45).

Apart from the laws just outlined, the conduct of sweepstakes, contests and promotions is governed by the Prize Competitions Act of 1955. The Lotteries (Control) Act also contains provisions that are relevant to advertisers who want to conduct such promotions. The Defamation Act of 1952, which regulates matters of slander and libel in general, has also been evoked by parties prosecuting advertisers for comparative advertising practices (Chakraborty 1994). In the case of financial advertising, the Securities and Exchange Board of India (SEBI) exercises significant control with regard to limiting the types of claims that advertisers can make, as well as stipulating certain statutory disclosures that must be made.

REGULATION BY THE MEDIA
PRINT MEDIA REGULATIONS. In addition to the regulations imposed on advertising by means of laws, the print and broadcast media also have codes of ethical conduct, by which advertisers must abide. Newspapers and magazines that are members of the INS are expected to conform to the Society's Code of Advertisement Ethics and Medical Standards (Shiva Ramu 1991). Most of the injunctions issued by the INS pertain to advertising claims of a medical nature, along the lines of the Drugs and Magic Remedies (Objectionable Advertisements) Act of 1954.

The print media are enjoined not to accept advertisements containing endorsements by doctors who are not recognized Indian Medical Practitioners. Further, according to the code, "no advertisement will be accepted containing claims or illustrations which are distorted or exaggerated in such a manner as to convey false impressions or containing statements of a 'knocking' or extravagant nature" (Shiva Ramu 1991).

BROADCAST MEDIA REGULATIONS. As the INS has no statutory powers to implement its code of ethics, compliance by member publications is purely voluntary. On the other hand, the broadcast media in India—AIR and Doordarshan—are virtually government monopolies, although there are now some moves to privatize these institutions. (Note: This does not include STAR-TV and other satellite/cable channels.) Even though AIR and Doordarshan do not have statutory enforcement powers, their near-monopoly status gives advertisers no alternative but to comply with their regulations. Both AIR and Doordarshan now use the Code of Ethics for Advertising in India issued by the ASCI, as the primary guideline for broadcast advertisers. In addition both the networks have their own regulations. These guidelines imposed by the AIR and Doordarshan codes can be classified into three categories: (a) restrictions on products and services, (b) restrictions based on target audience sensibilities, and (c) other executional restrictions.

Restrictions on products and services. Certain products and services cannot be advertised on the broadcast media. Prohibited products include cigarette and tobacco products, patent medicines, matrimonial agencies (the Indian equivalent of dating services), hypnotists, fortune tellers, foreign goods and foreign banks, betting tips, nongovernment lotteries, and most forms of financial services offered by nongovernmental organizations. Alcohol advertising is not permitted in any medium throughout India. On the other hand, medically approved contraceptive products *can* be advertised—hardly surprising in a densely populated country, whose government actively encourages citizens to limit the size of their families to one or two children. As of now these restrictions on advertising do not apply to satellite/cable channels.

According to an industry newsletter, Doordarshan is trying to increase its advertising revenue by removing the ban on advertising certain product categories. In 1994, Doordarshan declared its intention to permit the advertising of foreign products, including banks and financial institutions, jewelry, mutual funds, hair dyes, matrimonial agencies and astrological services (Rediffusion Precision Media 1994). This clearly represents the network's willingness to compromise some of its public policy goals in order to remain commercially viable.

Restrictions based on audience sensibilities. The codes for AIR and Doordarshan state that "advertising should be so designed as to conform to the laws of the country, and should not offend against morality, decency and religious susceptibilities of the people." Advertisements that deride any race, caste, color, creed or nationality are prohibited. This regulation is reflective of the government media's desire to play a pro-social role in the eradication of the caste system. Accordingly, advertisements should not criticize friendly countries, attack any religion or community, contain obscene or defamatory content, incite people to violence or violation of law and order, cast aspersions against the integrity of the President and Judiciary, criticize any person by name (Venkateswaran 1993).

Other executional guidelines. Advertisers are requested not to incorporate "any such effects which might startle the viewing public." Examples of such effects cited in the AIR and Doordarshan codes include rapid gunfire or rifle shots, sirens, bombardment, screams, raucous laughter and the like. Foreign commercials, or commercials primarily featuring foreign models were not accepted by Doordarshan, although there is nothing in the network's official code regarding this policy.

Advertisements on television are shown in a single pod at the beginning of a program, and no commercial interruptions are permitted within a program. Sometimes, commercial pods preceding popular programs can last as long as thirty minutes. Sponsors of television programs are also required to provide a visual break (or "wipe") between program content and commercial pods, to reduce the possibility of viewers confusing the two. (A similar stipulation exists in the United States with respect to advertising on child-oriented programs.) Doordarshan is reportedly planning to relax these rules, so as to allow commercials to be placed within programs.

Advertising and children. Doordarshan's code also contains a section on advertising and children, which stipulates that "no advertisement for a product or service shall be accepted if it suggests in any way that, unless children themselves buy or encourage other people to buy the products or services, they will be failing in their duty or lacking in loyalty to any person or organization." Also, "no advertisement shall be accepted which leads children to believe that if they do not own or use the product advertised, they will be inferior in some way to other children, or that they are liable to be condemned or ridiculed for not owning or using it." Clearly, it would be easy for advertisers to circumvent the spirit of these provisions while adhering to them to the letter (Venkateswaran 1993).

The regulations imposed by the government-owned broadcast media in India are motivated mainly by genuine pro-social concerns. However, in many instances, Doordarshan has been known to supplement its overall guidelines with periodic circulars issued by bureaucrats coming to grips with this relatively new advertising medium. Often these stem from an attempt to micro-manage advertising executions.

As a means of implementing its regulatory code, Doordarshan will not run advertisements unless the videotape for broadcast is accompanied by a storyboard that has the written approval of a Doordarshan official. This confers considerable discretionary authority upon the bureaucrats responsible for this "precensorship" process, although in practice, such powers are seldom misused. Advertisers wishing to avoid costly errors are advised to get such approval even before they start shooting the commercial. Approval of a storyboard by Doordarshan does not guarantee that the network will agree to run the commercial as shot, as there might be substantial differences between the storyboard and the finished commercial.

SELF-REGULATION
Self-regulation in advertising is a relatively recent phenomenon in India. The primary self-regulating body is the ASCI, which was established in 1985. The influence of the ASCI is demonstrated by the fact that its Code of Advertising Practice is referred to as a primary guideline, by both AIR and Doordarshan. The objectives of the ASCI, and its procedures for dealing with complaints about advertisements have been discussed earlier in this chapter.

Consumer Issues

CHANGING CONSUMER ATTITUDES
The increased commercialization of television, along with the extraordinary growth of television households in India, has created a consumer revolution (Narayan and Roy 1994). The all-pervasive medium has been able to bring the hitherto unknown lifestyle of the people of industrially developed nations into the living rooms of most middle- and upper-class Indians. Because middle classes in general are more prone to go in for "cultural borrowing" (de Mooij and Keegan 1991), the desire to imitate the lifestyle of their westernized counterparts has received a tremendous boost. An executive from a multinational alcohol marketing company described the Indian middle class as having "the right kind of attitude: they are willing to try out new brands, new tastes" (*Advertising Age International* 1994).

Until the late 1980s most Indian consumers were fiscally quite conservative. A typical Indian family would buy goods primarily from savings. Being in debt was socially unacceptable. Only housing loans were viewed as somewhat acceptable. Even big-ticket items such as electronics, appliances, motorcycles and automobiles were bought out of savings. These fiscal values are now going through a drastic transformation. In 1993, a study commissioned by the Housing Development and Finance Corporation (HDFC) estimated that 15 percent of middle-class homes had taken some kind of a loan to buy consumer durables, double the level of just 3 years ago. Forty-four percent of households owning television sets, 23 percent of those owning a refrigerator, and 10 percent of those owning cars had financed their purchases (Narayan and Roy 1994).

Private finance companies, including multinational banks, view this trend with great expectation. In 1994, GE Capital (a subsidiary of General Electric) entered into a joint venture with HDFC, known as Countrywide Consumer Financial Services (CCFS), to capitalize on the boom in consumer financing (Narayan and Roy 1994). Citibank, the world's largest issuer of credit cards, entered the Indian market in earnest in 1988–89. Today Citibank alone is estimated to have issued over 250,000 credit cards, making it the undisputed leader in a market that has doubled in less than 5 years (*Advertising and Marketing* 1993c). Many banks—foreign and domestic—have followed suit in the credit card business.

Not all Indian consumers are joining the credit-happy bandwagon. The market research study commissioned by HDFC classified Indian consumers into three segments, depending on their attitudes toward credit. Estimates of the relative size of each segment are not available. The three segments identified in the study are defined as follows:

1. *Hedonists:* These consumers are not inclined to postpone the gratification of their desires. Hedonists are not too concerned about the high interest rates involved in consumer financing (typically 22 percent or higher).

2. *Hard-nosed realists:* Unlike the hedonists, these consumers weigh the pros and cons of installment-purchase schemes. Under the right circumstances they are willing to pay the price for immediate gratification of his or her needs.

3. *The die-hard traditionalists:* Conservative and debt-averse, these consumers prefer to live within their means, even if it means putting off big-ticket purchases.

The findings of the HDFC study must be viewed with some caution, as they are based on a relatively small sample. It should also be noted that even in 1994, less than 30 percent of consumer durables purchases were financed (Narayan and Roy 1994).

It is too early to say whether the culture of conspicuous consumption and immediate need gratification will undermine India's high savings rate (nearly 20 percent), which is second only to Japan's, according to some estimates. However, the growth in consumption in some sectors has been quite remarkable. For example, in the 1980s the population increased by about 19 percent, but domestic electricity usage and the sales of personal goods, clothing, kitchen utensils and gadgets increased by eight to 10 times as much. In addition ready-made brand-name clothing sales more than doubled between 1985 and 1990, the number of washing machines in use more than tripled between 1987 and 1990, and the number of cars on Indian roads more than doubled between 1984 and 1991 (Operations Research Group 1991).

The growing appetite for consumer goods, especially among middle-class Indians, has invited criticism from many quarters. Critics view the Indian middle class as avaricious, insensitive and self-indulgent, but others argue that they are a dynamic group, whose hunger for consumption can only spur the economy toward higher growth (Dubey 1992).

CHANGES IN THE RURAL MARKET

It is an oft-quoted truism that India lives in her villages. Only around 20 percent of the country's 900 million people live in metropolitan centers. Yet most discussions of Indian advertising (and consumers) focus on the urban market, which has the maximum disposable income and propensity to spend. Recently, however, several marketers have begun to focus afresh on the relatively untapped rural market, due to its growth potential, as well as its impressive overall size. In terms of growth, rural shares of packaged consumer goods have increased from 28 percent in 1984 to over 42 percent in 1992. The sheer size of the market is illustrated by the fact that a 3 percent market share for a brand of bath soap translates to a rural consumer base of over 12 million consumers (Bhandari and Iyer 1994).

It is true that there are substantial logistic and communications hurdles in reaching rural consumers; the rural market is scattered over many small villages. At the same time, marketers are only now beginning to realize that in many states, over 65 percent of the population lives in 25 to 35 percent of the villages. According to Bose (1992), although marketers may not be able to reach out to all of rural India's 650 million consumers, they can nevertheless try to reach around 150 million of them.

From an advertising viewpoint, the major hurdles to reaching rural consumers are low literacy rates, and relatively low penetration of television sets. Radio is perhaps the medium best suited for reaching rural India, but most radio stations that are powerful enough to reach rural audiences accept advertising only on a limited basis. The major new media in India—including the new channels on the government-owned television network—have targeted the urban elite, and their impact on rural audiences has been incidental at best. This does not mean that television has had no impact on rural India. Many television programs, especially those based on Indian mythology, such as the Ramayana and Mahabharat, have been extremely popular. The impact of this medium is expected to increase with greater TV penetration of rural households. However, it is uncertain what impact urban-oriented advertising messages will have on rural audiences (Bose 1992). Bhandari and Iyer (1994) feel that marketers need to tailor their messages specifically to the needs of rural audiences, instead of trying to use common advertising for urban and rural consumers.

Some innovative entrepreneurs are already offering media alternatives that are appropriate for reaching rural consumers. These include video vans and point-of-purchase video displays. Using the latter concept, advertisers can screen their commercials in busy village markets, and communicate with them in a language appropriate for the region (unlike network television advertising, which is primarily in Hindi or English). As electrical outlets may not always be conveniently available, these entrepreneurs even equip their video displays with self-contained gasoline-powered generators.

Due to improvements in the transportation and communication infrastructure, the buying behavior of rural Indian households is also undergoing some transformation. Traditionally, male heads of households made all the key purchase decisions. An improvement in rural literacy, coupled with greater access to information, has resulted in a greater decision-making role for other family members. Better literacy has also made for better brand identification. Earlier many villagers identified brands primarily through their physical characteristics (for example, Unilever's Lifebuoy bath soap—India's largest selling brand—was universally identified by its red color; Nirma detergent powder was identified by its yellow color). Unscrupulous "guerrilla marketers" sometimes exploit the illiteracy of villagers by launching spurious brands that closely resembled successful brands in physical features as well as brand names. Thus, "Teta Salt" tried to capitalize on consumers' goodwill toward Tata Salt, and "Darbar Amla" hair oil rode in on the coattails of the highly successful Dabar Amla hair oil (Bhandari and Iyer 1994). The presence of literate rural consumers will probably render such tactics more difficult in the coming years.

CONSUMER PROTECTION ISSUES

The majority of Indian consumers are not gullible enough to be taken in by spurious brands, such as those just described. However, until recently, Indian consumers were relatively passive in their responses to unethical business and advertising practices. On the face of it, India has a large number of laws to protect consumers, but their implementation has been very poor (Sethi and Seetharaman 1994). The monopoly of government enterprises in key sectors (such as air and rail transportation, telecommunications, insurance services and electric utilities), and limited competition in many (but certainly not all) other sectors, resulted in markets where the interests of the seller were much better represented than those of the consumer. This scenario is changing slowly, but steadily. The consumer movement has made significant gains in making buyers far more aware of their rights, as well as in getting legislative protection.

The earliest Indian law dealing with the relationship between buyers and sellers is the Indian Sale of Goods Act of 1930, which is based on "the rules of justice, equity and good conscience" (Sethi and Seetharaman 1994). This law, nevertheless, contains the aphorism, *caveat emptor,* or "let the buyer beware." The MRTP Act further laid the ground for the consumer movement by defining unfair trade practices and by providing a mechanism for the redressal of consumer complaints, through the creation of the MRTP Commission, headed by a government-appointed Commissioner. Until the passage of the MRTP Act, consumers had no formal means of filing their complaints other than the courts of law. The Consumer Protection Act (COPRA) of 1986, probably the most important piece of consumer legislation, takes this concept one step further.

The Act provides for quick and inexpensive redressal of consumer grievances through quasi-judicial bodies set up at the district, state and national level. It provides this facility to three groups: individual consumers, registered voluntary consumer associations, and the central and state governments. Under CO-PRA, a consumer is defined as "any person who buys any goods or hires or avails of any service for a consideration." The Act differentiates between people buying goods for personal use, and those buying products for resale or commercial purposes. The latter group cannot seek relief from the consumer court. Consumers can complain against defective products, deficient services, restrictive and unfair trade practices, and overpricing (Girimaji 1993).

The first complaint under COPRA was filed in 1988, in Hyderabad, the capital of the southern Indian state of Andhra Pradesh. A large government enterprise, ECIL Limited, which sold television sets, was demanding service charges of 400 rupees from consumers, even during the warranty period when service was supposed to be free. A police intelligence officer who had bought an ECIL television set learned about COPRA from a newspaper article and decided to file a complaint. The district consumer forum directed ECIL to refund the amount, along with 12 percent interest. As COPRA was a new law, ECIL simply ignored the directive. The forum then ordered the seizure of a television set from the company's retail showroom. This was a rude awakening for ECIL managers, who promptly filed an appeal before the Andhra Pradesh State Commission. The state commission upheld the district forum's decision. Noting that the company's actions had made an impact not only on the complainant, but on many others, the state commission issued a class action order directing ECIL to pay back all the customers who had been charged unfairly. The class action portion of the commission's directive was later stayed by the Andhra Pradesh State High Court, which held that the other "victims" had not complained. The original complainant, however, emerged victorious (Mehta 1994). Due to this and other subsequent incidents, COPRA was amended in 1993 to permit class action suits for the first time in India (Girimaji 1993).

Since COPRA was passed in 1986, over 2.6 million Indian consumers have sought relief in the 400 district-level commissions set up under the Act. Courts have handed down rulings protecting consumers against a variety of private and government-owned establishments, including government-owned railways, insurance companies and public utility companies (Mehta 1994). Consumer activists are heartened by these statistics, but caution that many more millions are unaware of their rights under this law (Girimaji 1993). A recent book on the history of consumerism in India notes that the first formal consumer movement in India was as far back as the 1940s, but that growth since then has been rather slow (Sethi and Seetharaman 1994). Poverty, illiteracy, indifference of the affluent classes and the lack of organizational skills in consumer groups are some of the factors blamed for the slow growth of the movement. Some commentators feel that the Indian consumer movement is at last coming into its own, and that the pessimism expressed by Sethi and Seetharaman (1994) is probably not justified (Jayanthi 1994). According to a recent report there has been a sudden increase in the number of consumer organizations in India during the last decade. In the mid-1980s there were only about 80 registered organizations; in 1994, there were nearly 700 (Girimaji 1994).

The growth of the consumer movement, bolstered by legislative developments such as the 1993 Amendment to COPRA, is a positive development for the Indian consumer. At the same time, the increasing adoption of the ASCI's Code of Ethics is indicative of the growing influence of self-regulation among advertisers. Nevertheless, if a recent report about an increase in unethical business practices is any indication, both consumers and advertisers will have to remain vigilant in order to enjoy the benefits of economic liberalization (Roy and Mukerjea 1994).

Conclusions

Between 1950, when the first advertising agency started operating, and 1995, there have been dramatic changes in the Indian advertising scenario. Most of the changes, however, have occurred in the last 15 years with the government's open-door policy, liberalization and globalization. With each passing year the Indian economy is expanding at a rapid rate, especially due to the aggressiveness with which the Government of India is seeking foreign investment. While the winds of change bode well for the Indian advertising industry, it has started to feel the growing pains.

According to Shailendra Singh, the executive director of the Bombay-based Precept Advertising, "The pressures are getting worse. The risk factor in the business is growing." Sam Balsara, of Madison Advertising adds, "It's a pressure-cooker like atmosphere." With the runaway growth, the biggest problem facing the industry is the shortage of talent. Until very recently most agency executives were trained on the job. But with the per capita productivity that is required to stay in business, the agencies today prefer ready-made talents. A.G. Krishnamurthy, chief of Mudra Communications, believes that at least 1,800 new talents are needed by the industry each year. A few post-graduate institutes dedicated to develop advertising talents have opened up in the last few years, for example, the Mudra Institute of Communication & Advertising and the Narsee Monjee Institute of Management studies; however, many more will be needed in the coming years (Wanvari 1995).

In conclusion, these are exciting times for the Indian advertising industry.

With the help of advertising and other sophisticated marketing techniques, the culture of consumption has been internalized by the 150 million–strong Indian middle class. There is no turning back now.

Bibliography

Aaker, D.A. and J.G. Myers. 1987. *Advertising Management,* 3rd ed. Englewood Cliffs, NJ: Prentice-Hall.

Advertising Age International. 1994. Changing Demographics, October 17 (I): 11–16.

Advertising and Marketing. 1993a. The Fourth A&M Agency Report. December.

Advertising and Marketing. 1993b. Will Indian Brands Survive? October.

Advertising and Marketing. 1993c. Credit Worthy. December, pp. 160–166.

Advertising and Marketing. 1994. The Fifth A&M Agency Report. December 15.

Advertising Club of Bombay. 1994. *Annual Diary.* Bombay, India: Advertising Club of Bombay.

Ahluwalia, I.J. 1985. *Industrial Growth in India: Stagnation Since the Mid-Sixties.* New Delhi, India: Oxford University Press.

Banerjee, S. 1981. Advertising in India: Evolution and Technique. In: *Mass Media in India.* New Delhi: Ministry of Information and Broadcasting, Government of India.

Bardhan, P. 1984. *The Political Economy of Development in India.* Oxford: Basil Blackwell.

Basham, A.L. 1959. *The Wonder That Was India.* London: Sedgewick & Jackson.

Basham, A.L. 1970. Traditional India. In: Moore, C.D. and D. Eldredge, eds. *India: Yesterday and Today.* New York: Praeger Publishers, pp. 1–36.

Bhagawati, J. 1993. *India in Transition: Freeing the Economy.* New York, NY: Oxford University Press.

Bhandari, P. and R. Iyer. 1994. Rural Marketing: The Rules of the Game. *Advertising and Marketing,* July 15, 1993, pp. 23–25.

Bose, D.K. 1992. Reaching out to the Rural Millions. In: *The Best of Brand Equity '92,* (original article appeared on October 28, 1992). Bombay: *The Economic Times*/Bennett, Coleman and Co. Ltd., pp. 31–32.

Brown, J.M. 1994. *Modern India: The Origins of an Asian Democracy.* New York: Oxford University Press.

Carvalho, C. 1994. The Battle for the Beams. *Business Today,* July 22–August 6, pp. 60–63. New Delhi: Living Media.

Chakraborty, T. 1994. Negative Advertisements: Courts Can't Control the War of Words. *Pioneer,* New Delhi.

Chakravarty, S. 1987. *Development Planning: The Indian Experience.* New York: Oxford University Press.

Chan, J.M. 1994. National Responses and Accessibility to Star TV in Asia. *Journal of Communication,* 44 (3): 112–131.

Chiravuri, S. 1992. Cashing in on Client Confidence. In: *The Best of Brand Equity—'92,* (original article appeared on January 29, 1992). Bombay, India: *The Economic Times*/Bennett, Coleman and Co. Ltd., pp. 13–14.

D'Souza, L. 1994. Ad Agency Tie-Ups Spur Accounts Shifting. *The Times of India.*

Dean, V.M. 1959. *New Patterns of Democracy in India*. Cambridge, MA: Harvard University Press.

deMooij, Marieke K. and Warren J. Keegan. 1991. *Advertising Worldwide: Concepts, Theories and Practice of International, Multinational and Global Advertising*. London: Prentice Hall.

Dubey, S. 1992. The Middle Class. In: Gordon, L.A. and P. Oldenburg, eds. *India Briefing, 1992*. Boulder, CO: Westview Press, pp. 137–164.

Frankel, F.R. 1988. Middle Classes and Castes in India's Politics: Prospects for Political Accommodation. In: Kohli A., ed. *India's Democracy: An Analysis of Changing State-Society Relations*. Princeton, NJ: Princeton University Press, pp. 225–261.

Girimaji, P. 1993. A Guide to Consumer Protection Act. *The Times of India*, New Delhi, October 22.

Girimaji, P. 1994. Consumer Movement Gaining Momentum. *The Times of India*, New Delhi, August 20.

Jalan, B. 1990. *India's Economic Crisis*. New Delhi, India: Oxford University Press.

Jayanthi, C. 1994. Educating the Indian Consumer. *Pioneer*, New Delhi, June 18.

Khatkhate, D. 1992. India on an Economic Reform Trajectory. In: Gordon, L.A. and P. Oldenburg, eds. *India Briefing, 1992*. Boulder, CO: Westview Press, pp. 47–70.

Khushu, O.P. 1993. Satellite Communications in Asia: An Overview. *Media Asia*, 20 (1): 3–9.

Kishore, K. 1994. The Emerging Marketplace of Communication Satellites in the Asia Pacific: A Case Study of AsiaSatI and Star TV. In: Savage, J.G. and D.J. Wedemeyer, eds. *Proceedings of the 16th Annual Pacific Telecommunications Council Conference*, Honolulu, pp. 51–56.

Kurian, K. 1995. Letter to Kartik Pashupati, June 27.

Mehta, D.S. 1980. *Mass Communication and Journalism in India*. New Delhi, India: Allied Publishers Private Limited.

Mehta, P.S. 1994. Consumer Notes: Small, but Significant. *Pioneer*, New Delhi, November 5.

Menon, A. 1994. Street Smart Mice Stop Dancing to Piper's Tune. *Brand Equity, The Economic Times*, New Delhi, August 15.

Nagarajan, U. 1994. Boom Times on the Boob Tube, *Business World*, July 27–August 9, pp. 106–109.

Narayan, S. and M.G. Roy. 1994. The New Credit Culture. *Business World*, April 6–19, pp. 12–21.

Nehru, J. 1989. *The Discovery of India*. New Delhi, India: Oxford University Press.

News India Times. 1995. American Satellite Firm's "Direct-to-home" TV, March 22, p. 12.

Oke, H. 1994. Inter-office memorandum to Swaminathan A. Aiyar, Editor. *The Economic Times*, New Delhi, November 25.

Oommen, T.K. 1990. *State and Societies in India: Studies in Nation Building*. New Delhi, India: Sage Publications.

Operations Research Group. 1991. Expanding Consumer Markets, ORG Review, New Delhi: Operations Research Group, p. 1.

Price Waterhouse. 1990. *Doing Business in India*. Price Waterhouse World Firm Limited.

Rai, U. 1994. Government Hopes to Black Out Cigarette, Liquor Ads. *Indian Express*, New Delhi, May 9.

Reddi, U. 1989. Media and Culture in Indian Society: Conflict or Co-operation. *Media, Culture and Society,* 11: 395–413.

Rediffusion Precision Media. 1994. Zee Television: Rough Road Ahead, *Media Technology Group Bulletin,* March. Bombay: Rediffusion Advertising Private Limited.

Rothermund, D. 1993. *An Economic History of India: From the Pre-Colonial Times to 1991.* New York: Routledge.

Roy, M.G. and D.N. Mukerjea. 1994. From Smart Marketing to Dirty Tricks. *Business World,* July 27–August 9, pp. 22–29.

Roy, R. 1988. Three Visions of Needs and the Future: Liberalism, Marxism, and Gandhism. In: Coate, R.A. and J.A. Rosati, eds. *The Power of Human Needs in World Society,* Boulder, CO: Lynne Rienner Publishers, pp. 59–76.

Sen, A.D. 1992. A Copy for the Future. *Sunday Magazine, Indian Express,* New Delhi, March 1.

Sethi, M. and P. Seetharaman. 1994. *Consumerism—A Growing Concept.* New Delhi: Phoenix Publishing House.

Shiva Ramu, .S. 1991. *Advertising Agencies: Global and Indian Perspectives.* Jaipur, India: PWP Printwell.

Singh, P. 1994. Nodding, Shaking and Shrugging. *Brand Equity, The Economic Times,* New Delhi, August 15.

Singhal, A. and E.M. Rogers. 1989. *India's Information Revolution.* New Delhi, India: Sage Publications.

Singhal, A., J.K. Doshi, E.M. Rogers, and A.A. Rahman. 1988. The Diffusion of Television in India. *Media Asia,* 15 (4): 222–229.

Tansey, R. and M.R. Hyman. 1994. Dependency Theory and the Effects of Advertising by Foreign-Based Multinational Corporations in Latin America. *Journal of Advertising,* 23 (11): 27–42.

Tomlinson, B.R. 1993. *The Economy of Modern India, 1860–1970.* Cambridge, United Kingdom: Cambridge University Press.

Venkateswaran, K. S. 1993. *Mass Media Laws and Regulations in India.* Singapore: Asian Mass Communication Research and Information Centre (AMIC).

Vilanilam, J. 1989. Television Advertising and the Indian Poor. *Media, Culture and Society,* vol. 11. London: Sage Publications, pp. 485–497.

Wanvari, A. 1995. The Final Countdown, *Indian Advertising at the Crossroads,* Calcutta, India: Telegraph Supplement, Ananda Bazar Patrika Ltd.

Weiner, M. 1989. *The Indian Paradox: Essays in Indian Politics.* New Delhi, India: Sage Publications.

Xavier, F. and L. Eashwer. 1993. Communication Scene of INDIA. In: Goonasekhara, A. and D. Holaday, eds. *Asian Communication Handbook.* Singapore: Asian Mass Communication Research and Information Centre, pp. 29–57.

8

Advertising in the Philippines: Communication, Culture and Consumption

ELENA PERNIA

The Political Structure of the Philippines

GEOGRAPHY AND PEOPLE

Approximately 7,100 islands of various shapes and sizes comprise the Philippine archipelago. With a total land area of 300,000 square kilometers, the country is divided into three main island groupings. These are *Luzon*, the largest land mass forming the northern part of the country; *Visayas*, a group of smaller islands in the middle of the country; and *Mindanao*—the second largest land mass—located in the southern section. The Philippines lies east of mainland Southeast Asia, on roughly the same latitude as some of its Association of Southeast Asian Nations (ASEAN) partners such as Thailand, and peninsular Malaysia. It is north of the Indonesian archipelago and south of Taiwan. To its east is the vast expanse of the Pacific Ocean.

Filipinos are predominantly Malay with an intermingling of Spanish, Chinese, American, and other cultures and races. The latest population estimate (1992) is 64.3 million, growing at the rate of 2.3 percent annually. More than a hundred dialects and languages are spoken in the country, with Pilipino—which is largely based on Tagalog—as the national language. English is widely spoken, with Filipinos constituting the third largest English-speaking population in the world. Literacy is high at around 80 percent nationwide, reaching as much as 97 percent in the capital area, metropolitan Manila.

A Brief History

Prior to European colonialization in the 16th century, the islands were pop-

---

Dr. E. Pernia received support for this research from a grant by the General Carlos P. Romulo Chair for Associate Professor of Communication Research.

189

ulated by Malay groups that were predominantly Muslim in their politics and religion. Spanish rule, which lasted for 300 years from the 16th to 19th centuries, radically changed the political, social and cultural structures of the country. While the Spaniards consolidated control over the northern and middle parts of the archipelago (that is, Luzon and the Visayas), Malays reigned strong in the south (that is, Mindanao). The Philippines' Spanish heritage is still manifest in various cultural practices of Filipinos, the most evident being religion (80 percent of the population is Catholic).

American rule began around the turn of the 20th century when Spain ceded the Philippines to the United States after the Spanish defeat in the Spanish–American War. Filipino revolutionaries who fought for independence from Spain originally thought that the Americans were their allies; however, they soon realized that the United States had different intentions. A brief Filipino–American war ensued, with the Filipino forces overwhelmed by the superior weapons of the Americans. The colonialization of the Philippines by the United States, which was interrupted by the Japanese occupation during World War II, lasted for only 50 years, or a mere quarter of the length of Spanish rule. However, the influences of American rule are still evident. For example, the country's presidential system of government bears distinct similarities to that of the United States. Whereas Pilipino is the national language, English is also understood and spoken by the majority. The evolution of Philippine mass media, especially television and radio, has followed a largely American model in its format and content.

During the past 50 years (1940s to 1990s) the Philippines has undergone progress and prosperity, as well as tumult. A year after the end of World War II, the country gained independence from the United States. During the early postwar years, particularly during the 1950s, the Philippines had the most buoyant economy and the most democratic social structures compared with its ASEAN neighbors. However, a combination of political instability, abuse of political power and economic mismanagement, particularly during the 20 years of the Marcos dictatorship, led to the country's worst social crisis in its post-war history. The crisis peaked with negative economic growth in 1983—the year that saw the assassination of Benigno (Ninoy) Aquino, Marcos' longtime political adversary.

Popular discontent against the Marcos administration, awakened by the Aquino assassination, reached a climax in 1986 when millions of Filipinos congregated along the Epifanio de los Santos Avenue (EDSA), a 10-lane highway running from north to south of metropolitan Manila, in what is now referred to alternatively as the peaceful EDSA Revolution or the People Power Revolution. Along various points on the EDSA and other thoroughfares leading to it, in between two military camps, as well as in front of Malacanang, the Presidential Palace, Filipino civilians prayed and rallied for Marcos to step down; and for soldiers to turn their tanks around, put their guns down, break with the Marcos government, and rally behind Aquino's widow, Corazon. Linking arms and bodies to create a human barricade, these civilians, including a substantial number of priests, nuns and other members of the Catholic clergy, aimed to prevent certain bloodshed as military forces loyal to Marcos were sent out to quell breakaway military rebels. At the end of this 4-day revolution, the people had ousted the Marcos government and installed a new one with Corazon Aquino as the country's duly elected president.

The Aquino presidency was greeted by most Filipinos with much hope, as they counted upon her administration to turn around the economic and political misfortunes of the country. Her administration, however, encountered serious challenges, the most serious being the 1989 attempted coup d'état staged by right-wing military elements. President Aquino survived these threats, vaunting that the reinstallation and safeguarding of democracy in the country was her administration's legacy to the country. Her critics argue that she had only limited success in implementing policy reforms, particularly with regard to land reform and poverty alleviation. In 1992, Fidel V. Ramos, a former military general and one of the leaders of the breakaway military rebels in 1986, followed Aquino as president. Under Ramos the country has been experiencing a relatively stable peace and order situation, and steady positive economic growth.

NATIONAL IDEOLOGY

To most Filipinos democracy is a cherished ideal. The EDSA revolution, the ouster of the Marcoses and the installation of Corazon Aquino as president in 1986, and the holding of local and national elections are testaments to this. Even President Ramos, despite his military background, has committed his government to this ideal, saying that "we sailed against the authoritarian tide in Asia by striving to achieve development with democracy as our anchor and guide" (Ramos 1994a).

Corollary to democracy is people empowerment, which is itself in line with commitment to human rights and freedom. In the area of social reform, the task of government in empowering people is to help its citizens, especially the poorest of the poor, to help themselves by improving their access to social services (such as health care, education and housing), to land through agrarian reform, as well as to jobs and credit. More than assuring equitable access to resources, government is tasked to guarantee effective people's participation in decision making.

Peace through (re)conciliation is another national ideal. The national aversion to warfare and bloodshed was clearly manifest during the 1986 EDSA Revolution. Both the Aquino and Ramos governments have sought to eliminate insurgency and to ensure peace and political stability by forging conciliatory talks with different disaffected groups, including the communist factions, the secessionist Muslim groups, and right-wing military factions.

ECONOMIC GROWTH POLICY

President Ramos called his economic program a task of modernization "to make it more productive; to make it competitive in the world; and to make room for the small and middle-sized industries which are the building blocks of economic democracy" (Ramos 1994b). He has named his administration's vision to bring the country to newly industrializing country (NIC) status by 1998, "Philippines 2000." Sustained growth, improved productivity and efficiency—in the agricultural, industrial, manufacturing, and services sectors—are the Ramos administration's economic policy goals.

Toward these ends, economic policies have been aimed at deregulation and liberalization. Actually, the trend toward the dismantling of monopolies, beginning with the telecommunications sector, was initiated during the Aquino administration. President Ramos continued deregulation and liberalization in other areas, most notably in the transportation (land, water and air), energy, banking and investment sectors. For example, notable improvements in the shipping industry have resulted from investments worth over 5 billion pesos, such investment made possible by the liberalization of shipping rates and routes. Similar changes are expected with the deregulation and liberalization in Philippine aviation as well as in mass public transportation.

The administration is set to remove protectionist policies, including those shielding local infant industries, arguing that "protectionism for us had produced only retarded infant industries and a generation of political entrepreneurs who fattened on unearned income from tariff barriers, tax holidays, import licenses, and behest loans" (Ramos 1994b). In line with encouraging competitiveness, leveling the "playing field of enterprise," as well as meeting General Agreement on Tariff and Trade (GATT) requirements, the administration is also seeking to rationalize tariff rates, including removing both tariff and nontariff import and export barriers. Additionally, the executive branch has been lobbying the Congress to pass what it considers as urgent bills on antiracketeering, antitrust and antimonopolies.

Ensuring a place for the Philippines in the global economy, with the World Trade Organization (WTO) overseeing GATT, is a priority for the government. As the President has noted, the country

> began (its economic) recovery by reversing (its) inward-looking economy and turning it outwards to the world in recognition of the implacable reality of global economic competition. Globalism offers vast opportunities for trade, investments, jobs and progress. Equally, it contains dangers for laggard economies. . . . Without doubt, UR-GATT is a boon to both developed and developing economies. But the countries that adjust the quickest and trade effectively will benefit the most. [The] 1995 agenda, therefore, must encompass all these needs for adjustment, maintenance, and capacity-building in the world economy.
>
> (Ramos 1994a)

Cultural Context

RELIGIOUS AND PHILOSOPHIC UNDERPINNINGS AFFECTING CONSUMPTION AND COMMUNICATION

Filipinos, both Christian and Muslim, hold a strong belief in God. Among the Roman Catholic majority, belief in the divine and divine intervention is deeply ingrained in various aspects of life. It is in the character of Catholic Filipinos to manifest their religion in behaviors such as daily and weekly prayers, masses and novenas, community fiestas, Marian devotions and other forms of religious pledges, or *panatas*—both for supplication and for thanksgiving. With almost all Catholic Filipino homes having at least one altar on which religious statues are enthroned, sales of religious articles are brisk. Smaller religious items such as rosaries, prayer books, medallions and stampitas are very often souvenirs or tokens of remembrance distributed to guests during religious celebrations of baptisms, confirmations, first holy communions, weddings and even funerals. Especially in times of crises, Filipinos turn to the Almighty and even use religious statues and other articles of faith like rosary beads as shields or protection against physical harm. During the 1986 EDSA revolution, for example, an analyst noted that

> Wherever the rebellion took root, it became a curious blend of mass action and an expression of Catholic social conservatism. The barriers and burning tires flung across intersections to halt the expected onrush of Marcos' armored battalions could have been torn from the pages of press reports on Nicaragua or the streets of Paris in 1968. But the ornate images of the Santo Nino (Child Jesus) and Our Lady of Fatima carried dutifully into the streets would have felt at home in a 19th century cathedral.
>
> (Hernandez et al. 1986)

Filipinos are great believers of preordination or destiny, accepting that one's fate has been etched in the palm of one's hands (that is, *itinadhana ng langit* or *iginuhit ng tadhana*), yet they also believe that the individual has the freedom to shape his or her destiny. Although this is seemingly contradictory, it is consistent with the acceptance or belief that the Creator has given people free will to manage the course of their destiny:

> What Heaven has given us is Life. It has also given us, at the same time, the free will to do what we want with our life. Thus, if we view life from a negative perspective, we tend to have negative experiences. On the other hand, if we view life positively, we also have positive experiences. Simple, isn't it?
>
> (Jocano 1993a)

Related to the beliefs in God and in destiny is an often misunderstood concept, *bahala na*. It is not uncommon to hear this phrase in daily conversation. While it has been most popularly translated as "fatalism," it can also reflect religious undertones, that is, surrender to the will of God or the expectation that the Almighty will provide for all of one's needs so that all one has to do is to wait for His blessings. However, contrasted with these two interpretations is one that emphasizes inner strength to take up challenges. Jocano says:

> *Bahala na* is the psychological prop which we lean on in time of crisis when we are forced against the wall for a decision but the empirical evidences do not allow us to decide but decision is needed at the moment. How do we handle the anxiety of decision-making? What do we whisper to ourselves for reassurance that we are equal to the task? Isn't it *bahala na*? Saying *bahala na* is our only alternative and potent weapon for survival—for facing critical situations with confidence that we can overcome them.
>
> (Jocano 1993c)

INDIGENOUS CULTURAL VALUES (NATIONAL VALUES)

There has been a lot of concern over identifying and studying Filipino values, particularly as these can be used as a basis for social change and nation building. One such study, the Moral Recovery Program, identified the strengths of Filipinos as concern for others or *pakikipagkapwa-tao*; family orientation; joy and humor; flexibility, adaptability and creativity; hard work and industry; faith and religiosity; and ability to survive.

Concern for others, which strongly relates to *pakikisama* and the value given to smooth interpersonal relations, is also evidenced in another salient value termed *pakikiramay, malasakit* or compassion. Filipinos are easily moved by crises and by the sufferings of others, even of strangers.

> It is expected that during such times [of crisis], one should go out of his way to condole, to sympathize, or share the sorrows . . . [and] anyone who shows unconcern is generally talked about, if not ultimately ostracized by his close friends and peers.
>
> (Jocano 1993b)

These strengths or positive values have extremes, however, recognized as Filipino weaknesses or negative values. For example, family orientation may turn to extreme family centeredness resulting in the supremacy of personal or family concerns over national goals (*kanya-kanya* syndrome); joy and humor may become having too much of a good time such that one foregoes introspection and analysis of one's situation; an overemphasis of faith and religiosity can diminish individual industry as well as breed passivity and lack of initiative; flexibility, adaptability and creativity may become negative in that they can lead to lack of discipline as one may ignore rules and standard procedures. Hospitality is a tradition among Filipinos who are known to go out of their way to entertain guests, and even strangers, by being elaborate and overabundant in their food preparations, by offering the best living accommodations (even surrendering their sleeping quarters to house guests), and by generally striving to offer their best.

SOCIAL AND CULTURAL CONSTRAINTS TO ADVERTISING

Filipino culture puts weight on smooth interpersonal relationships, avoidance of conflict and gaining consensus in interpersonal and intergroup relations.

> [T]he acceptable way of transacting business in the community is through consultation. This is basic to Filipino expectation. Our communication technique is euphemism. Persuasion, not ordering, is considered the appropriate way for getting group consensus and action. Argumentation and debate, as favored by most Westerners, are avoided because the style often hurts Filipino sensitivities.
>
> (Jocano 1993a)

Filipinos find it difficult to be straightforward, to say no, as they are afraid to displease. The term *pakikisama* ("going along with") describes the importance of showing concern about, being supportive of, and—if necessary—conceding for the good of the group. This value given to good human relations is also the underlying reason for the focus on the reconciliation efforts in settling all forms of disputes—whether these are between individuals or groups, and whether of a personal or national consequence.

This importance given to conflict avoidance serves as a deterrence to the practice of comparative advertising in the country. J.J. Calero, chief executive officer of J. Walter Thompson Philippines, says that the outright naming of and comparison with a competitor in an advertisement is offensive to the Filipino audience. Being nonconfrontational, he notes, is a trait that the Filipinos share with their ASEAN neighbors. He adds that the Malaysians are even more nonconfrontational than Filipinos.

Colonial mentality or a preference for things foreign, particularly American, remains prevalent among Filipinos despite nationalistic efforts to eradicate such kinds of thinking. This is manifest in the popularity of foreign-brand items such as clothes, food and household appliances, as well as in the common practice of using Caucasian models and U.S. settings in advertising. There is, however, another view of this preference for foreign-produced products that runs along the lines of consumerism. Patronage of foreign goods, including viewership of Western-produced films and television programs, is not due to the Filipinos' colonial mentality, but rather to their concern to get the best value for the money.

Growth of the Advertising Industry

HISTORICAL ANALYSIS

Advertising via the mass media was American instigated, although there is evidence that even pre-Spanish Filipinos used crudely printed advertising forms to publicize their trade. During the Spanish period, despite the operation of printing presses and the circulation of various publications, advertising via some print media form was uncommon. Whatever advertisements there were in newsletters, journals, and magazines such as the *Excelsior* and *Renacimiento Filipino* were wholly business announcements. Publications at that time were generally short-lived and quite specialized in theme and audience. However, some forms of outdoor advertising were evident, such as posters put up in cockfighting rings, and in *moro-moro* plays. The beginnings of transit advertising were also evident during the last years of the Spanish rule in the form of the *paseo,* horse-drawn carriages on which barkers called public attention to their announcement with a drum.

During the last decade of the 19th century and the first of the 20th century, newspapers catering to various audiences, such as the Spanish-speaking elite and middle class, American servicemen, bureaucrats and businessmen, began to circulate. These publications carried advertisements, many of which were rather simple boxed business announcements (for example, the names, addresses and hours of operation of professionals such as doctors, dentists, barbers, sculptors and photographers, and goods for sale in department stores and import houses). Newspapers, including *The Manila Times* and the *Manila Daily Bulletin* founded at about this time, had these advertising announcements in a format similar to present-day classified advertisements.

By the 1920s, with several newspapers and magazines circulating, advertisements improved from simple announcements or notices to ones carrying pictures and illustrations. Moreover, advertisements could be found liberally scattered throughout every page of the publications. Outdoor advertising was in the form of posters or bills plastered on walls. The use of such bills became so rampant that commercial establishments plastered their own announcements on their walls—"*No Fijales Carteles,*" which meant "Post No Bills."

Being straightforward announcements, advertisements of the time were essentially more informative than persuasive in intent. An exception was the San Miguel advertisements that claimed it was "the best beer—you find it all over the world." Another was for Whatson's Blood Purifier, which said it "would not only purify your blood but also enable you successfully to resist all tropical diseases." With regard to the use of pictures in advertisements, the first use of some kind of artwork could actually be traced to the late 1800s when weeklies like the *Manila Alegre* and *Manililla*—both satirical publications—and *El Domingo* carried caricatures in their illustrated advertisements. During the American period, commercial art for advertisements was rendered in art nouveau style.

Most advertising at the time was in the print form. However, with the introduction of radio in 1922, entrepreneurs like Beck (an American who owned a department store), Araneta (a Spanish-Filipino mestizo who was in real estate), and Heacock (another American department-store owner) went into radio operations. As radio was a new medium with a limited audience, it was not regarded as profitable for advertising. In fact government granted station owners advertising subsidies.

From the onset of American rule until the 1940s, the burgeoning advertising industry was American dominated. Because the Philippines was a colonial state, the major advertisers as well as the most prominent advertising companies operating in the country were those of its colonial masters. In 1921, the first advertising agency in the country, Philippine Publicity Service Inc., was set up and managed by H. Edmund Bullis. Another of the major advertising players was Frank J. Herrier who set up the advertising and publicity department of the largest import–export company (and not coincidentally the largest advertiser) of the pre-war period, Pacifica Commercial, which was owned by another American, Horace B. Pond. Herrier later left Pacifica to set up the advertising department of La Vanguardia Press. Later Herier, together with two print media men, F. Theo Rogers and M.W. Jenkins, formed Philippine Agency Service, which served as a clearing house of U.S.–made advertisements for publication in the country.

More advertising companies, not all American, began to be set up. These included the International Advertising Agency, which was founded by Filipinos; the Jean Bisson Enterprises headed by a French artist (Bisson) who cornered the art side of Philippine advertising at the time; Brau and Rosendale Advertising; and Lu (for Luzon) Ocampo Advertising.

Filipino advertising pioneers during this pre-war period included people such as Manuel Buenaventura and Manuel Gonzales who trained under the Americans and who remained active in the industry until the 1970s. The advertising agencies at the time were often one-room affairs sustained by a limited number of clients; that is, usually just one or two large clients. Apart from Pacifica, the big accounts then included other import establishments (Sprungli and Co., Alfredo Roensch and Co.); specialty and department stores (such as Aguinaldo's, Berg's, Heacock's, Genato Commercial, and Hale Shoes); liquor and wine (San Miguel Beer, La Extremena); hotels (El Real, Metropole); oil companies (such as Caltex and Socony); manufacturing companies (such as Philippine Manufacturing Co., which was later bought by the American firm Procter & Gamble and Ysmael); tobacco (Liget and Myers Tobacco Co.); theaters (Times and Ideal); and drug stores/companies (Botica Inglesa and Botica Boie).

During the Japanese occupation, the media were Japanese controlled and the only type of promotion was government propaganda. By 1945, with the return of American rule and the task of reconstruction after the war, there was a resurgence of economic activity. At this time the print media rebounded, as did advertising. It is noteworthy that one of the first advertising agencies to open after the war was a Filipino-owned company (Philippine Promotions Bureau or Philprom). An exceptional feature of Philprom was that it was headed by Pedro Teodoro, an advertising pioneer who did not get his training from the Americans. Teodoro and Philprom prospered: its accounts were a combination of American and Filipino companies representing the manufacturing industry (paints, paper, drugs, alcohol, and liquor) as well as trading enterprises.

As many advertisements were for American products, a trend toward using American models developed and is still manifest today. With time, the pictures accompanying the advertisement copy got better so that the overall quality of print advertisements improved. Philippine radio soap opera was born during the 1950s, sponsored by giant consumer companies, Procter & Gamble Philippines and its competitor Philippine Refining Co. (an affiliate of Lever Brothers of the United States).

By the 1960s, in line with an economic boom evidenced by the growing numbers of products and services introduced to the market, advertising agencies became more sophisticated as they began to rely on empirically or "scientifically" collected data about consumers for their advertising campaigns. Moreover, agencies moved toward providing full service, that is, creative, research and media services. From the 1960s to the early 1970s, the advertising industry grew in revenue with the transnational companies—most of which were American—among the leaders. Factors affecting this growth included the public's increasing disposable income; the rise in the number of newspapers, radio and television stations; and the development of cinema and outdoor advertising media.

The 1950s and the 1960s were the golden years of Philippine advertising. With high regard for Filipino practitioners, advertisers from Singapore, Thailand, Taiwan and Indonesia had their promotional campaigns produced in the Philippines. The political and economic turmoil of the early 1970s just prior to the declaration of martial law was reflected in the advertising industry. Despite social strife, the advertising industry's activities did not decline and, in fact, media billings were on the rise. At this time, however, questions and doubts were raised by the public regarding advertising ethics and professionalism. Advertisements were branded as untruthful, poorly executed and even indecent. In the meantime martial law was declared, media establishments were closed and fears were raised regarding the future of the advertising industry.

The advertising industry was at a crossroads, necessitating radical action to restore its integrity and professionalism as well as to ensure its future in a new political environment. A code of ethics was needed. The Mass Media Council, a media censorship body created by the martial law government, convened a committee composed of representatives from the consumer sector, academe (that is, the University of the Philippines' Institute of Mass Communication), and the military (that is, the Office of Civil Relations) to formulate such a code. In March 1974, after more than a year, this code of ethics and rules and regulations for media and advertising agencies was approved by the government's Ministry of Public Information. Also in line with restoring professionalism, the Advertising Board of the Philippines was created in 1974. The Board adopted the code of ethics and took upon itself the functions of screening and regulating advertising in the country. (A more complete discussion of the Board is found later in this chapter.)

With the Philippine economy in a slump during the early 1980s, the advertising industry became sluggish. Things worsened after August 1983 when Benigno Aquino was assassinated. From 1983 to 1985, the country was in recession with massive retrenchments and closures in all sectors, the advertising industry included. Since 1986, there has been general economic recovery, dipping slightly in 1987, but continuing quite steadily thereafter.

CURRENT PUBLIC POLICIES TOWARD CORPORATE OWNERSHIP

A specific provision in the 1987 Philippine Constitution requires limited (30 percent) investment participation by foreigners in advertising companies. Moreover, there is a clear specification that the management of such companies be all Filipino:

> The advertising industry is impressed with public interest, and shall be regulated by law for the protection of consumers and the promotion of the general welfare. Only Filipino citizens or corporations or associations at least seventy (70) percent of the capital of which is owned by such citizens shall be allowed to engage in the advertising industry. The participation of foreign investors in the governing body of entities in such industry shall be limited to their proportionate share in the capital thereof, and all the executive and managing officers of such entities must be citizens of the Philippines.
>
> (*Constitution* 1987, Article XVI, Section 11[2])

While deliberating this provision, the constitutional commissioners recognized that at the time

• most of the agencies existing in the country were either multinational companies or joint-ventures with Filipinos;

• most of the advertisements were for foreign products produced or packaged by multinational companies;

• the number of advertisements seen daily by Filipinos exceeded those seen by Americans and Australians;

• the urban and Western lifestyles presented in the advertisements tended to reinforce a consumption-oriented mentality, elitism, urban bias, and overall favorable perception of foreign products;

• Filipino values of patriotism and nationalism might be jeopardized by the dominance of foreign advertising; and

• if Filipinos were to be economically self-reliant, faith in their capacity to manage and own advertising agencies must be shown.

By February 1992, advertising companies had to comply with the 70/30 percent local/foreign equity ratio, with the multinational agencies divesting themselves to the legal limit.

The Structure of the Media

THE PHILIPPINE MEDIA IN THE PAST 50 YEARS

The period immediately following World War II was one of the liveliest times in the Philippine press. Many newspaper companies were established or reopened, among them were several fly-by-night tabloids that did not survive long. Publishers of the more prestigious print media operations were also big names in business. Among the many other enterprises in which they were engaged were the agriculture, mining, shipping, manufacturing, public utilities, financing and food industries. Moreover, these publishers were involved in trimedia enterprises, as they also owned and controlled radio and television stations.

The post-war Philippine press enjoyed a reputation for being the freest in Asia, as it was able to criticize the government in general as well as its specific policies, programs and officials. At the same time, there was the perception that the press was becoming irresponsible and sensationalistic; that it was being used by its owners to protect their own economic and political interests. When Marcos declared martial law in 1972, the press experienced the brunt of the repression: journalists were harassed, arrested and detained; and all media establishments, except those sympathetic to the dictatorial government of Marcos, were closed down. The contents of newspapers became predictable—either drab press releases or elaborate praise for the Marcoses and their cronies.

In the broadcasting industry, the Marcos years were an era of monopolization. Ownership of the country's radio and television stations was concentrated in the hands of a few cronies. Telecommunication facilities were granted exclusive franchises. The Philippine Long Distance Telecommunications Corporation (PLDT) was the sole entity allowed to carry TV signals to and from satellite facilities. The Domestic Satellite Corporation (Domsat) was the only corporation allowed to purchase, operate and set up satellite TV stations. Sining Makulay, Inc. was the only cable company allowed to set up and operate nationwide. Needless to say, these monopolistic arrangements were detrimental to the growth and quality of service in the broadcasting industry.

In spite of the oppression, an alternative press upholding the libertarian tradition was born. The assassination of Ninoy Aquino emboldened other media practitioners so that the years between 1983 and 1986 saw the birth of more alternative newspapers. Another remarkable event of this period was the trend toward a more critical and outspoken analysis of government action and individual government personalities, begun by women journalists writing in the mainstream press.

Since the 1986 revolution, there has been a revival of media functioning as society's watchdog against government excesses. There has been a tremendous surge in the number of competing national dailies, a repeat of the post–World War II phenomenon. The Aquino government passed a bill deregulating the country's telecommunications facilities, resulting in the rise of new TV and cable operations nationwide. As it was during earlier post–World War II years, tendencies toward sensationalism and economic interests controlling the focus of reportage re-emerged.

OWNERSHIP OF THE MEDIA: LARGELY PRIVATE

The media in the country are largely owned and controlled by the private sector. There is, however, some (minimal) control by government of certain media establishments via actual ownership or by sequestration. Of the hundreds of radio stations operating nationwide, only 32 are government owned. Of the five television networks broadcasting throughout the country, one (People's Television 4) belongs to the government, and two (RPN 9 and IBC 13) have been sequestered by the government. In cases of sequestration, a government-appointed board of directors oversees the operations of the media company. The government does not publish a newspaper, but it does maintain its own press office.

GOVERNMENT POLICIES TOWARD THE MEDIA AND ADVERTISING

As just discussed, the end of the authoritarian regime of Marcos in early 1986 signaled the return of press freedom in the Philippines. Characteristic of libertarian press systems, the Philippine media—unconstrained by government regulation—enjoys a wide degree of freedom. Much like the American Constitution, the Philippines' 1987 Constitution guarantees press freedom as well as the people's right to information of public concern.

But in assuring freedom of the press, the Constitution implicitly realizes that the media may be used as instruments working contrary to public interests. Hence, there is a Constitutional prohibition against the ownership and management of mass media companies (including advertising) by non-Filipino citizens, in an attempt to guard against foreign influence via these mass channels. Moreover, there is a similar ban on the creation of media monopolies. The constitutional commissioners felt that

> a media monopoly is an abuse or perversion of the freedom of the press by a single individual or a company or companies owned by him. Its danger lies in placing in the hands of a man or a group of men a weapon for the widespread manipulation of vehicles of public opinion, to influence for the public mind and advance his or its selfish economic or political influence to the prejudice of the larger public interest and welfare.
>
> (*Constitution* 1987)

According to popular newspaper publisher–editor–columnist Maximo Soliven, the "Philippine press is combative, adversarial and, in certain quarters, malicious" (Soliven 1993). To protect against the potential for press (print and broadcast) abuse is the libel law, which provides that both journalist and publisher can be liable for a libelous article. Perhaps the most well-known application of this libel law was by President Aquino when she filed suit against popular columnist, the late Luis Beltran, and *The Philippine Star.* Beltran had written that President Aquino crawled and hid under her bed during the attempted military coup in 1987. Aquino took offense, claiming that the allegation that she hid "impeached her virtue, honor and reputation as President." Apart from filing suit, she invited television cameras into her bedroom to show that there was no way for her to have hidden under her bed. The Court decided in favor of Aquino. This decision was appealed, and the Court of Appeals reversed the decision. Soliven and the others were acquitted.

Apart from libel law, the only other constraint to free press is the National Emergency Act, introduced also during the Aquino presidency, which allows the president to take over any private company serving the public interest should national security warrant such an act.

During the presidency of Corazon Aquino and continuing into the incumbency of Fidel Ramos, the government has pursued an "open skies" policy with regard to media and telecommunications. Exclusive franchises earlier granted by the Marcos administration were revoked in line with the current administration's commitment to free trade and liberalization. Particularly in the broadcast and cable industries, the government encourages growth and expansion and provides regulation only in relation to programming and technical standards.

Although the government forbids crossover ownership between broadcast and print (in line with the Constitutional provision banning media monopolies), it encourages partnerships between broadcast and cable companies. Cross-ownership of print and broadcast media is disallowed in order to preserve media democracy, whereas broadcast–cable alliances are encouraged to maximize the synergy of broadcast, satellite and cable. For instance, cable companies are required to carry the signals of any TV station within the reach of the community. One beneficial result of such a requirement is that households serviced by cable companies have improved television signal reception. With the telecommunications deregulation, television networks have constructed their own up- and down-link facilities and have affiliated themselves with satellite–cable companies.

To oversee the broadcast, film and video media, the government has regulatory bodies lodged under the Department of Transportation and Communication. The National Telecommunications Commission (NTC) formulates guidelines and regulation for radio and television. The Movie and Television Regulatory and Classification Board (MTRCB) censors and classifies film and television programs. The Video Regulatory Board (VRB) monitors video rentals and sales in the country.

The media and advertising industries in the Philippines are averse to the government regulation (or censorship) that was the norm during the martial-law years. Nevertheless, the belief prevails that there is a need to guard against poor quality, untruthful, or morally and socially offensive media content. Toward this end, media companies have banded together among themselves to form private regulatory bodies in a move toward self-regulation, which they believe is better than government regulation. The Kapisanan ng mga Brodkaster sa Pilipinas (KBP or Association of Broadcasters in the Philippines) is a self-regulatory body composed of broadcasting practitioners.

In the advertising industry, the Advertising Board of the Philippines, or Adboard, is the most prominent regulatory body. The Adboard serves as an umbrella association for national organizations representing various advertising bodies. It comprises advertisers, media, advertising agencies, advertising support agencies and research organizations.

Some of the Leading Media in the Philippines Available to Advertisers

PRINT MEDIA

More than 20 national newspapers, including broadsheets and tabloids, circulate on a daily or almost daily basis. The total circulation of these newspapers is about 150,000 distributed in different parts of the country. These newspapers are self-proclaimed national dailies intended for distribution throughout the country. However, because of the archipelagic nature of the country and the concomitant problems related to print media distribution, the bulk of the regular readership of these newspapers is centered in and around the metropolitan Manila area.

Almost equal numbers of newspapers are published in English and in Pilipino; however, it is interesting to note that the broadsheets, including business newspapers, are published in English whereas the tabloids are all in Pilipino. As in other countries, Philippine broadsheets are considered more sedate than tabloids. In terms of circulation, it is the tabloids, more than the broadsheets, that enjoy the wider readership. In fact the leading two newspapers in terms of circulation, *People's Journal* (383,000) and *Abante* (350,000), are tabloids. Among the broadsheets, the three most popular in the country are *The Philippine Star* (275,000), *The Manila Bulletin* (240,000), and *The Philippine Daily Inquirer* (228,000). Of these three, the *Bulletin* is the oldest: Its origins can be traced to the first decade of 20th century. The *Star* and the *Inquirer* were founded in 1986, during the changeover from the Marcos to the Aquino government.

The dozens of magazines and trade journals are mostly published in English and on a weekly basis. It is not uncommon for print publishers to own other media. For example, four of the publishers of major dailies in the country, namely,

Philippine Journalists Inc. (*People's Journal*), Philippines Today Inc. (*The Philippine Star*), Bulletin Publishing Co. (*The Manila Bulletin*), and Metromedia Times Corp. (*The Manila Times*), are in the broadsheet, tabloid, as well as the magazine business. The magazines with the largest circulations in the Philippines are *Sports Life Weekly, Panorama, Starweek, Gossip, Scandals, Rumors, Sports Weekly* and *Teenstars*.

As advertising media, newspapers have higher average cost per full page advertisement than magazines ($1,414 for newspapers versus $454.70 for magazines). Of the leading broadsheets, the *Manila Bulletin* leads in terms of advertising content.

THE BROADCAST MEDIA

Between the print and the broadcast media, the latter are the more popular for news, information and entertainment. Radio enjoys the highest popularity in the country, as evidenced by its generally higher listenership figures than either print media readership or television viewership (Table 8.1). However, in terms of advertising billings, television has a 65 percent share, whereas newspapers control 18 percent and radio accounts for only 15 percent (*Manila Chronicle Supplement* 1993).

There are over 350 radio stations operating all over the archipelago, the bulk being private commercial radio stations. FM stations outnumber AM stations—365 and 251, respectively. The reach of many metropolitan Manila-based radio stations extends beyond the national capital region. Two of the leading AM stations—DZMM and DZRH—in fact broadcast nationwide and in stereo. Outside metropolitan Manila, the broadcasting power of the radio stations is usually limited to five or 10 kilowatts. As with newspapers, there is a strong language distinction within the radio medium. With few exceptions, AM radio is almost entirely in Pilipino or in the local dialect, whereas FM radio is typically in English.

Radio stations operating in the country are either independently owned or are affiliated with nationwide radio networks. The largest radio networks in the country are ABS-CBN, Radio Mindanao Network, Manila Broadcasting Co. and Bombo Radyo. ABS-CBN and Radio Mindanao are also involved in television broadcasting, while Manila Broadcasting and Bombo Radyo are radio operations exclusively.

Radio advertising rates are considerably less than television rates. Of the over 350 radio stations operating in the country, DZMM and DZRH charge the highest rates, for example, about $60 per 30-second spot. The advertising rates of other metropolitan Manila stations are only half that amount; and provincial radio stations, even those affiliated with these two stations, charge even less.

Intense competition exists between two of the largest networks, ABS-CBN and GMA. Both networks are privately owned companies. Majority ownership of ABS-CBN, which has been a public corporation since 1991, is with the Lopez

Table 8.1. Media Use in the Philippines by Area, Income and Gender

Mass Medium	Total Philippines	Metro Manila	Other Luzon	Visayas Area	Mindanao Area	By Income AB	By Income C	By Income DE	By Sex M	By Sex F
Readership										
National broadsheet	20.0	25.0	16.0	20.0	17.0	67.0	29.0	12.0	23.0	17.0
National tabloid	32.0	45.0	31.5	14.0	25.0	29.0	38.0	30.0	34.0	29.0
Provincial newspaper	3.0	1.0	NA	11.0	9.0	3.0	4.0	2.0	4.0	2.0
Sunday supplement	10.0	18.0	45.0	2.0	4.0	29.0	16.0	5.0	10.0	11.0
General interest magazine (English)	13.0	14.0	13.5	9.0	13.0	24.0	19.0	8.0	11.0	14.0
General interest magazine (Pilipino or dialect)	19.0	17.0	23.0	20.0	13.0	19.0	24.0	18.0	12.0	26.0
Sports magazine	6.0	7.0	8.0	5.0	3.0	9.0	10.0	5.0	9.0	4.0
Foreign magazine	5.0	5.0	5.0	5.0	6.0	13.0	7.0	3.0	7.0	3.0
Radio listenership	91.0	90.0	88.3	93.3	91.9	93.5	93.5	88.0	90.5	91.4
Television viewership	90.5	97.0	86.5	91.0	90.1	98.9	96.5	84.6	92.0	89.3

Source: Association of Accredited Advertising Agencies in the Philippines, 1994, *1993–1994 Media Factbook*, 21.

Note: NA = less than 5 percent; AB, high income bracket/AB = monthly earnings between P25,000(B) and P50,000(A); C, middle income bracket/C = monthly income between P6,000 and P24,999; DE, low income bracket/DE = those with monthly incomes below P6,000.

family. The business interests of the Lopezes are vast, ranging from media (apart from ABS-CBN, they are also the major stockholders of SkyCable, the largest cable company in the country; *The Manila Chronicle*; as well as movie production and post-production studios), a public utility (the electric company servicing metropolitan Manila), sugar mills, and financial institutions. The Lopezes are also into politics, with members of the family having served in several national and local elective positions. The main stockholders of GMA are Menardo Jimenez who is involved in agribusiness as well as real estate; Gualberto Duavit, also a businessman and politician; and Felipe Gozun, a lawyer who serves as the network's managing partner.

Both networks claim leadership in the television industry. ABS-CBN programs dominate in the audience viewership surveys and it was the first network to go into nationwide and international satellite broadcasting. GMA takes pride in the local and international awards and recognition that it has received, as well as in its shows that rate high in the audience surveys. Like ABS-CBN, GMA also broadcasts via satellite nationwide and, for special programs on seasonal holidays like Christmas, has gone into international satellite broadcasting aimed at Filipino communities overseas. Lately the competition of these two networks intensified as television programs and stars switched from one to the other.

RPN and IBC were sequestered by the government from Roberto Benedicto, an associate of former president Marcos. The networks rate low in the audience surveys and there are plans for both stations to soon be privatized. ABC is a relatively new television network owned by the Tan family. Calling itself the country's fastest-growing network, ABC has recently gone into nationwide satellite broadcasting. PTV is a government station, but it does not receive financial support from the government; hence, it operates like a commercial station.

The average advertising rates for prime time shows originating from metropolitan Manila stations range from US$900 to $1,600 per 30-second spot.

CABLE OR COMMUNITY NETWORK

There are more than 100 cable or community television operators throughout the country, offering anywhere from 12 to over 40 television channels to its subscribers. The metropolitan Manila and Cebu areas have the most and largest cable companies. SkyCable, a company affiliated with the Lopez-owned ABS-CBN television network, is the largest in the country. These cable companies normally carry the signals of free TV (that is, the six national networks whose broadcasts emanate from metropolitan Manila, as well as the local television affiliates broadcasting in the cable company's region of operation), satellite signals (for example, CNN, the Star Channels from Hong Kong, and other Palapa-transmitted signals), community billboards, as well as the cable company's own programs. These cable company programs include news, sports coverage and movies for which advertising is possible.

CINEMA

Movie watching in cinema houses is a very popular pastime among Filipinos. Moreover, it is inexpensive; for example, theater admission is P18 to P30 (US$0.75 to $1.00) in first-run movie houses in metropolitan Manila, and it is even lower in the provinces. There are over 300 movie houses in the various metropolitan centers, cities and other urban areas in the country. These accept both cinema as well as audio advertising.

NONTRADITIONAL AND OTHER ADVERTISING MEDIA

This category includes communication channels located out of the home that may be used for advertising. These advertising media are intended to be supplemental to the main media, to support promotions, and to penetrate narrow target groups with precision. They are thus used less frequently and with more care. The broad categories of these advertising media are the following:

• Billboards, including painted billboards, landscaped billboard, wall signs
• Neon signs
• Plastic back-lit signs, such as poster advertisements, airport advertisements, rota graphics, rota advertisements, and rotating triangular billboards
• Transit (public or mass transit) advertisements, such as bus advertisements, taxi advertisements, jeepney advertisements, tricycle advertisements, sealine advertisements, and light rail transit display advertisements
• Mediatron electronic billboards located in high motor vehicle–traffic areas, for example, the South Superhighway
• Street smart advertisements, the most common being the covered bus or jeepney stops and waiting sheds
• Balloons or airblimps, which are very sparingly used because of limitations, including weather and government regulation
• Trade directories or annuals
• Direct mail

Recent Growth of the Advertising Industry

Tables 8.2 and 8.3 show the growth of the advertising industry in recent years. Comparisons of purchases of time and space in various mass media over the years show that television traditionally has the largest (about 60 percent since 1987) share of the total. Print billings have been quite a distant second (about 20 percent since 1987), followed by radio (about 15 percent since 1987). Billings in other media, including cinema, have accounted for even smaller amounts, that is, less than 2 percent since 1987.

As indicated by gross media billings (Table 8.2), the industry has had steady

Table 8.2.   Comparison of Gross Billings of Philippines Advertising Agencies from 1987 to 1992

Year	Gross Billings in Current Terms (million pesos)	% Change	Gross Billings in Real Terms (million pesos)	% Change
1987	3,149	NA	3,430	NA
1988	4,194	33.19	4,194	22.26
1989	5,175	23.39	4,612	9.97
1990	6,189	19.59	4,831	4.75
1991	7,001	13.12	4,605	−4.67
1992	9,415	34.48	NA	NA

Source: *Advertising Industry Profile*, 1992 and 1993; "Advertising Industry Outpacing Economy" in *The Manila Chronicle*, 1993, February 4.
Note: NA, not available.

Table 8.3.   The Philippines Advertising Industry's Contribution to Gross Domestic Product (GDP), 1983-1992

Year	Media Advertising Expenditure (million pesos)	% Change	GDP at Current Prices (million pesos)	% Change	Media Advertising Expenditure as % of GDP
1983	995	NA	384,096	NA	0.259
1984	1,146	15.2	540,423	40.7	0.212
1985	1,499	30.8	609,459	12.8	0.246
1986	1,832	22.2	627,129	2.9	0.292
1987	2,207	20.5	708,368	13.0	0.312
1988	2,765	25.3	826,749	16.7	0.335
1989	3,886	40.5	964,500	16.7	0.403
1990	4,527	16.5	1,070,900	11.0	0.423
1991	5,176	14.3	1,239,100	15.7	0.416
1992	6,635	28.2	1,342,515	7.92	0.494

Source: *Advertising Industry Profile*, 1992 and 1993; "Advertising Industry Outpacing Economy" in *The Manila Chronicle*, 1993, February 4.
Note: NA, not available.

growth, averaging 39.48 percent over the 6-year period from 1987 to 1992. The greatest surges in growth were in the periods 1991–92 and 1987–88.

How the advertising industry has contributed to the general economy is indicated in Table 8.3. Media advertising expenditures have been steadily rising, from just under 1 billion pesos in 1983 to over 6.6 billion in 1992, at an average of about 20 percent per year. As a measure of the industry's contribution to the country's economic progress, media advertising expenditures in 1992 accounted for 0.494 percent of gross domestic product. This figure represents the highest, so far, since 1983.

LARGEST ADVERTISING AGENCIES

The top 10 advertising agencies, according to the Adboard, in the past 3 years are listed in Table 8.4. Several of these agencies have been leading names in the industry for over 20 years.

Table 8.4.   The Top 10 Agencies in the Past 3 Years

Rank	1991	1992	1993
1	McCann-Erickson	McCann-Erickson	McCann-Erickson
2	J. Walter Thompson	J. Walter Thompson	Basic Advertising
3	Basic/Foote Cone & Belding	Basic/Foote Cone & Belding	J. Walter Thompson
4	Ace Saatchi & Saatchi	Ace Saatchi & Saatchi	Lintas: Manila
5	Lintas: Manila	Lintas: Manila	AMA-DDB Needham
6	AMA-DDB Needham	Hemisphere-Leo Burnett	Hemisphere-Leo Burnett
7	Hemisphere-Leo Burnett	AMA-DDB Needham	Avellana & Associates
8	DY&R-Alcantara	DY&R-Alcantara	DY&R-Alcantara
9	PAC/BBDO	Avellana & Associates	Campaigns & Grey
10	Campaigns Universal	Avia Communications	Jiminez DMB & B

The Top 10 Agencies in the Past 3 years

McCann-Erickson Philippines has been operating since 1963. Another American company, J. Walter Thompson, has an even longer history in the country, having been set up in 1947. These American transnational companies moved to 70/30 percentage local/foreign partnership as of February 1993 in compliance with the provision in the 1986 Constitution.

Basic/Foote, Cone & Belding (FCB) began in August 1979 as an American-Filipino partnership. However, in 1993, the company became totally Filipino owned and renamed itself Basic Advertising. Like Basic before it cut its ties with FCB, Hemisphere-Leo Burnett (since June 1971) is an American-Filipino partnership. Its mother company is Leo Burnett Co. Inc. Lintas: Manila is another example of a partnership, but this time between Dutch and Filipino companies. Its mother company is Lintas Holding B.V. Rotterdam, a transnational with 179 offices in 50 countries. It has been operating in the Philippines since May 1978. Avia Communications, another top ranking advertising agency, is an affiliate of Lintas: Manila. However, Avia is a wholly owned Filipino company.

Some data on these leading advertising agencies are presented in Table 8.5.

LARGEST NATIONAL ADVERTISERS

Table 8.6 is a list of the top 10 categories of products advertised in the various mass media in 1992. Moreover, examples of advertisers for each category are included. Many of these companies (for example, Nestlé Philippines Inc., Procter & Gamble Philippines Inc., Colgate-Palmolive, Unilever Philippines, Philippine Refining Co., Mead Johnson Phils. Inc., Kimberly Clark, S.C. Johnson, Bayer, McDonald's, Wendy's, Toyota, Mitsubishi, Pepsi-Cola, Coca-Cola, Dole and Del Monte) are multinational companies manufacturing their products in the country. Others (such as San Miguel Corporation, United Laboratories, Philippine Long Distance Telephone Co., Fortune Tobacco Corp., Philippine Airlines, Jollibee, Asia Brewery, Purefoods, and Commonwealth Foods) are Filipino corporations.

The line of products manufactured or marketed by several of these compa-

Table 8.5. Leading Agencies in the Philippines and Their Foreign Affiliations

Agency	Year Established	Affiliate/Foreign Partner
Ace Saatchi &Saatchi	1949	Saatchi & Saatchi
AMA-DDB Needham Worldwide	1958	DDB Needham Worldwide
Avellana & Associates	1964	Avia Communications, AV Plus, Affiliated Advertising Agencies International
Avia Communications	1986	No foreign partner
Basic Advertising	1975	No foreign partner
Campaigns & Grey	1986	Grey
DY&R-Alcantara	1946	Dentsu, Young & Rubicam
Hemisphere-Leo Burnett	1971	Leo Burnett
J. Walter Thompson	1947	Studio Communication Arts, Lineshot Photoprint/J. Walter Thompson
Jimenez/DMB&B	1989	DMB&B
Lintas	1978	Lintas Holdings
McCann-Erickson Philippines	1963	McCann-Erickson
PCA/BBDO	1949	BBDO

nies is varied. For example, San Miguel Corporation, the largest company in the country, produces dairy products, beer, beverages and various food products. Procter & Gamble, Colgate-Palmolive and Unilever-Philippine Refining Co. make personal care products such as toothpaste, bath soaps and body spray, as well as laundry detergents and beverages.

Advertising Organizations

The *Adboard* is an umbrella organization of various associations dealing with advertising in the country. It is comprised of the Association of Accredited Advertising Agencies–Philippines (4A's–P), the Advertising Suppliers Association of the Philippines (ASAP), Marketing and Opinion Research Society of the Philippines (MORES), Print Media Organization (PRIMO), KBP, Outdoor Advertising Association of the Philippines (OAAP), Cinema Advertising Association of the Philippines (CAAP) and the Philippine Association of National Advertisers (PANA).

In light of the social and political situation of the country during its early martial law period, the advertising industry adopted the Code of Ethics formulated by the representatives of the industry, media, consumers, academe and the military. A unified organization—the Adboard—was set up to oversee the implementation of this Code in the spirit of self-regulation. This Code has been reviewed and revised a number of times to make it more attuned to changes in the industry.

The 1984 review of the Code resulted in the formation of two committees within the organization, that is, the Advertising Content Regulation Committee

Table 8.6   Leading Advertisers in the Philippines by Product Category, 1992

Personal Care Products	Medical Products and Equipment	Home Care	Dairy Products
Colgate-Palmolive Philippines	United Laboratories	S.C. Johnson	Nestlé Philippines
Philippine Refining Company	Myra Pharmaceutical	Bayer Philippines	General Milling Corp.
Kimberly Clark	Mead Johnson		Magnolia Corp.
Avon	Wyeth-Suaco		
Johnson & Johnson	Metro Laboratories		
Beer and Liquor	**Cars/Automobiles**	**Beverages**	**Cigarettes**
Tanduay Distillers	Toyota	Coca-Cola	Fortune
San Miguel Corp.	Nissan	Pepsi-Cola	Japan Tobacco
La Tondena	Mitsubishi	Del Monte	Philip Morris Co.
Asia Brewery		Dole	La Suerte
Corporate and Institutional	**Entertainment and Sports**	**Restaurants and Fast Food**	**Food products**
Philippine Long Distance Telephone Co.	Various film/movie companies	McDonald's	California Manufacturing Co.
San Miguel Corporation	Movie distributors	Jollibee	Kraft Foods
Johnson & Johnson		Wendy's	Commonwealth Foods Corporation
Banks		Pizza Hut	San Miguel Corporation
Petron Oil Company		Max's Fried Chicken	Purefoods

(ACRC) and the Trade Practices and Conduct Committee (TPCC), which essentially carry out the provisions of the Code of Ethics. The former deals with advertising content, prescreening all radio and television advertisements to ensure that they conform with the Code of Ethics; and the latter aims to ensure professionalism in the industry and concerns itself with sectoral (technical) matters outside advertising content. The ACRC formulates and implements the policies, rules and regulations pertaining to the screening of advertisements and sales promotions. (The procedures followed by ACRC are detailed later in this chapter in a discussion of censorship in advertising.) The TPCC formulates, interprets and implements intersectoral and interassociation trade practices and agreements not directly related to advertising content (for example, the collection and payment of accounts, publishing information on media rates, marketing media space/time, placing advertisements and signs, publishing rates for advertising services, and conducting research and publishing the results).

The origins of PANA may be traced to the Advertising Club set up in 1948, which was essentially a social group whose members included advertisers, media representatives, advertising agency representatives and "others in related areas." In 1958, PANA was set up with the following as its basic principles, to which it still subscribes:

• the belief that advertising is an essential factor in the marketing of goods and services and consequently, is an important factor in the economic life of the country;

• the belief that the interests of the consumers should be the primary concern of advertisers and in cases of conflict, the interests of the consumer should prevail;

• the belief that public confidence in advertising and advertised goods and services should be promoted and protected, and therefore any practices that tend to undermine that confidence should be prevented or corrected;

• the belief in the upliftment of the standards and practices of advertising.

Today over 200 companies in every major industry are PANA members. These companies represent a large majority (85 percent) of national advertisers.

Today 4A's–P is made up of 60 agencies. Members of 4A's–P are full-service advertising agencies, providing creative, media and research services; accredited with the print and broadcast media associations, PRIMO and KBP, respectively; and have a minimum paid-up capital of 100,000 pesos (about US$4,500). This association of advertising agencies was formed in 1977 with the merger of two influential groups, the Association of Philippine Advertising Agencies and the Lapian ng mga Advertaysing Praktisyoner na Pilipino sa Ikauunlad ng Sambayanan (LAPPIS, or the Association of Filipino Advertising Practitioners for the Philippine Progress). As a professional organization, 4A's–P in general aims to upgrade the practice of advertising and to promote the welfare of the association as a whole, as well as the welfare of its individual members. Toward these ends, there are several committees or groups within it, as follows:

• the Media Standards Authority, which is made up of all the media directors of its member agencies and which is tasked with projects such as arranging for media monitoring services, regular publication of a *Media Factbook,* and the formulation of print media guidelines

• the Creative Guild of the Philippines, whose members include all the creative directors of its member agencies and which gives out monthly (Creative's Choice) and yearly (Ad of the Year) awards in an attempt to upgrade the creative standards in all advertising media

• the Education and Manpower Development, Academe and Industry Committee, which conducts seminars through the Advertising Resources for Advancement through Learning (ARAL) for advertising executives and students

The research profession is represented in the advertising industry by *MORES.* Members of this organization believe that research, being an investment more than a cost, is essential to any business. Also established with the aim to upgrade the profession, MORES "provides for quick dissemination and exchange of ideas on the latest research techniques through seminars, workshops, conventions and colloquia." MORES was founded in 1977. Today, its membership of 67 includes research agencies as well as research groups based in advertisers' companies, advertising agencies, media and academe.

Broadcasters are represented in the advertising industry by the *KBP,* which is a private association of radio and television stations nationwide (government-owned radio and television are also members of the Association). As with the other sectoral organizations, KBP subscribes to self-regulation, having formulated and regularly updating its codes of ethics and standards for the broadcast industry (that is, Television Code, Radio Code, and Technical Standards). Within KBP, the Standards Authority acts as a quasi-judicial body that investigates and passes judgments on complaints referring to broadcasting. The KBP is a formidable broadcasting association, with roughly 120 members representing broadcast stations and networks nationwide.

Suppliers of services to the advertising industry, which include photography laboratories, photographers, graphic designers, audio recording studios, jingle writers, and talent and model agencies have banded themselves together into the *ASAP.* Since its creation in 1978, the association has aimed for professionalism in the sector by providing its members the standards and the environment for ethical business practices, healthy competition, and access to developments in crafts and technology locally and worldwide. The ASAP serves to protect their members from exploitation in the form of nonpayment and/or underpayment by their clients (that is, advertisers and advertising agencies), as well as from cutthroat competition among themselves. Today membership in ASAP is comprised of over 200 individuals and companies representing 14 services.

The *OAAP* is comprised of billboard operators and owners. This association was organized in 1964 with 15 founding members. Today, it lists some 30 members. As with the other sectoral organizations in the advertising industry, the OAAP believes in self-regulation and the need for its operations to fall within governmental laws and policies as well as within ethical bounds. Thus, OAAP drew up its Code of Ethics.

An association of the advertising managers of major newspapers and magazines nationwide, *PRIMO* was organized in 1973 with a view toward self-regulation within the print media, in particular print media advertising. The association oversees the standardizing of print media advertising rates, streamlining procedures for the accreditation of advertising agencies, and seeing to improvements in the quality of the print media materials. The membership of PRIMO currently stands at 27.

The smallest sectoral group within Adboard is *CAAP*. Currently comprised of five members, which are companies engaged in the production and exhibition of cinema commercials, CAAP was rather informally organized in 1972 because of a martial law ban on cinema advertising in theaters in metropolitan Manila, provincial capitals and other key cities. The lifting of the ban 3 years later resulted in vigorous advertising activities over this medium. However, cinema advertising experienced the most serious dislocation during the economic hardship years of the early 1980s. Moreover, the popularity of home video led to a drastic reduction in movie theater patronage, as significant numbers of the audiences began watching movies at home. During this time it was possible to rent pirated copies of movies currently showing in cinema houses. However, with government regulations controlling piracy, theater patronage started to increase steadily. Hence, cinema advertising began to pick up again. Also, CAAP sees to the standardization of advertising rates.

Public relations practitioners are represented in Adboard by the Public Relations Society of the Philippines (PRSP). As with the other advertising-related organizations, PRSP similarly aims toward professionalism among its practitioners and greater respect and recognition for public relations professionals within the advertising industry, as well as within the corporate organization. Since 1957, PRSP has been quite successful in elevating the position of the PR practitioner in the corporate organization by making him/her a part of the policy and decision-making team as a top-rated executive officer, as well as strengthening its professional development program by setting up an Accreditation System. Among its other projects is the ANVIL Awards competition, which aims to accord due recognition to outstanding PR programs that are tied to public interests.

Advertising Regulation and Public Policy Issues

ADVERTISING REGULATION

Over 50 bills, administrative orders and municipal orders pertaining to advertising regulation have either been enacted or proposed since 1986, many of them echoing or overlapping one another.

Except for a constitutional provision limiting foreign participation in the advertising industry and the Consumer Act of the Philippines, these bills are far from final and executory. Most of them are in their early stages of deliberation in national (that is, the House of Representatives and the Senate) and local (that is, city and municipality) legislatures.

Health concerns predominate: Eleven bills reflect health issues, and each seeks to regulate advertisements for cigarette and tobacco products, citing the warning that smoking is hazardous to the health. Two of these bills also address liquor consumption as a health hazard. The provisions of these bills may be classified as ranging from radical to moderate. While some bills call for the total ban of such advertising and promotions, others propose restrictions on their packaging, presentation and target audiences. Of these 11 bills, five seek the total ban of cigarette and tobacco advertising in various forms of media. The advertising industry does not deny the health hazard posed by smoking and alcohol consumption; it does, however, argue against the calls for the ban and/or further regulation of such advertising noting, among other things, that

• There is no clear research evidence linking advertising and cigarette/alcohol consumption.

• Cigarettes and tobacco products as well as liquor are legally manufactured and marketed products. Moreover, advertising is a lawful marketing tool.

• A total ban of cigarette and liquor advertising violates freedom of expression as well as harms media, which draws about 30 percent of its revenues from such advertising.

• Such a ban would also undermine the government's policy and support to the local tobacco industry.

• Specifications regarding the health warning, particularly provisions for frontal placement, tend to deface the packaging and may waste the presently available packs.

• It is of significance that the Adboard already has specific sections in its Code of Ethics regarding cigarette and liquor advertising.
(Advertising Board of the Philippines 1993a)

Public welfare concerns are evident in the bills that (a) seek to protect the rights of nonsmokers to smoke-free environments, (b) seek to ensure truthful information, and (c) call for the regulation of advertisements depicting sex and violence, and for penalizing the advertising agencies responsible. On this latter issue (pertaining to sex and violence), the advertising industry points out that such bills are superfluous, given that the Advertising Code of Ethics serves to protect against unnecessary sex and violence in advertising. The industry adds that the bills seeking to "penalize ad agencies, TV/radio stations and print publications that exploit women and glorify sex in their ads do not sufficiently define the punishable acts" (Advertising Board of the Philippines 1993a).

Eleven bills seek to ban or regulate the appearance of women and minors in advertisements, particularly in liquor and cigarette advertisements.

A strong sense of Filipino patriotism and nationalism prevails in six bills seeking to preserve and propagate Filipino cultural values and tradition. In particular, these bills refer to ownership of advertising agencies, the exclusive use of the Filipino language as well as Filipino talents and settings in advertisements. There is concern that Filipino values and traditions may be compromised if the management and content of advertising are not subjected to some form of regulation. With regard to the language restriction, the advertising industry argues that there are "sociocultural and economic realities that hinder [the bill's] immediate applicability" (Advertising Board of the Philippines 1993a). Among other things, most Filipinos are bilingual, while the mainstream media are still in English, which also happens to be the language of business.

Political advertising in the media is banned in the Philippines. Four senate proposals seek to modify this ban. Despite the fact that 1995 was election year (not presidential, however), not one of these Senate proposals nor those from the Commission on Elections was approved. It is interesting that all of these bills call for a relaxation of the bans against using media in political campaigns.

Two of the more significant of four bills pertaining to economic concerns are one that stipulates a minimum of 70 percent Filipino ownership of advertising agencies and another that seeks to impose a 10 percent tax on commercial or business advertisements.

Other recent bills aimed at regulating advertising include 11 that seek to protect minors involved in (and from) advertising, 11 protecting public welfare and the rights of others, and two that seek to limit the use of artistic works in cigarette advertisements.

ADVERTISING CENSORSHIP

Philippine advertising is self-regulated. No government agency screens advertisements prior to their airing or publication. As stated earlier, the Adboard screens advertisements, and following is their procedure:

1. An advertiser or advertising agency submits advertising materials, which may be the advertisement itself or the storyboard and other documents including research materials and testimonials of experts, to the Adboard.

2. The advertiser or advertising agency, more specifically "a duly authorized or designated presenter preferably of senior status," makes a presentation to the Adboard secretariat and executive director.

3. The executive director may recommend *approval, deferral,* or *referral* to a screening panel.

4. In the case of *approval of a storyboard,* the advertiser or advertising

agency may go ahead with the production of the advertisement. After production the finished advertisement is resubmitted to the Adboard for review; that is, to check whether it stayed within the approved storyboard. If this is the case, then the advertisement is given approval for airing/publication. However, if the advertisement has strayed from the approved storyboard, it is disapproved for airing/publication.

5. *Approval for airing/publication* via mass media may be given when the submitted material is advertisement itself.

6. Where the "material presented lacks or does not have support documents or substantiations required," the executive director may recommend *deferral*. The advertiser or advertising agency is given another chance to make a presentation, after which it may be given approval (that is, the substantiations required are submitted and deemed acceptable by the executive director), or another deferral. A third presentation is made, after which the decision may be approval or disapproval. In cases of disapproval, the advertiser or advertising agency may make an appeal to the main ACRC committee.

7. In cases where the advertising materials are "found to contain seemingly controversial elements or when the executive director thinks the material falls under the guidelines for review by a screening panel," *referral* is recommended. The executive director convenes a special panel consisting of "top executives known for their objectivity and mature judgment" from among the members of the Adboard (that is, representing the advertiser, advertising agency and media sectors) to screen the advertisement, storyboard and other submitted materials. This panel may initially recommend approval, deferral or disapproval. All cases of deferral, as just pointed out, are scheduled for representation (up to three times), after which the advertisement/storyboard may be approved or disapproved.

8. In all cases of *disapproval*, the advertiser or advertisement agency may make an appeal to the main ACRC committee, which conducts hearings on the matter. The decision of the ACRC may be approval or disapproval.

9. Anyone who disagrees with the decision of the executive director or the screening panel may approach the main ACRC committee with the complaint.

Complaints about advertisements and promotions made by competitors, government agencies, consumers and the general public may be submitted to this ACRC committee as well, which will hear the complaints and make the final decision regarding the advertisement or promotion.

Consumer Issues

CONSUMER BEHAVIOR
Studies that trace consumption patterns in the Philippines from the 1950s to

the 1980s have shown increases in income and consumption levels; however, the trend has not been consistent. From the late 1950s through the 1960s, improvements in the standard of living were indicated by increases in the average household consumption. Then during the 1970s and 1980s, the rise in prices resulted in a general erosion of the standard of living, especially in 1983 and immediately after. From 1986 onward, however, with the improved economic climate, consumers have enjoyed higher income and have been spending it on a larger number and variety of goods. However, despite the improved income situation, the Filipino consumer remains cautious and discriminating among the various products and brands. For the 1990s consumer, value for money has been the guiding principle.

Food has traditionally accounted for the largest proportion of consumption, especially for lower-income consumers. Economists confirm that "there exists a negative relationship between income and consumption in terms of basic needs, mainly food, but a positive association in terms of luxury and nonfood items" (Figeroa and Bernal 1992). In other words, the proportions of expenditure for food, clothing and shelter decrease as household incomes rise.

Forecasts of market conditions from 1990 to 2005 predict that although food expenditure will continue to account for the largest share of household budgets, it will decrease from 52 percent in 1990 to 45 percent in 2005. These forecasts project that the fastest rising expenditure items in consumer households will be for medical care (15.3 percent average annual growth rate), education (13.4 percent), housing (13.2 percent), transportation and communication (11.9 percent), clothing (11.1 percent) and alcohol and tobacco (10.6 percent) (Figeroa and Bernal 1992).

The housewife is regarded as the major household decision maker on purchasing and using consumer items. However, consumer studies have shown that women have increasingly sought help from the other members of the household regarding which products to buy and use. After all, "if a product is one that her family will use, it should satisfy as many members as possible"; moreover, "she does not want to risk choosing a product unacceptable to the family, for it will mean a waste of money" (Pascual 1990).

Children are influential with items ranging from food to personal care items, and even with the purchase of appliances and laundry detergents. This is because they are the heaviest users of television—a major advertising medium. The household help (especially in middle- and upper-income families) is similarly influential for they are the ones who are likely to use household products most. By contrast, the husband is the least involved in decision making over what household consumer goods are bought—except for items that he alone uses, and when decisions are made about major expenses for television sets, refrigerators and similar items.

Female influence in consumption decision making is projected to continue. And forecasts show that the biggest growth of expenditure will be in female-headed households (Figeroa and Bernal 1992).

LOCAL CONSUMER ASSOCIATIONS, CONSUMER ISSUES AND PUBLIC POLICY

A Philippine organization of women's clubs started the country's consumer movement: In the 1950s, the National Federation of Women's Clubs (NFWC) was the first to express the need for consumer education. During the 1960s, the Consumer's Federated Group of the Philippines (CFGP), organized by individual members of the NFWC, began to organize groups for consumer education and action all over the country. An outstanding achievement of the CFGP, together with the University of the Philippines' Law Center, was the drafting of a Consumer Code.

The CFGP was reactivated in the 1970s as the Consumer's Union of the Philippines (CUP). In 1970, the CUP and the Kilusan ng Mamimili ng Pilipinas (KMPI, or Consumer's Movement of the Philippines) were the most prominent consumer groups in the country. Despite the imposition of martial law in 1972, there was something of a surge in the establishment of mass-oriented and militant consumer organizations. By 1978, for instance, the following organizations had been created: the Church-Based Consumer Movement (CBCM), many of whose founders were the wives of protestant pastors; regional consumer movements in places outside metropolitan Manila, for example, Konsumo Dabaw (Consumer's Group in Davao in southern Philippines); the Consumers Movement of Negros Occidental (in central Philippines), and the Concerned Consumers of Benguet (in northern Philippines); and the Citizens' Alliance for Consumer Protection (CACP).

At present the most prominent consumer groups are KMPI, CFGP (both members of the International Organization of Consumers Unions or IOCU), CUP, CBCM and CACP. These consumer organizations are advocacy groups, utilizing various communication media (ranging from small group media—discussion forums and formal education classes—to mass media, like newspapers, radio, and television) to inform and educate the public regarding specific consumer issues and their rights as consumers. The causes or issues that these consumer organizations advocate include the following:

• The right to satisfy basic needs. "While attention (of consumer movements) must be given to unfair business practices, the overwhelming condition of poverty must first be addressed. This is what sets consumerism in third world countries like the Philippines apart from similar movements in industrialized countries. The provision of the basic needs in life, even if it means attacking poverty at its social roots, is the essence of the first consumer right" (Legaspi 1991).

• The right to safety and protection from products, processes and services that either endanger life or are health hazards. Consumer issues in this area include hygienic preparation of food products as well as the dumping of products containing unsafe drugs, banned pesticides and other chemical substances in third world countries like the Philippines. To serve as some kind of protection against such unsafe substances, the Consumer Act of the Philippines (RA 7394) has provisions to prevent their importation, advertising and sale.

• The right to information. A foremost consumer issue is the need to protect the public from patently dishonest or misleading advertising. In this regard the Consumer Act also has provisions guarding consumers from false and deceptive ads.

• The right to choose. This pertains to dismantling monopolies to ensure fair competition and therefore competitive prices of goods and services. Another issue reflecting consumer rights to information and choice touches on public health concerns. For example, aggressive advertising and promotion of transnational companies' infant milk formulas put the practice of breastfeeding at a disadvantage despite scientific evidence that breast milk is more healthful. Similarly, there is the case against advertising and promoting of tobacco and alcoholic products on health grounds. Apart from the special requirements for the advertising of cigarettes, food, drug, cosmetic, devices or hazardous substances set in the Consumer Act, bills specific to tobacco and alcohol aimed at further protecting public health are pending.

• The right to redress or fair settlement and compensation for false claims, unsatisfactory goods and services. The Civil Code and the Consumer Act have provisions pertaining to warranties. Additionally, until recently the practice in most stores had been not to accept sold goods for return, most receipts of sale having the words "no return, no exchange" clearly printed on them. At best, only some kind of exchange could be negotiated. Now, however, most stores accept returns and exchanges within reasonable time limits.

• The right to representation. That is, the involvement of consumer representatives in the formulation of social and economic policies that the Consumer Act provides for in its section on the establishment of a National Consumer Affairs Council. This council is made up of representatives from the Departments of Trade and Industry, Education, Health, and Agriculture, from business and industry, as well as from nationwide consumer organizations. Among the functions of this council are coordinating the enforcement of consumer laws, recommending new or amending consumer-related policy, monitoring and evaluating consumer programs, and undertaking consumer information and education programs.

• The right to consumer education. It is now law to integrate consumer education in the curricula of primary and secondary public and private schools, as well as in continuing education programs aimed at out-of-school youth and adults.

• The right to a healthy environment, which bears on environmental protection. This pertains to educating consumers and producers about environmental problems connected with the manufacture of goods and the delivery of services. Moreover, the right to a healthy environment calls for advocacy programs against pollution, including the use of nonbiodegradable packaging and chlorofluorocarbons (CFCs), and for garbage reduction and recycling.

Conclusions

As the Philippines moves toward the next century, the government's vision is to bring the nation to NIC status by the year 2000. This will involve sustained growth, and improved productivity and efficiency—in both the manufacturing and the services sectors. Toward these ends, economic policies aimed at deregulation and liberalization are being implemented. The administration is set to remove protectionist policies, including those shielding certain industries. Whether these liberalization policies will affect corporate ownership of advertising agencies remains to be seen. Certainly there are numerous issues that will affect the future of advertising in the Philippines, and many of these issues are currently being discussed and debated in the country.

Bibliography

Advertising Board of the Philippines. 1989. *Philippine Advertising Industry: Profile '89.* Manila: Advertising Board of the Philippines.

Advertising Board of the Philippines. 1992. *Philippine Advertising Industry: Profile '92.* Manila: Advertising Board of the Philippines.

Advertising Board of the Philippines. 1993a. *ACRC Manual of Procedures for Screening and Filing of Complaints and Appeals.* Manila: Advertising Board of the Philippines, September.

Advertising Board of the Philippines. 1993b. *Philippine Advertising Industry: Profile '93.* Manila: Advertising Board of the Philippines.

Asian Institute of Journalism. 1990. *Communication for the Common Good: Towards a Framework for a National Communication Policy.* Manila: Asian Institute of Journalism.

Association of Accredited Advertising Agencies in the Philippines. 1994. *1993–1994 Media Factbook.* Manila: Association of Accredited Advertising Agencies in the Philippines.

Constitution of the Republic of the Philippines 1987. Manila.

Figeroa, E.A.T. and N.B. Bernal. 1992. An Analysis of Consumption Expenditure Patterns of Households in the Philippines. In: Veloso, S.P., ed. *Forecasting Basic Household Needs.* Manila: National Economic and Development Authority (NEDA).

Hernandez, A., R. Moyer, and A.L. Neumann, REZA, G. Sacerdoti, S. Tucci, W. Vicoy, and N. Yamsuan. 1986. *Bayan Ko: Images of the Philippine Revolt.* Hong Kong: Project 28 Days Ltd.

Jocano, F.L. 1993a. *Issues and Challenges in Filipino Value Formation.* (Punlad Series No. 1: Series on Filipino Values). Quezon City: Punlad Research House.

Jocano, F.L. 1993b. *Notion of Value in Filipino Culture: The Concept of Pamatayan.* (Punlad Series No. 2: Series on Filipino Values). Quezon City: Punlad Research House.

Jocano, F.L. 1993c. *Diwa: The Spiritual Core of Filipino Value System.* (Punlad Series No. 5: Series on Filipino Values). Quezon City: Punlad Research House.

Lacson, J.R. Jr. 1994. Broadcast Satellite Communication: A Study of Media Technology Use and Adaptation. Ph.D. Dissertation. College of Mass Communication, University of the Philippines, Diliman, Quezon City.

Legaspi, E.P. 1991. Let the Seller Also Beware: The Essence of Consumer Rights. *Consumer Forum,* January–February.

Manila Chronicle Supplement. 1993. Advertising Outpacing Economy, February 4.

Maslog, C.C., ed. 1988. *Philippine Communication: An Introduction.* Los Banos: University of the Philippines (Philippine Association of Communication Educators).

Mercado, M.A., ed. 1986. *An Eyewitness History: People Power, the Philippine Revolution of 1986.* Manila: The James B. Reuter, S.J. Foundation.

Pascual, A.M. 1990. The Pinoy Consumer: What is (S)He Like? *Starweek,* January 21.

Pernia, E.E. 1991. Mass Media Infrastructure and Use in the Philippines. Unpublished paper. Communication Research Department, College of Mass Communication, University of the Philippines, Diliman, Quezon City.

Pernia, E.E. 1994. Socio-Cultural and Economic Impact of National and Transnational Broadcast Programming in the Philippines. Paper Presented at the ASEAN Regional Seminar on the Socio-Cultural and Economic Impact of Transnational Broadcast, April 4–7, Kuala Lumpur, Malaysia.

Philippine Monitoring Services. 1994. Ad Expenditures Up 17% in the First Quarter. *The Manila Times,* June 14.

Ramos, F.V. 1994a. To Sustain Our Growth, Address of His Excellency President Fidel V. Ramos in *Ulat sa Bayan.* Malacanang, Manila, January 4.

Ramos, F.V. 1994b. State of the Nation Address of His Excellency President Fidel V. Ramos at the Opening of the Third Session of the 9th Congress of the Philippines. Manila, July 25.

Soliven, M. 1993. Sex, Lies, and Videotape, but Truth Shall Prevail in the Filipino Media. In: Heuvel, J.V. and E.E. Dennis, eds. *The Unfolding Lotus: East Asia's Changing Media.* New York: The Freedom Forum Media Studies Center, Columbia University.

Talisayon, S.D. 1990. *Filipino Values: Determinants of Philippine Future.* Quezon City: Economic Development Foundation.

Tolentino, N.G. 1992. A Case Study on the Regulation of the Advertising Industry: Its Implications to Multinational Companies. Undergraduate Thesis. College of Mass Communication, University of the Philippines, Diliman, Quezon City.

Zubiri, B.R. 1993. Communication Scene in the Philippines. In *Asian Communication Handbook.* Singapore: Asian Communication Research and Information Center (AMIC).

9

The Blossoming of Advertising in Thailand

M.L. VITTRATORN CHIRAPRAVATI

Thailand in Brief

Located in Southeast Asia, Thailand covers approximately 551,430 square kilometers of the Indochinese Peninsula, with a population of 60 million. Bangkok is the capital. Thailand is bordered by Myanmar (Burma) to the west and north, Laos to the north and northeast, Malaysia to the south, and Cambodia to the east.

The country is a parliamentary democracy with a constitutional monarchy. Buddhism is the primary religion of more than 95 percent of all Thais; 4 percent are Muslim and less than 1 percent belong to other religions. Thailand uses the civil law system and the Prime Minister is the highest civil government official. Freedom of speech and freedom of the press are guaranteed, with the exception of the threatening of public order, good morals, public safety or the security of the state. The current issue of The Constitution of the Kingdom of Thailand 1978, Section 34, states that "People have freedom of speech, writing, printing and advertising."

Thai Economy

Thailand has produced a remarkable economic performance. Key factors driving the Thai economy are its stable macroeconomic environment, prudent monetary policy, the government's export policy, healthy service incomes from tourism and foreign remittances, inflows of foreign capital and technology transfer, and high inflows of foreign direct investment (World Bank/IMF 1991). In his book *Burning Bright, The Fifth Tiger: A Study of Thai Development Policy,* Muscat (1994) points out that Thailand is a new Southeast Asian candidate for Tiger status, joining the other four Tigers—South Korea, Taiwan, Singapore and Hong Kong. On the average, one new factory begins operating in Thailand every day. Some 50 companies became new listings on the Securities Exchange of Thailand

223

(SET) in 1991 (Rock 1992). Per capita income in Thailand rose 50 percent in the past decade (Lehner 1991). In 1994, per capita income in Thailand was 61,072 baht (US$2,443) and the gross domestic product (GDP) was 3,622 billion baht (US$145 billion). Thailand has been described in *The Wall Street Journal* as being "among the world's fastest-growing economies" and "one of the world's newest newly industrializing countries (NIC) and an area that is creating a new and booming opportunity for foreign investors" (Lehner 1991).

Thai Cultural Context and Advertising

Thailand is the only country in Southeast Asia that has remained independent throughout the colonial period. As a result, Thai culture and identity have remained essentially intact. There are three things that play important roles in Thai society. They are "nation," "religion," and "monarchy." These three things have contributed greatly to shaping and influencing Thai behavior. Therefore, many advertising restrictions have been created to maintain and protect the sacredness of the nation, the Buddhist religion and the King and his family.

Other salient Thai cultural characteristics are avoidance of confrontation; a high-context culture; hierarchical rigidity; and adaptiveness. Like other Asian countries Thailand has been characterized as a culture that avoids confrontation (Cooper 1991; Engholm 1991; Ketudat 1990; Thorelli and Sentell 1982). In Thailand open conflicts and aggressive forms of communication are perceived as disrespectful. This in turn is one reason why the use of comparative advertising is uncommon in Thailand, although it is not actually prohibited by law.

Thai culture can also be characterized as having a high-context language system. Thai people are likely to use indirect, implicit, ambiguous modes of expression and body language. Therefore, emotional appeals (the soft-sell approach), which emphasize image building, emotional elicitation and status symbols, tends to be utilized more often in advertisements in Thailand than are informative appeals (the hard-sell approach), which rely on product-related information (that is, price, quality, performance and so forth).

Hierarchical rigidity is another cultural characteristic that is salient in Thai society. Like Japan, Thailand has been characterized by a tight hierarchical social system (Komin 1991; Cooper 1991). Ketudat (1990) identified the main features that shape hierarchy in Thai society and noted that the roots of the traditional Thai sense of hierarchy are historical. The Thai monarchy was heavily influenced by the Khmer culture following the Thai subjugation of the Kingdom of Angkor several centuries ago. The Khmer political culture was structured around the concept of a god-king (*theewa-raacaa*), and since that time the Thai political culture and social organization have been characterized by steep hierarchical social arrangements.

Due to the hierarchical rigidity of Thai society, status appeals are often utilized in advertisements. Mueller (1987) describes the use of status appeals in advertisements as "advertisements that suggest the use of a particular product will improve some inherent quality of the user in the eyes of others. Positions and rank within the context of the group are stressed. This category also includes foreign status appeals, use of foreign words, phrases, models, and foreign celebrity endorsements."

The adaptiveness of Thai culture is also another essential value affecting advertising. According to Ketudat (1990), "The Thai people have the long history of openness toward other cultures, tolerance of cultural differences, and willingness to learn from the outside world." This notion is supported by a large number of standardized advertisements shown on Thai television. Many multinational companies operating in Thailand have imported their commercials from their headquarters and translated them into Thai.

Structure of the Thai Media

TELEVISION

Television stations in Thailand are government owned, and are assigned to various government agencies: Channels 5 and 7 to the Royal Thai Army; Channels 3 and 9 to the Mass Communication Organization of Thailand and Channel 11 to the Public Relations Department. These five television stations are located in Bangkok. The nine provincial stations are controlled by the Public Relations Department and are located in Khon Kaen, Nakhon Rachasima, Haadyai, Surat Thani, Songkhla, Phuket, Lampang, Chiang Mai and Rayong. These stations serve the people in their respective areas. Advertising provides nearly all revenue for operation of all television stations in Thailand, except Channel 11, the noncommercial station.

Advertising is limited to 10 minutes per hour on all commercial television channels. Usually, television commercials are 15, 30, 45 or 60 seconds in length. All television commercials must be submitted for pre- and post-censorship to committees consisting of representatives from the four national commercial television stations (Channels 3, 5, 7 and 9) and representatives from the Advertising Association of Thailand. Pre-censorship is scheduled on every Tuesday and Thursday and post-censorship on every Monday, Wednesday and Friday. In addition all advertising for food, drugs, cosmetics or potentially hazardous consumer products have to be approved by the Food and Drug Administration (FDA).

Approximately 95 percent of urban Thais have television sets, and the figure in rural areas ranges from 72 percent ownership of television in the northeast to 88 percent in central Thailand. The average cost for running a 30-second spot on prime-time television ranges from 68,000 baht (US$2,720) on Channel 3 to 85,000 baht (US$3,400) on Channel 7.

RADIO

Like television, all radio stations are 100 percent owned by governmental agencies. There are 498 stations scattered throughout the country; approximately 70 of these stations broadcast in Bangkok while the rest serve the rural areas. There are 249 FM and 249 AM stations, and 464 of these accept advertising both through sponsored programs and "loose" spots (Broadcasting Directing Board, 1994).

Approximately 80 percent of all urban households have access to radio and about 56 percent of rural dwellers listen to radio. The average cost for a loose spot on FM stations in Bangkok is 1,800 baht (US$72) and for commercial spots on sponsored programs (30 minutes) is 78,500 baht (US$3,140).

Recently two factors have contributed to the rising popularity of radio. One is Bangkok traffic jams and the other is format stations; that is, stations producing programming of a uniform content that is aimed at a certain target group. In the past radio was popular among peasants and workers in rural areas. However, a growing number of information radio programs today, such as traffic reports, business information and news, have captured the better-educated segments of the population (Mahaphant 1995).

NEWSPAPERS

Unlike the broadcasting media, newspapers in Thailand are owned by the private sector. There are about 37 national and more than 400 provincial newspapers including one Japanese, five Chinese and five English dailies. In the Thai-language sector, *Thai Rath* is the leader, selling more than 1 million copies a day. This is followed by *Daily News* and *Matichon*. Among the Thai-language business dailies, the leaders are *Phoo Jad Karn Daily* and *Krungthep Dhurakij*. Newspapers derive the majority of their revenue from advertising, with a small but significant proportion from subscriptions or single-copy sales at the cover price. The advertising rates of the major newspapers are shown in Table 9.1.

MAGAZINES

About 180 magazines are published in Thailand. They can be divided among various distinct categories such as women's, men's, business, communications, computer, entertainment, health, home and decoration, sports, automotive and travel. Like newspapers, magazines derive the majority of their revenues from advertising, with a small but significant proportion coming from subscription or single-copy sales at the cover price. The cost and readership of selected major magazines are shown in Table 9.2.

OUTDOOR/TRANSIT ADVERTISING

The use of outdoor and transit advertising has increased in parallel with Bangkok's traffic jams. It grew by more than 80 percent in 1993 (Miller 1994). Presently, there are many available outdoor advertising formats including liquid crystal display (LCD), light-emitting diode (LED), trivision, flexivision and flap

Table 9.1.   Major Newspaper Advertising Rates in Thailand, 1994

Publication	FP/B&W 1995 (baht[a])	FP/B&W 1994 (baht[a])	Approximate % Change
Thai Dailies			
Thai Rath	336,000	264,000	27.3
Daily News	264,000	204,000	29.4
Matichon	184,800	153,600	20.3
Siam Keela	150,000	120,000	25.0
Thai Business Dailies/Bi-Weeklies/Weeklies			
Phoo Jad Karn Daily	208,800	189,600	10.1
Krungthep Dhurakij	154,500[b]	132,000	17.0
Than Settakij	216,000	180,000	20.0
Prachachart Dhurakij	204,000	168,000	21.4
Phoo Jad Karn Weekly	145,600	135,000	7.9
Khoo Kaeng Dhurakij	204,000	168,000	21.4
English Dailies			
Bangkok Post	196,800	168,000	17.1
The Nation	161,500[b]	138,000	17.0

Source: Media News/Ogilvy & Mather, 1995.
Note: FP/B&W, full page/black and white.
[a]US$1 = 25 Thai baht.
[b]Estimate.

Table 9.2.   Selected Major Magazine Cost and Readership in Thailand, 1994

Magazine	Frequency of Publication	Circulation (000)	FP/BW (baht*)	FP/FC (baht*)
Business				
Dok Bia	Monthly	100	18,400	30,000
Khoo Kaeng	Monthly	85	34,500	42,000
Karn-Gaern Tanakarn	Monthly	95	19,550	35,000
Phoo Jad Karn	Monthly	120	33,000	43,000
Women's				
Di-Charn	Biweekly	102	16,100	31,000
Fashion Review	Monthly	100	17,250	30,000
Image	Monthly	50	17,250	30,000
Kullasatri	Biweekly	200	25,300	38,000
Kwan Ruen	Biweekly	185	17,250	35,000
Ploy Kham Petch	Biweekly	50	—	32,000
Preaw	Biweekly	150	17,710	34,000
Sakul Thai	Weekly	180	23,000	51,750

Source: Advertising Rate Cards, 1994.
Note: FP/BW, full page/black and white; FP/FC, full page/full color.
*US$1 = 25 Thai baht.

boards, as well as display panels at railway stations, bus terminal and airports. A variety of transport advertising is also available including bus backs, sides and bodies; bus stops and shelters; taxi tops and sun-blinds; train advertisements; and Tuk Tuks (small three-wheel taxi cabs). The outdoor and transit advertising rates are shown in Table 9.3.

Table 9.3. Outdoor and Transit Advertising
            Rates in Thailand, 1993

Advertising	Ad Rate Unit/Month (baht*)
Bus side	
Right side	3,500
Left side	2,300
Bus back	1,900
Busbody impact	22,000
Train ad	240
Tuk Tuk ad	750
Bus shelter	15,000
Bus terminal panel	16,000
Bus shelter, (up-country)	9,800
Train terminal panel	42,000
Billboard	100,000
Flap board	60,000

Source: Advertising Rate Cards, 1993.
*US$1 = 25 Thai baht.

CABLE TELEVISION

Cable television emerged in Thailand about a decade ago. Presently there are two established cable operators: International Broadcasting Corporation (IBC) of Shinawatra Group and Thai Sky TV of Siam Broadcasting and Communication. Due to the industry's fast growth and prosperity, the Mass Communication Organization of Thailand (MCOT) has granted another four licenses to cable companies including UCOM, Comlinks, Samart Corp. and Bangkok Entertainment Company.

The rapid growth in the cable television industry is due to two major factors: First, cable offers programs with better quality and, second, the programs are without advertising. Under Thai broadcasting laws, advertising is prohibited on subscription television channels because it would put the free television at a disadvantage. However, IBC has requested the government to deregulate the ban on airing advertisements on cable stations.

Growth of Advertising Industry

HISTORICAL ANALYSIS

The advertising industry in Thailand has been growing for over a century. Three significant movements can be observed: the movement in the 1960s to 1970s, or the "foreign" era; the movement from the late 1970s to the late 1980s, or the "Thai" era; and the movement in the mid-1990s to the mid-2000s, or the "growth" era.

FOREIGN ERA: ADVERTISING DURING 1943–1974

Advertising first started in Thailand in 1845 when Dr. Dan Beach Bradley, an American missionary, published the first newspaper in Thailand, *The Bangkok Recorder.* It carried the first advertisement in Thai, an advertisement for quinine (Shrestha 1994). After that, more and more advertisements for both local and imported products were carried in various newspapers.

The first modern agency, Groake Advertising, was established by an American named Graoke in the early 1950s (Thammasri and Yaowiwat 1992). In 1948, a U.S. company, Grant Advertising, was established, followed by the Cathay Advertising in 1953.

One event that made the advertising business flourish in this period was the beginning of television as a national medium. Following the introduction of television, many U.S. and Japanese transnational advertising agencies (TNAAs) opened their local branches in Thailand to serve U.S. and Japanese advertisers. These TNAAs included Chuo Senko, Asia 21, Thai Hakuhodo, Ogilvy & Mather, Leo Burnett and Dentsu (see Table 9.4). Thus, this period is considered the foreign era in Thailand because TNAAs played an important role in shaping and controlling the structure of advertising and agencies. In an interview Mr. Prakit Apisarnthanarax, the president of Prakit/FCB, noted, "In the beginning of the advertising business in Thailand, expatriates dominated the industry. All the top executive and creative admen were Europeans, Americans and Japanese. Only a few were Thais." Echoing Mr. Prakit is Mr. Pradit Rattanawijarn, executive director of corporate affairs at Leo Burnett (Thailand): "Back in 1965, the top management was one hundred percent expatriate" (Engholm 1991).

Table 9.4. Foreign Era: Advertising Agencies in Thailand, 1943–1974

Year Established	Agency	Parent Company
1943	Groake Advertising	Thailand
1948	Grant Advertising	United States
1953	Cathay Advertising (Ted Bates)	United States
1963	Chuo Senko	Japan
1964	Far East Advertising	Thailand
1965	McCann-Erickson	United States
1968	Asia 21 (Thailand) Co., Ltd.	Japan
1969	Mayford	United Kingdom
1970	Lintas: Bangkok	United Kingdom
1973	CP&S Co., Ltd.	Thailand
1973	Thai Hakuhodo	Japan
1973	Ogilvy & Mather (Thailand) Ltd.	United States
1974	Bay & Ben Ltd., Partnership	Thailand
1974	Diethelm/Leo Burnett Ltd.	United States
1974	Dentsu (Thailand) Ltd.	Japan

Source: *Annual Report & Membership Directory: The 25th Anniversary Issue,* 1991.

THAI ERA: ADVERTISING DURING 1977–1987

The second significant movement in the advertising industry in Thailand occurred from 1977–1987 when the advertising business flourished. Many experienced Thai advertising executives who had been trained by TNAAs established their own advertising agencies during this period. For example, Mr. Prakit Apisarnthanarax, chairman of Prakit and Associates (now Prakit/FCB), had worked 14 years for Diethelm/Leo Burnett; Chalerm Vatcharatanond of CVT & Bercia had worked for McCann-Erickson and Lintas; Vinit Surapongchai of Damask Advertising had worked for 11 years for Lintas, and so forth. Table 9.5 shows a number of Thai advertising agencies that were established during this period. This period is referred to as the Thai era.

Table 9.5. Thai Era: Advertising Agencies in Thailand, 1977–1987

Year Established	Agency	Parent Company
1977	Patterson and Partners Thailand	United States
1977	Indrayuth Co., Ltd.	Thailand
1978	Prakit and Associates	Thailand
1978	Amex Team Advertising	Thailand
1978	Patterns Advertising Co., Ltd.	Thailand
1979	Plan Grafik Co., Ltd.	Thailand
1980	Thai Image Advertising Co., Ltd.	Thailand
1980	The Ball WCRs Partnership	United States
1980	Isco Advertising Co., Ltd.	Thailand
1981	Spa Advertising Co., Ltd.	Thailand
1982	Major Advertising	Thailand
1982	PK Advertising	Thailand
1982	The Media	Thailand
1984	CVT & Bercia	Thailand
1984	DDB Needham Worldwide	United States
1986	Dai-Ichi Kikaku (Thailand)	Japan
1987	Damask Advertising	Thailand

Source: *Annual Report & Membership Directory: The 25th Anniversary Issue*, 1991.

GROWTH ERA: ADVERTISING IN 1988 TO 1993

The advertising business in Thailand experienced a steady growth in advertising expenditures from 1988 to 1993. Despite the 1991 world recession, total advertising expenditure in Thailand rose dramatically from 1988 to 1993 (Table 9.6). Jeff Fergus, a regional managing director of Leo Burnett, expressed confidence about the future of the advertising industry in Thailand in an interview with Sopittakamol (1995), noting:

> Thailand will join the list of the 20 largest advertising markets in the world within three years as economic growth continues to shift to Asia-Pacific. By then, total advertising expenditures in Thailand are forecast to reach 70 billion baht in 1994 and placing Thailand around 15th worldwide. It will join the other four Asian countries already on the list: Japan, ranked the second after the US, China (fourth), South Korea and Taiwan.
>
> (*Id.* 1995,17)

Owing to the continuous development of the Thai economy and advertising industry in this period, existing advertising agencies could not handle the fast growth in business. A great number of new transnational and Thai advertising agencies were thus founded, which in turn have rapidly expanded the industry.

Table 9.6.   Total Advertising Expenditure in Thailand,
             1988–1993

Year	Advertising Expenditure (million baht*)	Approximate % Growth Rate
1988	6,497.9	28
1989	8,632.6	33
1990	11,346.8	31
1991	14,322.8	26
1992	17,507.2	22
1993	23,062.3	32

Source: Khoo Khaeng Data Bank, 1994.
*US$1 = 25 Thai baht.

Although some of the TNAAs established their local branches in Thailand, many have formed partnerships with Thai advertising agencies. These agencies are, for example, J. Walter Thompson, Saatchi & Saatchi Advertising, Backer Spielvogel Bates (Thailand), Spaulding & Partners and Grey (Thailand). Presently, there are more than 200 advertising agencies in Thailand.

In contrast with the foreign era when TNAAs were controlled and managed by top expatriates from the United States and Japan, today most of the successful TNAAs are led by experienced Thai executives. Among those in the managerial positions are, for example, Charuvan Vanasin, a chairwoman of J. Walter Thompson; Mrs. Sunandha Tulayadhan, managing director of Ogilvy & Mather (the first woman to become managing director of an O&M national office anywhere in the world); Ms. Pornsiri Rojmeta, a managing director of Leo Burnett; and Mr. Vichai Suphasomboon, a managing director of Lintas. The creative directors of major agencies such as Leo Burnett, DY&R, DDB Needham Worldwide and Lintas are all Thais. Echoing this notion is Mr. Arnold Liong of Mc-Cann-Erickson: "expatriates will become a thing of the past" (Engholm 1991). This represents an advertising industry trend to promote more Thais into top positions.

In this growth era both transnational and well-established Thai advertising agencies have expanded their advertising business in other Indochinese countries such as Vietnam and Myanmar (Burma). Thanks to the ending of the U.S. trade embargo of Vietnam, DDB Needham, Ogilvy & Mather, J. Walter Thompson and Leo Burnett among others have established their headquarters in Hanoi (Miller 1994). Most of those branch offices use their Thai headquarters as centers due to their geographic proximity and the abundance of skilled personnel. Jeff Fergus, regional managing director of Leo Burnett, says that "Leo Burnett Thailand is a very well-placed agency to help develop a network in China and Indochina" (Sopittakamol 1995). According to an article in *Asian Advertising and Marketing* (1994), the Thai office of DDB will be serving as a coordination base for training in the region. Ogilvy & Mather, Leo Burnett and J. Walter Thompson are all planning to use Thailand as a springboard into Indochina.

Table 9.7 shows the largest agencies in terms of billings for the top 10 advertising agencies in 1992 and 1993. Among these, eight are transnational and two are Thai. Only minor reshuffling in the ranking of the top 10 agencies occurred between 1992 and 1993.

Lintas remained the country's largest advertising agency with billings of 3,148 million baht (US$12,592 million), signifying a 17 percent growth over 1992. Ogilvy & Mather, the second largest agency, with billings of 2,300 million

Table 9.7.   Current Largest Agencies in Thailand in Terms of Billings, 1992 and 1993

		Total Billings (million baht*)		Approximate
Ranking	Agency	1992	1993	% Change
1	Lintas	2,700	3,148	17
2	Ogilvy & Mather	1,667	2,300	38
3	Far East	1,050	1,200	14
4	Leo Burnett	1,000	1,200	20
5	Prakit/FCB	1,000	1,200	20
6	JWT	832	1,162	40
7	Spa Advertising	840	960	14
8	DY&R	777	930	20
9	McCann-Erickson	640	860	34
10	Dentsu (Thailand)	700	800	14

Source: *The Advertising Book 1994–95: Advertising, Marketing and Media Guide*, 1995, 23.
*US $1 = 25 Thai baht.

baht represented a 38 percent growth. The other top five agencies were Far East, Leo Burnett and Prakit/FCB, with not much difference in terms of billings and growth rate. J. Walter Thompson ranked sixth with an impressive growth rate of 40 percent, followed by Spa Advertising, DY&R, McCann-Erickson and Dentsu, respectively.

Table 9.8 shows that of the top 10 advertisers, six are multinational corporations and only four are Thai national corporations; but the recent growth of Thai companies shown here is encouraging.

Table 9.8.   Largest National Advertisers by Brands in Thailand, 1993

Rank	Brand	Billings (million baht*)
1	Vidal Sassoon/Shampoo and Conditioner	133.05
2	Toyota/Passenger Cars	114.99
3	Krating Daeng/Energy Drinks	112.60
4	PTT/Fuel Oil	109.93
5	Johnnie Walker/Whisky	106.86
6	Nissan/Passenger Cars	103.54
7	Central/Department Store	101.99
8	Fuji/Color Film	96.61
9	Muang Thong/Housing Projects	87.19
10	Oil of Ulan/Facial Moisturizers	83.6

Source: Khoo Khaeng Data Bank, 1993.
*US$ 1 = 25 Thai baht.

Advertising Expenditure by Medium

In 1993, total advertising expenditure in Thailand was 26 billion baht, an increase of 33 percent over 1992. Table 9.9 shows advertising expenditure by medium for television, newspapers, magazines, radio and cinema. Share of adspend in various media in 1993 remained remarkably similar to 1992, with television capturing 50 percent of the total media spending, newspapers 29 percent, radio 12 percent, and magazines 10 percent.

Although television has been the dominant medium, capturing about half of the total advertising expenditure, marketers and media planners have also allocated their advertising budgets toward other carriers like radio, daily business newspapers and direct marketing. The change in media allocation is due to a tremendous increase in television advertising rates. According to Suphasomboon, the President of the Advertising Association of Thailand (AAT) and managing director of Lintas (Thailand), "ad spending in business dailies grew at the highest rate; 148 percent from Bt 428 million in 1991 to Bt 1.06 billion in 1992, indicating that this type of newspaper has become more popular" (Thoopkrajae 1995).

Table 9.9. Advertising Expenditure by Medium in 1993

Medium	%
Television	50.00
Newspaper	28.85
Magazine	9.24
Radio	11.8
Cinema	0.06

Source: *Media Focus 1994*, 1994, 5.

Advertising Organizations in Thailand

There are two advertising associations in Thailand: the AAT and the Bangkok Art Directors Association. The Advertising Association of Thailand was established in 1966, with its main objectives being to establish a good relationship among members, to negotiate advertising-related issues with governmental agencies and to promote the advancement of professionalism in the advertising profession and the industry (*The Advertising Book: Thailand 1994–1995 Advertising, Marketing and Media Guide* 1995). The AAT has its own code of ethics, which serves as a voluntary set of guidelines for the advertising industry in Thailand. However, the enforcement of this code of ethics does not include punitive power; the only penalty for violating the code is the expulsion of the member from the association. Even though the AAT is a private organization, it works and coordinates with the government regulatory agencies. The Bangkok Art Directors Association was established in 1985, with its objective being to promote the quality of creativity by organizing seminars and work-shops for training young creative people, as well as to set up the annual Bangkok Art Directors Awards competitions.

Advertising Style

There have been two distinct styles of Thai advertisements. One is the use of an emotional or soft-sell approach and the other is the use of a cultural theme. According to Barry Owen (1993, 44), creative director of Ogilvy and Mather in Thailand who has worked in Thailand for more than 20 years:

> The first aspect of the "Thai style" that springs to mind is "soft-sell." But it works. It's been working for eighteen years . . . "soft-sell" works particularly well in Thailand. The local audience prefers to be wooed with catchy music and emotional images than with blatantly competitive mud-slinging.

John Englehart (1993) also says that

> Thais have a distinct style. Thai style TV advertising is characterized by a soft-sell approach—competitive advertising is considered too aggressive here. The theme music is most important, as are visual images relevant to Thai culture and high production values.

The reason behind the emotional or soft-sell approach of Thai advertisements may be due to the fact that Thailand is a high-context culture. Hall (1976) characterized high-context communication as "one in which most of the information is already in the person, while very little is in the coded, explicit, trans-mitted part of the message." Wells (1987) also explains that in high-context cultures, emphasis is placed on nonverbal expression, physical setting and social circumstances. Not surprisingly extensive use of music, cultural themes and celebrity endorsements is found in a great number of advertisements in Thailand.

Advertising Regulation and Public Policy Issues

In Thailand controls on advertising rely almost entirely on laws made ini-tially to protect consumers from certain acts or practices, rather than to encour-age competition. Before October 1994, there were three major governmental reg-ulatory agencies controlling advertising: the Consumer Protection Board (CPB), the FDA and the National Broadcasting Commission (NBC). Presently only the NBC has no direct authority over the control of advertising.

235

THE CONSUMER PROTECTION BOARD
The CPB, a dependent federal agency under the Secretary of the Prime Minister, was created by the Consumer Protection Act of 1979. There are two ad hoc committees that have descended from the Consumer Protection Act of 1979: the Committee on Advertisement and the Committee on Labels. The CPB has the power to regulate all advertising that is deceptive, misleading or offensive, found in any medium. However, it has no authority to censor program content. If advertisers are uncertain about any advertisements, they can propose draft advertisements that are then subject to approval by the CPB, and pay a fee to have their commercials reviewed.

The Consumer Protection Act of 1979 pertains to honesty in advertising. This Act established that an advertisement may not contain an untrue statement. According to Section 22 of the Consumer Protection Act 1979, untrue statements are:

1. any statement that is false or exaggerated;
2. any statement that will cause misunderstanding in the essential elements concerning goods or services, notwithstanding if it is based on or refers to any technical report, statistics or anything that is false or exaggerated;
3. any statement that directly or indirectly encourages the commission of an unlawful or immoral acts, or that adversely affects the national culture;
4. any statement that will cause disunity or that adversely affects the unity among the public; and
5. other statements as prescribed in the Ministerial Regulation.

If the Committee on Advertisement is of the opinion that an advertisement violates any CPB-established rule, the Committee has the power to issue one or several of the following orders to the violator (Consumer Protection Act, Section 27, 1979):

1. to alter the statement or method of advertisement;
2. to prohibit the use of certain statements that appear in the advertisement;
3. to prohibit the advertisement or the use of such method for the advertisement;
4. to correct by advertisement the possible misunderstanding to the consumers in accordance with the rules and procedure prescribed by the Committee on Advertisement;
5. to substantiate all claims made in the advertisement.

THE FOOD AND DRUG ADMINISTRATION
The FDA of Thailand is a federal regulatory agency related to advertising, and is under the auspices of the Ministry of Health. The FDA was given the

power to regulate and control the advertising of food, drugs, cosmetics and potentially hazardous consumer products. Before disseminating any advertisement for food, drugs, cosmetics or potentially hazardous consumer products, the advertiser must propose the content, sound or pictures of the advertised product to the FDA for approval. Violation of this Act will subject the offender to sanctions including fines, imprisonment, or both.

THE NATIONAL BROADCASTING COMMISSION

In 1975, the NBC (previously called the Broadcasting Directing Board, or BDB), a dependent federal agency under the Public Relations Department, was empowered with the right to exercise full authority to censor television commercials. At that time, an advertisement for any products to be advertised through television had to have the approval of the NBC prior to dissemination. Food, drugs, medical devices and cosmetics were scrutinized not only by the FDA, but also by the NBC. Although accepted by the FDA in terms of storyboards, the NBC could still examine them. However, the NBC's censorship process was terminated by the Fourteenth Ministerial Order B.E. 2537 in 1994.

Presently the censorship procedure for any television commercial is not supervised by the NBC. Instead it is conducted by the media, especially the commercialized television channels (Channels 3, 5, 7 and 9). These four television channels have jointly set up a committee for scrutinizing every television commercial. This committee is composed of representatives from each channel and those from the AAT. Though the NBC has not had direct authority over advertising since October 1994, its laws and regulations are still used by the committee.

Current Censorship Process for Television Commercials

There are two steps in the current censorship procedure. The first step is known as pre-censorship: In this step the committee scrutinizes the storyboard to approve both copy and visuals. Any word or picture that is found inappropriate must be changed. Material(s) may be requested from the advertiser to substantiate claims made in the advertisement, or the committees may recommend certain changes on the storyboard. The advertiser, after making the required revisions, may choose to resubmit the revised advertisement to the pre-censorship committees for re-evaluation, although this is not required.

The finished advertisement must be submitted prior to actual dissemination. The committee reviews the finished commercial before it is allowed to air.

Alcoholic Beverage Advertising

The advertising of beer and wine is permitted on all Thai radio and television networks for 24 hours a day. The advertising of hard liquor is also permitted; however, with a time restriction: Hard liquor commercials are restricted to late viewing hours, after 10:00 p.m. On-camera consumption of any kind of alcoholic beverage is forbidden. Advertising of alcoholic beverages is permitted on billboards and in publications.

Cigarette Advertising

In Thailand any promotion of cigarettes, including advertising in all types of media and at point of sale, is strictly banned by law. Offenders will face mandatory jail time and fines.

Comparative Advertising

The law in Thailand does not directly prohibit comparative advertising. However, Thai social customs of conflict avoidance or harmony seeking and *Kreing Chai* (akin to the Chinese notion of face saving) make these types of commercials uncommon. In addition to Thai culture, the Thai government has also done nothing to encourage comparative advertising. The government believes that the use of comparative advertising would likely lead to disparagement and deception. Only a few comparison advertisements have been permitted.

There are two major laws related to comparative advertising. One is the Radio and Television Act of 1978, created by the Broadcasting Directing Board of Thailand, specifying that advertisements disseminated through radio and television must not insult, despise or disparage any person, product or service. The other is the trademark law prohibiting any public use of another trade name. In Thailand the brand names of a firm's products are registered as trademarks—thus constituting a piece of property and part of the company's goodwill—which cannot be used by others for commercial purposes without the permission of the owner. Both enacted laws, though not directly forbidding comparative advertising, make it difficult for advertisers to use the comparative strategy.

Sweepstakes and Contest Advertising

There are two major pieces of legislation regarding the control of sweepstakes and contest promotions. One is the Gambling Act of 1935, and the other is the Consumer Protection Declaration of 1979.

Section 8 of the Gambling Act requires that the proposed sweepstakes or contest advertisement be reviewed by government officers preliminary to dissemination. The government officers in the province of Bangkok are officers of the Gambling Division of the Metropolitan Police Bureau (MPB). The government officers in the other provinces are officers of the local police stations; the local police stations do not have separate Gambling Divisions, though the officers perform the same duties as those in the MPB. The punishment for violating the Gambling Act can be a fine, imprisonment or both.

The Consumer Declaration of 1979 requires that when such promotions are used, the information must be disclosed in a clear and conspicuous manner. The information required by the Consumer Protection Board includes:

1. The exact number of the prizes to be awarded.
2. The value of the prizes to be awarded.
3. The schedule commencement and termination date of the game.
4. The geographic area covered by the game.

In addition such promotions have to be consistent with the requirements of the Gambling Act (Consumer Protection Act 1979).

Consumerism

Consumerism in Thailand is one of the available forces influencing advertising. According to Section 4 of the Consumer Protection Act of 1979, the consumer has the following rights of protection:

1. The right to receive correct and sufficient information and description as to the quality of goods or services; (2) the right to enjoy freedom in the choice of goods or services; (3) the right to expect safety in the use of goods or services; (4) the right to have the injury considered and compensated in accordance with the laws on such matters or with the provision of this Act.

However, Thai consumerism does not have a wide-based consumer support. Due to Thais' passive characteristics and their lack of influence over public policies, "they leave their consumer problems to be handled by the government sector or non-governmental organizations" (Vejpongsa 1994).

Most of the consumerists in Thailand are highly educated and include professors, college students and linguists. Usually they only express their opinions on advertising and propose changes to government officers in the relevant agencies; the officers then judge the legitimacy of the consumer complaints. In addition to highly educated consumerists, housewives are also a potent lobbying group—they are attempting to correct abuses in advertising, particularly those that are directed to children.

Recently there have been some active governmental and nongovernmental organizations that have raised consumer-protection problems. Among them are the Office of the Health Inspector General of the Thai Ministry of Health, the National Council of Women of Thailand, the Foundation for Children's Development (FCD), and the Drug Study Group. Ms. Samlee Jaidee of the Drug Study Group, for example, made a proposal to the Consumer Protection Board that "any companies found guilty of advertising misleading information about their products should have to run an advertisement in which they admit their misconduct to the public—in the same media, in the same time slot, and for the same duration as the original advertisement" (Asavaroengchai 1994). Ms. Assanee Saowaparb, the chairwoman of The National Council of Women of Thailand, is another activist who has tried to upgrade the portrayal of women's roles in the mass media. Saowaparb says that women's rights organizations have tried to promote awareness about the need to correct the unequal relationship between the sexes. Some of the campaigns attempted to discourage the use of women as sex objects in the media, films and advertisements. Another example is a cooperation between the NBC and Pa-Yai Creation Co., Ltd. in launching a weekly television program called *Taa Doo Hoo Fung* (Seeing Eyes, Listening Ears), encouraging consumers to give their opinions and complaints on media and on advertising, through television Channel 11.

Conclusion

Advertising in Thailand has experienced rapid growth during the past decades. Even though originally influenced by transnational advertising agencies, the structure of advertising and agencies, advertising and marketing techniques, creativity and technology, have today become less dependent. In terms of advertising laws and regulations, rules under government control have become less rigid. It is expected that censorship procedures will be gradually replaced by a less rigid form of self-regulation in the near future.

Bibliography

The Advertising Book: Thailand 1994–1995 Advertising, Marketing and Media Guide. 1995. Bangkok: AB Publications.
Annual Report & Membership Directory: The 25th Anniversary Issue. 1991. Bangkok: The Advertising Association of Thailand.
Asavaroengchai, S. 1994. Opening up the Legal Umbrella. *Bangkok Post,* September 26, p. 37.
Asian Advertising and Marketing. 1994. Thai Headquarters for Indochina Advertising, March 25.
Broadcasting Directing Board. 1994. Bangkok: Public Relations Department.
Consumer Protection Act of 1979. Ministerial Order B.E. 2522, Section 22(5).
Cooper, R. 1991. *Thais Mean Business: The Foreign Businessman's Guide to Doing Business in Thailand.* Singapore: Times Books International.

Engholm, C. 1991. *When Business East Meets Business West: The Guide to Practice and Protocol in the Pacific Rim.* New York: John Wiley & Sons, p. 49.

Englehart, J. 1993. Interview. *Manager.* February, p. 41.

Goldstein, C. and T. Rigoberto. 1989. Asian Advertising. *Far Eastern Economic Review,* 14 (26): 60–65.

Hall, E.T. 1976. *Beyond Culture.* Garden City, NY: Anchor Press/Doubleday, pp. 74–123.

Juers, J. 1995, Tapping into Vietnam. *Bangkok Post: Showcase Thailand, Board of Investment Fair 1995,* Bangkok: Bangkok Post Publications, p. 54.

Ketudat, S. 1990. The Middle Path for the Future of Thailand: Technology in Harmony with Culture and Environment, Chaing Mai, Thailand: Faculty of Social Science, Chaing Mai University.

Khoo Kaeng Data Bank. 1993. Bangkok: Khoo Kaeng.

Khoo Kaeng Data Bank. 1994. Bangkok: Khoo Kaeng.

Komin, S. 1991. *Psychology of the Thai People: Values and Behavioral Patterns.* Bangkok: Research Center, National Institute of Development Administration (NIDA).

Lehner, U.C. 1991. Thailand's Economy Surges and Country is Feeling the Strain. *Wall Street Journal,* June 12, p. 1.

Mahaphant, M. 1995. Account Execs Search for the Proper Media Balance. *The Nation,* January 30, p. B8.

Media Focus 1994. 1994. Thailand Advertising and Marketing, December.

Media News/Ogilvy & Mather. 1995. *The Nation,* January 12, p. B1.

Miller, L. 1994. Thailand: Special Report: Asian Advertising Review. *Asian Advertising and Marketing,* April 22, p. 26.

Mueller, B. 1987. Reflections of Culture: An Analysis of Japanese and American Advertising Appeals. *Journal of Advertising Research,* June/July, pp. 51–59.

Muscat, R. 1994. *Burning Bright, The Fifth Tiger: A Study of Thai Development Policy.* Armonk, NY: Eastgate Books.

Owen, B. 1993. Interview. *Manager,* February, pp. 44–45.

Rock, S. 1992. The Karma Before the Storm. *Director,* 45 (9): 48–51.

Shrestha, T. 1994. One Hundred and Fifty Years of Selling. In: *The Advertising Book: Thailand 1994–1995 Advertising, Marketing and Media Guide.* Bangkok: AB Publications.

Sopittakamol, S. 1995. Thai Ad Market on Verge of Global Top 20. *Bangkok Post,* January 12, p. 17.

Thammasri Y. and T. Yaowiwat. 1992. The Trend of Advertising Business in Thailand. In: *Advertising Business.* Bangkok: Sukhothai Thammathirat University Press, p. 788.

Thoopkrajae, V. 1995. Luring Disposable Income. In: *The Nation Yearbook 1994.* Bangkok: The Nation Publications, pp. 38–40.

Thorelli, H.B. and G.D. Sentell. 1982. *Consumer Emancipation and Economic Development: The Case of Thailand.* Greenwich, CT: Jai Press.

Vejpongsa, T. 1994. Consumer Protection from All Sides. *Bangkok Post,* September 26, p. 37.

Wells, W.D. 1987. Global Advertisers Should Pay Heed to Contextual Variations. *Marketing News,* February 13, p. 18.

World Bank/IMF. 1991. *Thailand: Standing out in Asia.* Bangkok, Thailand.

10

Malaysia: Advertising in a Multiracial Society

TECK HUA NGU

The Historical Context

Malaysia's thick mountain jungles, rich coastal plains and prolific sea life supported a succession of peoples for well over 5,000 years. The strategic position of the Malay peninsula adjacent to the Straits of Malacca, and its ancient and fabulously rich flow of trade between China, India and the Middle East, have long kept the Malay civilizations in contact with the world (M. Frith 1987).

The Malaysians of today share the centuries-long preoccupation of their ancestors: regional unity. In fact the forging of Malaysia from a collection of small independent states and colonies in 1957 represented the first major step toward the reunification of the Malay-speaking world since its disruption began with the Portuguese conquest of the Sultanate of Malacca in 1511. Today Malaysia consists of Peninsular Malaysia, which extends from Thailand in the north to the Singapore causeway in the south, and two additional Malaysian states, Sabah and Sarawak, which lie east across the South China Sea on the island of Borneo.

Since earliest times, regional commercial activity has centered around the Straits of Malacca, which for centuries controlled all the lucrative trade between China, India and the Middle East. The rise to power of the Sultanate of Malacca in the 1400s was to have a profound unifying influence on the scattered Malay world. Despite its supremacy for little over a century, Malacca was to bring a new and coherent unity to the people of the Malay world; and more importantly, it was responsible for cementing that bond by spreading Islam throughout the region.

Malacca was colonized by the Portuguese from 1511 to 1641. Ironically, the harsh imposition of Christianity and the ruthless treatment of the Malays are thought to have greatly strengthened Islam while Malacca was under Portuguese control. But the major damage to regional unity was undoubtedly the foothold for European colonists gained by the Portuguese (M. Frith 1987).

Under 150 years of Dutch control (1641–1824), the wealth and influence of

241

Malacca declined. Trade shrank disastrously under the tight monopolistic practices that replaced the old free-trade policies of the Sultanate and was largely captured by the British East India Company settlement at Penang. The influence of the British began with the founding of the city of Penang in the northwestern part of the Peninsula by Sir Francis Light in 1786, and culminated with the formation of the British Straits Settlement, consisting of Penang, Malacca and Singapore in 1858. The British spread their influence throughout the Peninsula and the area became known as British Malaya. The British were primarily interested in the commercial and strategic importance of the Malay Peninsula vis-à-vis the India–China trade (Sidhu 1980).

By the First World War, British Malaya had developed into the world's largest producer of tin and rubber, with Singapore emerging as a major trading center. Both developments were to introduce a new twist to the disunity in the Malay world. Ever since the first Europeans had settled Malaya, great waves of immigration—chiefly from China and India—had provided much of the labor for their developments. Although small settlements of Chinese had been on the Peninsula for many hundreds of years and Indians had a long history of involvement in the region, their combined impact on the social and political structure of the Malays had become almost nonexistent by the time the Europeans arrived. This was to change, however.

Under British rule the indigenous Malays were largely passed over in the development and modernization of the economy. By 1911, the Malay population of the peninsula (excluding Singapore) stood at only 59 percent of the entire population of 2.3 million (M. Frith 1987).

Although the political role of the Malay Sultans over the internal affairs of the states was guaranteed and respected by the British, the involvement of the indigenous Malaysian people in the administration of Malaya and in its emerging modern sector was minimal. The causes for Malay noninvolvement are not altogether clear. It is true that the British administrators favored the immigrant races for positions in the civil service and business; however, this discrimination may have been the result of the uneven access to modern education (M. Frith 1987). The education system set up by the British was centered in largely urban areas and the Malays favored a rural way of life. It is also felt that the existence of a well-established system of Koranic education and the Malays' natural suspicion of non-Islamic schooling may have dampened demand for British schools. In any event, as English became the lingua franca of colonial administration and commerce, Malay mobility in the modern sector became increasingly difficult (M. Frith 1987).

Malaya gained its independence from the British peacefully on August 31, 1957. In 1963, the nation of Malaysia was formed when Malaya, Singapore and the two British colonies in Borneo (Sarawak and Sabah) joined the Federation of Malaysia with Kuala Lumpur as its federal capital. Due to various disagreements with the federal government, Singapore left the Federation and became an independent nation in 1965. Islam was established as the official religion, and the King (or *Agong*, Paramount Ruler) as well as the Rulers (Sultans) and the heads of the states were appointed as the guardians of Islam.

Under the administration of the first prime minister, Tunku Abdul Rahman, the country underwent significant development and enjoyed relative peace until the racial riots of May 1969. One major cause cited for the racial riots was the income inequality between the two major racial groups: the Malays (who held the political power) and the Chinese (who wielded significant economic power). As a result of the racial riots, in which hundreds of people died, the government introduced the New Economic Policy (NEP). This policy has had the overall objectives of eradicating poverty regardless of race, and of restructuring the society so that no one particular race is identified with a particular profession. The government also set the objective of enabling the Malays to own 30 percent of the country's economic wealth by the year 1990. In 1991, NEP was replaced by the New Development Policy (NDP), which will be effective for the next 2 decades. The NDP will continue to pursue the objectives of the NEP, as the government has concluded that its objectives have not yet been fully met.

The Development of the Malaysian Advertising Industry

Advertising in Malaysia and Singapore is "almost as old as the trading tradition of the two countries," (The Advertisers Association 1971, 1). The earliest advertising primarily took the form of newspaper advertisements featuring imported products and shipping information from Britain to her colonies in Southeast Asia. For example, the first issue of the *Straits Times,* which was published in Singapore on July 15, 1845, contained various shipping movements on the front page. Other advertisements included hotels and medicinal products. The early advertising media included posters, handbills and sandwich boards. Although advertising was limited in scope then, "the basic principle that advertising was needed to sell goods still stood" (The Advertisers Association 1971, 1). The earliest evidence is that there were advertising agents and agencies in 1919 in Singapore. A Mr. J.R. Flynn Anderson advertised his services to help in advertising in the *Straits Times* on January 4, 1919. Another, Mr. Siow Choon Leng, also advertised his services as "an advertisement writer, publisher and printing press owner" and offered his expertise to "enterprising" merchants in the *Straits Times* on February 8, 1919 (The Advertisers Association 1971, 18). In those early days of advertising practice, most of the advertisements were prepared by the printers, such as Fraser & Neave, Limited: Good Printers. By 1934, the total number of firms offering advertising services had increased to 17 (The Advertisers Association 1971).

Advertising as an organized professional activity started in the late 1940s with the establishment of the Association of Accredited Advertising Agents

(4A's) in Singapore in 1948 (The Advertisers Association 1971). This was followed by the formation of the Malaysian Advertisers Association (MAA) in 1952, consisting mainly of transnational corporations (TNCs) such as Shell, Nestlé, and Lever Brothers (Anderson 1984). Western transnational advertising agencies (TNAAs) proliferated after the mid-1950s, when more TNAAs were established to service the increasing number of TNCs that had set up shop in Singapore. The establishment of such TNAAs usually follows their clients' overseas expansion; often the agencies are requested to set up foreign offices to service their clients' overseas accounts (Miracle 1977; Weinstein 1977).

Following the country's independence from Britain in 1957, the advertising industry experienced rapid growth as a result of the government's plans to develop the nation and to attract foreign investors. This growth was also spurred by the developing mass media, especially with the introduction of government television in 1963. Other media such as the government-run radio and the privately run Rediffusion (cable radio) also served as outlets for advertising. Among the earliest foreign TNAAs to set up branch offices in Kuala Lumpur, the federal capital, were Ogilvy & Mather, Ted Bates, Lintas and McCann-Erickson (Hashim 1994). Today, many of these TNAAs have become the largest advertising agencies in Malaysia.

The advertising industry has experienced formidable growth by riding the waves of development policies the country pursued in the last 3 decades. This can be seen by the total advertising expenditure in the mass media, which has increased by leaps and bounds over the past few decades. For example, in 1992, total advertising expenditure in the mass media reached a record-breaking 1,128 million ringgit Malaysia (US$434 million at the exchange rate of US$1 = RM2.6), an increase of 38 percent over the 1990 expenditure of RM817 million (US$314 million). In 1993, the total advertising expenditure in the mass media increased 28 percent to RM1,441 million. As for 1994, the total advertising expenditure in the media increased by 16 percent to RM1,674 million. For the first half of 1995, total advertising expenditure increased by 22 percent over the same period in 1994. Total billings for the year were expected to increase by 21 percent over the 1994 billings (*The Star* 1995a).

Today the most important advertising media are newspapers and television, together accounting for 86 percent of the total mass media advertising expenditure (54 percent and 32 percent, respectively). Magazine advertising shared another significant 6 percent, and advertising in all other media occupied the remaining 8 percent (Survey Research Malaysia, 1994). Furthermore, the deregulation of the mass media industry in Malaysia, such as the granting of more mass media licenses to the private sector as well as the launch of the first Malaysian satellite (MEASAT I) will open up more opportunities for the advertising industry, which has played an important role in the country's push toward modernization and industrialization. Since the Malaysian government has boldly embarked on a mission of becoming an industrialized country by the year 2020, the advertising industry in Malaysia is poised to enjoy further growth and more challenges.

Advertisers

Spearheading this growth are the transnational corporations, who have been and still are the biggest advertising spenders in the country. For example, of the 10 largest advertisers in Malaysia in 1993, all but one are TNCs. The only local company that made the list is Edaran Otomobil Nasional (EON), the national automobile distributor. Three of them are transnational tobacco corporations, and the other six are global consumer goods corporations that have become household names both in Malaysia and worldwide (see Table 10.1).

Table 10.1.   Top 10 Advertisers in Malaysia, 1993

Advertiser	Total Ad Expenditure (US $000)
Rothmans International	24,229
Nestlé SA	13,573
B.A.T. Industries	8,962
Unilever	8,581
Colgate-Palmolive Co.	6,772
RJR Nabisco	6,730
EON	5,192
Procter & Gamble Co.	4,586
Matsushita Electric Industrial Co.	4,543
Kao Corp.	4,054
Total:	87,222

Source: *Advertising Age International* 1994.

The important role played by the TNCs in advertising in Malaysia is even clearer if we examine the top 50 advertisers on Malaysian television in 1994 (January–November). The heaviest advertisers using the television medium are TNCs. The few local corporations that made the list are all privatized state monopolies, that is, Malaysian Airlines, Telekom (telephone monopoly), EON, Petronas (National Petrolium Corporation) and Malaysia National Insurance (Survey Research Malaysia 1994). This scenario has changed little from that of the last 2 decades; Anderson (1984) reported that in the 1970s, 95 percent of all television advertising revenues in Malaysia were from the TNCs. In 1994, of the RM276 million these top 50 advertisers spent on Malaysian television, the TNCs made up 93 percent. The 10 largest advertisers on television can be seen in Table 10.2.

Among the biggest TNC advertisers in Malaysia are the three transnational tobacco corporations. Advertising by the tobacco companies consistently tops the categories in terms of brand, product category and company. For example, Kim and Frith (1993) found that in 1990, nine out of the top 10 advertisers in the country were TNCs, seven of which were cigarette brands. According to the *SRM*

Table 10.2.   Top 10 Advertisers on Malaysian Television, Jan.–Nov., 1994

Advertiser	Ad Expenditure (RM*)
Cigarette Importers and Distributors	52,259,431
Nestlé	23,314,061
MTC (Malaysian Tobacco Company)	18,350,042
Colgate Palmolive	15,956,183
Procter & Gamble	13,701,117
R J Reynolds	13,475,408
Lever Brothers	13,107,816
EON (Edaran Otomobil Nasional)	7,611,147
AD HOC	6,074,050
Dutch Baby	5,947,369
Total	169,796,624

Source: *Survey Research Malaysia Adexcope*, 1994.
*RM, Malaysian ringgit.

ADEX Report 1992 (Survey Research Malaysia [SRM] 1992a), six of the top 10 advertisers by brand in the country are tobacco brands (SRM ADEX 1992a). They accounted for 73 percent (RM56.1 million or US$21.6 million) of the top 10 brands' total advertising expenditure or 19 percent of the total advertising expenditure in 1992 in Malaysia. In 1994, the transnational tobacco corporations (TTCs) made up nearly half (46 percent) of the total advertising expenditure of the top 10 advertisers. It is thus no wonder that the tobacco companies are affectionately referred to as the "tobacco boys" (Hashim 1994) by the advertising industry.

Advertising Agencies

The key advertising agencies in Malaysia are the TNAAs. Due to the strategy of international alignment of accounts adopted by most transnational corporations, the TNAAs in Malaysia also handled the accounts of the TNCs in their home countries. For example, McCann-Erickson handles the Coca-Cola account in Malaysia, as in all other countries where Coca-Cola is marketed. Because the TNCs can afford big advertising budgets, this invariably contributed to the dominance of the TNAAs in the Malaysian advertising industry. This is also a major reason that the local advertising agencies have remained relatively small compared with the TNAAs.

Anderson (1984) found that in the 1970s, six to seven TNAAs controlled 85 percent of the total advertising expenditure in Malaysia. This situation has changed little today. For example, in 1991, the TNAAs commanded RM800 million (or 80 percent) of the total advertising billings in Malaysia. In 1992, of the top 10 advertising agencies in Malaysia, all were TNAAs; they controlled 70 percent of the total advertising expenditure (Hashim 1994). For 1994, the foreign TNAAs commanded a combined billing of US$413.5 million (RM1,075 million). This represents nearly two-thirds of the total advertising expenditure in the country, leaving the rest to a myriad of small local agencies.

Even though government regulations require the TNAAs to be at least 51 percent owned by locals and that they be mainly staffed by locals, the TNAAs are actually run by the few expatriates who occupy the top positions in the agency (Anderson 1984; Hashim 1994; Kim and Frith 1993).The largest TNAAs in 1994 with their respective billings are presented in Table 10.3.

Table 10.3. Billings of the Transnational Advertising Agencies in Mal: ·sia, 1994

Agency	Billings (US$ 000)	Gross Income (US$ 000)
Bates Malaysia	95,000	11,875
Ogilvy & Mather	45,436	6,812
McCann-Erickson	32,891	4,931
Dentsu, Young & Rubicam	31,909	4,784
Lintas Malaysia	25,901	3,883
J.Walter Thompson Co.	25,358	3,802
Saatchi & Saatchi	22,400	2,800
AP:Foote, Cone & Belding	21,106	2,961
Leo Burnett Advertising	21,014	3,152
Batey Ads Malaysia	18,409	2,761
Grey Malaysia	16,794	2,518
Bozell	14,130	2,120
BBDO Malaysia	13,643	1,916
KHK BMB&B Advertising	9,232	1,384
Naga DDB Needham	6,870	1,030
Hakuhodo Malaysia	5,435	1,029
Euro RSCG Ball Partnership	4,616	691
Dai-Ichi Kikaku Malaysia	2,776	798
Dentsu Mandate Malaysia	583	87
Total:	413,503	59,334

Source: *Advertising Age*, 1995.

The Malaysian Consumers

A value and lifestyle study of the Malaysian consumers conducted by the Survey Research Malaysia (SRM) in 1990 yielded the following seven major groupings (Hashim 1994).

1. THE RURAL TRADITIONALISTS

This represents the biggest segment (32 percent) of the Malaysian market. They are the ethnic Malays who stay in rural villages. They are also largely conservative and traditional in outlook.

2. THE KAMPUNG [VILLAGE] TRENDSETTERS

This group makes up 16 percent of the market. About 60 percent of this group are ethnic Malays. However, they are from a younger age group and are largely rural dwellers. Unlike the Rural Traditionalists, they are ambitious, outgoing, and brand and fashion conscious, but are also family and community oriented.

3. THE REBEL HANGOUTS

The Rebel Hangouts also make up 16 percent of the market. This group consists mainly of young, urban ethnic Chinese with high personal incomes. They are nonconformists and the least religious and moralistic of the groups.

4. THE SLEEPWALKERS

This group makes up 12 percent of the market. They are mainly ethnic Chinese females over 40 years of age. The Sleepwalkers are described as pessimistic and least houseproud. They are also not very family or community oriented.

5. THE NOT QUITE THERES

The Not Quite Theres make up 10 percent of the market. They are largely young ethnic Malays with good personal incomes. They are described as moralistic, but are introverted and lacking in confidence.

6. THE INCONSPICUOUS

Like the Not Quite Theres, the Inconspicuous also make up 10 percent of the market. They comprise the urban female ethnic Malays with average income. They are also described as moralistic, introverted and lacking in confidence, but have high optimism.

7. THE UPPER ECHELONS

This last group makes up 5 percent of the market. They consist of urban ethnic Malays in the high income bracket. They are described as socially active, ambitious, confident and perceive of themselves as leaders. Similar to most ethnic Malays, they are family oriented, moralistic and nationalistic.

Structure of the Media

Reflecting Malaysia's multiracial, multicultural, multiethnic makeup, the mass media in Malaysia are also diverse and varied, with specific media catering to the needs of particular ethnic groups. Taking cognizance of the vast potential of the mass media in exploiting the delicate racial sensitivities, the government has instituted strict laws and regulations for the mass media. The majority of the media in Malaysia are either directly owned by the government—such as the Radio & Television Malaysia (RTM), which operates two of the existing three nationally televised television channels (TV1 and TV2) and all but two of the radio stations in the country—or indirectly owned by the political parties in power through their corporations. Even though changing conditions in the country have caused the government to relent somewhat on strict laws and regulations pertaining to ownership and freedom of the mass media, the government still keeps a tight rein over the media through numerous legislative measures.

In 1984, a private third television channel (TV3) was introduced to meet the increasing needs presented by the growing metropolis surrounding the Federal

Capital—the Klang valley. TV3 has since expanded its broadcast nationwide. A fourth channel—MetroVision—was launched in the middle of 1995. This channel is operated by the private sector, catering initially to the viewers in Klang Valley and hoping to expand later to the other parts of the country. In August of 1995, the first cable television service in the country—Mega TV—was launched by a private corporation. Mega TV offers five channels to its subscribers, four of which are 24-hour broadcasts. Originally limited to the Klang Valley, it hopes to cover the entire country by the middle of 1996 (*The Star* 1995b). In 1994, television accounted for 32 percent of the total advertising expenditure in the mass media. This situation will likely improve as more television channels are being planned with the 1995 launch of the first Malaysian satellite (MEASAT I) (Nasir 1995).

Ownership of the major privately owned media is heavily concentrated. A few media conglomerates own the most widely circulated print media. For example, the New Straits Times Group publishes six nationally circulated daily newspapers including the *New Straits Times, Malay Mail, Business Times, Shin Min Daily News, Berita Harian* and *Harian Metro*. The group also publishes leading magazines such as the *Malaysian Business, Malaysian Digest, Jelita*, and *Her World*. In addition it also indirectly owns a stake in TV3 through the parent company.

The newspaper is the most widely distributed and used medium, and hence, accounted for the bulk of the total advertising revenue (54 percent) in 1994. In 1995 there were 37 daily newspapers in Malaysia, in the major languages of Malay, English, Chinese (Mandarin) and Tamil. There are also 38 biweekly or weekly newspapers (Survey Research Malaysia, 1992b). In addition there are numerous magazines published in Malaysia, the most popular ones being women's and entertainment magazines. They captured up to 6 percent of the total advertising revenue in 1994.

Government Regulation of Advertising

Although the government has pursued policies of Western-style development in its efforts to develop and modernize the country, it is also at the same time taking a cautious stand toward Western influence, especially in the media and advertising. In fact as early as 1971, the government raised the issue of the Western influence on Malaysian advertising. This concern was expressed by the then Minister of Special Functions and Information, the Honorable Ghazali Shafie, who lamented that:

> we note in our newspapers, magazines, radios and on television that the images created have very often little relation with our environment or what we hope to achieve in our society. There is . . . a certain degree of mindless aping of bour-

geois values and styles of the West. I have noticed that certain products are associated through the mass media in this country with lifestyles of the middle and upper classes of the West, and this is being continuously presented to the Malaysian minds as something to model ourselves by.

(Anderson 1984, 219)

During those early years of Malaysia's independence as a sovereign nation from a colonial power, much of the country was still struggling from underdevelopment and poverty. Additionally, the multiracial and multicultural nature of the Malaysian society (which today consists of 56 percent Malays, 34 percent ethnic Chinese, 10 percent ethnic Indians and other indigenous races) also meant that advertising, if not well thought out, might offend the sensitivities of these diverse ethnic groups. In addition the advertising industry in early post-independence years was dominated by Western agencies that employed many foreign expatriates in the major decision-making positions. This often meant that Western-style advertisements were the norm.

With these factors in mind, the government instituted a set of regulations for all advertisements broadcast over radio and television. The regulations were spelled out in the *Advertising Code for Television and Radio* (revised 1990) issued by the Ministry of Information. This Ministry was given the important mandate of fostering and propagating the Malaysian identity and culture through the Ministry-owned RTM, which today still controls two of the three nationally broadcast television channels and all but two of the radio stations.

Cultural Values in Advertising

The *Advertising Code* is designed to safeguard advertising and the consumers against the influence of foreign cultural values. This is explicitly stated in the *Advertising Code,* which prohibits the "adaptation or projection of foreign culture which is not acceptable to a cross section of the major communities of the Malaysian society either in the form of words, slogans, clothing, activity or behavior" (6). In addition advertisements which depict "ways of life that are against or totally different from the ways of life followed by Malaysians (Malaysian Society)" (6) are also disallowed. As correctly pointed out by Deng et al. (1994), the government instituted this regulation because of the belief that not all its citizens are prepared to fully accept all aspects of Western culture.

Examples of the specific elements of the foreign culture that are unacceptable and prohibited by the *Advertising Code* include disco scenes; clothing imprinted with words or symbols conveying undesirable messages or impressions; scenes of an amorous, intimate or suggestive nature; and kissing between adults. Furthermore, advertising of the icon of Western culture—jeans—was prohibited. However, in recent years, the government allowed the advertising of all but blue denim jeans, provided they were presented as clean and neat. The ban on blue denim jeans was supposedly because of its association with the hippie culture of a past era. The government finally lifted the ban on blue denim jeans commercials at the end of 1994.

The *Advertising Code* also promotes cultural sensitivity in advertisements. It prohibits advertisements that "contain statements or suggestions which may offend the religious, racial, political or sentimental susceptibilities of any section of the community" (*Advertising Code for Television and Radio* 1990, 6). This is deemed to be vital in achieving racial and national harmony in a multiracial country such as Malaysia.

In addition the *Advertising Code* covers specific regulations concerning the technical requirements of the production of advertisements appearing in RTM, and general principles relating to the specific content of advertisements, such as issues of good taste and subliminal advertising. The code also covers the specific requirements and prohibitions regarding the use of children, men, women, professionals, medicines and pesticides.

Besides conforming to the existing laws and regulations, advertisements are also required to promote social responsibility. For instance, advertisements are required to "inject civic mindedness and desired behavioral attitudes in life, such as queuing up when boarding a bus etc. and keeping public places clean" (*Advertising Code for Radio and Television* 1990, 4). Perhaps the most far-ranging requirement is one that states that besides the commercial messages, all advertisements "must convey a second message such as messages calculated to bring about discipline, cleanliness, healthy living or industrious attitudes" (*Advertising Code for Radio and Television* 1990, 4). It is doubtful whether the advertisers adhere to these requirements.

Made-In-Malaysia Requirement

In an effort to reduce the elements of foreign culture being used in advertising, the Ministry of Information has, since the early 1970s, imposed the Made-in-Malaysia (MIM) rule, which requires all advertisements to be produced locally. This rule is also designed to protect the relatively new local film and advertising industry. The rule requires that the commercial be produced in Malaysia. The talent, creative team and the production staff must also be Malaysians. Foreign scenes or technologies can only be used after prior approval from the Ministry of Information. This approval is only granted when the technologies or footage are unavailable in the country.

An example is that of a Salem High Country Holidays commercial, which required the scene of snow-covered mountain peaks nonexistent in Malaysia. Thus, Salem was allowed to use some foreign footage in the commercial (K.T. Frith 1987). Even then, the foreign footage is limited to no more than 20 percent of the total commercial footage. If the language used in the commercials is English, then it must be "Malaysian-English" and the use of "British- or American-English" is prohibited (Parker 1982).

Islamic Values in Advertising

In addition to propagating Malaysian identity and culture, the *Advertising Code* is also heavily influenced by the government's effort to promote Islamic values throughout the country. This includes the imposition of stricter regulations on the mass media content (including advertising) based on Islamic principles and values. One example of this relates to the treatment of women in advertising. Unlike Western advertising, in which women are portrayed as sex symbols and sex objects, the women in Malaysian advertising must be portrayed as having "good behavior acceptable to local culture and society" (*Advertising Code for Radio and Television* 1990, 7). In addition to conform to Islamic standards, the female models in advertisements must also adhere to the *Advertising Code*'s decent dress code, which stipulates that a female model must be "covered until the neckline, which should not be too low, the length of a skirt worn should be below the knees, the arms may be exposed up to the edge of the shoulder but armpits cannot be exposed" (*Id.* 7).

In addition the women's costumes must not be "too revealing or suggestive" (*Advertising Code for Radio and Television* 1990, 7). These rules primarily conform to the Islamic value of covering the *aurat* (private parts of the body) for the women and Islam's prohibition of using women as sex symbols. Other rules concerning models in the advertisements include the proper use of the models and the prohibition of the use of scenes that could result in "undesirable thoughts" such as undressing.

The Ministry of Information is quite serious about protecting Islamic values. A few years ago the Seiko watch company began advertising in Malaysia using the company's worldwide slogan: "Man Invented Time, Seiko Perfected It." However, when the head of a local university's Islamic Studies Department complained that the advertisement was un-Islamic because God, not man, had invented time—the Ministry of Information required Seiko to withdraw all of their advertising. Seiko then revised its slogan for Malaysia to read: "Man Invented Time Keeping, Seiko Perfected It." This slogan was allowed to run because it fit within the Islamic value system (K.T. Frith 1987).

Additionally, all television commercials must pass through a lengthy process of screening and approval by the National Film Censorship Board (Filem Negara Malaysia) before they are allowed to be aired. This process is presented in Figure 10.1.

The Ministry of Information is in the process of converting the *Advertising Code* into law under the umbrella of the Broadcasting Act to enhance further the

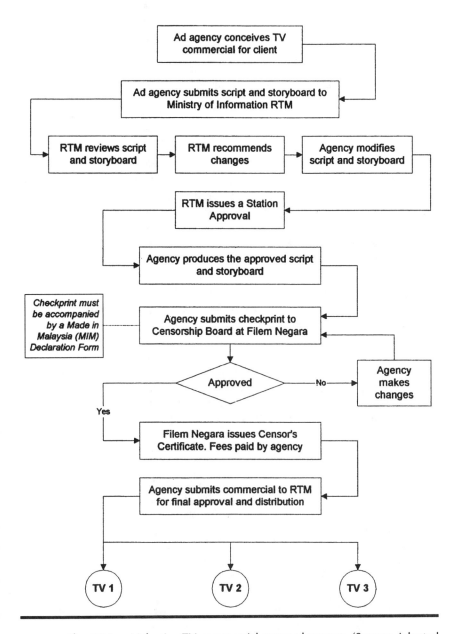

Fig. 10.1. Malaysian TV commercial approval process. (Source: Adapted from Frith, K.T., 1987, 102)

government's control of advertising on television and also to enable the government to prosecute the offenders in court. This is in addition to the Minister of Information's power and prerogative to remove all advertisements deemed unsuitable. While the *Advertising Code* is primarily designed for commercials aired in RTM and TV3, it has also become the standard document of reference for advertising in all the other media in the country.

Self-Regulation by the Advertising Industry

In addition to government regulation, the advertising industry has also set up a system of self-regulation. Advertising self-regulation formally began with the setting up of the Advertising Standards Authority of Malaysia (ASA) in 1974. It was established by the Association of Accredited Advertising Agencies (4A's), the Malaysian Advertisers Association (MAA) and the Malaysian Newspaper Publishers' Association (MNPA). The main function of ASA is to investigate complaints lodged with the authority by its own members, the various government departments, consumers and trade associations, as well as from members of the public. In addition the ASA is responsible for establishing and enforcing the Malaysian Code of Advertising Practice (MCAP), which serves as the self-regulation guideline for the industry.

Like the *Advertising Code,* the MCAP states that

> Advertisements must project the Malaysian culture and identity, reflect the multi-racial character of the population and advocate the philosophy of *"Rukunegara"* (the national ideology) which reads as follows: Belief in God; Loyalty to the King and country; Upholding the Constitution; Rule of law; Good behavior and morality.
>   (Advertising Standards Association of Malaysia 1990, 1)

The ASA enforces the MCAP "without there necessarily having been a complaint lodged with the authority" (Advertising Standards Association of Malaysia 1990, 3). Additionally, ASA is also responsible for the amendment of the MCAP to meet the changing values and needs of the society. However, in the 2 decades of its existence, the ASA has been criticized as a "toothless tiger" by the consumer associations, due to its impotence in enforcing the MCAP codes among its members. Its actions have been deemed to be self-protective instead of self-policing.

In view of the rapid growth and new challenges facing the industry, the ASA has recently taken steps to strengthen self-regulatory efforts further. In 1994, an agreement was reached by which the members of the MNPA (consisting of mass-media owners) would immediately withdraw all advertisements found violating the MCAP codes when so directed by the ASA. The ASA has also taken other proactive measures such as employing personnel to monitor all advertisements in the major mass media for violations.

Advertisements that violate the codes are investigated and advertisers who attempt to breach either the government's *Advertising Code* or the self-regulatory code of ASA, may find themselves denied advertising space or time in the media. The various mass media also have special terms and conditions to which the advertisements placed in their media must conform. For example, advertisements sent to the New Straits Times Group of newspapers are screened by the advertising department before they are printed.

Consumer Issues

The consumer associations in Malaysia are quite powerful and highly vocal. Each state in Malaysia has an active consumer association. The Federation of Malaysian Consumer Associations (FOMCA) is sponsored by the Ministry of Domestic Trade and Consumer Affairs. In particular, the Consumers' Association of Penang (CAP), which is independent of government funding and is not a member of FOMCA, is the most active in consumer issues. The CAP is also the most critical of and outspoken about the Malaysian advertising industry. Besides consumer activism at the grass-roots level, both FOMCA and CAP also publish monthly newspapers and other printed material. One such book published by the CAP is entitled: *Selling Dreams: How Advertising Misleads Us* (Consumers' Association of Penang 1986). This book decries the consumption culture perpetuated by the advertising industry and contends that multinational advertising in Malaysia has introduced negative cultural influences, such as Western values and the pursuit of materialism. Also, CAP has been particularly critical of the government's inaction in enforcing existing regulations.

Since 1977, CAP has been instrumental in waging an antismoking campaign and opposing cigarette advertising and promotions in Malaysia. CAP organized a national antismoking campaign in 1982 and has successfully lobbied the government to ban direct cigarette advertising and promotions on radio and television. In large part owing to pressure from the consumer associations, the Malaysian government again changed the laws regulating cigarette advertising and banned all direct cigarette advertising (except for point-of-sales promotions) in 1993. However, indirect advertising of the cigarette brand names is still permitted at sponsored events.

Conclusion

The advertising industry in Malaysia faces complex challenges, in particular the numerous government regulations make the practice of advertising more difficult in Malaysia than in some other Asian countries. On one hand, these regulations reflect the national aspirations of achieving a Malaysian identity and culture, while conforming to the values of Islam, the national religion. On the other hand, however, these regulations work against an advertiser who might be interested in producing a standard campaign to run across Southeast Asia. In such case, the advertiser would be required either to shoot the entire campaign in Malaysia in order to conform with the Made-in-Malaysia requirement, or alternately, to shoot single commercials separately for Malaysia.

Like other developing countries in the region, Malaysians realize that advertising can be a powerful force in shaping national values. It is the viewpoint of most Malaysians and of the Malaysian government that advertising needs to be harnessed to help construct a just society, not just a consumer society.

Bibliography

The Advertisers Association—Malaysia, Singapore. 1971. *A Review of Advertising in Singapore and, Malaysia During Early Times.* Malaysia: Federal Publications.

Advertising Age. 1995. Agency Rankings, April 10, S29. Detroit, MI: Crain Communications Inc.

Advertising Age International. 1994. November 21, I-14.

Advertising Code for Television and Radio. 1990. Kuala Lumpur: Ministry of Information.

Advertising Standards Authority (ASA). 1990. *Constitution, Terms of Reference & Modus Operandi.* Malaysia: ASA, January.

Advertising Standards Association of Malaysia. 1990. *Malaysian Code of Advertising Practice.* Petaling Jaya, Malaysia: Advertising Standards Authority of Malaysia, January.

Anderson, M.H. 1984. *Madison Avenue in Asia: Politics and Transnational Advertising,* Cranbury, NJ: Associated University Presses.

Consumers' Association of Penang (CAP). 1986. *Selling Dreams: How Advertising Misleads Us,* Penang, Malaysia: CAP.

Deng, S., S. Jivan and M.-L. Hassan. 1994. Advertising in Malaysia: A Cultural Perspective. *International Journal of Advertising,* 13 (2): 153–166.

Frith, K.T. 1987. The Social and Legal Constraints on Advertising in Malaysia. *Media Asia,* 14 (2): 100–104.

Frith, M. 1987. *The Academic Experience in Malaysia.* Kuala Lumpur: MACEE.

Hashim, A. 1994. *Advertising in Malaysia.* Petaling Jaya, Malaysia: Pelanduk Publications.

Kim, K.K. and K. Frith. 1993. An Analysis of the Growth of Transnational Advertising Agencies in Five Asian Countries: 1970–1990. *Media Asia,* 20 (1): 45–53.

Laws of Malaysia. 1983 [revised]. Act 290: Medicines (Advertisement and Sale) Act of 1956.

MAA Rules. Kuala Lumpur: Malaysian Advertisers Association.

Means, G.P. 1978. Public Policy Toward Religion in Malaysia. *Pacific Affairs,* 51 (3): 384–405.

Miracle, G.E. 1977. An Historical Analysis to Explain the Evolution of Advertising Agency Services. *Journal of Advertising,* 6 (3): 24–28.

Nagata, J. 1980. Religious Ideology and Social Change: The Islamic Revival in Malaysia. *Pacific Affairs* 53 (3): 405–439.

Nasir, H.M. 1995. Hughes on Target to Meet Satellite Launch Date. *The Star,* November 3.

Parker, E. 1982. Malaysia. In: Kurian, G.T., ed. *World Press Encyclopedia.* New York: Facts on File.

Sidhu, J.S. 1980. *Administration in the Federated Malay States 1896–1920.* Kuala Lumpur: Oxford University Press.

The Star. 1995a. Advertising Billings Rise. January 28, p. 8.

The Star. 1995b. Mega TV Confident of Good Subscriber Response. November 2.

Survey Research Malaysia (SRM). 1992a. *ADEX Report,* 1992. Kuala Lumpur: SRM.

Survey Research Malaysia (SRM). 1992b. *Media Index Database, 1992.* Kuala Lumpur: SRM.

Survey Research Malaysia (SRM). 1994. *ADEX Report, 1994.* Kuala Lumpur: SRM.

Weinstein, A.K. 1977. Foreign Investments by Service Firms: The Case of Multinational Advertising Agencies. *Journal of International Business Studies,* 8 (1): 83–91.

11

Advertising in Indonesia: Unity in Diversity

KATHERINE TOLAND FRITH

Introduction

Indonesia is the largest archipelago nation in the world, with its approximately 13,667 islands stretching 5,200 kilometers across the equator. About 6,000 of these islands are inhabited by different ethnic groups including the Javanese, Sudanese, Balinese and Bataks. In addition to the indigenous groups there are Melanesians, Micronesians, Chinese, Arabs and Indians. Together the Indonesians speak approximately 300 distinct languages and dialects and their cultures range from the formal court system of Java to the tribal systems of Irian Jaya (Butwell 1967).

Indonesia was inhabited for centuries before recorded history, as was demonstrated by archaeologists in 1891 and again in 1936 with the discovery of the fossilized remains of one of the earliest known types of primitive human— Java Man. This early humanoid species inhabited Indonesia more than half a million years ago (Danoesoegondo 1968).

Indonesia's recorded history dates back to the first century A.D. The main sources of early written history are Chinese chronicles of kingdoms on the islands of Sumatra, Java and Borneo (Danoesoegondo 1968). In the first century Indian traders searching for precious spices and metals brought their culture, traditions and religion to Indonesia. Thus began the history of absorption of foreign culture and religions by the people of Indonesia. Today Indonesians still have the ability to blend foreign influences with indigenous traditions, forming what Clifford Geertz and others have termed a "syncretic" culture (Geertz 1973).

Waves of traders and missionaries from India, China and the Middle East brought Buddhism and later, Islam, to Indonesia. Early Indonesian kingdoms built huge and impressive monuments such as Borobudur and the Prambanan temples on the island of Java, commemorating these religions. By the 15th century, however, most of Sumatra and Java had converted to Islam. The Hindu

259

faithful fled to the eastern end of Java and the island of Bali. Today Islam is practiced by the majority of the people of Indonesia. Although practically every religion in the world is practiced in Indonesia today, approximately 90 percent of the population are Muslim.

Colonization and Independence

The Portuguese arrived in Southeast Asia in the early 16th century and were followed by the Spanish, the Dutch and the British. The Dutch succeeded in monopolizing the highly valued spice trade and consolidated their trade in the Dutch East India Company, which was headquartered in Batavia (now Jakarta). For over 300 years Indonesia was ruled by the Netherlands. In 1945, after a bloody war with the Dutch, Indonesia proclaimed its independence from the Netherlands. The task of pulling together one nation from hundreds of ethnic groups spread over 13,000 separate islands fell into the able hands of the charismatic Javanese leader named Sukarno, the first president of The Republic of Indonesia. President Sukarno preached a nationalism that went beyond ethnic identity to embrace "all human beings who, according to geopolitics ordained by God Almighty, live throughout the entire archipelago of Indonesia from the northern tip of Sumatra to Papua" (*Far Eastern Economic Review* 1987).

Today Indonesia is the fourth most populous country in the world, with a population expected to exceed 200 million people by 1997. It has the world's largest Muslim population (Castle 1994). Nearly 60 percent of the country's population—approximately 100 million people—live on the island of Java. In addition to being the most densely populated island in the country, Java is the most densely populated island in the world, with an estimated population density approaching 900 people per square kilometer. Sumatra is the next most populous island with just over 20 percent of the country's population. Today's president of Indonesia, Javanese General Suharto, took charge of the country in 1965, when he quashed a communist-backed coup. Pak Suharto (the term *pak* or *bapak* means "father" in Indonesian and denotes both respect and endearment) became the country's second president in 1968 and will remain so until he chooses to step down. General Suharto's "New Order" government has largely been responsible for the sociopolitical stability and steady economic growth Indonesia has enjoyed over the past 25 years.

Among the peoples of Indonesia there are over 300 ethnic groups and numerous languages and dialects (Bunge 1983). It is fitting that the national symbol is a mythical golden bird, the Garuda, enshrined over a banner proclaiming "Unity in Diversity." This old Javanese motto was first used in the Mojopahit Kingdom in the 15th century and symbolizes the unity of the Indonesian people in spite of their varied and diverse ethnic and cultural origins.

Pancasila: The National Ideology

The national ideology of *Pancasila* (meaning "Five Principles") was introduced by President Sukarno and has been retained by Suharto as the basis for civilized rule in Indonesia. This state ideology, which pioneered state ideological development in the Association of Southeast Asian Nations (ASEAN) region, is displayed on practically every building and street corner in the country. Pancasila urges Indonesians to follow these five *sila,* or principles:

1. Belief in One Supreme God
2. Humanitarianism: A Just and Civilized Society
3. The Unity of Indonesia
4. Democracy, guided by the wisdom of unanimity from discussion (*musjawarah*) and mutual assistance (*gotong royong*)
5. Social Justice, the equality of political rights and the citizenship, as well as social and cultural equality

Because Pancasila affects almost every aspect of Indonesian life, a fuller discussion of the principles and their meaning to Indonesian culture is essential. Sila one means that all religions have equal status in Indonesia. Some authors have suggested that the first sila was an effort by Sukarno to avoid having Indonesia become a Muslim state with all the complications of *sharia* law (*Far Eastern Economic Review* 1987). Under Pancasila today, the Muslim majority has equal status with Buddhists, Christians, Hindus and other mystical beliefs.

Sila two involves the acceptance of community or village mores, including respect for elders and people in power. In a culture that values deference over directness and considers strident criticism as taboo, the practice of this sila is extremely important. Indonesians seek balance and harmony in their daily life and tend to avoid situations that may cause friction or personal embarrassment. No action becomes superior to an action that might have negative consequences (Fitch and Webb 1989). The Javanese concept of *tepo seliro,* or sensitivity to the feelings of others especially when offering advice or criticism, is a core belief that relates to this principle. The belief that a just and civilized society is built upon the virtues of moderation, composure, even-handedness and tolerance is uniquely Indonesian (Douglas 1994, 11).

Sila three is the enterprise of uniting hundreds of ethnic groups into one nation. In an effort to promote unity and nationalism, the government requires that all schoolchildren, university students and civil servants periodically study or attend Pancasila training programs known as P4 (*Pedoman Penghayatan dan Pengalaman Pancasila,* or "Guidance for the Perception and Practice of Pancasila"). The dynamics of implementing this enormous enterprise are daunting, yet 72 percent of Indonesian adults claim to have been "reached" by the P4 program (Douglas 1994, 26).

Sila four has its origins in local communities, or *kampungs,* where the community comes first and the individual second (Fitch and Webb 1989). This sila includes *gotong royong,* the well-known practice of mutual assistance and collective enterprise that is the cornerstone of Indonesian village life (Anderson 1990). A visitor to Indonesia might see *gotong royong* being demonstrated in a government TV advertisement for nation building where throngs of villagers literally lift a stranded bus out of the mud and move it back onto the road. The second concept inherent in Sila four is *musyawarah* and *mufakat,* which mean "consultation" and "consensus." In the villages all community decisions are made by consultation and consensus. This is the prevalent group spirit that forms the backbone of Indonesian democracy.

Sila five, social justice, guarantees equality of political rights and citizenship, as well as social and cultural equality. Some Westerners might argue that this principle overlooks economic realities. As the *World Bank Report* noted, the richest 10 percent of Indonesians receive 40.7 percent of the nations income, while the poorest 40 percent receive 17.3 percent (*Media Scene* 1994–95). This disparity of income creates a social class system that leaves some people overemployed and others underemployed (Fitch and Webb 1989). However, it is important to note that the World Bank has also reported a dramatic decrease in the poverty level over the past 20 years, with some 70 million living below the poverty line in 1970 and only 27 million in 1990 (*Media Scene* 1994–95).

Economic Context

Indonesia has a mixed, free-market economy. In terms of exports, the country has vast natural resources of crude oil and natural gas and timber. It is also the world's third largest producer of tin and a major exporter of textiles, rubber, coconut, rice, sugarcane, tea and coffee. Economic policy is based on a system of 5-year plans known as *Repelita,* which operate within a broader 25-year Long Term Development Plan (*Media Scene* 1994–95). The country has completed five *Repelita* and is entering the sixth cycle known as the "Take Off Era of Industrialization." The country has targeted an annual growth rate of 6.2 percent for the years 1994 to 1999, during which time the government hopes to increase per capita yearly income to US$670 and to create 12 million new jobs. President Suharto has predicted that the country will reach the Newly Industrialized stage by the year 2019 (*Media Scene* 1994–95).

Advertising in Indonesia

As Michael Anderson noted in an earlier history of advertising in Indonesia:

Modern advertising—meaning Western defined and imported—arrived in the sprawling archipelago called Indonesia to serve the growing needs of non-indigenous manufacturers and distributors. By 1938 the advertising agency as a specialized business organization had reached Indonesia.

(Anderson 1984, 153)

The first international agency to set up shop in Indonesia was Lintas International, a London-based agency. Lintas opened an in-house agency in Jakarta to handle the expanding business of its client Unilever (formerly known as Lever Brothers). While other transnational advertising agencies were all but nonexistent during the Dutch colonial period and throughout most of Sukarno's rule, Lintas was working exclusively for Unilever and developing resources that even today are second to none in Indonesia (Anderson 1984).

The history of the advertising industry in Indonesia has been fraught with tensions. Each step forward has led to at least one step back. Under President Sukarno's policy of Guided Democracy, transnational corporations such as Unilever were put under the control of various government agencies. In general, Sukarno's liberation politics were idealistic, and for the most part aimed at trying to end foreign domination and unite Indonesia's thousands of islands and peoples. These policies, however, failed to bring about much economic growth. In 1966, Sukarno was overthrown and President Suharto and his New Order took power.

Advertising began to grow again under the New Order. In 1970, P.T. Fortune, an agency affiliated with the Australian agency of the same name, was established. In addition to Lintas and Fortune, a few indigenous agencies emerged during the 1960s and early 1970s, including Intervista Advertising started by a young Indonesian intellectual named Nurmadi, known today as the father of Indonesian advertising. Nurmadi was also instrumental in setting up the Asian Advertising Congress in Jakarta in 1974 (Anderson 1984).

Under Suharto's more liberal policy toward foreign investment, the door to the West was reopened. The decision to return expropriated businesses to their original foreign owners, and the decision to permit some nongovernmental commercial radio stations fostered the first flush of growth and expansion in the Indonesian advertising industry. Prior to the New Order, advertising expenditures in Indonesia were perhaps only one million dollars a year, but between 1969 and 1972 they increased more than tenfold. By 1977, approximately $70 million was being spent on mass media advertising (Anderson 1984).

During the 1970s transnational agencies such as Dentsu, McCann-Erickson, and Ogilvy & Mather set up management agreements with Indonesian partners to handle foreign clients such as Toyota, Kao, Goodyear, Gillette and Coca-Cola. However, the restrictive work permit policy for foreigners and the restrictions against wholly owned subsidiaries restrained the growth of transnational agency business in Indonesia.

As transnational corporations and advertising agencies began to expand, local advertising agencies—quite reasonably—wanted a share of the action. In 1972, the government helped organize the Persatuan Perusahaan Periklanan Indonesia (PPPI), the Indonesian Association of Advertising Agencies, in an effort to bring order to "the chaotic young advertising industry" (Anderson 1984, 164). Tensions mounted between the PPPI members, who were for the most part small indigenous agencies, and the multinational agencies. For example, the PPPI refused to grant membership to Lintas because it was foreign owned. In addition to antiforeign feelings, there was also some anti-Chinese sentiment aimed at local Chinese-owned agencies.

These antiforeign sentiments were not restricted to the advertising industry, but certainly the industry was a key source of frustration to many Indonesians. Antiforeign tensions erupted in Jakarta with the "Malari" demonstrations in January of 1974. Students and others took to the streets during the visit of Japanese Prime Minister Tanaka. One of the prime targets of the demonstrations were the 30-foot outdoor advertisements for Toyota products that were displayed atop the tallest building in Jakarta, the Nusantara Building. Earlier, in 1973, students from the "National Pride Committee" had hoisted an Indonesian flag atop the building to protest "foreign domination as symbolized by the Japanese products" (Anderson 1984, 173). The Nusantara Building and its Japanese advertisements again figured prominently in the Malari demonstrations.

Following the demonstrations, in which over 800 people were arrested, the Suharto government called for a move from luxury-style living to a "simple, plain lifestyle" (Anderson 1984, 173). The import of luxury cars was stopped and tighter restrictions on the number of expatriate employees were implemented. After the demonstrations advertising was increasingly seen as part of a larger system that

> generated consumption—particularly in Jakarta where conspicuous consumption was most visible and people were confronted daily with perhaps two thousand advertising messages.
>
> (Anderson 1984, 173)

Finally, to help reduce public frustration and the growing belief that the government was indifferent to the poor, the government banned all TV commercials for luxury products.

By the late 1970s the government had again tightened foreign ownership restrictions on agencies, and in June of 1978 Lintas became the last of the transnational advertising agencies (TNAAs) to comply publicly with the policies. Lintas shut its Jakarta office and once again became the in-house agency for Unilever. Public sentiment against advertising continued into the late 1970s. Mochtar Lubis, an outspoken journalist, summarized the sentiment in this way:

We are shuddering under the impact of international consumerism. Every night on TV and in the cinemas, the commercials entice our people to join the great bandwagon of wasteful consumerism, to buy goods they do not really need, to want more, to buy more, to waste money. In the world of "free market forces," where your only protection is your own strength, Indonesia is but a weak link in the great chain of international finance, international marketing, and international technology.

(Lubis 1977, 45)

By the early 1980s the negative public sentiment toward advertising had grown into a significant public issue (Anderson 1984). In 1981, President Suharto, bending to political pressures, surprised everyone by his announcement that effective in April of that year, all television commercials would be banned from the airwaves. The ban on television advertising lasted for over a decade and devastated the fledgling advertising industry. During this time most transnational agencies either closed up shop or left a single expatriate "technical assistant" to maintain a presence in the country.

In 1991, the ban on television advertising was lifted and today commercial television messages appear on all but one of the government run television stations. The multinational agencies have returned, and government policies toward foreign ownership are being liberalized. Indonesia is now in its 3rd decade of political stability under Suharto's New Order government and there have been no major political disturbances in the last quarter of a decade (Castle 1994).

Today agencies with transnational affiliation play an important role in Indonesian advertising. The 10 largest agencies are listed in Table 11.1 with their multinational affiliations.

Table 11.1. The Top 10 Agencies in Indonesia, 1994

Agency	Gross Income (US $000)	Affiliation
1. Citra:Lintas Indonesia	7,005	Lintas Worldwide
2. Ad Force	3,607	J. W. Thompson
3. P.T. Indo Ad	3,239	Ogilvy & Mather (WPP)
4. InterAdmark	1,591	Dentsu
5. Grafik	1,509	McCann-Erickson
6. Perwanal	1,404	D'Arcy Masius B&B
7. Metro	1,245	Dentsu, Young & Rubicam
8. Rama & Grey	1,178	Grey Advertising
9. BSB Indonesia	1,125	Backer Spielvogel Bates
10. The Agency	733	Saatchi & Saatchi

Source: *Advertising Age*, 1994, 26.

The Indonesian Consumer

The process of urbanization has taken place more rapidly in Indonesia than had been expected. Although overall population growth figures remained relatively stable, the rate of migration from rural to urban areas was significant. In 1980, an estimated 22 percent of the population lived in urban areas; that share is now estimated at 35 percent. The implications for the development of the consumer market are substantial. Urban areas now account for between 50 percent and 80 percent of consumption, depending on the product (Castle 1994).

Indonesia cannot yet be considered a truly national market; however, access to television and other media as well as a proliferation of retail outlets such as department stores and supermarkets is changing consumer behavior. Sales records show Java to be the major market for most consumer goods. It is the most densely populated island and has the highest percentage of household expenditures. Although poverty is still a major problem in many areas of Java, the emerging middle class has created the largest single consumer market in the country.

There are three major market classifications for the Indonesian consumer: those living in the large urban areas; secondary city dwellers; and rural people. The urban consumers in Indonesia tend to enjoy a higher standard of living than do their rural counterparts. Another consumer classification system developed by Survey Research Indonesia (SRI) segments consumers by monthly expenditures (see Table 11.2). This classification system differs from other Survey Research Group studies in Asia because experience with official income data in Indonesia has been unreliable. SRI reports that the reluctance to divulge income figures and an absence of reliable and timely official income statistics are drawbacks to using an income-based classification to segment Indonesian consumers.

Approximately 23 percent of "A" consumers have a university education and the largest percentage of school leavers are in the "E" classification. The "A" consumers tend to live in the urban areas of Jakarta, Bandung, Surabaya and Medan (*Media Scene* 1994–95).

The Indonesian population is still relatively young; however, it is moving toward an older structure. The aging of the population is due in large part to successful family planning programs by the government as well as to increased life expectancy.

Today's generation of young Indonesians is better educated than previous

Table 11.2. Consumer Classification by Monthly Household Expenditures in Indonesia, 1993

Consumer Groups*	Monthly Family Expenditures (US$)
A1	340+
A2	243–340
B1	146–243
C1	97–146
C2	73–97
D	49–73
E	<49

Source: *Media Scene,* 1994–95.
*16% of the population are in the A groups, 20% are in the B group, 37% are in the C groups, and 27% are in the D and E groups.

ones. Literacy rates have climbed to 84.1 percent, up from 71.2 percent 10 years ago, and compulsory education has expanded, particularly at the elementary level. In 1991, the percentage of urban heads of households with a high school education was 25.7 percent, up from 19.4 percent in 1986 (Castle 1994).

One of the most significant changes over the past decade has been a dramatic increase in the number of households with electricity. Of the households surveyed by SRI, 95 percent now have electricity as compared with only 80 percent in 1983 (Castle 1994). Another lifestyle change of interest is the increasing appeal of Western fast-food restaurants. Urbanization and rising income have led to changing preferences in consumer purchases, food and entertainment choices. Over the past 15 years, fast-food outlets have proliferated, beginning with Kentucky Fried Chicken in 1979 and being joined by McDonald's, Wendy's and Pizza Hut more recently.

Advertising and Islam

Although 90 percent of the population of Indonesia practices Islam, there has not been the strong fundamentalist movement here that has emerged in some parts of the Middle East. Indonesian Islam is Sunni (rather than Shi'a, which prevails, for example, in Iran). The character of Indonesian Islam has been shaped by the Javanese, the dominant ethnic group in Indonesia:

> The Javanese have evolved an elaborate compromise with the Islam that was first embraced by their ancestors some seven centuries ago. Their compromise blends the newer Islam with heavy doses of the personalistic mystic ritual and practice contained in the rich blend of Hinduism and indigenous animism that preceded Islam.
>
> (Castle 1994, 34)

Today, while the rest of the Muslim world becomes ever more devout, Indonesians remain sybaritic and secular. *The Far Eastern Economic Review* (1987) points out that: "In the fasting month of Ramadan you may smoke, eat and drink with impunity almost anywhere in Indonesia." Only in Aceh, on the northern tip of Sumatra, where more-rigid forms of Islam have taken root, is religious rigor the order of the day. In most other parts of the country, the religion is still occasionally mixed with local ethnic rituals and practices.

Indonesians take their national ideology of Pancasila quite seriously, and thus respect and tolerate all religions and religious practices. Although most Indonesian Muslims respect the right to profit from work and economic activity, and do not in principle oppose banks or the charging of interest, there is a generally conservative streak in Indonesia that frowns upon consumerism and products that are viewed as luxuries rather than necessities (Castle 1994). The 10-year ban on television advertising had its roots in this general opposition to promoting luxury goods to people who could ill afford them. Consumerism is seen as "Western," and therefore threatening to local values. As noted by Castle:

> It is important to remember that in Indonesia it is usually the advertising/promotion process itself which is seen as negative, not the product per se. While conspicuous consumption earns the same social stigma in Indonesia as in many other parts of the world, goods themselves are rarely seen as corrupting. It is the individual who is seen as weak and advertising which is seen as pandering to or exploiting this weakness.
>
> (Castle 1994, 36)

In general, Indonesian Islam has not been an obstacle to economic growth, but it has been seen as a restraining factor on the promotion of consumption.

Indonesian women have traditionally played a more active role in social and economic activity than have their counterparts in the Middle East (Castle 1994). Few women are veiled, and the strict separation of the sexes, common in some Islamic countries, is not practiced in either education or business in Indonesia.

The Indonesian respect for all religions has led to a calendar full of religious holidays, although none has quite as much impact on the society as Ramadan, the fasting month for Muslims, and its culmination in the feasting day of Lebaran (*Idul Fitri*). The impact of this feasting holiday on Indonesian business is quite strong. All Muslims strive to be with their families on Lebaran and, though gifts are not normally exchanged as they are on Christmas, nonetheless it is customary to buy new clothes for oneself and one's family, improve or repair one's home, serve special foods and buy new furniture (Castle 1994). Overall sales during Ramadan generally increase dramatically.

The Indonesian Media

By 1993, the Indonesian government had awarded television broadcast licenses to five commercial networks. Rajawali Citra Televisi Indonesia (RCTI) was the first private local station in Indonesia. It has been on the air since November 1988 and runs for approximately 95 hours per week. About 15 percent of the air time is allocated for commercials. Penetration is limited to Greater Jakarta. RCTI-Bandung is a local station that went on air in May 1992; it covers Bandung and West Java. Surya Citra Televisi (SCTV) is a private TV station that was introduced in 1990 and serves Surabaya and the surrounding area. SCTV-Denpasar is mainly for relaying programs from SCTV to Bali and the surrounding area. Televisi Pendidikan Indonesia (TPI), which is considered the educational channel, is the only private station with a nationwide reach. Two new commercial networks, Cakrawala Andalas Televisi (ANteve) and INDOSIAR Visual Mandiri (IVM) were launched in 1993 and 1994, respectively. Televisi Republik Indonesia (TVRI) is the noncommercial government-owned network, which broadcasts nationally a mix of educational and general interest programs. It still does not carry advertising.

The commercial TV industry is subject to various restrictions related to on-air broadcasting. For example, all TV programming must be broadcast in Bahasa Indonesian, the national language, or in English with Indonesian subtitles. All foreign TV programs and TV commercials are subject to approval of the Film Censorship Board (BSF), a branch of the Ministry of Information. Private stations are required to air a minimum of 1 hour per day of government news programming. Commercial time on these networks is restricted to a maximum of 20 percent of total air time (*Media Scene* 1994–95).

In addition to the national networks, many urban-dwelling Indonesians purchase small satellite dishes for their rooftops. Because of the Indonesian PALAPA communications satellites, viewers with receiver dishes can pick up broadcasts from Malaysia, Hong Kong and Australia as well as CNN and BBC.

Recently a new company, Indovision (Matahari Lintas Cakrawala PT) was launched to offer pay TV services for international networks such as CNN, ESPN, HBO, TNT, Cartoon Network and the Disney Channel. The company broadcasts on a decoder subscription channel. Star TV, broadcast out of Hong Kong, is also available in some parts of Indonesia.

The average price for a 30-second TV spot runs from 500,000 to 2,500,000 rupiah (US$250–1,250) depending on network, program and time slot (*Media Scene* 1994–95).

The total number of radio stations in Indonesia is listed as 840 (*Media Scene* 1994–95). Most of these stations are privately owned and are AM, although FM stations have recently become more numerous. Commercial time on radio is restricted to a maximum of 25 percent of total air time. The average cost of a 30-second FM spot in the Jakarta area is approximately Rp.50,000 and in the other areas of the country about Rp.30,000. An AM spot might run approximately Rp.10,000 in Jakarta and about Rp.6,000 in local areas.

There are a total of 162 newspapers published in Indonesia. The newspapers with the largest circulation are *Kompas*, which has a nationwide circulation, and *Pos Kota*, which has the second largest circulation but is mainly concentrated in Jakarta. Other important regional newspapers are *Jawa Pos*, the largest East Java regional newspaper, and *Pikiran Rakyat*, the largest West Java newspaper. *The Jakarta Post* is the leading English-language newspaper. Advertising space is restricted to 35 percent of total newsprint. Prices for newspaper advertising runs from approximately Rp.2,000 to 12,000 per column millimeter for black and white and about Rp. 3,000 to 25,000 per column millimeter for full color.

In addition to newspapers, there are over 116 magazines published in Indonesia; most of these are published in Jakarta. Some of the leading magazines are *SWA* and *Warta Ekonomi*, which are both business magazines, and *Femina*, *Kartini* and *Sarinah*, which are all leading women's magazines. Advertising space in magazines is restricted to 35 percent of total space. The cost of a full-page black-and-white ad in a leading magazine would vary from Rp.550,000 to

9,500,000 and for a full-color page from Rp.2,000,000 to 15,200,000 (*Media Scene* 1994–95).

Besides the major media, advertising time and space is available at cinemas, exhibitions, sports events and trade shows, and in directories. There are outdoor signs available to advertisers in Jakarta, and city buses carry advertisements. Recently direct mail has become a popular way to reach selected target audiences and some of the larger agencies have started direct mail operations for their clients.

Advertising expenditures have grown nearly sixfold over the past decade. In fact the advertising industry in Indonesia has been transformed since the opening of RCTI in 1988. Television commercials increased from only 6 percent of the total advertising expenditures in 1990 to 25.4 percent in 1992. The advertising expenditures in Indonesia for the year 1994 are listed in Table 11.3.

Table 11.3.   Advertising Expenditure by Media in Indonesia, 1994

Media	1994
Newspaper	32.5%
Magazine	6.6%
Radio	5.5%
Cinema	0.4%
Television	48.3%
Outdoor	6.8%

Source: *Media Scene,* 1994–95.

Indonesian Advertising Regulation

In an effort to create "correct, healthy and responsible" advertising, The Code of Ethics and Practices of Advertising was formulated in 1981 during an advertising convention organized by the Association of Indonesian Advertisers (ASPINDO), the Indonesian Association of Advertising Agencies (PPPI) and organizations representing the major mass media in Indonesia.

The preamble to the Code begins with the words: "With God's Grace" and notes that advertising has certain social responsibilities including "protecting the cultural values of the nation based on Pancasila and the 1945 Constitution." It further proclaims that advertising should be in accordance with the principles of national development.

The Code is divided into General Principles, General Outlines and Specific Outlines. The General Principles urge that all advertisements be "truthful, responsible, and not in conflict with current legal regulations; not be offensive or degrade religious faiths, moral ethics, traditions, culture and any race or interest group; and keep with the spirit of healthy competitiveness."

The General Outlines are more specific and define each of the terms used in the General Principles. For example, *truthful* is defined as not deliberately misleading, and *responsible* as not violating public trust. The General Outlines also describe certain situations and claims that are not acceptable, such as that advertisements should not encourage violence; should not play on people's fears and superstitions; should not use the word "free" if in reality the consumer will pay some amount of money; should not portray dangerous situations or condone disregard toward public safety; and should not portray elements considered to be disturbing or damaging to children. The General Outlines also cover topics such as consumer testimonies, price comparisons, refunds/warranty claims, guarantee claims, statistics and scientific terms and nonavailability of products (*Economic and Business Review Indonesia* 1993).

The Specific Outlines refer to specific advertising situations; for example, that children in advertisements should not be portrayed in dangerous situations and should not be used to advertise products not fit for children's consumption; doctors, pharmacists and paramedicals should not be used to advertise medicines; advertisements offering investment opportunities should not mislead and should fully and clearly state the conditions of the investment; alcoholic beverage and cigarette advertisements should not influence or encourage the public to begin consumption of these products or suggest that they are healthy and should not be directed toward children or pregnant women. The Specific Outlines also include detailed requirements for mail order advertising, advertising for real estate, drugs, vitamins and minerals, cosmetics, medical treatments, medical equipment, house-to-house promotions, sweepstakes and prizes and advertisements for jobs.

Although the Code of Ethics is very detailed, the enforcement is limited for the most part to television commercials. All TV commercials must be previewed by the government Censor Board and must receive a Certificate of Approval before they can be aired on television. Print advertisements for products, other than health products, can run in the print media without any previous approval by government agencies.

Health product advertising, which includes baby foods, foods and drinks as well as medicines, vitamins and mineral supplements must be approved at the storyboard level by the Pengawasa Obat Makanan (POM). No health products may be aired on TV without a letter of approval from POM. The POM committee is made up of 10 members who are doctors, nurses, pharmacists and one PPPI representative. The committee meets once a week to review storyboards, radio scripts and television commercials for health products. The approval process from storyboard to finished commercial often takes up to 3 months. Print advertisements for health products must also be reviewed by POM.

It is interesting that while advertising for health products is carefully scrutinized, packaging is not carefully screened by any government agency. There are traditional medicines on the market that make outlandish claims on their packaging. In fact the copy on one local brand of cigarettes claims the product can actually increase longevity and improve health!

Conclusions

Although there are relatively little reliable data on the shifting socioeconomic status of Indonesians, there are many indicators that consumer lifestyles are improving and that the middle class is indeed growing. The World Bank estimates that the percentage of those defined as poor in Indonesia has decreased from 42.5 percent in 1976 to about 15 percent in 1990. In addition, over the past 2 decades, Indonesia has achieved a rapid improvement in health care and life expectancy. In a recent government survey of welfare perceptions by the people, the majority of respondents felt that their lifestyle has either remained favorable or moderately improved over the past 3 years (*Media Scene* 1994–95). All data point to continuing economic progress and the burgeoning of the middle class. For advertising, the relaxing of restrictions on foreign involvement and the opening of new media channels point to continuing growth for the advertising industry as a whole.

Bibliography

Advertising Age. 1994. Annual Report, April 13, p. 26.

Anderson, B. 1990. *Language and Power: Exploring Political Cultures in Indonesia,* Ithaca, NY: Cornell University Press.

Anderson, M. 1984. *Madison Avenue in Asia: Politics and Transnational Advertising,* Cranbury, NJ: Associated University Presses.

Bunge, F.A., ed. 1983. *Indonesia: A Country Study,* Washington, DC: American University.

Butwell, R. 1967. *Today's World in Focus: Indonesia.* Boston: Ginn & Co.

Carsten, J. 1994. Special Report: *Asian Advertising Review,* April 22.

Castle, J. 1994. *The Indonesian Consumer.* Jakaarta: Survey Research Indonesia.

Danoesoegondo, P. 1968. *Indonesia.* Sydney, Australia: Southern Cross International.

Douglas, S.A. 1994. *The State of the Myths: Official Nationalism in Southeast Asia.* Unpublished Manuscript. University of Illinois.

Economic and Business Review Indonesia. 1993. Raised on TV. No. 43, February 6.

Far Eastern Economic Review. 1987. Indonesia: Two Fathers—Sukarno and Suharto, August 15.

Fitch, R.M. and S. Webb. 1989. Cultural Immersion in Indonesia through Pancasil: State Ideology. *Journal of Educational Thought,* 23 (1): 44–51.

Geertz, C. 1973. *The Interpretation of Cultures.* New York: Basic Books.

Lubis, M. 1977. Between Myths and Realities: Indonesia's Intellectual Community Today. *Asian Affairs,* September/October, p. 45.

Media Scene: The Official Guide to Advertising Media in Indonesia. 1994–95. Jakarta: PPPI Secretariat.

Palmer, L. 1965. *Indonesia.* London: Thames and Hudson.

Widyahartono, B. 1993. Indonesia's Management Distinctive. *Jakarta Post,* June 14.

12

Advertising in Singapore

FELIX STRAVENS

Introduction

Over the past centuries various groups of people have migrated to Singapore, most notably the Chinese, the Malays and the Indians. Today, Singapore is a multiracial, multicultural society that has developed into a major market for international companies. The economy is dynamic, and growth continues at a rate envied by many countries in Asia as well as the rest of the world. In Singapore, as in many other areas, understanding culture is the key to understanding the needs and hearts of consumers. The question therefore arises of whether it is necessary to develop specific marketing concepts/strategies for identified groups or whether a global strategy without modification will suffice.

This chapter attempts to address this issue and provide an overview for those interested in marketing successfully in Singapore. First, we analyze Singapore's environment and infrastructure for consumer marketing. We then discuss the segmentation of its consumers. Finally, the implications for setting the marketing mix are suggested in accordance with the changing environment and consumer profiles.

The Environment for Consumer Marketing

While some aspects of the marketing macro-environment have been changing gradually over the years, others have been changing dramatically. The most noticeable ones can be summed up in five major categories, namely, demographic, economic, technological, political and cultural environments.

DEMOGRAPHIC ENVIRONMENT

DECLINING GROWTH RATE. The population growth in Singapore has slowed down over the past few years. The population in 1993 stood at 2,873,800. The natural increase rate fell gradually from 4.4 percent in 1957 to 2.0 percent in 1992. The government's efforts to reverse declining birth rates in the 1980s with selective

273

pro-naturalist policies had led women to have an average of 1.4 children in 1987. It increased to 2.0 in 1993, but this is still below the ideal replacement rate of 2.1 children. It is estimated that the total population will be four million in the year 2000, with a natural growth rate of 2.1 percent.

MATURING AND AGING OF THE POPULATION. The age structure in Singapore is inclined to maturing and aging. The median age was 26.1 years in 1983, and in 1993, 31.0 years. The percentage of the population over 60 years of age has also increased gradually. This percentage was 7.6 percent in 1981 and increased to 9.5 percent in 1993. Meanwhile the percentage of people under the age of 14 has gradually dropped over the years to 23.1 percent in 1993. It is estimated that by the year 2030, because of the maturation of the baby boomers of the 1950s and 1960s, the proportion of people aged greater than 60 years will increase to 25 percent of the population. According to data compiled by the United States Bureau of Census, the percentage increase in the elderly population in Singapore (at 348 percent) is the second highest in the world, next only to Guatemala (357 percent). Factors contributing to the graying of the population include a falling infant mortality rate and increased life expectancy due to better health care and improved standards of living. Also a decline in the fertility rate resulting from deliberate population control policies such as legalized abortion and the introduction of disincentives aimed at promoting small family size in the early 1970s has led to minimal population growth.

HIGHER FIRST-TIME MARRIAGE AND DIVORCE RATE. The average age for first-time marriages in 1993 was 30.3 years old for males, compared with 28.1 years in 1983; and for females 26.9 years compared with 24.9 years. The divorce rate has also been rising, with the gross divorce rate increasing from 84 couples per 1,000 persons in 1984 to 170 couples per 1,000 in 1991 (Department of Statistics 1993).

HIGHER EDUCATIONAL LEVEL. Education has been a major item of public expenditure, accounting for about one-fifth of the total government recurrent expenditure. A child in Singapore normally undergoes at least 6 years of primary education and 4 years of secondary education. A substantial portion of the cost of education is subsidized by the state.

A fundamental feature of the Singapore education system is the bilingual policy. Each student learns English and a second language, such as Mandarin for the Chinese and Malay or Tamil for the others.

The educational level of people in Singapore has risen rapidly. The illiteracy rate in Singapore dropped from 14.5 percent in 1983 to 8.4 percent in 1993. At the same time, the number of males graduating from institutes of higher learning increased from 4,085 in 1982 to 9,720 in 1992. For females, the number graduating from institutes of higher learning increased from 2,866 in 1982 to 8,597 in 1992 (Department of Statistics 1993). The population is better educated, creating a more-informed and more-discerning consumer population. This in turn will result in a greater demand for quality goods and services.

MORE WORKING WOMEN AND FEMALE EXECUTIVES. More employment opportunities, a higher educational level and a changing attitude toward female employment have enabled more female citizens to take up jobs. The participating rate of female labor above the age of 15 years increased from 45.7 percent in 1983 to 50.6 percent in 1993 (Department of Statistics 1993). At the same time, a better educational background and working efficiency have elevated many female employees to supervisory and managerial positions in private and public organizations. This has brought about greater affluence as dual-income families have increased. There has also been a greater demand for time-saving household gadgets, domestic help and, ultimately, child-care facilities.

ECONOMIC ENVIRONMENT
CONTINUING ECONOMIC GROWTH. In the early 1980s, Singapore's economic growth increased at the average rate of 10 percent. In 1985, a negative growth of −1.6 percent was recorded owing to a sustained recession in the world economy. Singapore regained its economic momentum with a growth rate of 9.4 percent in 1987 and 11.1 in 1988. The 1993 growth was 9.9 percent (Department of Statistics 1993).

INCREASING PER CAPITA INCOME. The gross national product (GNP) has increased rapidly from S$36.6 billion in 1983 to S$90.2 billion in 1993. The per capita income and per capita GNP have also increased continuously. For instance, today, an average Singaporean has an income of about S$20,000 a year—six times greater than in 1965. The per capita GNP was S$9,854 in 1981 and jumped to S$20,031 in 1991. The unemployment rate has also dropped from 3 percent in 1980 to 1.7 percent in 1990 (Department of Statistics 1993).

CHANGING FAMILY EXPENDITURE PATTERN. The composition of family expenditure in Singapore has changed greatly in the wake of fast economic development and higher personal income. Less than half of this expenditure goes to meeting basic needs such as food and housing, compared with two-thirds in 1965. The percentage of expenditure for food and beverage items has decreased from 31.8 percent in 1981 to 22.5 percent in 1991, and that for transport and communications from 16.4 percent to 16.0 percent. Expenditure for recreation and education activities has increased from 15.0 percent to 19.3 percent during the same period. The ratio of expenditure between food and nonfood items was 30 to 70 in 1981. It is projected to be 25 to 75 in the year of 2000 (Department of Statistics 1993).

INCREASING CONSUMER AFFLUENCE

Most Singaporeans would have been satisfied with a small one- or two-room apartment in 1965. Today such apartment blocks are being torn down to make way for more-spacious apartments in better-landscaped surroundings. Telephones and televisions used to be luxuries. In the 1960s, there was only one telephone for every 22 persons and a television set for every 30 persons. Today there is a telephone for every two persons and a television set for every six persons. Consumer durable ownership, which is an indication of wealth, is high in many areas. Color television ownership has increased from 51 percent of the population in 1981 to 99 percent in 1991. Air conditioner ownership has grown from 10 percent to 29 percent over the same period, washing machines from 31 percent to 84 percent, and VCRs from 3 percent to a high of 78 percent (Department of Statistics 1993).

TECHNOLOGICAL ENVIRONMENT

Since the late 1970s, Singapore has been involved in an industrial revolution emphasizing growth in higher-technology industries, both products and services. The government has provided impetus for this through channels such as the Singapore Economic Development Board and participation in the US-ASEAN Centre for Technology Exchange. The government's involvement now is mainly in providing infrastructure, guidelines and incentives to further diversification, and smoothing out the vagaries of the business cycle. The private sector is expected to lead Singapore through this stage in her economic development. This may require that noncompetitive companies and/or industries be allowed to dissolve so that new ones may develop that are more in tune with Singapore's plans for the future.

Another issue that must be addressed is that of intellectual property rights. Singapore may someday be a center for software development for domestic and foreign companies. For this to be possible the government would have to ensure and provide a mandate for effective protection of intellectual property. This will encourage foreign investment in Singapore, as well as development of domestic industries related to this business. Singapore will face growing pressure from the developed countries to assume the status of a developed country for purposes of Generalized System of Preferences (GSP) treatment. In Singapore the feeling now seems to be that a reasonable time frame for attainment of that goal is around the year 2000.

POLITICAL ENVIRONMENT

Singapore has had a stable government for the last 30 years. The People's Action Party (PAP) contested the parliamentary elections in May 1959 and won an overwhelming victory by gaining 43 of the 51 seats. Lee Kuan Yew was appointed Prime Minister as a result of that election and remained the chief executive in Singapore until 1991. The PAP dominated all intervening elections held in 1963, 1968, 1972, 1976, 1980, 1984 and 1988. Since 1959 they have occupied all the seats in Parliament, that is, there were no opposition party members elected. This changed in 1980 when two opposition members were elected. In 1991, there was a change in leadership of the PAP with Lee Kuan Yew retiring as the Prime Minister and giving way to new blood: Goh Cheok Tong, his Deputy who then took over as Prime Minister. At the general elections held in the same year, four opposition members were elected.

CULTURAL ENVIRONMENT
MORE LEISURE TIME AND INCREASED TOURISM ACTIVITIES. In the wake of technological advancement and productivity improvement, people's working hours have become shorter, and leisure time has thus become more abundant. People's interest in foreign travel has also been increasing. The number of outgoing tourists has increased significantly over the years. It is expected that more people will spend their time in foreign travel because of rising educational levels, more personal income and greater leisure time.

CONTINUED INFUSION OF FOREIGN CULTURES. Various foreign cultures, especially Japanese, British and American, have affected all walks of life in Singapore. This infusion of foreign cultures exerts an influence on the traditional local culture. It is expected that in the future, Singapore will become even more international in its makeup. The government has therefore taken steps to ensure that although Singapore may have an international outlook, the traditional cultures of the various races will still be preserved. A list has been drawn up in an attempt to show what are considered to be both good and bad Asian values and good and bad Western values.

- *Bad Asian values*: Caste system in Hindu culture; inferior status of women; practice of nepotism; tradition of authoritarian rulers; parental shame toward children with disabilities and general lack of sympathy for the disabled; attitude of subservience to those in authority; and the deep-rooted Chinese belief that "good boys" should never be soldiers.
- *Good Asian values*: Work ethic; thrift; strong family ties and support; modesty and humility; respect for education; respect for one's elders, teachers and righteous rulers; and communitarian values.
- *Bad Western values*: Too much emphasis on the rights and interests of the individual and too little emphasis on the rights and interests of the community and the state; lack of respect for one's elders, teachers and upright rulers; mistaken belief that competition in education is bad; inability to make sacrifices in the short-term for long-term benefits; excessive materialism and hedonism; and living beyond one's means.
- *Good Western values*: Political system based on democracy; independent judiciary; rule of law; civil service based on merit and free of corruption; equal

rights for women; pursuit of science and technology; management based on merit, team work and delegation of power; punctuality and public hygiene; empathy with and support for the disabled; and egalitarian belief of affording equality of opportunity to all.

Consumer Segmentation

The government of Singapore has over the years sought to promote racial harmony and religious tolerance among ethnic groups. It realizes that for the country to succeed, there should be no internal strife. However, the existence of three main groups of people, each with their own culture and beliefs, makes it difficult for marketers to launch one campaign or product that will have universal appeal.

In order to reach various targeted groups, marketers segment consumers in various ways on the basis of geographic variables, demographic variables, psychographic variables and behavioristic variables. Segmenting the market allows marketers to gauge the differences in buyer attitude, their motivations, their value patterns of usage, their aesthetic preference and their degree of susceptibility. For the Singapore market there would be no need to do a geographic segmentation, as its size does not justify it. Furthermore, the bulk of the population is already living in the urban areas and there is very little rural area left. The segmentation of the Singapore market is therefore examined here in terms of other demographic variables. A cultural segmentation of the consumer market is also done, based on which it is then possible to evaluate the attractiveness of marketing products to each group. This discussion may also be useful for advertisers who wish to develop correct strategies that appeal to each segment.

DEMOGRAPHIC VARIABLES

The Chinese make up the largest proportion of the population, accounting for 2,228,600 people, or 77.5 percent as of 1993. The next largest group is the Malays, constituting 407,600, or 14.2 percent of the population, followed next by the Indians with 204,100 people, or 7.1 percent of the population. Others make up the remaining 33,500 people, or 1.2 percent of the population. The Chinese have a slower growth rate, 2.0 percent, when compared with the growth rate of the Malays and the Indians of 2.2 percent (Department of Statistics 1993).

Singapore has a fairly young population. The median age of the total population was 31 years as of 1993. Approximately 68 percent of the population are below 40 years of age. The majority of the population are in the 20- to 39-year-old age group, which accounted for 1,096,500 people, or 38 percent of the population. The 15- to 19-year-old group accounted for 204,400 people, or 7.1 percent of the population; the 20- to 29-year-old group 234,500, or 8 percent; the

30- to 39-year-old group 587,600, or 20 percent; the 40- to 49-year-old group 400,700, or 14 percent; and those aged 50 years and over accounted for 390,200 people, or 13.5 percent of the population (Department of Statistics 1993).

Singaporeans are affluent when compared with other Asian countries. As of 1991, the monthly personal income median for the total population was $928 (S$) and the monthly household income median was $1,898 (S$). In terms of personal income breakdown, 734,000 adults aged 15 years and above earned less than $1,000 (S$) per month; 421,000 earned between $1,001 and $2000 (S$) and the remaining 262,000 earned $2001 (S$) and above. For household income, 266,000 adults aged 15 years and above lived in households with income of less than $1,000 (S$) per month. The group of households accounting for an income of $1,001–$2,000 (S$) had some 704,000 people living in them. There were 458,000 adults living in homes with a household income of between $2,001 and $3,000 (S$) and another 620,000 adults living in households with income of more then $3,000 (S$) per month. Of the total population, as of 1991, 33 percent were white-collar workers; another 33 percent were blue-collar workers; housewives accounted for 21 percent; and students made up the remainder (Department of Statistics 1993).

PSYCHOGRAPHIC VARIABLES

In Singapore 10 different groups have been identified, each with their own characteristics and motivations.

THE TRADITIONAL CHINESE. This group is comprised of the more traditional Chinese. They show a certain degree of pride in their ethnic origins, although this can to a certain extent border on chauvinism. This group contains the most businessmen and displays some of the more stereotypical behaviors associated with the Chinese in terms of leisure activities and product purchases. They enjoy the race track on the weekends; gambling with friends and associates-either with cards or mah-jongg; and prefer Chinese herbs and other traditional Chinese cures.

THE MODERN MALAY. This is a youngish Malay group who are family-centered. They show a desire to get on in life but have no need for outward or overt displays of success. They are usually thrifty with food and beverage expenses, instead spending the major portion of their money purchasing modern appliances for the home. This type of purchase tends to be their only way of showing their success.

THE COMFORTABLE CAREERISTS. This group has done well for themselves and this is reflected in both their value system as well as their consumer behavior. Their affluence gives them more opportunities and relieves them of some of the worries and concerns that strongly affect other sectors of society. It is believed that their contentment springs not only from their material success, but also from their secure and supportive domestic situations.

THE HARD-PRESSED PROVIDERS. These are the "good" people. The hard-pressed providers are probably very law abiding. They are most intent on caring for their families and bringing them up correctly. They are not well off, however, and their desire to give their families the best that they can afford means that they are always short of money. This in turn affects many of their consumption values.

THE POSSESSION PARADERS. These are basically the administrative class rather than the executive class. They are comfortably well off and have all the "right" consumer durables but don't have the status that is commanded by a high-level decision-maker's job or deep-rooted family wealth. This latter aspect has probably made them a bit self-conscious and hence their need for "face." It is important for them to "keep up with the Tans."

THE DEPENDENT MATRIARCHS. These people are generally the older housewives whose once dominant role in the family hierarchy has now been greatly diminished. Though still the "titular" head of the family, the "executive" decisions are made by the more affluent and better-educated younger family members. The Dependent Matriarchs are very relaxed about life, resulting from the lack of pressure on them to succeed and probably also from the experiences they have encountered over the years.

THE "BO CHAPS." This is a relatively young, apathetic underachieving group. They are relatively self-centered and not very interested in their surroundings. They are always on the lookout for the "easy way out" or a short cut to help finish something quickly with the least inconvenience to themselves.

THE DISAFFECTED. This is a young group who have not enjoyed much academic success and thus tend to have lower-status jobs than many of their contemporaries. They are aware of the different standards of living that can accrue in such circumstances and probably resent the situation in which they find themselves.

THE JING DI WA (FROGS IN THE WELL). The Jing Di Wa are a group of mixed ethnic background. They are guided in their values by society's norms and appear to have few deeply held personal views or convictions. They probably keep a fairly low profile and live in a very tightly defined world rotating around their family and close relatives. Like a frog at the bottom of a well, they are very familiar with their own immediate surroundings, but their perception of the world outside is only the tiny circle of blue sky they see above them.

THE BRAT PACK. The Brat Pack is a young and clearly upwardly mobile group. Although they display considerable "antiestablishment" values in some areas, they nevertheless know on which side their bread is buttered. They will in time most likely grow up to become affluent model citizens, in some cases, pillars of society.

All of these groups have very distinct differences and therefore marketers can, in fact, market products that will appeal to each group or a number of groups.

BEHAVIOR VARIABLES

In understanding consumer behavior in Singapore, it is important to understand the family because of the influence it can have on the buying process; its social influence on family members; its mediating effects; and its effects on normal role relations. The family has received considerable attention in consumer behavior literature in recent years. Many authors have emphasized the need to focus on the family as a decision-making and consumption unit. A study of family purchasing dynamics is natural to the study of many consumer decisions, which in Asia are more likely to be family consumption decisions than individual consumption decisions.

For the Singapore market, the family exerts great influence on the purchasing and consumption of products. There are five sources of family influence: cultural, biological, psychological, social and situational, and each can heavily influence an individual's cognitions and affect behaviors. The family performs a mediating function that links its members with larger social systems by screening the information available to the family members. It is through this mediating function that family members learn roles appropriate to adult life.

DYNAMICS OF FAMILY DECISION MAKING. The husband–wife role relationship is central to the family social system. There are four husband–wife role structures that have become a popular typology in the consumer behavior literature. These are husband-dominated decisions, wife-dominated decisions, autonomic decisions (in which either the husband or the wife is the primary decision maker, but not both), and joint or syncratic decisions (in which husbands and wives are equally influential).

Often marital roles are influenced by the interaction of the comparative resources of husbands and wives and the cultural expectations about those roles. This "relative contribution theory" would have a major impact on family decision-making structures in modern societies due to several underlying cultural factors. These include the transition toward an egalitarian marital ethic, a high degree of flexibility about the distribution of marital power, and the importance of education, occupation, and income in defining a person's status.

The United States is widely believed to be in late transitional egalitarianism, moving toward egalitarianism vis à vis women. This transition has been activated by the women's liberation movement, the "sexual revolution," and the dynamic value orientation of America's youth. These movements are believed to be causing profound changes in family ideologies in America. All evidence suggests that the Singaporean culture is quite different. Singaporeans of Chinese descent (overwhelmingly the largest cultural group in Singapore) largely embrace the cultural values of traditional China. The concept of the family is deeply rooted, with family members culturally bound to preserve the family. In this culture it is still deeply held that the husband is the head of the family; his ideology and authority command respect by other family members. The wife is highly valued as household manager. Consequently, it can be expected that Singaporean husbands participate less in household duties compared with their American counterparts.

Singapore is in a state of transition, however. It is under increasing influence from Western cultures that emphasize the individual, progress and achievement. The popularization of television and Western programming, magazines, music, the women's liberation movement and the roles of family members at home are all part of this influence. Traditional patriarchal family norms in Singapore have also been affected by this egalitarian ethic. The result is that the contemporary Singaporean has become less traditional and more Westernized. As such, Singapore would likely be classified as a modified patriarchal society whereby power roles in the family are ascribed, as the male household head still holds legitimate authority within his family by virtue of his position. However, these patriarchal norms have recently been modified by egalitarian norms, thus blurring the traditional roles of men and women. Classifying Americans in "transitional egalitarianism" and the Singaporean Chinese in "modified patriarchy," suggests two observations about the two groups: (a) greater joint decision making should exist in the American families than in the Singaporean Chinese families, and (b) greater husband dominance should exist among Singaporean Chinese husbands than among American husbands.

Singaporean Chinese couples make more individual than joint decisions, whereas American couples make more joint than individual decisions. The American husbands are less influential in decision making than their Singaporean Chinese counterparts. And American couples are more likely to engage in joint decision making than are Singaporean Chinese couples. Most of all it should be noted that family decision making is a culture-specific phenomenon. Conclusions about family role behaviors from one culture should not be applied to another. Marketers will benefit by understanding culture-specific family role dynamics for their products and should include such information in the design of their strategies and campaigns.

The Mass Media in Singapore

The infrastructure including media technologies are more advanced in Singapore than in many other developing countries in the region. This infrastructure is critical for corporations, particularly foreign ones, if they are to tap into the market and maximize marketing efficiency and effectiveness. Over the years the government has actively developed the media to cater to the various races in Singapore.

PRESS

Approximately 84 percent of Singaporeans read at least one newspaper each day. Time spent reading newspapers seems to have decreased marginally as the choice of media has widened. Readership of English-language dailies is now 48 percent, and readership of Chinese-language dailies is at 45 percent. All newspapers, with the exception of the Tamil-language newspaper, belong to one holding company—Singapore Press Holdings. The company is headed by a former government minister and produces the newspapers identified in Table 12.1.

Table 12.1.   Newspapers Produced by Singapore Press Holdings

Language	Name	When Published
Dailies		
English	*The Straits Times*	Morning
	Business Times	Morning
	The New Paper	Afternoon
Chinese	*Lian He Zao Bao*	Morning
	Lian He Wan Bao	Afternoon
	Shin Min Daily News	Afternoon
Malay	*Berita Harian*	Morning
Weeklies		
English	*The Sunday Times*	Morning
Chinese	*Lian He Zao Bao*	Morning
	Lian He Wan Bao	Afternoon
	Shin Min Daily News	Afternoon
Malay	*Berita Minggu*	Morning

As mentioned earlier, there is also an independent Tamil-language newspaper, *Tamil Murasu,* produced daily in the morning as well as on the weekend.

BROADCAST MEDIA

The first radio station was set up in Singapore and operated by a private operator, the British Malaya Broadcasting Corporation. The government then took over the operations in 1940 and it underwent several stages of change. In 1959, Radio & Television of Singapore (RTS) was formed. This body was only for radio broadcast. It was converted to a statutory board in 1980 and was renamed Singapore Broadcasting Corporation (SBC). In 1986, a separate body—SBC Enterprise—was formed to look after the marketing and selling of commercial air time. The government privatized SBC in October 1994. With the privatization of SBC, the body was divided into four operating subsidiaries. All four companies come under a holding company, Singapore International Media Pte Ltd (SIM). The four bodies are Television Corporation of Singapore (TCS); Television Twelve (TV12); Radio Corporation of Singapore (RCS); and SIM Communications (SIMCOM).

COMMERCIAL TELEVISION

There are two main broadcasting operators—TCS and TV 12. TCS owns and manages two channels—Channel 5 and Channel 8. Channel 5 telecasts programs in the English language and Channel 8 in Chinese. TV 12, which also manages two channels, telecasts programs in all four languages and focuses on cultural programming. All stations ensure that there is a balance in news and a variety of information and entertainment programs in various language media to cater to a multiracial and multilingual audience. There is also a teletext service, INtv, which transmits 800 pages of news and information from 6:00 a.m. to 12:00 midnight daily over two channels. In addition Singaporeans are also able to pick up three additional television channels from Malaysia—two government-owned and one private station. Satellite television is not allowed into Singapore. Cable television is available but is in its infant state.

In an average week, 98 percent of the population watch television. On a weekly basis, Channel 8, with its Chinese programs, has a 90 percent penetration of the population; Channel 5 has 74 percent; and Channel 12, 64 percent.

RADIO

Less than 10 years ago the Singapore radio industry was represented by only four stations, broadcasting on different bands catering to the different language groups. Today there are 14 stations in Singapore, including the British Broadcasting Corporation (BBC). Listeners are also able to receive broadcasts from two stations in Batam, Indonesia, and one in Johor, Malaysia. The Radio Corporation of Singapore (RCS) owns and operates 10 radio stations. This body is the successor of the government's Singapore Broadcasting Corporation.

In July 1990, another radio company was set up in Singapore. It is run by the National Trade Union Congress (NTUC) and is the first private wireless radio station in Singapore. It operates two private wireless radio stations in Singapore, broadcasting in the four official languages. Its mission is to inform, educate and help listeners to better understand labor policies and current issues, as well as to provide them with entertaining radio programs. Another station, Power 98FM broadcasting in English, is run by the Singapore Armed Forces.

On a daily basis, 77 percent of all adults listen to radio. Most of this is confined to peak time when consumers are traveling to and from work. Radio listenership is slightly more popular among the male than the female population. The two most popular radio stations are Perfect 10 (English) and FM 93.3 (Chinese) with listenership of 11 percent and 18 percent, respectively. The two NTUC radio stations have a combined reach of 10 percent of the population. Listenership for Malaysian radio and the two Batam radio stations has declined to 1 percent each day.

REDIFFUSION

There is a commercial audio broadcasting station, which has been under government franchise since 1949. It provides direct sound broadcasts via cable to subscribers on two networks. One network broadcasts Mandarin programs daily from 6:00 a.m. to 12:00 midnight and the other carries 24 hours of non-stop English programs. Their application to convert to a wireless station and compete more effectively with the radio stations has been turned down by the government. Their listenership is at 4 percent on an average day; the majority of Rediffusion listeners are predominantly the older-generation Chinese population. Subscriptions to Rediffusion have dropped from 95,030 in 1983 to 33,423 in 1993 (Department of Statistics 1993).

CINEMA

Like most countries, this medium caters mainly to the younger audience of either students or blue-collar workers. About 13 percent of the total adult population visit the cinema every week (Department of Statistics 1993). There are 103 cinema halls in Singapore and the majority of them screen Chinese or English films. Occasionally Malay and Tamil films are screened. There is an increasing trend toward watching English movies, though Chinese movies remain as popular.

OUTDOOR AND TRANSIT

All the buses that ply Singapore roads accept advertising. The main bus service, put together by the government, is the Singapore Bus Services (SBS). They own 3,000 buses (100 of which are double-decker buses) and operate 226 service routes island-wide. On any single day, they serve 2.4 million passengers (*Singapore 1993* 1993). Advertising is accepted on the back, the sides and the interior of these buses. In addition SBS also provides wholly painted buses for advertising messages. The minimum contract period is 3 months for single-deck and interior and 6 months for double-decks. To supplement this main bus service, there are two other bus services, the Singapore Shuttle Bus Service with six service routes and the Trans-Island Bus Service with 13 service routes. Both of these companies accept advertising on their buses.

Taxi-top advertising is now available in Singapore. In addition taxis also accept advertising inside their taxis with facilities to carry brochures or leaflets for commuters. There are also some 1,600 baggage trolleys available in Changi Airport that accept advertising. The minimum book is 50 trolleys for 13 consecutive weeks. Additional trolleys required can only be booked in lots of 50 trolleys.

Poster advertising is readily available in most areas in Singapore. There are poster sites in the airport, shopping centers, malls, underpasses and bus interchanges. These are all rear-illuminated light boxes and are available in various set sizes.

The Mass Rapid Transit (MRT) has become a popular mode of transportation in Singapore. On an average day, 347,000 people commute on the MRT. In an average week, about 894,000 people use the MRT (*Singapore 1993* 1993). This makes the MRT Posters a medium that has wide exposure to the population. The MRT accepts advertising in various sizes, 12-sheet (on track sites), four-sheet, on the bulk heads and inside the train. Minimum display period is 8 weeks for four-sheets and 26 weeks for bulkheads. All panels are rear illuminated. In addition there is a license fee of S$20 per month per panel.

There are limited sites for large outdoor posters, or sky signs, available in Singapore as the government discourages this type of advertising. Advertisers are normally on long-term contracts and have to negotiate privately with the owner of the sites. Approval from two government departments is necessary before a site can be established.

Advertisers are allowed to use any language in their outdoor advertising. However, all advertising must be submitted to the government for approval and all require a license fee. Neon advertising is allowed but must be of a nonmoving nature. Strict regulation is done to control outdoor advertising in order to maintain the beauty of the island.

DIRECT MAIL

The government has recently privatized the postal service in Singapore. It is a very speedy system and there is a relatively low cost involved in executing a direct mail program. They also offer an express delivery, which is becoming indispensable for overseas and domestic communication. The telecommunication system is operated by the government. Its services are very convenient and the rates seem to be reasonable. In recent years they have upgraded and improved the services offered, and pagers, facsimile machines and cellular telephones have mushroomed and become essential equipment for business executives.

Over the years Singapore Telecom has collaborated with the national Computer Board to develop Singapore into an "intelligent island." It is expected that by the end of 1996, the island will be totally wired with optic fiber cables. This will then provide the island with more information access.

Advertising and Research Agencies

The number of advertising agencies has grown rapidly in recent years. This is particularly true for the local agencies that have mushroomed over the years to serve the needs of local companies with small advertising budgets. Both the foreign branches/subsidiaries and the local counterparts are rather creative and competitive in terms of advertising concepts and technology. There are some 100 Accredited Advertising Agents, who receive a 15 percent agency commission from the media and 60-day credit terms. Another 100 or more agencies are nonaccredited and therefore place advertising through associate agencies. The top 10 agencies account for 80 percent of the advertising expenditure. Of this, only one agency, Batey Ads, is a local agency set up initially by an expatriate to service the Singapore Airlines account. Batey is now the top agency in Singapore in terms of billing (see Table 12.2).

There are a number of market research agencies operating in Singapore including the Survey Research Group (SRG). This research house provides most of the industry data including media indexes, product indexes, competitive spend and other syndicated studies. Other research houses include Frank Small & Associates, Consumer Probe, Acorn and many others. These research houses provide qualitative as well as quantitative research studies.

Table 12.2.   Top 10 Agencies in Singapore, 1994

Agency	Billings (million US$)
Batey Ads	81.96
Ogilvy & Mather	67.62
Saatchi & Saatchi	57.17
J. Walter Thompson	49.18
DDB Needham Worldwide GAF	47.81
McCann-Erickson	45.28
Dentsu, Young & Rubicam	41.12
Euro RSCG Ball Partnership	28.69
Leo Burnett	27.46
BBDO	21.17

Source: *Advertising and Marketing*, 1994.

Infrastructure to Support Marketing Activities

DISTRIBUTION

On an island of 540 square kilometers, Singapore's transportation system is sophisticated and unique. There are highways, double-tier roads, underground roads, railways and maritime and air freight. The companies providing services for distribution are experts in meeting the needs of their customers, whether geared toward a particular type of goods or areas of the island or the rest of the world.

RETAILING

Over the years Singapore has undergone an amazing process of development. One-stop shopping centers and other planned suburban shopping centers have mushroomed all over the island. The unplanned and bazaar types of outlets declined in numbers as they were gradually phased out by development programs. They were replaced by the better planned shopping facilities in the Housing and Development Board (HDB) estates and by the shopping centers in downtown areas.

BUSINESS EDUCATION

Singapore has no natural resources and its only real resource is its people. Traditionally the government has placed great emphasis on education and intellectuals. Due to the importance of trade and related business activities throughout the course of Singapore's economic development, formal business education at the university level is well established. The government set up a new university, The Nanyang Technological University (NTU), in July 1991 to handle the business subjects; NTU places a top priority on relating its professional courses to the requirements of industry and business. In 1994, the Open University was set up. Funded by the government, it will be run by a private institution. There are also three polytechnics in Singapore, all offering a wide range of business and management courses at diploma and post-diploma levels. In addition many foreign universities also offer business courses in Singapore. The dissemination of management systems and practices from the subsidiaries of foreign firms or international joint ventures has also contributed to the development of business education.

The government has also recognized that there is a need for retraining older workers whose skills and knowledge can become obsolete very quickly in the wake of rapid technological change. The proper identification of training needs, the provision of counseling to allay fears of being retrained, and the availability of training programs suited to the learning abilities of the workers all are essential management efforts toward the upgrading of the work force. The government, through the National Productivity Board (NPB), has packaged some special programs for efficient delivery. There is the Basic Education for Skills Training (BEST) and Worker Improvement through Secondary Education (WISE) programs, which are basic education courses in English and mathematics. The Core Skills for Effectiveness and Change (COSEC) program, launched by NPB in 1986, teaches workers problem solving, computer literacy, communication, quality, personal effectiveness and work economics—the generic skills required by every worker. Some 100,000 workers have participated so far in the COSEC program. As well, NPB has launched a series of video-based programs. These include Successful Supervision, Successful Selling, WORKperfect, Easy English, Working English, Easy Math and Express Math. All this training and retraining are subsidized by the government to ensure a more efficient and productive work force.

Advertising Regulation and Control

Controls on advertising and its practice normally take one of two forms. There are legislative and regulatory processes and voluntary controls. In Singapore there are sufficient laws and regulations in existence to moderate advertising practice. Voluntary control is practiced by the advertisers and the advertising agencies. The major media owners have also set up their own code of advertising practice to ensure that advertising is controlled. Excessive legislative controls can stifle and discourage the practice of advertising and can prevent the advancement of advertising and technology. The existence of too many regulations may frustrate the role and enthusiasm of the advertising professionals.

A total reliance on voluntary controls on the other hand, may not be ideal, as the excessive competition in the market may lead agencies, media owners and marketers to resort to finding ways to circumvent the code. Therefore, it appears that a suitable balance of legislative and voluntary controls is required to promote the interest of advertising.

In Singapore the advertising laws and regulations are monitored and enforced mainly by The Ministry of Health, The Ministry of the Environment and the Department of Customs and Excise. The media owners, Television Corporation of Singapore (TCS), Radio Corporation of Singapore (RCS) and the Singapore Press Holdings (SPH), have their own in-house guidelines for advertisers and advertising agencies. These have been in effect since 1964. This system is effective and has been acceptable to the advertising industry.

In 1976, the Consumers' Association of Singapore (CASE) initiated the formation of the Advertising Standards Authority of Singapore (ASAS). Its main objective is to protect the consumer from advertisers whose advertisements mislead, misrepresent or offend. Today the solution that seems the best for Singapore would be for voluntary controls to exist side by side with legislative control. It has also been suggested by those in the advertising industry that voluntary control should take precedence over legislative control.

Problems in advertising control do not normally stem from the implementation of official policy or the code of advertising practice, but rather from the misinterpretation or lack of guidelines and references on advertising practice in the codes. Problems in other areas such as language, food and health, product claims and guarantees, services, hire purchase, "new products," mail order and other government rulings and campaigns also exist and make voluntary controls somewhat difficult to implement. Hence, it was found that an independent and influential body had to be established to regulate advertising in Singapore and ensure fair treatment to all within the industry.

THE ADVERTISING STANDARDS AUTHORITY OF SINGAPORE

All advertising in Singapore must be legal, decent, honest and truthful. If it isn't, it must be withdrawn. That is why the ASAS exists. Its main objective, as just mentioned, is to protect the public from advertisers whose advertisements mislead, misrepresent or offend whether in the press, on TV, in print or in the cinema. The ASAS is an advisory council to CASE. Its members are representatives of the following organizations:

Singapore Advertiser's Association
Association of Accredited Advertising Agents, Singapore
Advertising Media Owners' Association of Singapore
Consumers' Association of Singapore
Singapore Manufacturers' Association
Singapore Medical Association
Pharmaceutical Society of Singapore
Singapore Association of Pharmaceutical Industries

Ministry of Health
Ministry of the Environment
Singapore Broadcasting Corporation
Direct Marketing Association of Singapore

Set up by the advertising industry, ASAS is not a government body and therefore has no legal jurisdiction; hence, people are sometimes skeptical about its effectiveness. However, because its constituents control the media, ASAS can stop any offending advertisement from appearing in the media. How, one might ask, can ASAS be objective about advertising if it was set up by the industry? In fact it was agreed when ASAS was first set up that not more than half of the Council should have any connection with advertising at all. And in practice, less than one-quarter of its membership does. For instance, ASAS has a pharmacist, a lawyer and a food technologist on the Council.

Each person is elected to serve on the Council because he or she can offer unbiased judgment on advertisements that come under scrutiny. And no one serves as the voice of any particular interest. The set of rules used by ASAS is the Singapore Code of Advertising Practice, which covers not only matters such as offensiveness and truthfulness, but also the particular problems that arise from advertising certain products such as medicines and alcohol. Advertisers, agencies and the media have agreed to observe the spirit as well as the letter of the Code.

The volume of advertising that runs in Singapore makes it impossible for ASAS to evaluate every individual advertisement before it is published. One way it keeps a thorough check on advertising is to respond to consumers' and competitors' complaints. Any complaint that is sent to ASAS is considered carefully. If there is a case to answer, a full investigation is made. To make doubly sure that the system is working and that advertisers and agencies are adhering to the Code, ASAS monitors a wide range of advertisements on a continuous basis, paying particular attention to areas of current concern. As well, ASAS provides individual advice and guidance to advertisers, advertising agencies and the media who are in doubt as to the acceptability of advertising, particularly prior to publication. Also, to make sure that the Council members and the Code are up to date with current opinion, ASAS conducts research from time to time.

UNACCEPTABLE ADVERTISING

When an advertisement is found to be problematic, the advertiser is asked to amend or withdraw the offending advertisement from the media. Failing to do so, the media owners are informed. They will not make space available in a publication, on TV or in the cinema for any advertisement that ASAS has ruled contravenes the Singapore Code of Advertising Practice. This system happens to be not only very effective, but is also quick and inexpensive.

In addition to the voluntary codes, advertisers also need to get clearance from government and statutory boards for some forms of advertisements such as certain food and health products.

Conclusions

In sum, the marketing infrastructure in Singapore concerning media availability, advertising and research agencies, communication, physical distribution, and business education is fairly well developed and many aspects of it match the level of developed countries. It is expected that the level of these infrastructures will become even more sophisticated in the future.

Bibliography

Advertising Age. 1993. Singapore: Fear Sells in Singapore, October 11. Detroit, MI: Crain Communications, Inc.

Advertising and Marketing. 1994. Agency Rankings, April 22, 19.

Bellows, Thomas J. 1989. Bridging Tradition and Modernization: The Singapore Bureaucracy. In Hung-chao Tai, ed. *Confucianism and Economic Development: The Oriental Alternative?* Washington, DC: The Washington Institute for Values in Public Policy, 195–223.

Birch, David. 1993. *Singapore Media: Communication Strategies and Practices.* Melbourne, Australia: Longman Chesire Pty Ltd.

Brown, David. 1993. The Corporatist Management of Ethnicity in Contemporary Singapore. In Rodan, G., ed. *Singapore Changes Guard: Social, Political and Economic Directions in the 1990s.* Melbourne, Australia: Longman Cheshire Pty Ltd.

Department of Statistics. 1993. *Yearbook of Statistics Singapore.* Singapore.

Kuo, Eddie, C.Y. 1986. Confucianism and the Chinese Family in Singapore: Continuities and Change. Paper presented to the International Conference on the Psycho-Cultural Dynamics of the Family: Past and Present, Yongpyong, Kangon Province, Korea.

Meng, Ho Wing. 1990. Value Premises Underlying the Transformation of Singapore. In Sandhu, K.S. and P. Wheatley, eds. *Management of Success: The Molding of Modern Singapore.* Boulder, CO: Westview Press, 671–691.

Milne, R.S. and Diane K. Mauzy. 1990. *Singapore: The Legacy of Lee Kuan Yew,* Boulder, CO: Westview Press.

Sandhu, K.S. and P. Wheatley, eds. 1990. *Management of Success: The Molding of Modern Singapore.* Boulder, CO: Westview Press.

Singapore 1993. 1993. Singapore: Publicity Division, Ministry of Information and Arts.

The Straits Times. 1994a. Three lessons for Singapore, August 22, 24.

The Straits Times. 1994b. Sustagen Ad PM objected to will be withdrawn, August 23, 3.

The Straits Times. 1994c. The Asian Values Debate Revisited, January 28, 4.

Tu, Wei-ming. 1984. *Confucian Ethics Today: The Singapore Challenge,* Singapore: Federal Publications.

INDEX

AAAI (Advertising Agencies Association of India), 173, 175
AAT (Advertising Association of Thailand), 225, 233, 236
Abante newspaper (Philippines), 203
ABC (Audit Bureau of Circulation) system (Taiwan), 117
ABS-CBN radio network (Philippines), 204, 206
ABS-CBN satellite broadcasting (Philippines), 163
ACC (American Chamber of Commerce), 132, 142
Acorn agency (Singapore), 287
Adboard (Advertising Board of the Philippines), 199, 203, 210, 216-17
Advertising. *See also specific country* global integration and, 9
Advertising Agencies Association of India (AAAI), 173, 175
Advertising and Marketing magazine (India), 165, 168-69
Advertising Association of Thailand (AAT), 225, 233, 236
Advertising associations
  in China, 89-90, 92
  in India, 174-175
  in Indonesia, 270-71
  in Japan, 36-37
  in Korea, 146
  in Malaysia, 243-44, 254-55
  in the Philippines, 210-14
  in Singapore, 286-88
  in Taiwan, 119-20
  in Thailand, 233-34
Advertising Board of the Philippines (Adboard), 199, 203, 210, 216-17
Advertising Code for Television and Radio (Malaysia), 250-51, 252, 254, 255
Advertising Federation of Japan, 36
Advertising Law of People's Republic of China, 93-94
Advertising Standards Authority of Malaysia (ASA), 254-55

Advertising Standards Authority of Singapore (ASAS), 289-90
Advertising Standards Council of India (ASCI), 175, 178, 180
Advertising Suppliers Association of the Philippines (ASAP), 210, 213
AFTA (ASEAN Free Trade Area) agreement, 6
Age demographics
  in Hong Kong, 44, 63, 64, 65, 67
  in India, 156
  in Singapore, 274, 278-79
AIR (All India Radio), 162, 178, 179, 180
Akashvani radio (India), 162
All India Radio (AIR), 162, 178, 179, 180
All Japan Radio & Television Commercial Council, 36
American Chamber of Commerce (ACC), 132, 142
Anderson, Michael, *Madison Avenue in Asia: Politics and Transnational Advertising,* 3-4
ANteve (Cakrawala Andalas Televisi, Indonesia), 268
Anti-Monopoly Act (Japan), 12, 28
Apisarnthanarax, Prakit, 229-30
Aquino, Benigno (Ninoy), 190, 199, 200-201
Aquino, Corazone, 190-91, 202
Aryan influence, in India, 155-56
ASA (Advertising Standards Authority of Malaysia), 254-55
Asahi Shimbun newspaper (Japan), 15, 32, 33
ASAP (Advertising Suppliers Association of the Philippines), 210, 213
ASAS (Advertising Standards Authority of Singapore), 289-90
Asatsu agency (Japan), 16
ASCI (Advertising Standards Council of India), 175, 178, 180
ASEAN (Association of Southeast Asian Nations), 3,6,7. *See also specific nation*
ASEAN Free Trade Area (AFTA) agreement, 6
Asia Television Limited (ATV, Hong Kong), 55, 57, 58-59, 60
Asia 21 agency (Thailand), 229

ASPINDO (Association of Indonesian Advertisers), 270
Association of Accredited Advertising Agencies (4A's, Philippines), 210, 212-13
Association of Accredited Advertising Agents (4A's)
  in Malaysia, 243-44, 254
  in Singapore, 289
  in Taiwan, 116, 118, 119-20
Association of Indonesian Advertisers (ASPINDO), 270
Association of Southeast Asian Nations (ASEAN), 6. *See also specific country*
  GDP statistics and, 7
  GNP statistics and, 3
ATV (Asia Television Limited, Hong Kong), 55, 57, 58-59, 60
Audience behavior, in Taiwan, 113
Audit Bureau of Circulation (ABC) system (Taiwan), 117
Avia Communications (Philippines), 209, 210
Awakening Foundation (Taiwan), 120

B. Dataram and Company advertising agency (India), 164
Backer Spielvogel Bates agency
  in Korea, 138
  in Taiwan, 114
Bangkok Art Directors Association, 233-34
Basic Advertising (Philippines), 209, 210
Basic Education for Skills Training (BEST, Singapore), 288
Bates Malaysia, 244, 247
Batey Ads agency (Singapore), 286, 287
BBDO (Batten, Barton, Durstein and Osborn agency)
  in India, 166, 167, 168, 169
  in Japan, 16
  in Korea, 138, 139
  in Malaysia, 247
  in Singapore, 287
  in Taiwan, 114
Beck Spielvogel Bates agency (Thailand), 231
Beltran, Luis, 202
Bengal Gazette, 164
BEST (Basic Education for Skills Training, Singapore), 288
Bombay Samachar newspaper, 161
Brau and Rosendale Advertising (Philippines), 197

British East India Company, 156-57, 242
British Malaya Broadcasting Corporation, 283
Broadcast Act (Japan), 34
Broadcasting Authority (Hong Kong), 68
Broadcasting Corporation of China (Taiwan), 111-12
Broadcasting Directing Board of Thailand, 237
Brooke Bond-Lipton India, 173
BSF (Film Censorship Board, Indonesia), 269
Buddhism
  in Indonesia, 259
  in Korea, 128
  in Thailand, 223, 224
Buenaventura, Manuel, 197
Bullis, H. Edmund, 197
Bunka-Hoso radio (Japan), 15
Burnett, Leo, 83

CAA (China Advertising Association), 89
CAAP (Cinema Advertising Association of the Philippines), 210, 214
Cable television
  in Hong Kong, 59-60
  in Malaysia, 249
  in the Philippines, 201, 202, 206
  in Singapore, 284
  in Taiwan, 109, 112, 113
  in Thailand, 228
Cable television (CATV)
  in Japan, 36
  in Korea, 149-50
CACP (Citizens' Alliance for Consumer Protection), 219
Cakrawala Andalas Televisi (ANteve, Indonesia), 268
Calcutta Advertising Agency, 164
Calcutta General Advertiser, 164
Canal Television International (France), 163
CAP (Consumers' Association of Penang, Malaysia), 255
Carl Crow, Inc. (China), 76
CASE (Consumers' Association of Singapore), 289
Cathay Advertising (Thailand), 229
CATV. *See* Cable television (CATV)
CBCM (Church-Based Consumer Movement, Philippines), 219
CCA (Chinese Consumer Association), 92
CCTV (China Central Television), 88
Censorship. *See* Regulatory process

Center for Monitoring the Indian Economy
(CMIE), 172
CFAA (China National Advertising Association
for Foreign Economic Relations and
Trade), 89
CFGP (Consumer's Federation Group of the
Philippines), 219
Chaebol (Korea), 5
advertising industry and, 127, 133
economic development and, 126-27
Cheil Communications agency (Korea), 130
expenditures and market share of, 136
growth rate of, 138
as in-house agency, 133, 134, 135, 137
market research of, 141
Cheng-Sheng Broadcast Network (Taiwan),
112
Chiang Ching-kuo, 104, 105
Chiang Kai-shek, 104, 105
China. *See also* Guangdong Province
advertising associations in, 89-90
advertising expenditures of, 131
advertising industry in, conclusions regarding, 98-99
advertising industry in: historical perspective
on
earliest evidence of, 74-75
in early post-Mao years, 78-79
growth of, 79-80
modern emergence of, 75-77
in 1950s-1980s, 77-78
advertising industry in: structure of
agencies and, 76, 81-83
constitution stipulations and, 80-81
domestic advertising and, 82
foreign trade advertising and, 82-83
Ministry of Foreign Economic Relations
and Trade and, 81-82
political ideology and, 81
suppliers and, 83
bureaucracy in, 6
Communism in, 21, 73-74
consumer behavior in
consumption materialism and, 93-94
cultural value changes and, 96-98
inflation and, 96
public policy affected by, 96-98
purchasing power control and, 96
Western brand preference of, 95-96
"Cultural China" components and, 4-5
geographic setting and, 73

"Greater China" concept and
Hong Kong and, 4, 41, 103
Macao and, 41
Singapore and, 4, 41
Taiwan and, 4, 41, 103
historical perspective on, 73-74
Hong Kong and
advertising spending and, 54
early Chinese advertising in, 75
historical perspective on, 39-40
immigrants and, 43
mass media in, 83-84
magazines, 76, 84-85
mass transit, 89
newspapers, 75-76, 84, 85, 88
outdoor advertising, 89
radio, 76, 85-86
satellite TV, 163
television, 86-88
merchant class of, 5
new capitalism in, 6
population statistics of, ix
regulation and policy issues and, 90-94
Taiwan and, 104
China Advertising Association (CAA), 89
China Central Television (CCTV), 88
China Commercial Advertising Agency
(CCAA), 76
China International Advertising Corporation,
82
China National Advertising Association for
Foreign Economic Relations and Trade
(CFAA), 89
China National United Advertising Corpora-
tion, 82
China Television Corporation (CTV, Taiwan),
112
China Times News (Taiwan), 110, 116
Chinese Communist Party, 73-74, 77, 79, 80
Chinese Consumer Association (CCA), 92
Chinese Television Services (CTS, Taiwan),
112
Christianity
in India, 157
in Malaysia, 241
in the Philippines, 190, 193
Chubu Nihon Hoso radio (Japan), 15
Chun Doo Whan, 127, 143-44
Chuo Senko agency (Thailand), 229
Church-Based Consumer Movement (CBCM,
Philippines), 219

Chu Senko agency (Thailand), 229
Cinema advertising
    in Hong Kong, 57, 65-66, 67
    in Indonesia, 270
    in the Philippines, 198, 207, 214
    in Singapore, 285
    in Thailand, 233
Cinema Advertising Association of the Philippines (CAAP), 210, 214
Citizens' Alliance for Consumer Protection (CACP), 219
Civil Code (Philippines), 220
Clarion Advertising Services (India), 164, 166, 167
Clea Advertising (India), 170
CMIE (Center for Monitoring the Indian Economy), 172
Coca-Cola
    in China, 95
    global impact of, 9
    Hong Kong advertising by, 56
    in India, 165, 172
    in Indonesia, 263
    in Korea, 130
    in Malaysia, 246
    in the Philippines, 209, 211
Code of Advertising Practice (Singapore), 290
Code of Advertising Practice (Taiwan), 119-20
Code of Ethics (Philippines), 210, 212, 215
Code of Ethics and Practices of Advertising (Indonesia), 270
Collectivism/relationship-centeredness, 48-49
Commercial Radio (Hong Kong), 60-61
Communications technology, 8-9
Concept Communications agency (India), 170
Concerned Consumers of Benguet (Philippines), 219
Conference of Advertising Workers in Socialist Countries, 77
Confucianism
    changes of in China, 97, 99
    "Confucian Work Dynamism" and, 50
    in Korea, 128-29
    Wu Lun principles of, 49-50
Consolidated National Advertising Company (PRC), 76
Consumer Act of the Philippines, 215, 220
Consumer Code (Philippines), 219
Consumer issues
    Chinese consumer behavior and, 96-98
    Hong Kong consumer demographics and, 42-47, 63-67

    in India, 180-85
    Korean consumption culture changes and, 146-48
    in Malaysia, 247-48
    in the Philippines, 217-20
    Taiwanese interest groups and, 120-21
Consumer Probe (Singapore), 287
Consumer Protection Act (COPRA, India), 184-85
Consumer Protection Act (Thailand), 235, 238
Consumer Protection Board (CPB, Thailand), 235, 238, 239
Consumer Protection Declaration (Thailand), 238
Consumers' Association of Penang (CAP, Malaysia), 255
Consumers' Association of Singapore (CASE), 289
Consumer's Federation Group of the Philippines (CFGP), 219
Consumers Movement of Negros Occidental (Philippines), 219
Consumer's Movement of the Philippines, 219
Consumer's Union of the Philippines (CUP), 219
Contract Advertising (India), 169
Convergence theory, 8-9
COPRA (Consumer Protection Act, India), 184-85
Core Skills for Effectiveness and Change (COSEC, Singapore), 288
COSEC (Core Skills for Effectiveness and Change, Singapore), 288
Council of Better Business Bureaus (United States), 30
Council for International Exchange of Scholars, xii
CPB (Consumer Protection Board, Thailand), 235, 238, 239
Creativity Award of 4A's (Taiwan), 116, 120
CTS (Chinese Television Services, Taiwan), 112
CTV (China Television Corporation, Taiwan), 112
Cultural and Educational Foundation for Consumers (CEFC, Taiwan), 120
Cultural factors. *See also* Religious factors
    in Asian advertising, xi
    in China, 4-5, 96-98
    economic growth and, 4-5
    in Hong Kong, 48
        authority, respect for, 50-51

collectivism/relationship-centeredness,
    48-49
conformity, 51
"face" behavior, 49
hierarchy, power and status, 50
modernization, 47-48
motivation, 51-52
patriarchy, respect for, 50
personalism, 50
practical ethics, 51
reciprocity, 49
relationship intensity and status, 49
"shame" culture, 49
social harmony, 48-49
structural harmony, 49-50
trust, 51
in India, 178-80
    consumption behavior, 181-82
    fiscal values, 180-81
    gender and age, 156
    rural vs. urban markets, 182-83
in Indonesia
    conflict avoidance, 261
    consumerism stigma, 267-68
    Islam, 21, 259-60, 267-68
    mutual assistance, 262
    national unity, 261
    Pancasila national ideology, 261-62, 267,
        270-71
    social justice, 262
in Japan, 21-22
    changing lifestyles, 24-25
    gift-giving and entertainment customs,
        23-24
    group consciousness, 22-23
    homogeneity, 23
    language barrier, 19
    lifetime employment, 18, 22
    social constraints, 25-28
in Korea
    advertising regulation, 145
    birthday party behavior, 147
    competition criticism, 146
    Confucian principles, 128-29
    consumption culture changes, 146-48
    "face" behavior, 147
    foreign models, 142
    "my car" behavior, 147
    teenage buying behavior, 147
    transnational advertiser barriers and, 140
    wedding culture, 147-48

in Malaysia
    conflict avoidance, 195
    consumer issues and, 255
    consumer profiles and, 247-48
    foreign culture unacceptabilities, 250-51
    Islamic values, 252-54, 256
    racial sensitivity, 251
    social responsibility, 251
mass media affecting, 8
in the Philippines
    compassion, 194
    conflict avoidance, 195
    divine intervention, 193-94
    family centeredness, 194
    flexibility and adaptability, 194-95
    foreign brand preference, 195
    hospitality, 195
    inner strength, 194
    joy and humor, 194
    national values, 191, 194-95, 216
in Singapore
    cultural group segmentation and, 279-81
    family decision making dynamics and,
        281-82
    foreign values and, 277
    lifestyle changes and, 275-76, 277
in Taiwan
    eating habits, 108
    family structure, 106-107
    leisure behavior and time orientation,
        108-109
    teen behaviors, 107-108
    women's role, 107
in Thailand
    adaptiveness, 224-25
    conflict avoidance, 224, 234, 237
    hierarchical rigidity, 224
    high-context culture, 224, 234
    status appeal, 224-25
Cultural Revolution (PRC), 74, 77-78, 79, 90
CUP (Consumer's Union of the Philippines),
    219
CVT & Bercia agency (Thailand), 230

Daehong Advertising (Korea)
    expenditures and market share of, 136
    growth rate of, 138
    as in-house agency, 133, 134, 137
    market research of, 141
Daewoo Group (Korea), 133, 134
Daiko agency (Japan), 17

Daily News (Thailand), 226
Damask Advertising (Thailand), 230
DDB Needham agency
    in Korea, 138, 139
    in Malaysia, 247
    in Singapore, 287
    in Taiwan, 114
    in Thailand, 231
    in Vietnam, 231
Defamation Act (India), 177
Democracy
    in Indonesia, 261
    in the Philippines, 190-91
    in Taiwan, 103-14
    in Thailand, 223
Democratic Progressive Party (Taiwan), 112
Deng Xiaoping
    economic strategy of, 74, 94
    "Open Door" policies of, 40
    post-Mao reform of, 79
Dentsu Inc. (Japan), 16. *See also* Densu, Young
    & Rubicam (DY&R)
    Dentsu-Ho publication of, 21
    impact of, 20-21
    service expansion of, 19
    size of, 17, 18
Dentsu, Young & Rubicam (DY&R)
    in China, 83
    in India, 166, 168
    in Indonesia, 263
    in Korea, 139
    in Malaysia, 247
    in Singapore, 287
    in Thailand, 229, 231, 232
Department of Health (DOH, Taiwan), 117,
    118, 119
Dependency theory
    convergency theory and, 8-9
    culture and economic connection and, 4-5
    elite-oriented culture and, 7-8
    intra-Asian trade connections and, 5-6
    TNAA employment practices and, 6-7
    TNC advertising and, 3
Deregulation
    in Japan, 30-32
    in Taiwan, 109
        magazines, 111
        newspapers, 110
        radio, 111-12
Dewe Rogerson (India), 170
Diamond Advertising (Korea), 133, 134, 135,
    136, 137, 138

Digitalization, ix
Direct mail advertising
    in China, 89
    in Indonesia, 270
    in the Philippines, 207
    in Singapore, 286
    in Taiwan, 113
    in Thailand, 233
Divorce rate
    in Singapore, 274
    in Taiwan, 106-7
DMB&B (D'Arcy Masius Benton & Bowles)
    advertising agency (Hong Kong), 40
    in India, 166
    in Korea, 133, 134, 136, 137, 138, 139, 141
Domestic Satellite Corporation (Domsat,
    Philippines), 200
Domsat (Domestic Satellite Corporation,
    Philippines), 200
Dongbang Ad (Korea), 133, 134, 136, 137, 138
Doordarshan television network (India), 162,
    163, 173, 178-80
Drugs and Magic Remedies Act (India), 177
Drug Study Group (Thailand), 239
Dutch East India Company, 260
DY&R. *See* Dentsu, Young & Rubicam
    (DY&R)

East Asia
    economic growth in, 4-8
    GNP statistics of, 3
    intra-Asian trade and, 6
Eating habits (Taiwan), 108
Economic development
    of China, 73-74, 79
    of Hong Kong, 41-42
    of India, 158-61
    of Indonesia, 7, 262, 272
    of Japan, 11-14
    of Korea, 125-27
    of the Philippines, 191-92, 221
    of Singapore, 275
    of Taiwan, 104-5
    of Thailand, 223-24
Economic Planning Board (Korea), 126
Edge Communications, The (India), 169
EDSA Revolution (Philippines), 190-91, 193
Education demographics
    in Hong Kong, 44-45, 48
    in India, 157
    in Singapore, 274-75

in Taiwan, 107
El Domingo publication (Philippines), 196
Electronic media, in Japan, 36
Emblems and Names Act (India), 177
Employment demographics
in Hong Kong, 46
in Japan, 18, 22
in Singapore, 275
in Taiwan, 107
Entertainment customs, of Japan, 23-24
Everest Advertising (India), 166, 167

"Face" behavior
in Hong Kong, 49
in Korea, 147
Fair Trade Commission (FTC, Taiwan), 117, 118-119
Fair Trade Law (Taiwan), 118-119
Far East agency (Thailand), 232
FCB advertising agency, in Korea, 138
FCD (Foundation for Children's Development, Thailand), 239
FDA (Food and Drug Administration, Thailand), 225, 235-36
Federation of Bankers Associations of Japan, The, 30
Federation of Malaysian Consumer Associations (FOMCA), 255
Federation of Pharmaceutical Manufacturers Associations of Japan, The, 30
FERA (Foreign Exchange Regulation Act, India), 159, 165, 170
Film Censorship Board (BSF, Indonesia), 269
First Five-Year Plan (China), 74
"Five Principles" (*Pancasila*) national ideology (Indonesia), 261-63, 267, 270-71
FOMCA (Federation of Malaysian Consumer Associations), 255
Food and Drug Administration (FDA, Thailand), 225, 235-36
Foreign Exchange and Foreign Trade Control Law (Japan), 13
Foreign Exchange Regulation Act (FERA, India), 159, 165, 170
Foundation for Children's Development (FCD, Thailand), 239
Fountainhead Communications (India), 168
4A's (Association of Accredited Advertising Agencies, Philippines), 210, 212-13
4A's (Association of Accredited Advertising Agents)

in Malaysia, 243-44, 254
in Singapore, 289
in Taiwan, 116, 118, 119-20
Four Dragons, 4. *See also* Hong Kong; Singapore; South Korea; Taiwan
"Four Modernizations" (China), 98
Frank Small & Associates (Singapore), 287
Freedom of the press
in the Philippines, 200, 201, 202
in Thailand, 223
Freedom of speech
in India, 176
in Thailand, 223
FTC (Fair Trade Commission, Taiwan), 117, 118-119

Galtung's structural theory of imperialism, 4
Gambling Act (Thailand), 237-38
Gandhi, Indira, 159
Gandhi, Mahatma, 157, 159
Gandhi, Rajiv, 160
GATT (General Agreement on Tariff and Trade), 192
Gender demographics
in Hong Kong, 44, 63, 64, 65, 67
in India, 156
in Singapore, 275
General Agreement on Tariff and Trade (GATT), 192
Generalized System of Preferences (GSP) tax system, 132, 276
Geoson advertising agency (Korea), 134, 137, 138, 139
Gift-giving customs
in Japan, 23-24
in the Philippines, 193
GIO (Government Information Office, Taiwan), 117, 118
Global integration, 8, 9
GMA radio network (Philippines), 204, 206
GNP (Gross national product). *See* Gross national product (GNP)
Goh Cheok Tong, 277
Gonzales, Manuel, 197
Government Information Office (GIO, Taiwan), 117, 118
Grant Advertising (Thailand), 229
Grant, Kenyon and Eckhardt (India) Private Limited, 164
Great Britain
Hong Kong and, 39-41

Great Britain (*continued*)
 in India, 156-58
 in Malaysia, 242, 243
Great Leap Forward (PRC), 74
Great Wall in Ruins, The (Chu and Ju), 96-98
Grey agency
 in Korea, 138, 139
 in Malaysia, 247
 in Taiwan, 114
 in Thailand, 231
Grey-Daiko agency (Japan), 16
Groake Advertising (Thailand), 229
Gross domestic product (GDP)
 of ASEAN nations, 7
 of Hong Kong, 41-42
 of India, 160
 of the Philippines, 208
 of Thailand, 224
Gross national product (GNP)
 of China, 79, 80, 94
 of Hong Kong, 41
 of India, 159
 of Japan, 13, 14, 24
 of Korea, 126
 of Singapore, 275
 of Taiwan, 105
 world statistics of, 3
GSP (Generalized System of Preferences) tax
 system, 132
Guangdong Province
 foreign agencies in, 83
 Hong Kong and, 40, 42, 46
Guanxi (new capitalism), in China, 6
Guanxi (relationship status intensity), in Hong
 Kong, 49

Hakuhodo advertising agency (Japan), 15, 16,
 17, 18
Hansavision agency (India), 169
Hapdong Advertising Bureau (Korea), 130
HDFC (Housing Development and Finance
 Corporation, India), 180, 181
Heisei Boom (Japan), 13
Hemisphere-Leo Burnett agency (Philippines),
 209, 210
Herrier, Frank J., 197
Hierarchy of human needs, 51-52
Hinduism
 in India, 156-57
 in Indonesia, 267
 in Singapore, 277

Hindustan Lever (India), 172, 173
Hindustan Thompson Associates (HTA, India),
 164, 165, 166, 167, 168
 Contract Advertising subsidiary of, 169
Hong Kong
 advertising expenditures of, 131
 advertising industry in
  agency "musical chairs" in, 54, 55
  expenditures by medium of, 54-56
  expenditures by product categories of, 56
  rate structure of, 54
  regulation of, 68
  Singapore, compared to, 68-69
  structure of, 52-54
 China and
  advertising spending and, 54
  earliest advertising in, 75
  as "Greater China" component, 4, 41, 103
  immigrants from, 40, 43
 consumer dynamics in
  age and, 44, 63, 64, 65, 67
  cultural impact on, 48
  density of, 44
  education and, 44-45, 48
  employment and, 46
  gender and, 44, 63, 64, 65, 67
  household expenditures and, 46
  housing and, 46
  income and, 4, 45, 46, 48, 63, 64, 65, 67
  literacy and, 45
  market segmentation in, 43-44
  population and, 42-43, 46-47
  race and, 44, 63, 64, 65, 67
 cultural factors in, 48
  authority, respect for, 50-51
  collectivism/relationship-centeredness,
   48-49
  conformity, 51
  "face" behavior, 49
  filial piety, 49
  hierarchy, power and status, 50-51
  modernization and, 47-48
  motivation, 51-52
  patriarchy, respect for, 50
  personalism, 50
  practical ethics, 51
  reciprocity, 49
  relationship status and intensity, 49
  "shame" culture, 49
  social harmony, 48-49
  structural harmony, 49-50
  trust, 51

economic development in, 41-42
  future of, 68-69
  financial capital of, 39
  as Four Dragons component, 4
  Guangdong Province and, 40, 42
  historical perspective on, 39-41
  local business competition in, 5
  mass media in, 56-57
    cable TV, 59-60
    cinema, 57, 65-66, 67
    coverage by, 57
    Kowloon-Canton Railway and, 57, 66-67
    listener compositional profile of, 62
    magazines, 48, 56, 63-65, 66
    newspapers, 48, 55, 56, 57, 62-63
    outdoor advertising, 57, 67-68
    radio, 40, 48, 54, 57, 60-62, 63
    satellite TV, 59, 149, 163
    television, 40, 48, 54-56, 57-59, 60, 61
    transit advertising, 57, 66, 67, 68
  Western agencies in, 19
  Western business interests in, 39
Housing Development and Finance Corpora-
  tion (HDFC, India), 180, 181
HTA (Hindustan Thompson Associates, India),
  164, 165, 166, 167, 168
  Contract Advertising subsidiary of, 169
Human needs hierarchy, 51-52
Hyundai Group (Korea), 133

IBC (International Broadcasting Corporation,
  Thailand), 228
IBM, in India, 165
ICRT (International Community Radio of
  Taipei, Taiwan), 112
Imegeads (India), 170
Impact agency (Korea), 130
IMRB (India Market Research Bureau), 163
Ind-Advertising Agency (India), 164
Indecent Representation of Women Act (India),
  177
India
  advertising associations in, 174-175
  advertising industry in
    early period of, 164-65
    growth period of, 165-68, 185-86
    financial agencies of, 170
    largest agencies of, 167, 168-69
    specialized agencies of, 171
    subsidiary agencies of, 169
  consumer issues in

  attitude changes of, 180-82
    protection issues and, 183-85
    rural market changes and, 182-83
  cultural factors in, 178-80
    consumption behavior and, 181-82
    fiscal values, 180-81
    gender and age, 156
    rural vs. urban markets and, 182-83
  economic development in, 158-61
    under Indira Gandhi, 159-60
    under Mahatma Gandhi, 159
    under Nehru, 158-59
    under P.V. Narasimha Rao, 160-61
    under Rajiv Gandhi, 160
  geographic setting of, 115
  Hinduism, origins and, 155-56
  historical perspective on, 155-57
  mass media in
    magazines, 161-62, 177-78
    newspapers, 161-62, 177-78
    radio, 162, 178, 182
    satellite TV, 162-63
    television, 162-63, 178, 182-83
  national advertisers in, 171-72
    media buying developments and, 172-74
    product categories of, 171
  political development in, 157-58
  population statistics of, ix
  regulatory process in
    of broadcast media, 178-80
    freedom of speech and, 176
    laws of, 176-77
    of print media, 177-78
    self-regulation and, 180
  socialist development in, 158-60, 165
  TNAA management in, 7
India Market Research Bureau (IMRB), 163
Indian Broadcasting Service, 162
Indian Express, The, 161
Indian Newspaper Society (INS), 165, 169,
  174-75, 177
Indian Sale of Goods Act, 183
Indian Society of Advertisers (ISA), 174
Indonesia
  advertising expenditures of, 131
  advertising industry in, 262-65
    Islam and, 267-68
  consumer behavior in, 265-67
    lifestyle changes and, 267, 272
    market classifications and, 266
    population demographics and, 266-67
    urbanization and, 266

Indonesia (*continued*)
  cultural factors in
    conflict avoidance, 261
    consumerism, stigma of, 267-68
    Islam and, 21, 259-60, 267-68
    mutual assistance, 262
    national unity, 261
    Pancasila national ideology of, 261-62,
      267, 270-71
    social justice, 262
  economic development of, 7, 262, 272
  geographic setting of, 259
  historic perspective on, 259-60
  mass media in, 268-70
    cinema advertising, 270
    direct mail, 270
    magazines, 269-70
    newspapers, 269, 270
    outdoor advertising, 270
    radio, 263, 269, 270
    satellite TV, 163, 269
    television, 7, 264-65, 267-69, 271
  Philippine advertising and, 198
  regulatory process in, 270-71
Indonesian Association of Advertising Agen-
  cies (PPPI), 264, 270, 271
INDOSIAR Visual Mandiri (IVM, Indonesia),
  268
Indovision (Indonesia), 269
INS (Indian Newspaper Society), 165, 169,
  174-75, 177
Institute of Technology Bandung (Indonesia),
  xii
Institute of Technology MARA (Malaysia), xii
Intellectual property rights, in Singapore, 276
Interact-Vision agency (India), 169
Interim Regulations for Advertising Manage-
  ment (PRC), 90-91
International Advertising Agency (Philippines),
  197
International Advertising Association (PRC),
  90
International Broadcasting Corporation (IBC,
  Thailand), 228
International Community Radio of Taipei
  (ICRT, Taiwan), 112
International Organization of Consumers
  Unions (IOCU, Philippines), 219
IOCU (International Organization of Con-
  sumers Unions, Philippines), 219

ISA (Indian Society of Advertisers), 174
Islam
  in India, 156-57
  in Indonesia, 21, 259-60, 267-68
  in Malaysia, 241, 242, 243, 252-54, 256
  in the Philippines, 190, 193
  in Thailand, 223
IVM (INDOSIAR Visual Mandiri, Indonesia),
  268

J. Walter Thompson agency
  in India, 164, 165, 166, 169
  in Japan, 16
  in Korea, 138, 139
  in Malaysia, 247
  in the Philippines, 195, 209, 210
  in Singapore, 287
  in Taiwan, 114, 115, 122
  in Thailand, 231, 232
  in Vietnam, 231
Jakarta Post, The (Indonesia), 269
Japan
  advertising expenditures of, 131
  advertising industry in: features of
    agency services range, 19
    Dentsu's role in, 17, 20-21
    major agencies' market share and, 17-18
    media-buying practices and, 19-20
    no "one product per category" system,
      18-19
    U.S. model for, 17, 28, 37
    Western agencies and, 19
  advertising industry in, growth of, 15-17
  advertising industry in: social and cultural
    constraints on, 25-28
    comparative advertising, 26, 31-32
    discriminatory words, 27-28
    indirect speech, 26, 32
    nature associations, 26-27
    number associations, 26
    positive vs. negative connotation words,
      26-27
  bureaucracy in, 5-6
  conclusions regarding, 37
  cultural factors in
    changing lifestyles, 24-25
    gift-giving and entertainment customs,
      23-24
    group consciousness, 22-23

homogeneity, 21-22, 23
language barrier, 19
lifetime employment, 18, 22
religion, 21-22
deregulation in, 30-32
economic growth in, 11, 12-14
geographic and strategic setting of, 11-12
Indonesia and, 264
mass media in
advertising associations and, 36-37
magazines, 33-34
new electronic media, 36
newspapers, 32-33
radio, 15, 34-35
satellite TV, 149, 163
television, 15-16, 34, 35-36
Philippines and, 197
regulatory process in, 28
self-regulation in, 28-30
Japan Advertising Council, The, 36
Japan Advertising Review Organization
(JARO), 28-30
Japan Fair Trade Commission (JFTC), 28, 31
Japan International Advertising Association,
36-37
Japan Marketing Association, The, 37
Japan Newspaper Publishers and Editors Asso-
ciation, 30, 32
Japan Radio Network, 34
Japan Satellite Broadcasting Co., 36
Japanese Satellite Television, 149
JARO (Japan Advertising Review Organiza-
tion), 28-30
Jean Bisson Enterprises (Philippines), 197
Jenkins, M. W., 197
JFTC (Japan Fair Trade Commission), 28, 31
John Tung Foundation (Taiwan), 120

KABC (Korea Audit Bureau of Circulation),
141
Kapisanan ng mga Brodkaster sa Pilipinas
(KBP, Philippines), 203, 210, 212, 213
Karisma Advertising (India), 169
KBACOL (Korean Broadcasting Advertising
Corporation Law), 144
KBP (Kapisanan ng mga Brodkaster sa Pilip-
inas, Philippines), 203, 210, 212, 213
KBS-TV (Korean Broadcasting System), 128,
130

KCC (Korea Cable Communications Commis-
sion), 149
KCR (Kowloon-Canton Railway), 57, 66
Kentucky Fried Chicken, 96, 108
Ketchum International, in Korea, 138
KFCPA (Korean Federation of Consumer Pro-
tection Associations), 143, 144
Kilusan ng Mamimili ng Pilipinas (KMPI,
Philippines), 219
Kim Young Sam, 128
KMPI (Kilusan ng Mamimili ng Pilipinas,
Philippines), 219
KMT (Kuomintang)/Nationalist party (Tai-
wan), 104, 105
KOBACO (Korean Broadcasting Advertising
Corporation), 131, 144, 145, 150
Kohodo advertising agency (Japan), 15
Kokoku-sha advertising agency (Japan), 15
Kompas newspaper (Indonesia), 269
Konsumo Dabaw (Philippines), 219
Korea
advertising expenditures in, 131
advertising industry in, historical perspective
of, 129-33
advertising industry in: after market liberalization
account transfer and, 140-41
broadcast time increase and, 142
foreign model and language use and,
142-43
modernization and, 141
personnel turnover and, 140-41
advertising industry in: regulation of, 143-44
of broadcast advertising, 145-46
of print advertising, 144-45
advertising industry in: structure of
alliance between, 137-40
in-house agencies and, 133-36
independent agencies and, 136-37
consumer issues and, 146-48
cultural factors in, 145-147
Confucian principles, 128-29
consumption behavior, 147-48
"face" behavior, 147
foreign models and, 142
"my car" behavior, 147
teenage buying behavior, 147
transnational advertiser barriers of, 140
wedding culture, 147-48
economic development of, 125-27

Korea, economic development of (*continued*)
  chaebol and, 5, 126-27, 133
  industrialization and, 125-26
  mass media in
    cable television, 149-50
    future of, 148-50
    magazines, 149
    newspapers, 141, 148-49
    radio, 129, 135-37, 144
    satellite TV, 149
    television, 129-30, 141, 144, 145, 146
  political development of, 127-28
Korea Audit Bureau of Circulation (KABC),
  141
Korea Cable Communications Commission
  (KCC), 149
Korea First Advertising, 130
Korean Advertisers Association, 146
Korean Association of Advertising Agencies,
  146
Korean Broadcasting Advertising Corporation
  (KOBACO), 131, 144, 145, 150
Korean Broadcasting Advertising Corporation
  Law (KBACOL), 144
Korean Broadcasting Commission, 142, 144,
  145
Korean Broadcasting System (KBS-TV), 128,
  130
Korean Council of Women's Organizations,
  148
Korean Federation of Advertising Associations,
  146
Korean Federation of Consumer Protection As-
  sociations (KFCPA), 143, 144
Korean Press Ethics Commission, 146
Korean War
  consumer market after, ix
  Japan and, 12-13
Korea Survey Gallup Polls (KSG), 141
Korea Telecom, 149
Kowloon-Canton Railway (KCR), 57, 66
KSG (Korea Survey Gallup Polls), 141
Kuomintang (KMT)/Nationalist party (Tai-
  wan,) 104, 105
  newspaper of, 110
  radio of, 111

La Vanguardia Press (Philippines), 197
Labor reform (Japan), 12
Labor Relations Adjustment Law (Japan), 12
Labor Standards Law (Japan), 12

Land reform, (Japan), 12
Lee Kuan Yew, 276-77
Lee Teng-hui, 104
Leisure behavior (Taiwan), 108-109
Leo Burnett agency, 7
  in Korea, 139
  in Malaysia, 247
  in the Philippines, 209, 210
  in Singapore, 287
  in Taiwan, 115
  in Thailand, 229, 230, 231, 232
  in Vietnam, 231
LGAd (Korea)
  expenditures and market share of, 136
  growth rate of, 138
  as large in-house agency, 133, 134, 137
Lifetime employment (Japan), 18, 22
Ling, C. P., 76
Lintas agency
  in Indonesia, 263, 264
  in Korea, 139
  in Malaysia, 244, 247
  in the Philippines, 209, 210
  in Taiwan, 114, 122
  in Thailand, 230, 231, 232, 233
Lintas India Limited, 164, 165, 167, 168
  Karishma Advertising subsidiary of, 169
Literacy rate
  in Hong Kong, 45
  in India, 161, 182-83, 184
  in Indonesia, 267
  in Japan, 12
  in the Philippines, 189
  in Singapore, 274-75
Lotte Group (Korea), 133, 134
Lotteries Control Act (India), 177
Lu Ocampo Advertising (Philippines), 197
Lubis, Mochtar, 264-65
Lucky-Goldstar (Korea), 133, 134

MAA (Malaysian Advertisers Association),
  244, 254
Macao, as "Greater China" component, 41
McCann-Erickson agency
  Hakuhodo joint venture with, 19
  in India, 164, 166, 167, 168, 175
  in Indonesia, 263
  in Japan, 16, 19
  in Korea, 130, 138, 139, 141
  in Malaysia, 244, 246, 247
  in the Philippines, 209, 210

in Singapore, 287
in Taiwan, 114, 115
in Thailand, 230, 231, 232
McDonald's
in Indonesia, 267
in the Philippines, 209, 211
in Taiwan, 108
Madison Avenue in Asia: Politics and Transnational Advertising (Anderson), 3-4
Magazine Advertising Association of Japan, 33
Magazines
in China, 76, 84-85
in Hong Kong, 48, 56, 63-65, 66
in India, 161-62, 177-78
in Indonesia, 269-70
in Japan, 15, 33-34
in Korea, 149
in Malaysia, 244, 249
in the Philippines, 196, 203-204, 205, 214
in Taiwan, 109, 110-11, 113
in Thailand, 226, 227, 233
Mainichi Shimbun newspaper (Japan), 15, 32, 33
Malaysia
advertisers in, 245-46
advertising expenditures of, 131
advertising industry growth in, 243-45
agencies in, 246-47
consumer issues in, 255
cultural factors in
conflict avoidance, 195
consumer profiles, 247-48
foreign culture unacceptabilities, 250-51
Islamic values, 252-54, 256
racial sensitivity, 251
social responsibility, 251
economic development in
GDP of, 7
New Development Policy and, 243
New Economic Policy and, 243
historical context of, 241-43
Islam in, 241, 242, 243
Christianity and, 241
values of, 252-54, 256
Made-in-Malaysia rule in, 251-52, 256
mass media in
magazines, 244, 249
newspapers, 243, 244, 249
radio, 244, 248
satellite TV, 163, 244, 249
structure of, 248-49
television, 244, 245, 246, 248-49, 252-53

regional unity and, 241
regulatory process in
government regulation and, 244, 249-50, 255-56
self-regulation and, 254-55
TNAAs (transnational advertising agencies) management in, 7
western agencies in, 19
Malaysian Advertisers Association (MAA), 244, 254
Malaysian Code of Advertising Practice (MCAP), 254
Malaysian Newspapers Publishers' Association (MNPA), 254
Man-nen-sha advertising agency (Japan), 15
Manbosa Advertising (Korea), 130
Manila Alegre publication, 196
Manila Daily Bulletin, 196, 203, 204
Manila Times, The, 196
Manililla publication, 196
Mao Zedong, 74, 79
Marcos, Ferdinand, 190-91, 200, 201, 202
Marketing and Opinion Research Society of the Philippines (MORES), 210, 213
Maslow, Abraham, 51-52
Mass Communication Organization of Thailand (MCOT), 228
Mass media. *See specific country, media type*
Mass Media Council (Philippines), 198
Mass transit advertising. *See* Transit advertising
Matichon newspaper (Thailand), 226
MBC-TV (Munwha Broadcasting Corporation, Korea), 128-29, 130
MCAP (Malaysian Code of Advertising Practice), 254
MCOT (Mass Communication Organization of Thailand), 228
Media professionalism, of TNAAs, 5-6
Media Services Korea (MSK), 141
Meiji Restoration, Shintoism and, 21
Metro Radio (Hong Kong), 60-61
Millington Ltd. (PRC), 76
Ministry of Foreign Economic Relations and Trade (MOFERT, China), 81-82, 89, 90
Ministry of International Trade and Industry (MITI, Japan), 14, 28
MITI (Ministry of International Trade and Industry, Japan), 14, 28
MNPA (Malaysian Newspapers Publishers' Association), 254

MOFERT (Ministry of Foreign Economic Relations and Trade, China), 81-82, 89, 90
Monopolies
in India, 159, 176-77, 183-84
in the Philippines, 192, 200, 201, 220
TNCs (transnational corporations) and, 5
Monopolies and Restrictive Trade Practices Act (MRTP, India), 159, 176-77, 183-84
Moral Recovery Program (Philippines), 194
MORES (Marketing and Opinion Research Society of the Philippines), 210, 213
Movie and Television Regulatory and Classification Board (MTRCB, Philippines), 202
MRTP (Monopolies and Restrictive Trade Practices Act, India), 159, 176-77, 183-84
MSK (Media Services Korea), 141
MTRCB (Movie and Television Regulatory and Classification Board, Philippines), 202
Mudra Communications (India), 169, 185
Mughal India, 156
Multinational advertising agencies. See Transnational advertising agencies (TNAAs)
Multinational corporations. See also Transnational corporations (TNCs)
barricades to, 5-6
in India, 160-61
mass market of, 3
opportunities for, xi
Munwha Broadcasting Corporation (MBC-TV, Korea), 128-29, 130
Muslims. See Islam
Myanmar, 231

NACK (National Advertising Council of Korea), 132
Nanyang Technological University (NTU, Singapore), 287-88
Nara advertising agency (Korea), 137, 138
National Advertising Council of Korea (NACK), 132
National Association of Commercial Broadcasters (Japan), 30
National Broadcasting Commission (NBC, Thailand), 236, 239
National Consumer Affairs Council (Philippines), 220
National Council of Women of Thailand, 239
National Emergency Act (Philippines), 202

National Federation of Women's Clubs (NFWC, Philippines), 219
National Productivity Board (NPB, Singapore), 288
National Radio Network (NRN, Japan), 34
National Telecommunications Commission (NTC, Philippines), 202
National Trade Union Congress (NTUC, Singapore), 284
NBC (National Broadcasting Commission, Thailand), 236, 239
NDP (New Development Policy, Malaysia), 243
Near Instantaneously Compounded Audio Multiplex (NICAM), 57, 59
Nehru, Jawaharlal, 157, 158
NEP (New Economic Policy, Malaysia), 243
New Development Policy (NDP, Malaysia), 243
New Economic Policy (NEP, Malaysia), 243
New Straits Times Group (Malaysia), 249, 255
Newspaper Association of Taipei, 119
Newspapers
in China, 75-76, 84, 85, 88
in Hong Kong, 48, 55, 56, 57, 62-63
in India, 161-62, 174-75, 177-78
in Indonesia, 269, 270
in Japan, 15, 32-33
in Korea, 141, 148-49
in Malaysia, 243, 244, 249
in the Philippines, 196, 198, 200, 201, 203-4, 205, 207, 214, 233
in Singapore, 283
in Taiwan, 109, 110, 113
in Thailand, 226, 227, 229
NFWC (National Federation of Women's Clubs, Philippines), 219
Nihon Hoso Kyokai (Japan), 16, 34, 36
Nikkei newspaper (Japan), 32, 33
Nippon Arts Council, The, 36
Nippon Television Network (NTV), 15
No Sense of Place (Meyrowitz), 9
NPB (National Productivity Board, Singapore), 288
NRN (National Radio Network), 34
NTC (National Telecommunications Commission, Philippines), 202
NTU (Nanyang Technological University, Singapore), 287-88
NTUC (National Trade Union Congress, Singapore), 284

NTV (Nippon Television Network), 15

OAAP (Outdoor Advertising Association of the
    Philippines), 210, 213-14
OBM (Ogilvy, Benson and Mather Private
    Limited, India), 164
Ogilvy & Mather (O&M)
    in India, 164, 165, 167, 171
    in Indonesia, 263
    in Korea, 134, 135, 136, 138, 139
    in Malaysia, 244, 247
    in Singapore, 287
    in Taiwan, 114, 115, 122
    in Thailand, 6, 229, 231, 232, 234
    in Vietnam, 231
Ogilvy, Benson and Mather Private Limited
    (OBM, India), 164
Opium, Hong Kong and, 39
Oricom Advertising (Korea), 130, 134, 135,
    136, 137, 138
O'Sammon, Michael, 130
Outdoor advertising
    in China, 89
    in Hong Kong, 67-68
    in Indonesia, 270
    in the Philippines, 196, 198, 207, 213-14
    in Singapore, 285-86
    in Thailand, 226-27, 228
Outdoor Advertising Association of the Philip-
    pines (OAAP), 210, 213-14

Pacifica Commercial import-export company
    (Philippines), 197
Pacific Chemical, 133
PANA (Philippine Association of National Ad-
    vertisers), 210, 212
PanAmSat (United States), 163
Pancasila ("Five Principles") national ideology
    (Indonesia), 261-62, 267, 270-71
Park Chung Hee, 125, 127
Pengawasa Obat Makanan (POM, Indonesia),
    271
People's Action Party (PAP, Singapore), 276-77
People's Journal (Philippines), 203
People's Republic of China (PRC). See China;
    Guangdong Province
People's Television 4 (Philippines), 201
Pepsi-Cola
    in India, 168

in Korea, 130
in the Philippines, 209, 211
Pharmaceutical Affairs Law (Taiwan), 118, 119
Philippine Agency Service, 197
Philippine Association of National Advertisers
    (PANA), 210, 212
Philippine Daily Inquirer, The, 203
Philippine Long Distance Telecommunications
    Corporation (PLDT), 200
Philippine Promotions Bureau, 198
Philippine Publicity Service Inc., 197
Philippines
    advertising expenditures in, 131
    advertising industry growth in
        conclusions regarding, 221
        corporate ownership policies and, 199-200
        GDP and, 7, 208
        gross media billings and, 207-8
        historical analysis of, 196-99
        largest advertisers and, 209-10
        largest agencies and, 208-9
    advertising organizations in, 210-14
    consumer issues in
        consumer associations and, 219-20
        consumer behavior and, 217-18
    cultural factors in
        compassion, 194
        conflict avoidance, 195
        divine intervention, 193-94
        family centeredness, 194
        flexibility and adaptability, 194-95
        foreign brand preference, 195
        hospitality, 195
        inner strength, 194
        joy and humor, 194
        national values, 191, 194-95, 216
        religion and philosophy, 193-94
        social and cultural constraints, 195
    geographic setting of, 189
    history of, 189-91
        economic growth policy and, 191-92
        national ideology and, 191
    mass media in
        cable TV, 202, 206
        cinema, 198, 207, 214
        community network and, 206
        government policies toward, 201-3
        historic perspective on, 200-201
        magazines, 196, 203-4, 205, 214
        newspapers, 196, 198, 200, 201, 203-4,
            205, 207, 214

Philippines, mass media in (*continued*)
  nontraditional media, 207
  outdoor advertising, 196, 198, 207,
    213-14
  ownership of, 201
  radio, 197, 198, 200, 201, 204, 205, 206,
    207, 213
  satellite TV, 163, 200, 206
  structure of, 200-203
  television, 198, 200, 201, 202, 204-6, 207,
    213
  transit advertising, 196
  regulatory process in
    censorship and, 216-17
    foreign ownership and, 199-200
    health issues and, 214-16, 219-20
    of the 1970s, 198-99
    self-regulation and, 202-3, 210-14, 216-17
  Western agencies in, 19
Philippine Star, The newspaper, 202, 203
Philprom, 198
PLDT (Philippine Long Distance Telecommunications Corporation), 200
Political development
  in the Philippines, 189-91
  in Singapore, 276-77
Political factors
  in Asian advertising, xi
  in China, 81
  in India, 157-58
  in Korea, 127-28
  in Taiwan, 103-4
POM (Pengawasa Obat Makanan, Indonesia),
  271
Pond, Horace B., 197
Pos Kota newspaper (Indonesia), 269
PPPI (Indonesian Association of Advertising
  Agencies), 264, 270, 271
Prakit Apisarnthanarax, 229-30
Prakit/FCB agency (Thailand), 229, 230, 232
PRC (People's Republic of China). *See* China
Press Council (Taiwan), 118, 119, 120
Pressman Advertising and Marketing (India),
  170
PRIMO (Print Media Organization, Philip-
  pines), 210, 212, 214
Print Media Organization (PRIMO, Philip-
  pines), 210, 212, 214
Prize Competitions Act (India), 177
Procter & Gamble (P&G)
  in India, 172, 173

in Malaysia, 245, 246
in the Philippines, 197, 198, 209, 210
PRSP (Public Relations Society of the Philip-
  pines), 214
P.T. Fortune agency (Indonesia), 263
Public Relations Society of Japan, The, 37
Public Relations Society of the Philippines
  (PRSP), 214

Race demographics, of Hong Kong consumers,
  44, 63, 64, 65, 67
Radio
  in China, 76, 85-86
  in Hong Kong, 40, 48, 54, 57, 60-62, 63
  in India, 162, 178, 182
  in Indonesia, 263, 269, 270
  in Japan, 15, 34-35
  in Korea, 129, 135-37, 144
  in Malaysia, 244, 248
  in the Philippines, 197, 198, 200, 201, 204,
    205, 206, 207, 213
  in Singapore, 283-84
  in Taiwan, 15, 109, 111-12, 113, 289
  in Thailand, 226, 233, 236
Radio and Television Act (Thailand), 237
Radio & Television Malaysia (RTM), 163, 248
Radio & Television of Singapore (RTS), 283
Radio Corporation of Singapore (RCS), 283,
  284, 289
Radio Television Hong Kong (RTHK), 55,
  61-62
Radio Tokyo, 15, 21
Rajawali Citra Televisi Indonesia (RCTI), 163,
  268
Ramos, Fidel V., 191-92, 202
RCA, in Korea, 129
RCS (Radio Corporation of Singapore), 283,
  284, 289
RCTI (Rajawali Citra Televisi Indonesia) satel-
  lite broadcasting, 163, 268
Rediffusion Advertising (India), 166, 167, 168,
  173
Rediffusion cable radio (Malaysia), 244
Rediffusion cable radio (Singapore), 284-85
Regulations for Advertising Management
  (PRC), 91-93, 94
Regulatory process
  in China, 90-94
  in Hong Kong, 68
  in India

of broadcast media, 178-80
freedom of speech and, 176
laws of, 176-77
of print media, 177-78
self-regulation and, 180
in Indonesia, 270-71
in Japan, 28
in Korea, 143-44, 145-46
in Malaysia
government regulation, 249-50
self-regulation, 254-55
in the Philippines
in the 1970s, 198-99
censorship and, 216-17
on health issues, 214-16, 219-20
in Singapore, 288-89, 290-91
in Taiwan, 119-21
Religious factors. *See also specific religion*
in Asian advertising, xi
in Hong Kong, 48
in India, 155-56
in Japan, 21-22
in the Philippines, 190, 193-94
Ritual model, of communication, 8-9
R K Swamy Advertising Associates (India),
166, 167, 168, 169
Rogers, F. Theo, 197
Roh Tae Woo, 128
RTHK (Radio Television Hong Kong), 55,
61-62
RTM (Radio & Television Malaysia), 163, 248
RTS (Radio & Television of Singapore), 283

Saatchi & Saatchi, 83
in India, 166
in Korea, 138, 139
in Malaysia, 247
in Singapore, 287
in Taiwan, 114, 115
in Thailand, 231
SAIC (State Administration for Industry and
Commerce, China), 82, 84, 90, 93, 94
Samhee Communications advertising agency
(Korea), 134, 136, 137, 138
Samsung Group, 133, 134
San Miguel Corporation (Philippines), 210, 211
Sankei newspaper (Japan), 32, 33
Satellite Instructional Television Experiment
(SITE, India), 162
Satellite Master Antenna Television systems

(SMATV, Hong Kong), 59
Satellite telecasting, ix
in Hong Kong, 59
in India, 162-63
in Indonesia, 269
in Japan, 36
in Korea, 149
in Malaysia, 163, 244, 249
in the Philippines, 163, 200, 206
in Singapore, 284
in Taiwan, 109, 112, 113, 163
Satellite Television Asian Region Television
(STAR TV)
in Hong Kong, 113, 146, 149
in India, 163, 178
SBC (Singapore Broadcasting Corporation),
283, 290
SBS (Seoul Broadcasting System), 142, 149
SCTV (Surya Citra Televisi, Indonesia), 268
SEBI (Securities and Exchange Board of India), 177
Securities and Exchange Board of India
(SEBI), 177
Self-regulation
in India, 180
in Japan, 28-30
in Malaysia, 254-55
in the Philippines, 202-3, 210-14, 216-17
in Taiwan, 119-20
Seoul Broadcasting System (SBS), 142, 149
"Shame" culture, in Hong Kong, 49
Shanghai
advertising agencies in, 76-77
advertising reemergence in, 78
foreign agencies in, 83
Hong Kong and, 40
magazines in, 76
radio in, 76
Shanghai Advertising Corporation, 77, 78
Shanghai Television Station, 86
S.H. Benson advertising agency (India), 164
Shinnihon Hoso radio (Japan), 15
Shintoism, in Japan, 21
Siam Broadcasting and Communication (Thai-
land), 228
SIM Communications (SIMCOM, Singapore),
283
SIM (Singapore International Media Pte Ltd),
283
SIMCOM (SIM Communications, Singapore),
283

Singapore
  advertising agencies in, 286-87
  advertising industry in, 243
    development of, 243-44
    Hong Kong compared to, 68-69
  consumer marketing environment in
    consumer affluence increase and, 276
    cultural changes and, 277-78
    demographics of, 273-75
    economic development and, 7, 275
    education levels and, 274-75
    lifestyle changes and, 267, 275
    marriage and divorce rates and, 274
    political development and, 276-77
    population growth decline and, 273-74
    population maturation and, 274
    technological advancements and, 276
    working and executive women and, 275
  consumer segmentation and
    behavior variables and, 281-82
    demographic variables and, 278-79
    family decision-making dynamics and,
      281-82
    psychographic variables and, 279-81
  cultural factors in
    of consumer groups, 279-80
    foreign values and, 277
    lifestyle changes and, 275-76, 277
  as Four Dragons component, 4
  as "Greater China" component, 4, 41
  infrastructure of, 287-88
  Malaysia and, 242
  mass media in, 282-83
    cable TV, 284
    cinema, 285
    direct mail, 286
    newspapers, 283
    outdoor advertising, 285-86
    radio, 283-84, 289
    Rediffusion and, 284-85
    satellite TV, 284
    television, 276, 283-84, 289
    transit advertising, 285-86
  Philippine advertising and, 198
  regulatory process in, 288-89
    ASAS and, 289-90
    unacceptable advertising and, 290-91
  TNAA management in, 7
  western agencies in, 19
Singapore Broadcasting Corporation (SBC),
  283, 290
Singapore Code of Advertising Practice, 290

Singapore Economic Development Board, 276
Singapore International Media Pte Ltd (SIM),
  283
Singapore Press Holdings (SPH), 283, 289
Singapore Telecom, 286
Sining Makulay, Inc. cable company (Philip-
  pines), 200
SITE (Satellite Instructional Television Experi-
  ment, India), 162
S/K Associates (Korea), 130
SkyCable (Philippines), 206
SMATV (Satellite Master Antenna Television
  systems, Hong Kong), 59
Sobhayga Advertising (India), 170
Socialism. See India; China
Socialist Education Campaign (PRC), 74
Soliven, Maximo, 201-2
South Korea, 4
Spa Advertising (Thailand), 232
Spaulding & Partners agency, in Thailand, 231
SPH (Singapore Press Holdings), 283, 289
SRG (Survey Research Group, Singapore), 287
SRI (Survey Research Indonesia), 266
STAR TV (Satellite Television Asian Region
    Television)
  in Hong Kong, 113, 146, 149
  in India, 163, 178
  in Indonesia, 269
  in the Philippines, 206
State Administration for Industry and Com-
    merce (SAIC, China), 82, 84, 90, 93, 94
Sticker, John C., 130
Straits Times newspaper (Malaysia), 243
Stratagem Media (India), 173
Suharto, Pak, 260, 261, 262, 263, 264, 265
Sukarno, Achmad, 260, 261, 263
Sun Yat-sen, 104
Survey Research Group (SRG, Singapore), 287
Survey Research Indonesia (SRI), 266
Surya Citra Televisi (SCTV, Indonesia), 268

Taiwan
  advertising expenditures in, 131
  advertising industry in, 114-17
  economic development in, 104-15
  as Four Dragons component, 4
  future directions of, 121-22
  as "Greater China" component, 4, 41, 103,
    121-22
  local business competition in, 5

mass media in, 109
  audience behavior and, 113
  cable television, 109, 112, 113
  magazines, 109, 110-11, 113
  newspapers, 109, 110, 113
  radio, 15, 109, 111-12, 113
  satellite TV, 109, 112, 113, 163
  television, 109, 112-13
  Philippine advertising and, 198
  political development in, 103-4
  regulatory process in
   associations and, 119-20
   consumer interest groups and, 120-21
   future priorities of, 122
   governmental agencies and laws regard-
    ing, 117-19
   self-regulation and, 119-20
  sociocultural changes in, 106-9
  TNAA management in, 7
Taiwan Television Corporation (TTV), 112
Tara Sinha McCann-Erickson agency (India),
  166, 167, 175
Tata Oil Mills Company (TOMCO, India), 172,
  173
TBC-TV (Tongyang Broadcasting Corporation,
  Korea), 127-28, 130
TCS (Television Corporation of Singapore),
  283, 284, 289
Teens, in Taiwan, 107-108
Television
  in China, 86-88
  in Hong Kong, 40, 48, 54-59, 60, 61
  in India, 162-63, 178-80, 182-83
  in Indonesia, 7, 264-65, 267-69, 271
  in Japan, 15-16, 35-36
  in Korea, 129-30, 141, 144, 145, 146
  in Malaysia, 244, 245, 246, 248-49, 252-53
  in the Philippines, 198, 200, 201, 202,
   204-6, 207, 213
  in Singapore, 183-84, 276, 289
  in Taiwan, 109, 112-13
  in Thailand, 225, 233, 236
Television Broadcasts Limited (TVB, Hong
  Kong), 55, 57, 58-59, 60
Television Corporation of Singapore (TCS),
  283, 284, 289
Television Twelve (Singapore), 283, 284
Televisi Pendidikan Indonesia (TPI), 268
Televisi Republik Indonesia (TVRI), 268
Teodoro, Pedro, 198
Thai Hakuhodo agency (Thailand), 229
Thailand

advertising industry in: growth of
  foreign era (1943-1974), 228-29
  Thai era (1977-1987), 229-30
  growth era (1988-1993), 230-33, 239
advertising industry in, 233-34
alcoholic beverage advertising in, 236-237
cigarette advertising in, 37
comparative advertising in, 237
consumer behavior in, 238-39
cultural factors in
  adaptiveness, 224-25
  conflict avoidance, 224, 234, 237
  hierarchical rigidity, 224
  high-context culture, 224, 234
  status appeal, 224-25
economic development of, 223-24
GDP of, 7
geographic setting of, 223
local business contacts in, 6-7
mass media in
  cable TV, 228
  cinema, 233
  direct mail, 233
  magazines, 226, 227, 233
  newspapers, 226, 227, 229, 233
  outdoor advertising, 226-27, 228
  radio, 226, 233, 236
  television, 225, 233, 236
  transit advertising, 226-27, 228
Philippine advertising and, 198
regulatory process in, 234
  Consumer Protection Board and, 235
  Food and Drug Administration and,
   235-36
  National Broadcasting Commission and,
   236
  television censorship process and, 236
  sweepstakes and contest advertising in,
   237-38
Thai Rath newspaper (Thailand), 226
Thai Sky TV (Thailand), 228
Third World Advertising Congress (Beijing),
  89
Third World countries
  1970s and 1980s advertising and, 4
  dependency theory regarding, 3-8
Time orientation, in Taiwan, 108-9
Times Advertising Award, 116
Times of India, The, 161
TNAAs. *See* Transnational advertising agencies
  (TNAAs)
TNCs. *See* Transnational corporations (TNCs)

Tokyo Broadcasting System, 15, 34
Tokyu Agency (Japan), 17, 18
TOMCO (Tata Oil Mills Company, India), 172, 173
Tongyang Broadcasting Corporation (TBC-TV, Korea), 127-28, 130
TPI (Televisi Pendidikan Indonesia), 268
Trade Union Law (Japan), 12
Transit advertising
  in China, 89
  in Hong Kong, 57, 66-68
  in the Philippines, 196, 207
  in Singapore, 285-86
  in Thailand, 226-27, 228
Transmission model, of communication, 8
Transnational advertising agencies (TNAAs)
  in China, 82-83
  consumer culture spread by, 7
  employment practices of, 6-7
  in India
    early days of, 164-65
    growth period of, 165-68
    financial agencies and, 170
    largest agencies and, 168-69
    specialized agencies and, 171
    subsidiary agencies and, 169
  indigenous culture destroyed by, 7-8
  in Indonesia, 263-65
  in Korea, 132-33, 135, 137-41
  in Malaysia, 244, 246-47
  in the Philippines, 197-98, 209-10
    regulation of, 199-200
  in Singapore, 286-87
  in Taiwan, 114-15
  in Thailand, 229-32
Transnational corporations (TNCs). *See also* Multinational corporations
  impact of, 4-5
  in India, 160-61, 172
  in Indonesia, 263-65
  in Korea, 130
  local competition and, 5
  in Malaysia, 244, 245-46
  in Singapore, 244
Treaty of Nanking, 39
Trikaya Grey agency (India), 170, 171
TTV (Taiwan Television Corporation), 112
Tu Wei-ming, 4-5
TV12 (Singapore), 283, 284
TV 3 satellite broadcasting (Malaysia), 163
TVB (Television Broadcasts Limited, Hong Kong), 55, 57, 58-59, 60
TVRI (Televisi Republik Indonesia), 268

Unilever
  in India, 172, 173, 183
  in Indonesia, 263, 265
  in the Philippines, 209, 210
Union Advertising agency (Korea), 130, 133
United Advertising Agency (Taiwan), 115
United Daily News (Taiwan), 110
United States
  Asian advertising money of, 3
  Council of Better Business Bureaus in, 30
  family ideologic changes in, 281-82
  GNP comparisons of, 3, 24
  Japan and
    noncoupon policy and, 31
    occupation of, 12
  Korea and
    agency liberalization and, 130-33, 137-38
    broadcasting and, 129
    political and economic interests and, 127, 150
  media-buying companies in, 19
  and the Philippines
    foreign-brand preference and, 195
    political development and, 190
    transnational agencies from, 198
  Taiwan and, 104

Video Regulatory Board (VRB, Philippines), 202
Vietnam
  economic growth of, 7
  TNAAs in, 231
Vietnam War, consumer market after, ix
VRB (Video Regulatory Board, Philippines), 202

Wide-band blockage, ix
Wireless Telegraphy Act (Japan), The, 34
WISE (Worker Improvement through Secondary Education, Singapore), 288
Women
  in Indian advertising, 177
  of Indonesia, 268
  in Korean advertising, 146, 148
  in Malaysian advertising, 252

in Philippine advertising, 216
as Philippine consumers, 218
in Singapore, 275, 281-82
in Taiwan advertising, 107
Thai advertising and, 238, 239
Worker Improvement through Secondary Education (WISE, Singapore), 288
World Bank, GNP statistics and, 3
World War II
  Chinese advertising and, 77
  consumer market after, ix
  Japan after, 11
  Philippines after, 190, 200, 201

Yomiuri Shimbun newspaper (Japan), 15, 27, 33
Young & Rubicam agency. *See also* Dentsu, Young & Rubicam (DY&R)
  Dentsu joint venture with, 17, 83
Young Women's Christian Association (YWCA, Korea), 148
YWCA (Young Women's Christian Association, Korea), 148

Zaibatsu dissolution, in Japan, 12
ZEE TV (India), 163